Everl

Legacy of Bl… and Hope

Melanie Frome

ISBN: 978-1-9992492-6-7

Cover Design: Georgie Barnes

For the ones still figuring themselves out—may you embrace every detour, cosmic prank, and unexpected rewrite along the way.
And for my son—my favorite plot twist, my unexpected guide, and the one who somehow became the wise old wizard while I'm still out here making 'questionable main character choices.'

***

For the curious, the brave, and the mildly concerned...
Scan this QR code and head over to the *Extras*—inside, there's the playlist that got me through writing Sady's chaos—and the Pinterest board where her world started to make sense. Sort of.
Call it a cosmic prank survival kit.
Spoiler-free. Mostly.

"They call it Prophecy. I call it the world's longest setup for a punchline I'm not gonna like."

Prologue

I was never meant to exist.

For years, my parents waded through the cruel tides of infertility, longing for a child that never came. Then, eighteen years ago, against every expectation—against science itself—I arrived. A miracle, they were told. A statistical anomaly.

But miracles are not always welcomed with open arms.

The moment my mother's pregnancy was confirmed, a flurry of specialists, geneticists, and high-ranking doctors entered the picture, each one peering into the unknown that was me. Tests. Scans. Second opinions. Worry thick in every whispered conversation behind closed doors. The prognosis was grim. The risks, too high. The consequences, irreversible.

Termination, they said, would be the most logical choice.

It wasn't fair—to them or to me. How could I ever hope for a normal life when my very existence had been met with doubt?

So when I tell you that growing up as the child who was never meant to be brings its own set of complications—and, dare I say, impossible expectations—take my word for it.

As if being a teenager wasn't hard enough already.

Chapter 1

"Sady baby," Mom's voice echoed from the back of the moving truck. "Would you please come and grab your boxes?"

Every damn year, we have packed up our lives, moved, and tried not to leave any skeletons in the closet. Except this time, the closet might actually have skeletons. This house was over a hundred years old, after all. After eighteen years, you'd think I'd be used to it. But no matter how often my family has tried to make it feel normal, it wasn't.

We have moved all over the world. Last year, it was Paris—the enchanting city of love and liberty, according to the latest travel guidebooks. So how the hell did we end up in Brampton, Ontario, Canada, this time?

We had been here just under two weeks, and frankly, I was baffled. Mom was the family's culture snob, and Dad—well, he was our family history nerd. This town didn't have enough of either to fill a coffee cup.

I felt like someone, probably Dad, had been playing blindfolded pin-the-tail-on-the-donkey with a map when they chose the place we'd call home for the next twelve months. Granted, it did have easy access to transportation—trains, planes, and automobiles—guess it still met the requisites set out before I was born.

Somehow, despite the modern suburban cookie-cutter vibe

of this city, Dad—or maybe Mom—had found a century-old, well-maintained relic of a house with enough character and quirks to make it tolerable. I *hoped*. Located on a quiet cul-de-sac just off the main downtown road, less than a five-minute walk from the bus and train stations and within a twenty-five-minute drive to the airport, our new home fit the bill.

My parents cared about that part, a lot. As for me, I happened to like the way the deep emerald ivy clung to the weathered red brick facade—a cloak of greenery wrapping nearly half the house facing the street. It was as if nature was shrouding secrets from prying eyes, even before our family decided to call this place home. *Couldn't help but wonder what kind of secrets.*

I had already claimed the loft-style attic space as my bedroom. The low-angled ceilings on both sides would make navigating the room a challenge for Dad, so this was an easy win. The creaky, narrow wooden stairs leading from the middle floor to the top opened onto a small landing with barely enough room for two people to stand side by side. The door blocked entry to the room, while the low ceiling posed a health hazard to anyone over six feet tall. *Also, a challenge for Dad.*

Once inside, the space spanned almost the full width of the house. I grudgingly admitted that the windows on both ends of the room, combined with the skylight just above my bed, created rather spectacular patterns of light on the floor and ceiling. *Grudgingly*, because I didn't want to like this house. I didn't want to like this town.

Both windows were large enough for me to climb out. *Hell*, I thought even Dad might fit through one of them, and that was saying something. My bed was precisely where I liked it—in the middle of the room, not touching a single wall. When your life already felt like a cage; you didn't want to feel boxed in. Besides, it came with strategic benefits, as Mom liked to point out every single time we set up another bedroom for me.

Flopping onto the new mattress, wishing I were anywhere but here, I gazed up. The exposed wooden beams crisscrossed above, forming patterns against the ceiling, and the roof peaked directly over my pillow. From this vantage point, I was reminded of medieval cathedrals and rustic churches in the French countryside.

Memories flooded back of countless weekend trips Mom and I had squeezed in this past year, visiting every holy site imaginable. You'd think it was lovely mother-daughter bonding time, but truth be told, Mom's near-obsession with Mary Magdalene always took center stage. Often, I felt like a spectator in our shared adventures. Sometimes, she forgot I was even there—literally. It had taken her over thirty minutes to realize she had left Saint-Maximin-la-Sainte-Baume without me. *Thank hell for cell phones.*

Huh. That's new. A skylight directly above my bed. It clearly clashed with the building's original architecture. The rainbow catcher hanging on the latch rope, gleaming a kaleidoscope of colors, was a curious addition.

Testing a theory, I knelt on the mattress and pulled myself up with the deceptively delicate-looking rope to flip the skylight open with little effort. It was just big enough for me to crawl onto the roof—but nearly impossible for anyone to follow. Leave it to Mom to disguise an escape hatch.

"Sady doll, don't you even think about terrifying our new neighbors! I can hear you on the roof—get back inside!"

Damn Dad and his hearing. *Grudgingly*, there was that word again, I dropped onto my bed and tried to get my bearings.

From the front window, I had a panoramic, 180-degree view. An advantageous vantage point. A huge oak tree stood close enough that I could jump onto the branch overhanging the front yard without too much effort. Beyond the line of houses, the train station peeked into view. *Wonder if the trains will wake me at night.*

The back window opened onto a fire escape leading down into the enclosed backyard. A breeze flowed from one end of the room to the other when both windows were open—a handy feature if the air conditioning failed. I had read online that the weather here could get pretty sticky and humid, which was bad news for my wavy hair. It was the bane of my existence. Well, one of them.

This house already held more than met the eye. As with every other move, there were renovations and modifications—discreet ones, without the help of contractors. If you knew what to look for, you'd see hints of protection—signs that this was no ordinary family home. The kind of reinforcements woven into its walls would put even the most paranoid doomsday preppers to shame. Whatever worst-case scenario they were bracing for, we had them beat—not that anyone outside the family would ever know. It was a familiar dance, one we had perfected over the years.

Take my bedroom door, for example. The original had already been replaced with one framed in internal steel—the kind used in panic rooms. I'd had one like that since I was in a crib.

The moving van was long gone. Unloading the boxes, furniture, and all our belongings was next—Mom's favorite part. My room was a minimalist's dream. A single narrow wardrobe and a chest of drawers held all my clothes, all of which fit neatly into two suitcases. My desk was just as simple. I'd had a clean-desk policy since kindergarten.

The ensuite bathroom, consisting of a shower, toilet and sink with a mirror was a feat of modern proportions, given the odd angles they had to be built around. It was quirky. *I liked quirky.*

No school medals or awards, despite disobeying Mom's "no public attention" directive a few times, were on display. No stuffed animals littered my bed. No makeup was scattered across the desk—I didn't wear any, thanks to my disdain for chemical-laden products. And you certainly wouldn't find a starry-eyed girl's diary anywhere.

"Oh, Sam, don't you dare—"

And that was my cue to shut my door or vacate the premises. When either of my parents started a sentence with *don't you dare,* it usually meant things were about to get X-rated. No teenager should have to listen to that.

The master bedroom on the middle floor, with its own en suite bathroom, clawfoot tub, and vintage tiles, was already being christened. *Great.*

Thank hell Dad had finished the other renovations. Only the most discerning eye would notice that the walls in their bedroom extended slightly beyond the original framework. Soundproofing, of course—their bedroom door included.

Don't get me wrong—I was happy my parents' passion was alive and well after all these years. But seriously, did they have no shame? Their room was just inches away from the stairs leading to the attic—and therefore, to my room. I swore, as I got older, my hearing got sharper, like some cruel evolutionary prank designed to torture me. Soundproofing or not.

On a completely different note, the stairs leading up to my room betrayed any attempt at stealth with their thunderous creaks. My door could probably stop a small hippo from crashing through, but it didn't do much for sound. I might ask Dad to fix that for our next move. Our next *home.*

This was the first real chance I'd had to explore the rest of the house. With Mom and Dad otherwise occupied, I seized the moment to take a look around on my way out.

On the ground level, a spare room had been repurposed into an office—a communal space where most of my homework assignments would probably get done. A large L-shaped desk near the window, and a sofa bed in the back corner. The faint scent of fresh caulking and paint lingered, a reminder of recent renovations. The windows, fortified with shatterproof glass, had two separate locks.

Huh, that's new.

The glazing, I was sure, had a two-way mirror effect. *Note to self*—check on my way out if anyone can see into these windows. This room wouldn't be used as a guest room—nobody visited us anyway. *That's against the rules.*

The grand double doors at the front entrance, framed in sturdy oak, boasted stained-glass panels adorned with intricate rose patterns. Reinforced with steel, similar to my bedroom but with some extra touches invisible to the naked eye. On closer inspection, I could see hidden metal lines etched within the glass—a detail invisible to all but the most perceptive eye. The deep ruby hue of the roses cast a mesmerizing glow onto the dark wooden floors of the foyer. It was beautiful but eerie. *Like blood.*

So, not only was the door stunning, but it was also a formidable obstacle for anyone trying to get through without our permission. A fortress disguised as a home. Or was the home disguising the fortress?

The front foyer seamlessly transitioned into the living room and kitchen, creating an expansive and inviting space with a small bathroom, complete with toilet and shower, veered off to the left. I liked the kitchen. It was yellow—like liquid sunshine—and it made me smile. Big, charming windows overlooked the garden, already filled with herb pots, courtesy of Dad. I could smell mint, thyme, basil, and rosemary wafting through the air.

What the hell? He's planted autumn crocus too. That was new. Now I'd have to be extra careful when grabbing herbs. You wouldn't find that one in garden shops for good reason—it was poisonous. Nobody grew it anywhere near kitchen herbs. *Except apparently Dad.*

The kitchen boasted a gleaming vintage stove and fridge—both silver—that perfectly complemented the antique dark-wood cabinetry with silver knobs and handles. A corner cabinet with a stained-glass facade matching the front door held what looked like wine glasses. And if I knew my parents, that would be the designated cabinet. *Just in case. If it happens.*

And beyond the kitchen island lay the dining area. *Ah hell,* I thought we were done with bar tables. Despite my fervent protests two years ago in Italy, a bar table and matching chairs now occupied the space that should have been reserved for a proper dining area. I'd wager it was Mom's idea. Dad was a bit more sympathetic to my height deficiency.

Not that Mom cared. "Just hop up," she'd say, like I was some kind of parkour prodigy. Sure, let me just vault onto a chair that was practically at eye level and hope I don't faceplant in the process. Short people deserve dignity too.

At the far end of the kitchen was the door leading to the backyard—a private sanctuary surrounded by a high fence and dense foliage. The surrounding trees and bushes shielded us from prying eyes. Beyond them sat the garage and, a few steps away, the shed.

The garage was Dad's domain when it came to his motorcycles, but the shed? That had been entirely converted into his workspace.

A normally boring garden shed had been meticulously transformed into his personal sanctuary—a fully operational workshop where he would disappear daily to work in seclusion with his surveillance equipment. His fascination with technology wasn't just a hobby—it was his job. As a private contractor, he designed and deployed high-end surveillance systems, sometimes for corporations, sometimes for individuals who could afford his expertise. He never talked about his clients, and I knew better than to ask.

But even without the work angle, Dad was the ultimate family geek. He loved all things electronic and could fix almost anything, often taking gadgets apart just to see how they worked—sometimes even putting them back together in better condition than before. We could lose him for hours in those little pawnshops or second-hand stores, where he'd dig through forgotten treasures, sometimes resurfacing with some antique gadget that kept him occupied for days.

Mom, on the other hand, had a far simpler approach to technology—if it didn't do what she wanted, her first instinct was to put her fist through it.

As for me? I practiced Dad's curiosity and patience, but honestly, weird things tended to happen whenever I was around electronics. Glitches, random shutdowns, entire devices just... stopping. It was enough to convince me there was some kind of tech-based conspiracy against me. And well, in those moments, my personality leaned a lot more toward Mom.

I had, quite literally, put my fist through a computer monitor more than once. Dad had replaced at least three monitors, two TVs, and four—no, wait, five—phones because of my temper. The list of what had needed replacing because of Mom was longer than my arm.

I was seven or eight when curiosity got the better of me, and I snuck in to watch him work. He wasn't pleased. After that, he moved his workspace out of the house.

The basement, once barren, now held the most extensive—and secretive—renovations. The previously unfinished concrete foundation had been transformed into a fully equipped exercise room with free weights, a squat rack, weight machines, and more. Against one wall loomed a locked cabinet spanning over six feet in width and height. *Just in case. If it happens.*

Ah, there it was—the subtle seam in the floor, almost imperceptible to the untrained eye. Soon, it would be hidden beneath heavy gym mats. Under this unassuming surface lay a concrete block concealing a small vault, secured with a cutting-edge, gene-printing security code lock—not even on the market yet.

The first few days in a new house were always the same. Mom and Dad were distracted by unpacking and organizing everything. It was endearing in a way, their childlike excitement palpable with each move. For all our sakes, I spent these first days wandering around town, familiarizing myself with bus routes, grocery stores, police stations, cemeteries—anything that might prove useful. You'd be surprised how much construction caused delays and detours.

Truth be told, I relished these solitary bike rides. Finding a path, choosing a direction, and riding until it ended before turning back. My sense of direction was impeccable, and my healthy appetite usually led me to some tucked-away restaurant or café offering something you wouldn't find listed in The Lonely Planet travel guides.

This solitary time gave me a fleeting chance to reconcile myself to another move. Thankfully, Mom had stopped calling them relocations when I was ten—it sounded way too military. We were now on move number nineteen, though the tally hardly mattered anymore. It didn't get easier, even though memorizing every part of my surroundings without trying had become second nature. Like breathing.

Every move meant starting over—blending in, fitting in with kids my age. Even if I managed that, the rule remained: keep them at arm's length. Acquaintances, not friends. *What's the point?*

Every year, always after my birthday. August. Except for that one time in first grade when they found us just before Christmas. In New York.

Despite the upheaval, my love for the outdoors kept me sane. My skin, a soft bronze just slightly lighter than Dad's tawny shade, sported freckles across my nose and cheeks. My parents had tried to give me as normal a life as possible, but it was a futile effort. When I was born, they had decided that moving every year was the only way to keep us safe. But contingency plans started the moment they knew Mom was pregnant.

While it had been twelve years since they last found us, the threat loomed. There had been close calls—mostly when I had deviated from the routine or the rules. *Note to self*—witness protection could learn a thing or two from a six-year-old.

With groceries stowed, school supplies replenished, and both parents settled into their routines, I supposed I was as prepared as I'd ever be for the new school year. Registration had been a formality, completed before our move, as always.

I had just turned eighteen, and tomorrow was the first day of my final year of high school. While other kids my age were planning for college, university, or backpacking through Europe, I felt stuck—directionless, devoid of plans, with no glimpse of the future beyond my next birthday.

Then, we'd start again.

We never talked about what came after.

One year at a time, that was how we lived. Not once had we discussed college or anything beyond.

After all, I was never supposed to live, let alone survive this long. It was all just borrowed time.

Maybe this year would be different.

Despite the seamless transition to our new home, there was something in the air. A change. Palpable, yet intangible. Like a storm brewing on the horizon. *Or maybe it's just wishful thinking.*

Mom had started her latest UN assignment at their Toronto office last week. She was already working insane hours. Don't ask what she did—she'd just smile and say, *"I'd love to tell you, but then I'd have to kill you."* You'd think she was joking.

She had gone back to work when I was four. It hadn't taken long for my parents to figure out that Dad would be better suited for hands-on parenting. His temperament was better for raising a child—especially one as spirited as me. Mom called me a *problem.* Dad called me *precocious.* I knew which word I preferred.

Mom was renowned for her problem-solving skills—the kind governments liked to keep out of public view. Dad said she was trying to atone for her past. Every time I asked what she could have done that was so terrible, he just said he'd tell me when I was older.

So, you could imagine that dealing with a toddler didn't exactly provide her with the kind of redemption that saving lives did. If memory served, her way of handling a two-year-old throwing spaghetti at the wall was to opt for a sledgehammer assault on said wall—instead of just wiping it down.

For two years, they had juggled their schedules to split time with me, but after the incident in first grade—when *they* found us—Dad had officially become my primary caregiver. His calm nature and observational skills weren't just assets in his line of work—surveillance and security—but also in raising me. A babysitter or nanny had been out of the question. Too risky. Remember, I was *precocious.*

Despite daily meditation sessions with Dad, my temper could still flare out of control. Like hers. *Mom.* We've had our share of arguments—throwing things, yelling some pretty hurtful insults at each other. Often in at least three languages. Dad could usually judge the mettle of the fight and knew it was about to hit a bad spot when we started slinging some ancient Latin cuss words. He was a master at de-escalation—always knowing how to calm things down without being condescending. That would have only made things worse, especially with Mom.

We always made up over hot chocolate—Mom's with almond milk, mine with vegan dark chocolate and coconut milk. Neither of us liked marshmallows, but Dad ate them straight out of the bag. Nothing went to waste.

From the moment I was born, they had been vigilant. Watching me for *signs*. Of being different. Meanwhile, I've often wondered what it might be like to introduce my parents to a schoolmate—grappling with the daunting task of explaining their idiosyncrasies rather than fretting over my own.

Plopping onto the enormous couch, it had to be that big to fit Dad's ginormous frame and Mom's giraffe legs, I contemplated the looming day ahead. The first day of my last year of high school.

By now, I'd outgrown the nerves that came with being the new kid. We used to review and rehearse our fabricated backstory together as a family every night for a week before that first day. We'd stopped when I started high school and Mom realized her drilling me on the finer details was pointless. I knew my lines. And the rules. My near photographic memory made this a breeze.

The New York incident had left its mark.

Stay as close to the truth as possible—lying was harder to remember. That's how liars got caught. They strayed too far from the truth and tripped up. Or they start sentences with *'The truth is.'* That's a dead giveaway.

We had started watching *Lie to Me* a couple of years ago. Tim Roth played a body language and micro-expressions expert who consulted for law enforcement. My parents could run circles around him, but we still loved the show—and the eccentricity of the main character.

Dad, of course, couldn't resist pointing out the similarities. "See that?" he'd say with a grin whenever the main character got in someone's face, reading them like an open book with zero patience for their nonsense. "Remind you of anyone?"

Mom would roll her eyes, but she never denied it. Because, honestly? He wasn't wrong. Like Lightman, she had a habit of picking people apart before they even opened their mouths, and she had no tolerance for liars. But where he had a smug, chaotic genius vibe, Mom had more of an *if-you-waste-my-time-I-will-end-you* energy. I think that's why she liked the show.

They were, for all intents and purposes, human lie detectors, thanks to their extensive pre-parenthood life.

And that had rendered any attempted normal teenage rebellion futile. *Oh wait,* never mind—I'd actually have to have friends for that to even be a worthwhile gambit with my parents.

So, why this strange tingling of nerves now? This new school shouldn't have been any different. All my courses were already selected. It was just another year, wasn't it? Yet something felt... *off.*

It wasn't just that I was tired of moving—something else was brewing.

Like I don't have enough to worry about just being a teenager?

According to public transit schedules, the school was thirty minutes away, but after spending a day scouting it out, I knew the trip took closer to forty. Important detail. Our family was punctual. Even one minute could make the difference between life and death.

Dramatic, I know. Sorry.

Scouting local malls for fashion trends was part of my pre-school checklist. Thankfully, my standard uniform of jeans, T-shirts, and Chucks blended in just fine.

Thanks to a rather bizarre combination of genetics, my features leaned toward the odd side of the appearance spectrum, but I'd gotten absolutely none of their height. Being the same size as a preteen had its perks—give me a baseball cap and I could disappear in a crowd and stay unremarkable.

With nearly three thousand students, this school promised to make it easy to fade into the background. Its location—close to a major highway, along a bike path, and with three nearby bus stops—offered plenty of options for a quick exit. *Should it be needed.*

Years of practice had honed my ability to avoid crowds and perfected my knack for going unnoticed, particularly around my peers. It wasn't disdain—it was necessity. *Safer for everyone involved.*

So, it was with some annoyance and mild confusion when I'd found myself targeted by the resident mean girl at my last school. Her boyfriend had apparently given her the impression that I had a crush on him, which couldn't have been further from the truth.

Not just because he was about as interesting as dry toast, but because, well... that had never been a thing for me. The whole heart-racing, stomach-flipping, can't-think-straight attraction that people always talked about? Never happened. Not once. I understood it in theory—just like I understood how to fake a smile when necessary—but I'd never felt it.

So, the idea that I would suddenly fixate on *her* boyfriend? Laughable. But try telling that to someone who'd already made up her mind. She had no idea how close she came to my fist breaking her picture-perfect nose.

Mom and Dad hadn't been thrilled about the attention it brought to our family. They both saw how much it tested my patience. But high school politics? That was something I'd stopped trying to make sense of a long time ago. Cliques, rumors, social hierarchies—none of it mattered when you were never in one place long enough for it to stick.

So, no matter how much I longed for normalcy, a chance to live like any other teenager, I knew that our family's past would always loom large, casting its shadow over our uncertain future.

I still couldn't shake this feeling.

A creeping sense of something coming.

Chapter 2

I was jolted awake by the blaring intrusion of my alarm clock, clinging desperately to the last remnants of sleep. My body resisted, reluctant to surrender its grip on slumber. This was the one day of the year Mom granted me a reprieve from our usual early-morning workout, so I seized the opportunity to burrow deeper under my comforter, groaning in protest.

The snooze button blinked its betrayal, and I finally accepted that it was time to get up—before Dad decided to intervene in his usual, overenthusiastic way. Though more laid-back than Mom, he had a habit of hovering just enough to be mildly exasperating.

Perched on the edge of my bed, I caught a glimpse of myself in the oval mirror hanging on my wardrobe door. My face looked as exhausted as I felt—dark smudges under my eyes, lips pressed into a frown, shoulders slumped forward like I was far older than my meagre eighteen years on this earth.

Oh great, it's gonna be one of those days, huh?

My usually relaxed waves had morphed into wild curls, thanks to the lingering summer humidity in the air. *Fantastic.*

"Hey, Sady doll!" Dad's booming voice ricocheted up the stairs, shattering the morning stillness. "Coffee with breakfast?"

How does that man always know when I've slept like crap?

"Yeah, sure!" I shouted back, already tugging on jeans, a plain black T-shirt, and my favorite red high-top Chucks. I headed to the bathroom to attempt the taming of the shrew—known as my hair. When nothing seemed to work, I let out another groan.

"Are you all right?"

Damn his hearing.

"Yeah, I'll be down in a minute!" I snapped, rolling my eyes. Armed with a hair tie, I managed to corral my mane into a semblance of a side braid that should stay put for the day, with a little help from the trusty coconut oil that lived in my bathroom—not the kitchen.

When I finally made it downstairs, he was standing in the back kitchen doorway, grinning around a mouthful of frittata. Or more accurately, he was filling the entire doorframe. Standing at a lofty six foot five with shoulders broad enough to block most doorways, the man might as well have been part Sasquatch.

You'd never guess he was an ovo-vegetarian. Not by choice, mind you—his body simply refused to cooperate with anything else. For reasons buried in his genetics, he couldn't digest or absorb meat, and the only animal product that didn't trigger his gag reflex was eggs. Unlike most allergies, which show up as hives, rashes, or an unfortunate trip to the bathroom, Dad's reaction was far more... *explosive*. Also known as projectile vomit.

Normally a morning person, today's lethargy slowed everything down, and it showed. Moving sluggishly, I grabbed the laziest and least nourishing breakfast meal ever—cereal—while sipping my coffee and watching Dad with a wary eye. He was bouncing on his toes like an overgrown kid, putting the doorframe at serious risk of denting.

"I'm going to drive you to school!" he declared. Or should I say shouted?

"Dad, you really don't have to," I protested, but my words fell on deaf ears as he laughed and then did that weird snort that always caught in his throat.

Wait a minute—was he getting emotional?

"This is your last year of high school!" Then he paused long enough to give me the look. "Please let your old man do this one more time?"

He was giving me *the look*—wide-eyed, overly earnest, with just the right amount of tragic puppy-dog energy. If his bottom lip started quivering, I was done for. With a sigh, I relented before he could weaponize the pout.

The grin that spread across his face was comical, stretching to his hairline where his curly blonde hair stuck out in all directions. Dad always waited too long between haircuts, leaving him looking like a straw man who got a bad perm.

Meet Sam Smith, a.k.a. *Dad*. Weighing in at a solid two hundred forty pounds, and if it weren't for his perpetual goofy grin, he could probably scare the most violent offender with his sheer size and presence. A man with an unusual fondness for Guinness and hands so big that his pinky fit behind my left ear and his thumb behind my right ear—yeah, that's right, he could use my whole head as a bowling ball.

Last year, a former classmate, Genevieve, had made the cringeworthy remark that Dad could give Thor a run for his money. Imagine Chris Hemsworth—if he were even taller, had bushier curls, a permanent tan, and about fifty extra pounds of muscle. *Wait, don't. That's disturbing.*

Yeah, thanks for that image, Genevieve.

Because *every* teenage girl wants to think of her father as some Hollywood heartthrob. No, thank you. That was an image I did *not* need seared into my brain.

So, given his size, you might appreciate Mom's sense of humor when she bought him a new vehicle for his birthday three years back when we were in London.

It was a Smart car.

Watching him attempt to cram his hulk-size frame into the pint-sized vehicle was comedy gold. His knees nearly reached his chest, his elbows jabbed against the door, and when he tried to adjust the seat, the whole car groaned in protest. But he got the last laugh when he persuaded Mom to join him for a *romantic* car ride. Witnessing them contort and curse in multiple languages, reminiscent of clowns squeezing into a tiny circus car, was a spectacle that still sent me into giggle fits anytime I thought about it. Sadly, any attempt to capture the chaos on my phone would have violated the rules. Needless to say, the car was promptly returned the following day with vows to never inflict that kind of torture on each other again. Eco-friendly efforts be damned.

"Fine," I grumbled, letting him win.

"Yes! You won't regret it! Let's go!" For a pretty quiet guy, the dude sure could shout. "Don't want to be late on your first day, do you?"

"Dad, I've never been late for school a day in my life. And if I'm late today, it's on you."

Am I imagining things, or is he actually dancing on his toes?

His grin was wide enough to split his face, and his excitement practically radiated off him. His shoulders wiggled, his hips gave an exaggerated little shake, and for a brief second, he looked like a hyperactive, but grizzly-sized, golden retriever about to be let outside.

Like for real, what is that ridiculous little wiggle in his hips?

"Sady doll, we won't be late. Trust me. I got a surprise waiting for us in the garage."

Ah hell, what could that be now?

In my family, surprises were synonymous with chaos. At least I could blame them for my warped sense of humor—but not sure how or from where they got theirs.

Dad had already bolted out to the garage without bothering to check if I was following him or not.

"I'm coming!" Homemade lunches were essential for the first week of school because you never knew what cafeteria food would be like. "Just grabbing my backpack."

And under my breath, I mumbled, "This better not be another Smart car."

I grimaced as Dad suddenly reappeared, blocking the doorway and stepping into my personal space. With his arms crossed, he looked downright intimidating. If only he weren't my father—or holding back that gleeful energy. I swore I could count his nose hairs.

Just further proof of how different I was, even in my own family.

I had stopped growing when I was about thirteen, and Mom had made a big deal out of it. She even used the word *defective*—completely straight-faced, like she was diagnosing a manufacturing flaw. There was a pause. Then something left my hand. I won't confirm what, but let's just say it made an impact. Dad, ever the peacekeeper, had stepped in before things escalated.

Standing barely over five feet tall, I looked like I was adopted. *Sort of.* Apparently, our extended family—whom I've never met—didn't share my height deficiency either.

Except Ramira, and she's taller than Mom.

"Ah, Dad, put me down!" I squealed as he effortlessly hoisted me onto his shoulders, then flipped me upside-down behind his back. Dangling precariously, I flailed, but he knew this wasn't what I expected—and he was loving it.

"Close your eyes," Dad giggled. Hearing a man of his stature giggle was equal parts absurd and endearing—and contagious as hell.

Over the years, I'd become pretty good at squirming and thrashing about, thanks to daily practice with techniques like jujitsu, grappling, and bizarre moves Dad had learned in Mongolia years ago. But today, I was just slow enough for him to haul me into the garage before I could escape. My hope for solid ground was interrupted when he swung to the side, and I caught sight of the surprise waiting for me.

It wasn't another Smart car.

Even upside down, I could tell what it was. My jaw dropped in awe, and I relented.

Gently, he set me back on solid ground, and I stepped closer, drawn to the machine like a magnet.

"Dad, it looks like a Harley Davidson... but—" I began, but he cut me off mid-sentence.

"It's not on the market yet," he interrupted, grinning like he was in on the world's best-kept secret. "This is the first Harley hybrid—gas and electric. A cleaner ride, but it still has its signature rumble." His pride was tangible, and he sounded thoroughly satisfied with himself. *Rightly so.*

"No way! This is so wild." I ran my hands over the matte finish, inspecting the admittedly badass motorcycle. "Where did you get it? How—?"

Considering our family's commitment to environmental consciousness and minimizing our carbon footprint, this was... *epic.* "How the hell did you get your hands on this?"

"Can you please not use that word?" he quipped, rolling his

eyes. "As for the bike... let's just say the designer had some personal motivation."

"Wait, what? Dad—are you kidding me?" My disbelief mounted. "This was the design you were talking about last year? You didn't mention you actually submitted it to the company!"

"Well, this is just the prototype, Sady doll." He shrugged, trying to sound nonchalant but failing miserably. "I nearly didn't nail the specs until one of their other contractors shared what turned out to be the missing link. We haven't quite perfected the sound yet, but to be honest, is a Harley even a Harley if it doesn't rumble? Anyway, it won't hit the market for another eight or nine years."

"They obviously loved it, or you wouldn't have the prototype in our garage." I made sure he caught my genuine admiration. "Okay, Dad, I am officially impressed."

"Glad I haven't completely lost my edge." He chuckled, tossing my helmet with the force of a cannon. "Catch!"

Thank hell my reflexes were sharp; I snatched it just in time to avoid a broken nose. Dad had the arm strength of a titan but forgot it every time he got excited—like an overgrown toddler. One time, he got so carried away in a 'friendly' game of tug-of-war with me that I ended up airborne for a solid three seconds before landing in a heap. And let's not forget the time he enthusiastically clapped me on the back for acing my chemistry final and sent me face-first into the fridge. Subtlety was not in his skill set, at least not in that way.

I pulled the helmet over my head, carefully threading my loose side braid through the back to keep it from getting crushed. A few quick adjustments, and it fit snugly into place. Slinging my backpack onto my shoulders, I climbed onto the bike behind him. The engine growled to life—a deep, familiar rumble laced with a futuristic hum—before we launched forward, the world blurring around us.

As we sped toward school, the wind rushed past, cool but not cold. Dad was always a furnace, so I wouldn't have felt the chill anyway. I exhaled, debating whether I could talk him into ditching school altogether—just this once. But before I could even get the words out, he was already slowing down, pulling into the parking lot.

Damn, that ride was too short.

He killed the engine, and every head within sight swiveled toward us. As Dad's towering frame stepped off the unusual Harley, both were impossible to ignore.

Silently cursing myself for not asking him to park in the back lot, I unfastened my helmet and pulled it off, adjusting my loose side braid as I took in the scene. My skin prickled with apprehension. Perfect. An audience. I clipped the helmet into the holder on the back of the bike, already bracing for whatever nonsense was about to unfold.

Yup. They were taking bets on whether the giant on the bike was my boyfriend. Judging by the way some of them were whispering and sneaking glances, the odds were probably shifting in real time. Fantastic. Just what I needed—fuel for the rumor mill. By lunch, I'd probably have an entire fabricated love story starring me and my so-called 'mystery man.' *Teenagers suck sometimes.*

Ugh. Gross.

"Uhm, Dad?" I pleaded. "Think you can leave your helmet on and just give me a quick hug?"

His hands were already on his helmet, but he paused, tilting his head dramatically. "Sady doll, are you embarrassed by your old man?" he asked, feigning an affronted look.

Before I could answer, his gaze flicked around the parking lot. He did a double take, posture shifting, suddenly on high alert.

Not what I intended.

"Wait, what's wrong?" he asked.

"Nothing, but there's no hiding a bike like this. I just don't want to draw any more attention than we need to," I said quickly, trying to diffuse the situation. "And in case you forgot, or think you shrunk in height or width—which you've not, you are not exactly the blend-into-the-crowd type."

I adored my dad, but you'd think a man with his years and experience would have picked up on some social cues along the way. Apparently not.

Dad sighed but relented. "Fine. A quick hug. But you owe me another one later."

Leaning down, he wrapped me in his signature bear hug.

One. Two. Three.

"Uhm, Dad?"

Four. Five.

"Dad—?"

The man hugged me like a bear, putting me in danger of a cracked rib.

Ah, hell. Now I was trying to squirm out of his arms without causing a scene. Fantastic. Because nothing screams *cool new student* like getting publicly smothered by your oversized father on day one. His sweater all but swallowed me, the thick fabric muffling my protests as I struggled against the sheer wall of muscle trapping me. Maybe if I played dead, he'd get the hint and drop me.

"You can let go now," I managed through gritted teeth, my voice barely escaping the wool cocoon I was trapped in. The crowd gathering behind us wasn't helping. Not exactly the low-key start I'd envisioned for my first day at a new school.

"Sure, sorry," he said sheepishly, climbing back onto the bike.

That's when I felt it.

A SURGE—so subtle I almost missed it.

It wasn't physical, exactly, but more like an unseen ripple moving through the air, brushing against my skin. A static hum danced at the edge of my awareness, not quite sound, not quite sensation. My body tensed, and a faint pressure built behind my eyes, as if the world had just shifted half an inch sideways and I hadn't moved with it.

I had felt this before. *Sorta.*

First grade. The day *they* found us. The memory sat buried, untouched for years, but even now, it slithered through the cracks when I least expected it. A shadow against the edges of my mind, cold and sharp, whispering that some things don't stay forgotten forever.

But back then, it had been different. *Colder. Sharper.* Like a blast of sub-zero air flooding through my skull, turning my thoughts brittle, as if they might crack under the weight of the unnatural chill. It had left behind an ache, a bone-deep frostbite that lingered long after the moment had passed.

This wasn't that.

This was... *muted.* A whisper instead of a howl. There was no painful sting of ice slicing through my veins, no instinct to recoil from the invasive cold, no gut-clenching certainty of danger. Instead, it felt—*kind.* As if something, or someone, had just brushed against the outer edge of my consciousness.

And then it was gone.

Too fast. Too fleeting.

It didn't leave that telltale frostbite in my mind the way *they* always did. But the fact that it had happened at all was enough to set my nerves on edge.

It caught me sideways, making my steps falter. Dad noticed immediately.

"Something wrong?" His voice was laced with concern.

For a split second, I considered telling him.

But what would I even say? *Hey Dad, I think I just felt something, but don't worry, it's not like last time. Probably.*

Yeah. That would go over well.

He'd only worry. And worry meant *scrutiny*. It meant *questions*. It meant Mom getting involved.

Nope. Not happening.

So instead, I forced a small, easy smile—the kind he wouldn't question. *I hoped.*

"Uhm." I whipped around, trying to sound casual. "Love you, Dad."

I couldn't tell him. It would only send both my parents into a panic. Besides, it was probably just first-day-of-school nerves. *Or anything else but this.*

He hesitated, eyes flicking over me like he knew I wasn't telling the full truth. But after a beat, he just nodded.

"All right, holler if you need me," Dad said, his voice warm and reassuring. "From home to here, I can make it in less than three minutes if I push it."

The Harley's engine rumbled to life, vibrating through the pavement beneath my feet.

I stood there for a moment, watching him go, the fading hum of the bike swallowed by the chatter of students. The air around me settled—quiet, still—like whatever had brushed against me was never there at all. *But it was there.*

My fingers curled into my palms, the urge to shake off the feeling creeping up my spine.

Don't overthink it. It's just nerves.

Or the crowd. Or maybe just the fatigue of another first day at another new school.

Yeah. That's all it was.

I inhaled, slow and deep, rolling my shoulders as if I could physically shrug it off.

The first time I'd felt something like that, I had been too young to fully understand what it meant. But now?

Now, I chose not to understand. I could have turned the thought over, examined it from every angle, let it fester like an itch that refused to be scratched. But that would mean opening a door I wasn't ready to walk through.

Because acknowledging it—*really* acknowledging it—meant considering what it could mean. And I wasn't ready for that.

Not yet.

So instead, I let out a breath, plastered on my best neutral expression, and took my first step toward the building.

To hell with it. *Ignorance is bliss, right?*

Scanning the building, I took in my first real look at the school. It was unlike any other I'd attended. Gone were the historic façades, private campuses, and elaborate architecture. This was a plain, boxy structure of muted brown brick—a rectangle of mediocrity. I tried not to judge the student body by the building, but I failed spectacularly.

Before heading inside, I glanced at the sky and muttered a half-hearted plea, half-expecting some cosmic force to roll its eyes at me. *Like I was rolling my eyes at it.*

"If you're listening... please let me finish my final year of high school. Preferably drama-free. And alive."

Entering through the main doors, I spotted the reception area easily. Behind the desk sat one of the most miserable-looking receptionists I'd ever encountered. She seemed grimmer than the building itself, with a resting bitch face to match. I wondered if she got enough fiber in her diet or if she just thrived on misery.

Time to play my part. I'd rehearsed this so often I probably mumbled it in my sleep.

"Hi, my name is Sady Smith. I'm new here. The registration email said I needed to come to the office first to grab my schedule?"

She didn't even look up, her fingers clacking on the keyboard.

"Let's see here. I don't have a Sady Smith, but I do have a Sadatana Smith. Would that be you?"

The sly curve of her lips told me she was loving this.

"Yes, that's me," I replied with exaggerated politeness.

She could try all she wanted, but I was going to kill her with kindness. There was nothing sweeter than watching someone try to aggravate you, only for you to respond with good manners instead of the snark they wanted to provoke. I'd learned this long ago and always kept it in mind when people were miserable around me.

If that fails, there's always voodoo. Not that I have a collection of tiny dolls hidden under my bed or anything. And even if I did, it's not like I'd actually use them. *Probably*.

Besides, letting my temper loose would only bring trouble.

She handed me a printout of my schedule, her snide grimace unwavering.

"Welcome to Brampton Central."

I weaved through the hallways, surprised by how easy they were to navigate. The building was a big box, after all—an ugly one, but a box nonetheless.

My first class was homeroom, which also happened to be history. Convenient, considering it was my favorite subject, especially anything to do with ancient civilizations. Here's hoping the teacher isn't a total bore or, worse, one of those know-it-alls who hates students smarter than him.

Inevitably, I *was* smarter. Not just in history—though that was where I thrived—but in most subjects. That wasn't ego, just fact. Last year, I corrected a teacher's equation before he even finished writing it, and instead of thanking me, he spent the rest of the semester pretending I didn't exist. So yeah, I've learned to tread lightly.

Finding the room faster than expected, I still managed to arrive two minutes after the bell.

Opening the door, I breathed a sigh of relief—the teacher wasn't at the desk by the huge black chalkboard at the front. Being late, even with a note from the office, usually resulted in the teacher picking on me, and I liked to avoid that. *Attention I don't want. Or need.*

Taking a few steps into the room, I started to look for an empty chair while avoiding the curious gazes of just about every other student already seated.

Oh, great. The obligatory new-kid stare-down. Just what I wanted. Do I keep my eyes down and pretend I don't notice? Offer a polite nod like some lost diplomat? Maybe pull out my phone and fake an urgent text from the President?

The faintest rustle, a barely contained chuckle—something just at the edge of my awareness—was about to make the choice for me. Whatever it was, I had the distinct feeling I was about to become today's main event.

Fantastic.

Chapter 3

"Welcome, ye latecomer. Present thyself with a proper introduction to thy fellow students," a voice rang out, dripping with sarcasm and an exaggerated accent from somewhere near the back of the room.

Startled, I froze mid-step, my search for a seat momentarily forgotten. Turning toward the source of the remark, my eyes scanned the room, navigating through a maze of desks and students. Finally, I found him—perched atop a short, broad filing cabinet, his feet dangling casually over the edge.

The voice. The fake accent. *Ah hell*, this guy is going to be trouble. Of course, my first day at a new school couldn't just be normal. Nope. The universe had to drop a walking, talking headache into my lap—complete with a flair for dramatics and an obvious need for attention.

He looked like the human embodiment of chaos. Slim-cut black jeans hugged his long legs, while a black T-shirt and light-blue denim jacket completed his outfit—well, almost. Over the jeans, he wore a maroon skirt. *A skirt.* And that wasn't even the most bizarre part. A blonde-and-magenta mohawk crowned his head, striking and vivid against the drab classroom walls. Black nail polish adorned his fingers, which were decked out with silver rings that caught the fluorescent light whenever he moved.

Yes, definitely trouble. The kind of trouble that rewrites the rules before you even realize you're playing the game.

I'd seen guys like him before—at least from a distance. The reckless ones who thrived on standing out. The ones who set off fireworks in the bathroom for *science*, got suspended for arguing with the principal, or turned hallways into their personal fashion runways. Basically, the type of guy who, in any teen drama, would either be the misunderstood rebel with a tragic backstory or the wildcard side character who existed solely to stir the pot. Either way, nothing good for me.

There had enough unpredictability in my life—none of it the fun kind—and I wasn't about to invite more into my orbit. So, to be avoided at all costs.

I felt my jaw tighten as I forced myself to stay calm. Clenching my fists, I resisted the overwhelming urge to tell him exactly where he could shove his theatrics. Instead, I locked onto the empty chair at the back of the room.

Just keep walking.

As I moved toward my intended desk, I risked another glance at him. His unnervingly bright blue eyes sparkled with mischief, and a smirk played on his lips.

Oh no. No, no, no.

This was bad. Really bad.

The teacher was still nowhere to be seen—a strange anomaly on the first day of class. They were usually militant about punctuality. Almost reaching the desk, I allowed myself a small sigh of relief.

Maybe I could avoid—

And then he moved.

In one swift, fluid motion, he hopped down from the filing cabinet, took two steps, leaped over another desk, and landed squarely on the desk I was about to claim as mine.

My mouth opened, but no words came out.

What just happened? And how?

"My fair lady, thou shalt make pilgrimage to the fore," he declared, with all the pomp of a Shakespearean actor. His hand extended in a dramatic flourish, pointing toward the chalkboard and the empty teacher's desk. "Proper introduction is thy solemn duty."

I stared at him, momentarily stunned.

Who the hell does this guy think he is?

Drawing in a deep breath, I prepared to tell him to go suck on a vacuum cleaner—or something significantly more obscene.

But then he winked at me. My stomach dropped like I'd just missed a step on the stairs. *Fantastic.* Not only was the universe out to humiliate me, but it had apparently assigned this guy as my personal tormentor.

The air seemed to leave the room.

As fantasies of throttling this idiot floated through my mind—or perhaps dangling him outside the second-floor window—a collective gasp rippled through the classroom, accompanied by muffled giggles and snickering. Swallowing my words, my pulse quickened.

Everyone seemed to know something I didn't.

He was closer now. *Too close.* Close enough that I could smell him—a warm, woodsy scent with a faint trace of something spicy.

It smelled good. *Too good.*

Heat flooded my face as I realized I was blushing.

What. The. Hell.

Meeting his gaze, I found myself locked in a silent standoff with those brilliant blue eyes. They were annoyingly captivating. Time stretched, seconds turning into what felt like an eternity, before he leaned in and whispered,

"Boo."

Naturally, that was the exact moment my composure deserted me, and I jumped with a tiny squeal—a sound I was fairly convinced had not graced my vocal repertoire since kindergarten.

His laughter erupted, loud and unapologetic. His eyes crinkled at the corners as he beamed at me, clearly reveling in my discomfort.

A disquieting notion fluttered at the edge of my consciousness.

He wasn't as young as I'd initially thought.

There was an edge to his appearance, something older and rougher than the boyish grin he wore. And upon closer inspection, his face held more lines than one would assume at first glance.

No.

Holy hell.

No.

It couldn't be.

"Frankly, my dear," he said, cutting through my spiraling thoughts with an infuriatingly smooth tone, delivering his words with the suave demeanor of Rhett Butler from Gone with the Wind. "I don't give a damn who you think I am. I am your teacher, Mr. Black—though I prefer my students call me Greyson."

He punctuated the declaration with another smirk and, of course, another wink.

Like he just read my mind. *Why does he have to wink at me?* Once might've been an accident. Twice felt like a choice. If this was going to be a thing, I was going to need a strategy.

As he walked to the front of the room, I found myself staring.

Correction.Dad would have called it *ogling*.

His loose, confident stride had a magnetic quality, drawing my gaze even as I internally screamed at myself to look away. Then my eyes landed on his shoes, and my stomach dropped.

Red Chucks.

Bright, bold, unmistakable.

Matching mine.

Oh no.

No, no, no.

Have I stumbled into my own personal hell?

Heat bloomed beneath my skin, and I could feel my face flushing a shade of scarlet that surely rivaled the hue of our matching footwear.

"Miss, given your tardiness, I say again, the privilege of introduction falls upon you," Greyson said, turning to face me with an expectant grin. His tone was light, almost playful, but there was an undeniable authority beneath it, while maintaining that Rhett Butler charm.

Extending his hand toward me, I swore my cheeks had found a new shade of red not currently on the color wheel.

As I hesitated, he furrowed his brow and drew a deep breath.

I was almost certain I was annoying him now, so I left my backpack stationed on the floor by what I *hoped* would be my desk at the back. Avoiding his hand, still outstretched, I made my way toward the front of the class.

My voice was clipped and rushed as I spoke. "My name is Sady Smith. My family just moved here from Paris."

I delivered the words like a rapid-fire monologue, not even pausing for breath. *Damn it*. I'd forgotten to mention the job transfer excuse.

"Not so fast, Miss Sady," he said, perching precariously on the edge of his desk. His eyes glinted with curiosity. "The attendance list shows a different name. Care to explain what Sadatana means?"

I swallowed a groan, accompanied by the start of a classic teenage eyeroll.

Here we go again.

"Uhm, yeah sure." *If it was at all possible to roll my eyes further back, I could have stared at my own ass.*

"It's derived from Sanskrit. It means Everlasting or Eternal. My parents are dorks, okay?"

Muffled giggles filled the room, offering a glimmer of hope that perhaps some of my classmates might be sympathetic. Or at the very least, have a compatible sense of humor.

"Please, do elaborate further," Greyson continued, his smirk unwavering. "Where were you born? Parents? Siblings? Allergies? Favorite food? Secrets no one else knows? This is history class, after all, and learning your history will be on tomorrow's pop quiz."

My irritation flared.

"Oh, well, uhm—" I started. "I was born in Romania. Parents are alive and still happily married—to each other, I might add. Only child. Parents were both only children, which means no living relatives. No allergies, unless you count pompous jerks. Favorite food? Cherries. Favorite color? Red. As for secrets, you haven't earned them. Satisfied?"

The last sentence hissed out of my mouth in a rather embarrassing display of frustration—or should I say, embarrassment.

"Why thank you, Miss Sady!" A quick hop, and he was standing again. "I wonder if you might tell us why you do not have an accent, Romanian or French, if you do indeed hail from the old world continent?"

"I said I moved from there." My jaw practically snapped at him. *Is this guy for real?* Why won't he just let me sit down? "I didn't say I grew up there."

"Pardon me for the assumption." He obviously had no clue how uncomfortable this was making me. "You may be seated, with my gratitude."

Is the moment over? Man, that was awkward.

"Miss Sady?" I was like a deer caught in headlights when he winked at me and I realized that I hadn't moved. "I said, you may be seated."

Did my teacher seriously just wink at me? Maybe he had some kind of involuntary eye twitch. Or a medical condition. Yeah, let's go with that.

Turning on my heel, I was eager to escape the spotlight.

I settled into my seat, exhaling a sigh of relief. Now to survive the next hour without calling further attention to myself.

"Don't worry, you'll get used to him." The girl sitting beside me leaned in, her voice warm with reassurance. "I've been in his class since ninth grade. He has this weird way of making everyone feel completely on the spot, but somehow, you never feel humiliated. It's like... he wants you to push past the awkwardness, not drown in it."

I glanced at her, surprised by the kindness and insight in her tone. Not usual for teen girls, I should add.

"He's different," she admitted with a small smile. "But in a way that makes you feel safe. He has this way of pulling people out of their shells. Most of us actually thrive here."

I smiled back, my nerves still buzzing but just a little less edged.

Her gaze lingered on me for a moment before she suddenly leaned in closer, curiosity written across her features. "Oh wow," she said, her voice hushed. "You have heterochromia, don't you? Your eyes—they're different colors!"

I blinked, startled by her observation. "Uhm, yeah," I murmured.

Not really a fan of being inspected at such close range, but my neighbor leaned in with the kind of easy confidence that made it feel less invasive—more like curiosity than scrutiny. There was something refreshingly open about her, the kind of person who made conversation feel effortless.

"That's so cool!" she exclaimed, her grin widening. "It's like something out of a superhero movie."

"Can we please not make a big deal out of this?" I whispered at her, hoping that Mr. Black did not hear us at the back. The last thing I wanted was to gain even more attention than I already had.

"Consider it done." And now it was her turn to wink at me.

This time I didn't blush, but I did smile back.

The rest of the class passed in a blur.

Greyson didn't teach so much as perform, moving through the room with an effortless, magnetic energy that was impossible to ignore. He leapt onto desks to demonstrate historical events, swung a chalk-covered ruler to mimic sword fights, and delivered dramatic monologues in a way that would make Broadway actors jealous.

It was... captivating.

And that was *the problem.*

I caught myself leaning forward—just slightly—and immediately snapped back, forcing my spine straight. *Oh no. Nope. Nope.*

This is my teacher.

This is not happening. If there was a higher power listening, now would be a great time to smite me where I stand. Or at least drop a conveniently placed distraction, like a fire drill. Or an alien invasion. Anything, really.

A strange warmth curled in my belly, foreign and unwelcome.

I shoved it down immediately, filing it away under the *things-we-will-never-acknowledge*-section of my brain.

Across the room, I noticed I wasn't alone in my reaction. Several students, both girls and guys, watched him with varying levels of amusement, admiration, or barely concealed infatuation. One girl near the window was doodling something in the corner of her notebook—yep, definitely the outline of his mohawk surrounded by small hearts.

Even my seat neighbor seemed entertained.

She caught my eye and grinned, her sleeves swallowing her hands as she nudged me lightly with an elbow. The baggy sweater she wore draped over her frame, the cuffs well past her wrists, hiding half her fingers like she was permanently tucked into a cocoon of fabric.

"Told you," she whispered, nudging me lightly with her elbow. "Weird, but worth it."

I exhaled with a half-scoff, half-laugh. "Yeah, he's... something."

"Don't worry, the shamelessly eccentric thing grows on you," she said with a smirk. "Besides, you'll notice something about his class—no one fails. Even the kids who normally struggle? They get it in here."

That caught my attention. I scanned the room, noting that everyone was engaged, even the students who had seemed disinterested earlier. Greyson had an uncanny way of making everyone feel like they were part of something, like they mattered.

That didn't make my reaction to him any less *bizarre*, though.

She glanced at me again, tilting her head slightly. "You okay? You've got that 'I'm internally screaming' look."

I forced a casual shrug. "Just processing the most ridiculous class I've ever been in."

She grinned. "Yeah, that's about right."

As she turned back to her notebook, the noise of the classroom faded into the background. My thoughts, however, refused to follow suit.

The rest of the day slipped by in a haze. I couldn't concentrate in my other classes, and the details of each period blurred together. My thoughts kept circling back to Greyson. His energy, his presence, the strange way he'd made me feel.

What even was that?

A fluke? Some weird chemical reaction? Maybe my nervous system had short-circuited from the sheer absurdity of the situation. I'd never felt anything like it before—so why now? Why him?

My teacher.

Ah, hell. How wrong is that?

By the time the final bell rang, I was more than ready to leave. Locating my locker at the end of the day turned out to be easier than I thought. The school had already put a lock on it, but no matter how many different ways I tried the combination, the blasted contraption wouldn't open. And given my extensive school experience, I'd learned every trick in the book to open a lock.

Glancing around to ensure the hallway was empty, I took a deep breath, flexed my fingers, and yanked.

The lock snapped with a satisfying crack.

Dad always kept a few spares for situations like this—although, admittedly, they were usually for Mom.

I went to shove it into my bag, reminding myself to replace it tomorrow, when the faint sound of snickering behind me caused me to pause. Standing up quickly and turning around, my face nearly collided with the chest of none other than Mr. Black.

He wasn't nearly as tall as my parents, standing maybe five-foot-nine, and his slim build made for a more embarrassing moment than a threatening one.

"Leaving us so soon, Miss Sady?" he asked, his voice low and teasing.

"N-no," I stammered. "My lock broke, so I'm just taking everything home."

He smells so good, and his proximity is tempting me to bury my face in his shirt. *Note to self*—don't do that.

His lips quirked into an amused grin as he inspected the broken lock in my hand. "That lock looks like the devil himself pulled it off," he said, raising an eyebrow.

I fought the urge to groan. My thumbprint had left an unmistakable dent in the metal.

Damn it.

"Well," he continued, his tone light, "Must've been a manufacturer defect, right? I'm sure the office can replace it in the morning."

I nodded mutely, watching as he turned and strolled down the hallway. His walk was loose and easy, with just the faintest hint of swagger.

What am I doing? No. Stop it.

Exiting the school, I managed to trip over my own feet.

This was unusual—grace was one of the few things I could count on. Years of yoga, martial arts, and Pilates backed by genetics have made me coordinated and steady, more so than girls my age.

But today, my thoughts were scrambled, and it felt like my usual balance had abandoned me.

I caught myself before I could fall, glancing around to make sure no one saw my embarrassing misstep. With a huff, I adjusted my backpack and slid on my sunglasses, shielding myself from the late-afternoon glare. My focus shifted to the bus stop at the edge of the lot—then I saw him.

Dad.

Staring straight at me, having witnessed my misstep.

He was perched on the Harley, his massive frame relaxed but too still. One arm rested casually against the handlebar, but the other gripped his helmet, fingers tense against the leather strap. His hawk-like eyes scanned the sea of students, darting over the crowd like he was searching for something—or *someone.*

A group of kids nearby whispered and pointed, their attention torn between the sleek black motorcycle and the towering man astride it. I couldn't tell which fascinated them more.

But something about his posture felt *off.* It was too rigid, too deliberate. His jaw set, and I recognized that look—the one he gets when he's assessing a threat.

My stomach tightened. *Why is he here? Why does he look like he's expecting trouble?*

I didn't have time to dwell on it.

Because that's when I heard it.

SO TINY. SHE'S SO MUCH SMALLER THAN I EXPECTED.

The words were soft, almost a whisper, but they cut through the noise around me as if the world had gone silent.

But… that was all they were. *Soft.*

There was no biting chill creeping into my skull, no sharp sting of something foreign invading my thoughts. No suffocating pressure, no distant echoes of malice hiding in the undertones.

It was *just* a voice. *Well hell*, that was new.

Curious. Gentle. As if whoever it belonged to was simply wondering about me.

I hesitated. Instinct had always told me to recoil, to brace for pain, to prepare for *them*—but this didn't *feel* like them. Not even close.

I reached out, just a little.

The world shifted. A familiar hum vibrated in my skull, rippling through my senses as I pushed past the veil of what is seen and reached into what *is*.

And—*whoa*.

Warm sapphire blue with soft swirls of brushed silver.

The colors drifted around me, smooth and steady, like sunlight gliding over the surface of a still lake.

Nothing about it felt threatening.

I let out a slow breath.

This wasn't the same. This was *different*.

This felt *safe*?

The weight in my chest eased, the tension which felt like it had coiled in my muscles for years, but was only seconds, finally loosening—

A bellow cut through the air, shattering the moment.

"Get on the bike. Now."

The soft hum of awareness vanished in an instant, ripped away like a tide retreating too fast. The parking lot, the crowd, the real world crashed back into focus, and suddenly, I was standing there, my dad's voice ringing in my ears.

Dad's order was clear. Commanding. *That was usually Mom's job.*

Any argument died on my lips—he was already moving.

He strode toward me, the easygoing demeanor he wore like a second skin gone. His usual calm had been replaced with a controlled urgency.

I barely had time to react before he grabbed my helmet, jamming it onto my head with firm hands. Then, without waiting for my consent, he hoisted me onto the Harley. One steadying hand gripped my arm as he swung himself onto the seat in front of me.

"Dad, it's okay!" I shouted over the rumbling engine as he started the bike. "I'm fine! It's not—"

"It's not okay, Sady!"

His voice cut through the noise, hard and unyielding. "Hang on!"

The bike lurched forward, and I barely had time to grab hold of him before we tore out of the parking lot.

The world blurred. Wind roared in my ears, pressing against my helmet as he pushed the bike beyond the speed limit. My pulse kicked up, adrenaline and unease flooding my veins.

"Dad, stop! Please!"

My voice was lost to the rush of air and the roar of the city.

I squeezed my eyes shut, my mind spinning. The voice. The words. The tension in Dad's posture.

Something was happening—and for the first time in years, I felt it.

The shadow of the past creeping back into my life.

It was here.

Chapter 4

Dad reached out to Mom—not with his voice, but with his mind. His thoughts carried across the space between them, reverberating so powerfully that even I caught faint echoes, despite the roar of the engine.

RENDEZVOUS POINT B.

The message didn't travel through air or sound. It crossed kilometers in an instant, carried along the unseen current that bound our family—a connection stronger than distance, as natural as breathing.

Mom's acknowledgment was immediate. She didn't waste time questioning or debating—not when it was serious. Her response was precise:

ETA FIVE MINUTES.

As Dad steered us through traffic, my stomach churned. He had already broken half a dozen traffic laws, and I could feel the urgency radiating from him. I tried to focus on the passing scenery, mentally tracking landmarks and estimating how long it would take to reach our destination. My calculations aligned with Mom's. *Five minutes.*

A pang of genuine worry gripped me. Mom, the tougher of the two, possessed a tunnel vision sharper and narrower than Dad's, especially when it came to *them.*

When we finally pulled into the sprawling parking lot of Terminal 3 at Pearson International Airport, I felt it—the unspoken truth lingering like a storm cloud.

We would run. *Again*.

That was what this meant.

The thought hit me harder than expected. Moving meant leaving. Leaving meant starting over. *Again*. Leaving meant erasing every small trace of normalcy I'd managed to carve out in less than a day.

Leaving meant I wouldn't see him again.

Mr. Black.

My teacher.

That realization landed somewhere between mild panic and sheer absurdity, like finding out you'd developed an allergy to oxygen.

I had known him for less than a day, and yet the idea of never seeing him again tugged at something deep inside me—unsettling and unexpected. It didn't make sense. I wasn't *that* girl—the type who got flustered over a teacher, of all people. I wasn't the type to let someone matter that quickly.

But none of this was normal, was it?

I had felt the SURGE, heard a voice in my mind that wasn't my own—and my parents had no idea.

But somehow, they still knew enough to react.

Now, my parents were ready to drop everything. *Again*.

This had always been my life. Long before I was born—before I could even understand the danger—my parents had been running from *them*.

And I understood that. I really did.

But right now?

Right now, all I could think about was the fact that I wasn't ready to leave.

For the first time in as long as I could remember, I had something I wanted to stay for. And the conflict of it—the sheer selfishness—gnawed at me.

Some of those teen shows, like The Vampire Diaries, were starting to make some disturbing sense. *Damn it.*

The bike slowed to a stop, the engine rumbling beneath us as Dad surveyed the lot. My eyes scanned the area, searching for Mom.

She stood cloaked in shadows, nonchalantly leaning against a pillar with one ankle crossed over the other. However, her crossed arms betrayed the inner turmoil brewing beneath her calm demeanor.

Two reasons prompted someone to cross their arms.

So, ask yourself—what did a person with a propensity for violence do to restrain themselves from having previously mentioned violent outbursts?

Cross their arms.

The wind toyed with her braid, tugging at the loose strands until they whipped around her face. It was only then that I noticed we were sporting the same hairstyle—a tiny, absurd detail that briefly distracted me from the tension.

Mom remained perfectly still, her eyes scanning the area with predatory precision. It was a stance I had seen countless times, but it never failed to unsettle me.

She didn't move until Dad killed the engine. Then, in one swift motion, she pushed off the pillar and strode toward us.

She enveloped Dad in a fierce embrace, her body momentarily softening against his. But her focused gaze didn't falter—it darted around the lot, ensuring no one had followed us.

Despite her agitation, I found some comfort in the predictability of her actions, even if the implications weren't reassuring.

When she turned to me, her hands cradled my face with surprising gentleness. She pressed a kiss to my right eyebrow, just above the violet eye.

"Would you two please explain," she began, her voice cold and direct, "why I had to leave the Russian ambassador in my office mid-sentence?"

Her glare could have rivaled Medusa's. The tension in her shoulders, the tightness in her jaw—it was all there, barely restrained.

Dad spoke first, his tone calm but firm. "Our daughter felt a SURGE today. Twice, if I'm not mistaken. And—" he glanced at me "—she reached out."

Mom's features hardened. Her violet eyes narrowed, and I felt the sting of her scrutiny, like a spotlight I couldn't escape.

Damn it. Dad always knows.

His years of watching people, of studying every micro-expression, made it impossible to hide anything from him.

"Whoa, whoa, hold on!" I blurted out, throwing my hands up defensively. "Dad's blowing this way out of proportion. He's totally overreacting!"

Dad leaned back against the bike. Now his arms were crossed. He didn't need to say anything.

Mom's silence was louder than any words he could utter.

"This is different," I insisted, my voice trembling under the intensity of their stares. "Both of you, just listen to me for a second!"

Only too late did I realize that neither of them had uttered a single word yet.

Mom's gaze pierced through me. "By all means," she said, her voice dangerously soft. "Enlighten us. Why is this 'different'? And why, by all the shadows of Tartarus, did you think it was a good idea to reach out?"

Her quiet was worse than shouting. It was a silence that crackled with suppressed anger.

"Well, uhm, you see…" I faltered, the words tangling in my throat, feeling the weight of their expectant gazes pressing down on me. "This morning, it didn't even feel like a SURGE. It was all hazy-like. It was like… a baby SURGE."

Mom cracked her knuckles—a snapping, deliberate sound that sent shivers down my spine.

"What exactly did you feel?" Dad's calm voice offered a stark contrast to Mom's intensity.

"Honestly?" I threw my hands up in exasperation. "It felt like a nauseating flutter just above my belly button, okay? Like when your belly does a little weird flip on a rollercoaster. Not painful, not forceful, or freezing; it was kinda lame in comparison to the first time and lasted only a second, maybe two. So, Dad, with it being my last year of high school, I chalked it up to nerves."

"Sady doll," his giant paw of a hand came down gently on my shoulder. "I'm worried. It's unlike you to keep secrets. So, what happened when I came to pick you up?"

"It's stupid, okay?" I snapped, frustration bubbling to the surface. *They're going to make me say it, damn it.* "It didn't feel bad. It wasn't threatening."

"What was it?" Mom pressed, her voice edged with steel. "What did you feel?"

I hesitated, my gaze dropping to the ground.

"It said…" I muttered indignantly. "'Tiny. She's so much smaller than I expected.'"

Mom stiffened.

"A freakin' voice now?! And you didn't think to tell Dad immediately?" she demanded through clenched teeth.

"Seriously, Mom?!" I burst out, the words tumbling out so fast even Dad flinched. "Besides the fact that he practically cracked my skull jamming my helmet on, and dragged me onto the Harley without even letting me speak?"

At least he had the decency to look remorseful, although he knew it would take more than that to crack my skull.

"Have you ever considered the possibility that I am sick and tired of moving every year?" My temper flared, and my voice grew louder. "You insist on me attending school and living as if everything's normal. But we're not normal. Moving every damn year isn't normal. Every day is a lie, and I'm sick of it."

Hot tears spilled down my cheeks, my voice rising with every word. "When I felt it the first time, I ignored it because I knew what it would mean. But the second time, I reached out to assess the risk—just like you taught me."

Mom and Dad stood closer together, unprepared for my emotional outburst, especially when snot started dribbling from my nose. *Very graceful, Sady.*

"Look, they are cold enough to freeze hell over, right?" I dug my heels in. "Shades of dark gray and deep crimson slicing through the air? Well, this was warm sapphire blues with brushed silver. Not even remotely the same, okay? And clearly, there was no aggression—unless you count picking on my size as aggressive."

My voice trailed off into a whimper.

"Wait, what?" Mom's scrutiny shifted from anger to curiosity as she stopped cracking her knuckles. "Your size?"

"Yeah, hello? The words 'tiny' don't ring a bell?" I was so upset the tears had stopped, replaced by hiccups—an unfortunate side effect that drove both of them nuts since they had never experienced them. "Must have been referring to me. Clearly, I am a disappointment, and not just to you, Mom. I'm sorry I'm defective, okay?"

They froze. Not a breath, not a bat of an eyelash. Time stood still for five, maybe ten seconds. The tension in the air abruptly faded, because Mom had started snickering under her breath. She didn't even have the nerve to hide it.

"Sady baby, I'm sorry—" she began, but the lack of conviction in her tone ruined the effect. Meanwhile, I was shaking and hiccuping, and poor Dad looked from one to the other, utterly bewildered. Not that I blamed him.

"You're not defective," Mom added, her lips twitching as she tried to suppress her amusement. "You're precious."

Oh, for the love of—

"Okay, dolls," Dad interjected, seeing where this was headed. "No immediate action is required. We'll monitor, assess the situation, and go from there."

"Agreed," I blurted out, my relief evident. If they knew my true reason for wanting to stay, they might still make us move. They cannot know about Greyson. *No way. Not ever.*

Mom's keen gaze lingered on me a moment longer, her violet eyes narrowing as if searching for cracks in my argument. Then, with a faint sigh, she let her arms drop to her sides.

The storm had passed—for now. But not without conditions.

"Sady," Mom said, her tone shifting into something far more measured—her strategist voice. "From this point forward, if you feel another SURGE, you will not—under any circumstances—reach out.

You will not probe. You will not attempt to 'assess the risk' like you did today."

I swallowed hard. "But—"

"No. Exceptions." Her gaze bore into mine, sharp as tempered steel. "You come straight to us. Understood?"

I hesitated for half a second too long.

"Sady," Dad warned.

"Fine," I mumbled. *Like I had a choice anyway.*

Mom studied me for another beat, then gave a small nod as if mentally filing away loose ends. She already had a plan in mind—she always did.

"Sam," she continued, turning toward Dad. "We'll talk later about contingencies."

His expression flickered, but he nodded once. That was the thing about them—Mom made the plans, Dad made sure they worked.

And me?

I was just along for the ride.

"Since we're all here, and my calendar has been preemptively cleared," Mom said, her tone softer now, "how about dinner?"

Dad raised an eyebrow, clearly amused by the abrupt shift in her mood. "Dinner?"

"Yes, dinner," Mom replied, a wry smile tugging at her lips. "Preferably somewhere that doesn't require me to cook. And we can talk about our *wee* daughter's first day of school."

Her faux Scottish accent added a touch of humor to the jab about my size—more amusing than it should have been. I couldn't help but offer up an eye roll at that. Mom's aversion to cooking was legendary. Dad and I had long since accepted that if food preparation was left to her, we were either eating burnt toast or ordering takeout.

Dad took off solo on his Harley, the deep rumble of the engine fading into the distance as I slid into the backseat of Mom's SUV. She spared me any forced conversation, for which I was grateful, and the ride passed in blessed, if not stifled, silence.

Lucky for us, there was a gem of a restaurant nearby that catered perfectly to our eclectic dietary preferences. By the time we were seated, the tension from earlier had dissipated enough for us to slip into the rhythm of normalcy—at least, as close to normal as we ever got.

The server approached, visibly flustered under the brightness of Dad's green gaze. "May I offer you something to drink?" she stammered, her eyes darting between us. "And can I interest you in any of our specials?"

Dad's calm, measured tone immediately put her at ease as he ordered for the table. To anyone watching, we were just another family out for dinner—laughing, chatting, enjoying a rare night out together.

But caution was second nature to us.

Dinner began with small talk. Mom regaled Dad with stories from her latest UN assignment, her voice animated as she described the political intricacies of her work. Dad listened intently, his sharp mind piecing together the subtleties with ease.

And, as always, we played our little game—shifting languages mid-conversation, layering an extra barrier between us and anyone who might be listening. *Just in case.*

I was fluent in eight languages—English, French, German, Russian, Italian, Portuguese, Spanish, and Latin—with decent proficiency in Mandarin, Sanskrit, and Aramaic. Mom and I often defaulted to Latin, while Dad preferred to speak Aramaic with me. It was second nature by now, an invisible shield we had perfected over the years.

The poor server did a double take more than once, clearly thrown off by our casual transitions. At one point, she hesitated before setting down a dish, as if debating whether to ask what on earth we were talking about. Each time, Dad put her at ease again. He had his charms.

I, on the other hand, found myself lost in thought, absentmindedly folding the edge of my napkin into tiny, precise creases. My fork nudged at my food, but I barely took a bite. My mind was elsewhere—back in the classroom with Greyson.

Was he single?

The thought crept in, unbidden and unwelcome. I shoved it aside as quickly as it came. But it didn't leave. His cerulean-blue eyes, the way his voice seemed to wrap around every word, the faint scent of cedar and spice—*it was all I could think about.*

"What do you think, Sady baby?"

Uh oh. *Crap.* Who asked me what now? I blinked, realizing both of them were looking at me expectantly.

"Just discussing the idea of jetting off somewhere for the Christmas holidays this year," Mom said, as though everything was utterly ordinary. She was a master at masking her concerns. "Maybe a visit with Ramira?"

"That sounds... great," I replied automatically, though my enthusiasm was noticeably absent. Normally, the prospect of visiting Ramira—the closest and only thing we had to family—would excite me. But tonight, my mind was too preoccupied to muster much interest.

Mom's gaze lingered on me for a beat longer, her composure cracking just slightly. A faint twitch near one of her eyes betrayed her irritation, though she quickly reined it in. She was a master at maintaining her facade, exuding an effortless grace that I had always envied. Even in moments of frustration, she seemed untouchable.

Meet Sera Smith, a.k.a. *Mom.* At just six feet tall, her presence was commanding in a way that turned heads wherever she went. Her jet-black hair, straight as an arrow, cascaded almost to her waist, framing a face so striking it was almost unreal. Her violet eyes—so much like my right—were framed by lashes so thick and flawless they belonged in a mascara commercial. *Maybe she was born with it. Maybe it was some cosmic cheat code.*

Her porcelain skin only added to the ethereal quality about her, and when she smiled—a genuine, unguarded smile—Dad fell a little more in love with her. Which was saying something, because they had been together like... forever.

Her voice was rich and velvety, carrying a faint rasp with a subtle, almost-impossible-to-place accent that only added to her mystique. Even without trying, she commanded attention. I had seen her quiet a room full of people with a single word. Oh, and if I had a nickel for every time someone, regardless of age, tried to flirt with her, I'd be a millionaire.

But for all the attention she drew, there was one constant—me.

No matter how chaotic her work schedule got, Mom had always made it a priority to spend our mornings together. From the time I could walk, she had woken me up at the ungodly hour of five a.m. to join her in rigorous workouts. She claimed it was her way of "exercising her demons," but I thought it was also her way of keeping us connected. Her notion of quality mother-daughter time.

I guess, in a way, movement had always been her language.

Amidst the fervent rituals of her workouts, Mom found a special kind of peace in dance. There was something almost hypnotic about the way she moved, as if the music wove through her very bones.

It didn't matter what kind of music it was; if it had rhythm, she found a way to lose herself in it. When she danced, her movements became something otherworldly, almost weightless. Watching her was like watching a panther glide through the jungle—graceful, powerful, and entirely untouchable.

I remember the first time music moved me. Not in some vague, foggy childhood memory, but crystal clear—like it happened yesterday. One second, I was a wobbly, floor-bound potato, and the next, I was up, my chubby little legs stumbling forward, arms flailing, tiny diapered butt shaking like the universe had personally issued me a dance challenge.

Not walk. *Dance.*

So, yeah. I guess it runs in the family.

As for Dad, well, his love of music had instilled in me an appreciation for an eclectic array of genres, styles, and artists, no matter how obscure they seemed.

It was funny, really—Mom and Dad had taught me so much about everything, yet nothing they had ever said or done could have prepared me for *this*. This thing I was feeling. This strange, electric pull I couldn't quite explain. None of their lessons on self-discipline, emotional regulation, or situational awareness had equipped me to deal with the fluttering chaos that was my brain right now.

Greyson Black.

Why does his name sound like a melody I can't stop humming? Why does my skin prickle with warmth every time I think about him?

Why does my first crush have to be on a teacher?

This feels almost as pathetic as Elena Gilbert pining after the Salvatore brothers. This can't be what my life has been reduced to?

Back at the dinner table, the conversation flowed effortlessly between Mom and Dad, switching between languages as they discussed plans for the holidays. My parents, and I, were masters of code-switching, their words a careful blend of casual chatter and subtle strategy. It was second nature to them, a skill honed over years of living in shadows.

I listened absently, nodding when prompted, but my thoughts were miles away. And then I caught my reflection in the restaurant's windowpane.

For a moment, I tried to see myself as someone else might. Against the backdrop of my parents—two of the most beautiful people on the planet—I felt like a pale, petite imitation.

Remember when I said I inherited equal parts of both of them? I did—*quite literally.*

Mom's jet-black hair mixed with Dad's unruly curls had left me with a mostly untamable mass of waves. A single streak of light blonde grew stubbornly over my left eye, defying every attempt we had made to color or hide it. Thanks to that streak, I had earned endless comparisons to Rogue from *X-Men*—a favorite among comic book nerds at previous schools.

My eyes were another oddity. Mom's deep violet was mirrored in my right eye, while my left took after Dad's bright emerald green. It was a striking combination, I supposed, but it was also another thing that set me apart. People tended to stare, though most were too polite to comment. The ones who did usually asked if I was wearing colored contacts. *I wasn't.* We had tried those too, but let's just say... they didn't take.

My face was round, with what Dad insisted on calling "cherubic" cheeks. Mom, less tactfully, had referred to them as "chubby." *Thanks, Mom.* Neither term felt flattering. My lips, meanwhile, were average at best, lacking the fullness that might lend them some drama. And then there was my dimple, from Dad's full-dimpled smile. Just one, on the left side, sitting beneath my green eye. It was cute, I guessed, but it felt mismatched—like the rest of me.

Even my ears seemed determined to be different. They were subtly pointed, just enough to draw comparisons to elves or faeries. Another feature I had spent time agonizing over, wishing they were rounder, or just... *normal*, so I mostly kept them tucked under my aforementioned hair.

As for my complexion, I fell somewhere between my parents. Mom's porcelain skin didn't tan, while Dad's naturally deep bronzed tone seemed to glow year-round. I sat awkwardly in the middle—olive-toned, but not enough to be striking. Just enough to look like I had spent a little too much time in the sun.

I let out a small sigh and turned back to my meal, pushing the reflection—and the insecurities that came with it—out of my mind. It's just my face. *Why does it matter all of a sudden?*

Dinner carried on with its usual rhythm, Mom and Dad debating global politics between bites of food, while I pretended to be present. But my mind wasn't on the conversation. It kept circling back to everything that had happened today—the SURGE, the voice, and I couldn't exclude the growing infatuation with Greyson.

By the time we finally left the restaurant, I was more exhausted than I should have been. Not physically, but mentally. Emotionally. It was as if my brain had spent the entire meal running in circles, trying to untangle a knot that refused to loosen.

Back home, I retreated to my bedroom with every intention of tackling homework. But my thoughts refused to focus. What should've been a simple assignment stretched into hours as I replayed the events of the day over and over in my mind.

Greyson. Those blue eyes. I think they are cerulean-blue. His voice. *His scent.*

I sprawled on my bed upside down, feet propped against the headboard, staring up at the skylight. The night sky beyond was clear, the barely visible stars scattered like flecks of silver on black velvet. I tried to focus on my breathing, grounding myself the way Dad had taught me, but it was useless. My mind spiraled.

Why does my first crush have to be on a teacher? Of all the people in the world, why him?

Sleep eventually claimed me, though my dreams were no respite.

My dreams were filled with shadows and whispers, with flickers of sapphire and silver. And somewhere, just on the edge of consciousness, I felt another SURGE.

It was soft but distinct, resonating through the shadows like a ripple in still water. A shiver passed through me—not of fear, but of something else. Something that felt impossibly vast and deeply unfamiliar.

It faded as quickly as it came, leaving me adrift in the silence of my subconscious.

CHAPTER 5

The morning sun slipped through my window, its warmth creeping beneath my covers, dragging me from restless sleep. *Odd*—Mom hadn't woken me for our customary training session. *That was unusual.*

Sitting up in bed, my body protested the movement for the second day in a row. Sleep had been elusive since arriving in this town, restless and filled with fragmented dreams. A lingering sense of something vast and unfathomable clung to the edges of my mind, slipping through my grasp like mist. Sapphire and brushed silver flickered in the recesses of memory—distant, fleeting. The whispers of a SURGE hummed just beneath my skin, faint but persistent, like a song I couldn't quite recall.

Had it even been real? Or had I imagined it, just another trick of exhaustion warping my senses?

But it hadn't been just one dream. There had been others—dreams that felt *different*. The first had been steeped in something weightless, a world of symbols and shifting light of sapphire and silver, where meaning floated just beyond reach. Those had felt... *otherworldly*. Like echoes of something bigger than me.

Then there was *him*.

Greyson.

His presence had bled into my subconscious, unraveling the edges of those other dreams and leaving something far more tangible in their place. No strange symbols, no mystical weight—just him. Too real. Too close. Like my mind had decided to betray me in ways I didn't have the patience to unpack.

Why couldn't I be like a normal teenage girl, harboring crushes on boy-band members or actors?

At least, I assumed that was normal. I wouldn't know for sure. Normal was a foreign concept to me, but I was pretty certain that crushing on a teacher didn't fit into its definition.

Preparing for another day of school, my mind whirred with relentless thoughts.

For the past few years, I'd assumed I might be asexual. I had never entertained a proper crush, never felt that rush of attraction everyone always talked about. Our constant moving made attachments impossible, fostering an inevitable sense of detachment.

But it wasn't just the leaving that hurt—it was the knowledge that anyone I let get close might not survive the crossfire. They could get hurt because of me, drawn into danger they never asked for.

And beyond all that? I had never so much as kissed anyone.

And then there was the sheer drama of teenage relationships. Observed in many school hallways, locker rooms, and TV shows filled with exaggerated teen angst. *Who willingly signs up for that?* Not me. *No, thank you.*

My hair was even less cooperative than usual this morning, stray strands sticking out at impossible angles, mocking my every attempt to tame them. After wrestling with a defiant braid, I finally gave up and resorted to a red velvet headband. Functional, if uninspired.

Reaching for my backpack, my eyes fell on the single family photograph on my dresser. The only one we had. It had survived four years and just as many moves, which in itself felt like a miracle. We never kept journals, never had keepsake boxes, and certainly never held onto anything that would leave traces of where we had been. That was the rule. Efficiency over sentiment. Yet somehow, this one photo had made it through.

It had been taken when I was fourteen, during a our month-long stint in Santorini. At the time, we were living in Athens, though "living" always felt like a temporary state. The trip had been an anomaly—a rare, impulsive getaway where we weren't training or preparing for the next inevitable move. For a whole month, we had existed like any other family, indulging in ridiculous amounts of gelato from Lolita's.

We had spent slow afternoons stretched out on the warm sand, reading as the waves lapped at the shore, the scent of salt thick in the air. Evenings were spent at Santorini Mou, watching the sun sink into the caldera, the sky streaked in molten gold and deep rose. We wandered through the narrow alleyways of Oia, ducking into tiny artisan shops filled with hand-painted ceramics, woven textiles, and bottles of fragrant olive oil. On a whim, we ferried to Pyrgos, climbing its winding paths to the ruins of the old Venetian castle, where the wind howled through broken stone.

One morning, we wandered through the island's orchards, our fingers grazing sun-warmed fruit. The figs were the size of Mom's fist, so sweet they tasted almost unreal. We were explorers then, unburdened, pretending—just for a little while—that we belonged to the world instead of skirting its edges. And, of course, we had indulged in ridiculous amounts of gelato from Lolita's, savoring every creamy bite as if trying to make the memory last. *Speaking of memories.*

Mom had asked a passing tourist to take the picture, something she never did. I was the only one looking directly at the camera. My parents, ever the embodiment of devotion, were gazing at each other like the rest of the world didn't exist.

When your parents were basically the human equivalent of a grand romance novel—epic love, swoon-worthy devotion, the whole nauseating package—anything less felt like a waste of time. It was like craving a steak but being handed a soggy burger from a fast-food joint. *What was the point?*

I wondered sometimes if the people we met in each country ever thought of us, or if we vanished from their memories as easily as we vanished from the places themselves. Dwelling wasn't useful. That was another rule.

Rummaging through my wardrobe, I couldn't help but note the irony. I had always found it amusing how other girls fussed over their crushes, obsessing over their outfits, hair, and makeup, as if teenage boys would ever notice the difference. And yet, here I was, standing in my underwear, trying to decide if my sweater should match my socks.

It wasn't until I found myself standing on my bed in a simple red-and-black bra and matching panties that I realized I'd spent an hour trying on every possible outfit combination. My room looked like a tornado had torn through it.

Then I heard the creak of the stairs.

"Sady baby?" Mom's voice cut through my frantic scrambling. "Coming in!"

Leaping from my bed, I knew if she caught this mess, it would launch an interrogation. With a steadying breath, I determined this warranted drastic action. Drawing on the suppressing shield that Dad had taught me, I moved several paces faster than a human to get dressed, just managing to slip on my socks before she opened the door fully. My heart pounded as the door swung open, but I managed to appear calm—at least, I *hoped* so.

"Wow, you're just getting ready now?" Mom teased, planting a kiss above my violet eye. "Did you sleep all right?"

Define 'all right'. Those dreams were something else.

"It's all good, Mom. Just a tad tired, that's all," I said, hoping to evoke a hint of maternal guilt for veering from our routine. "Thanks for letting me sleep in."

"Oh, Sady baby," she said, wrapping me in one of her long, comforting hugs. "I completely forgot. Had a two a.m. conference call with another crisis."

Her gaze lingered on me a moment longer than usual, her head tilting slightly in suspicion, as though she were straining to hear an unspoken truth. *She knows something is off.*

But for now, she decided to let it slide. Impeccably dressed in damson and white, she glided out of my room, her steps impossibly graceful.

I followed, shooting her an irritated glare at her backside. Every day, she looks like she stepped out of Vogue, while I was still grappling with puberty's uncertainty at eighteen, struggling to define my style. The only constant seemed to be the size of my feet, still fitting into kids' shoes.

Downstairs, the morning unfolded in its usual rhythm. I fumbled through breakfast, lost in thought.

"Sady baby, aren't you packing a lunch?" Mom never asked me about food in the morning, usually because she was already gone to work immediately after our workouts.

"Nah, it's fine. I've got lunch plans," I replied, fibbing to Mom for the first time and trying not to hold my breath to see if she caught on.

"Sady doll—" Dad's voice startled me as he emerged from the shadows of the kitchen.

My heart lurched. I wasn't the kind of person who got snuck up on. Years of training had sharpened my instincts, widened my peripheral awareness, made me attuned to the smallest shifts in movement and sound. And yet, somehow, I hadn't noticed him. That was never a good sign.

"Ack! Dad, can you please not do that?"

"Now I am positive that something is going on."

Dad surprising me wasn't just rare—it was deliberate. He didn't waste opportunities like this, and if he was testing me, it meant I was already slipping. *Bad.*

He stepped forward, drawing Mom into his arms, their united front pressing in like walls closing around me.

"Please," he said gently, "don't shut us out."

Wait a minute. Mom's not at work yet, and her two o'clock meeting was likely a pretext. She runs on minimal sleep.

My throat tightened. *Damn it.* They knew something was off with me. How the hell am I going to wriggle out of this?

"Okay, well," I clutched my backpack defensively, shielding my most vulnerable parts—my abdomen and heart. *Mama didn't raise a fool.* Self-preservation dictated a cautious mix of truth and omission. "Well, I am still a little rattled by what happened yesterday—."

"What else happened?" Mom's tone did a total one-eighty.

Great. She just entered what I like to call 'bitch mode'.

"Mom, I'm your daughter!" I snapped, categorically despising it when she flipped that switch. "I won't answer you like one of your stupid soldiers."

Dad's steady hand landed on my shoulder. "Sady, we're not your enemies. We're your family. And you—you're our Everlasting."

The word settled between us like an unspoken truth, heavier than I expected. *Everlasting*. *Sadatana*. They had always called me that, but in moments like this, it felt more like a responsibility than an endearment. A role I was meant to play, even if I didn't fully understand the script.

I swallowed hard, my fingers tightening around the strap of my bag. *No pressure or anything.*

"I'm sorry," I murmured. "I needed time to process. I didn't know how to put it into words—not until I could make sense of it myself."

Mom moved to speak, but Dad silenced her with a gentle hand over her mouth—a brave gesture, considering her penchant for biting. She rolled her eyes but stayed put. Now, why couldn't she do that this time? Bite him again, *that is.* That would totally divert attention away from me.

"Mom, Dad." I steadied myself. "There's someone at school. After careful consideration, it appears that I have developed an absurd infatuation. A crush, to be precise. Rest assured, I have this under control. It won't interfere with my studies."

Was I speaking as a daughter or a soldier? The line blurred in moments like these.

Holding my breath, I waited for the backlash.

Dad's hand fell away, his face betraying nothing. Mom's mouth opened—then erupted into a fit of giggles. She even snorted. It occurred to me, somewhat vaguely, that this was the first time I had actually seen or heard her laugh like that. *So that's where I get the giggle-snorts from.*

Dad's face contorted into something that resembled a fish gasping for air, leaving me bewildered. I stared at both of them, my cheeks growing hotter by the second. Mom was in full hysterics now, tears streaming down her face as she doubled over, and Dad almost lost his grip on her waist.

This was not the reaction I had expected.

"I won't stand here while you gawk at me like a circus act. I'm going to school," I declared, spinning on my heels and stomping out the door. The porch steps splintered beneath my dramatic exit. Let them deal with that.

I grabbed my bike from the porch, pedaling furiously away from my source of embarrassment, the morning's chaos trailing behind me like a storm cloud. The familiar rhythm of the ride should have been soothing, but my thoughts kept spiraling. Before I knew it, I was pulling into the school lot later than I had realized. Despite the emotionally-influenced speed of my tires, I somehow arrived after the bell.

Arriving fashionably late to class wasn't my style, but this morning's events had heightened my stress. Standing in front of the classroom door, I took a deep breath to gather my wits and calm the hell down. Stepping through, my eyes immediately sought the teacher's desk—Greyson's desk.

I should have known better.

He was not where any normal teacher would be.

"Thank you for gracing us with your presence, Miss Sady," his voice greeted me, and a quick scan of the room revealed him leaning against my desk.

Oh. Oh no.

He looked good. *Too* good. The kind of good that made my brain short-circuit for a second. White pants with zippers and pockets everywhere, a black leather jacket over a crisp white t-shirt—casual but effortlessly cool. And somehow, the contrast made his blue eyes even more ridiculous.

Wait. Hold on. Was I just *ogling* my teacher? *Again*?

I blinked, heat creeping up my neck. *Yup.* That's *exactly* what I was doing. And judging by the way he started walking past me, I was probably still doing it. *Fantastic.*

"Uhm, sorry, Mr. Black. Family situation at home," I muttered, sinking into my chair, determined to focus. It was only the second day of school, after all.

"Very well, let us begin." With a dramatic sweep of his hand, he began etching words onto the chalkboard, their edges blurring as my concentration waned. I sank a little lower into my seat, silently grateful that the spotlight had shifted away from me.

"Hey," a voice beside me broke through the haze of my thoughts, grounding me before I drifted too far. "You good?"

She had one of those effortlessly studious looks—like the kind of girl who actually read the recommended books, not just the assigned ones. Even behind her thick glasses, her doe-brown eyes, too big for her face, shone with warmth, framed by thick lashes. An auburn bob skimmed her jaw, slightly tousled, like she had tried to tame it this morning but given up halfway through. The oversized sweater she wore swallowed her arms, the cuffs stretched past her wrists, as if she were perpetually cocooned in a blanket of comfort.

She looked... normal. In the best way. The kind of normal that made her blend into a crowd but still feel approachable.

"Uhm," I fumbled for a response. "Yeah. Just—" *Just what?* Just feeling ridiculous for the way I had been staring at our teacher? Just internally spiraling because of my own lack of emotional experience?

She must have seen my struggle because she offered a small, knowing smile. "You're not the first person to get a little thrown off by him. Mr. Black has this... way about him."

That was an understatement.

"Yeah," I admitted, exhaling. "He really does."

She nodded slightly, thoughtful. "There's something about him—he makes you want to be better, you know? Like he sees something in you that you didn't even know was there."

I glanced toward our teacher, still at the front of the room, completely at ease as he scribbled something onto the board. *That tracks.*

"Just—" she hesitated for a second, as if choosing her words carefully. "Enjoy learning from him. But try to keep your head clear, okay?"

The words settled between us, and for a moment, I couldn't tell if she meant them as a warning or a reassurance. *Maybe both.*

I studied her for a beat, surprised by how easily she had read me. "Thanks," I murmured, feeling more settled than I had a moment ago.

"I'm Kelsey, by the way." She turned back to face the front, leaving me with a faint smile.

I tried to refocus on the lesson, but the words on the board blurred together, barely registering. Every so often, my gaze drifted toward Greyson as he spoke, his voice threading through my thoughts like a song stuck on repeat. *How does he make even the most mundane topics sound interesting?*

I took notes—or at least, I pretended to. Judging by the half-scribbled sentences and the tiny doodles filling the margins, my attention span had long since abandoned me. Kelsey, on the other hand, was furiously jotting things down, occasionally nudging my elbow when I zoned out for too long.

Before I knew it, the bell rang, marking the end of class and yet another day where I couldn't remember half of what was said.

I sighed, gathering my things and tucking my books and pencil case back into my bag—just as Greyson's voice cut through the commotion.

"Miss Sady, could you stay for a moment?"

His tone was casual, almost nonchalant, but it halted me mid-motion. He didn't even look up from his notes as the rest of the students shuffled out.

Crap. What now?

It wasn't that I minded spending more time in his presence—it was the fear of saying something utterly stupid or inappropriate. Worse, what if I did something embarrassing? Like bury my face in his shirt and inhale his woodsy-spice scent.

Note to self—do not, under any circumstances, do that.

"Uhm, sure, Mr. Black," I managed, hovering near the door like a trapped bird. My heart pounded as I watched the last student leave, the door clicking shut behind them. Now it was just us.

"Please, Miss Sady," he said, finally looking up. His cerulean-blue eyes met mine, their intensity disarming. "Take a seat."

I hesitated, torn between compliance and the desire to bolt. Eventually, I sank into the nearest chair, trying to project an air of calm that I definitely did not feel.

He set his notebook aside and leaned against the desk, his stance relaxed but attentive. The proximity was unsettling, the faint scent of his skin making my thoughts blur.

Does he have any concept of personal space?

"I understand you're new here, and it's only the second day of school. We haven't had the chance to establish the rapport that might assure you of my genuine concern for all my students' well-being. Is there something troubling you at home that you'd like to share?"

His question caught me off guard. *Well, this conversation just took a turn I wasn't expecting.* Definitely not where I thought this was going.

"Why do you think something's wrong?" My voice came out higher-pitched than I intended—almost a squeak. *Great. So, smooth Sady.*

"Well," he started, a faint smile tugging at his lips. "Tardiness alone wouldn't give me too much concern, especially given your excellent school records. After all, teens have an art for defying punctuality. But you did tell the class you were late because of a family situation, which implies something might be amiss. And then there's..." He gestured vaguely toward me.

I frowned, confused. "And then there's what?"

Greyson stepped to the other side of his desk, his movements unhurried as he continued. "Your appearance, for starters. Not to sound superficial, but it's... eclectic today."

"Eclectic?" I repeated, my brows furrowing.

"Yes, eclectic," he said, his tone teasing but not unkind. "For instance, you're wearing two different shoes—one orange neon running shoe and one purple Vans. Your socks don't match either, and your sweater appears to be on inside out and backwards."

My jaw dropped as I glanced down at myself. Then I blinked, flabbergasted—which just proved his point. Glancing down again, my jaw slackened. In my rush to get dressed this morning, I had undeniably grabbed one of everything. And not a single peep from my parents. *Were they oblivious?*

Damn it. How did I not notice?

"And there's this," he added, gesturing toward my head. "You've got toothpaste in your braid."

Toothpaste?!

Mortification flooded me, and I resisted the urge to bolt. I reached up to check, my fingers brushing against the sticky residue.

Great. Just great.

Greyson chuckled softly, a sound that felt too warm, too kind for this moment. "Relax, Miss Sady. I'm not here to humiliate you. Everyone has off days."

"Off days," I muttered, more to myself than to him. *Sure, let's call it that.*

His gaze swept over me again, more observant than judgmental. "It appears you either dressed in the dark or in considerable haste—perhaps both. That, combined with the fact that your notes look more like abstract art than actual classwork, suggests something was... distracting you."

I stiffened slightly, but before I could formulate a response, he continued, his tone still even. "And then there's the way you've been sitting in class—like you're here, but not really here." His lips quirked in that unreadable half-smile. "I'd say you're either deeply lost in thought or mildly in shock."

The thought of retreating home to burrow under my blankets for the next two decades sounded really enticing right about now.

I tried to form a coherent response, but my brain had short-circuited. "I, uhm... overslept," I finally managed, my voice weak. "I got dressed in a hurry. And, uhm, my parents were having... a very animated discussion about my personal life. You know how parents get."

Greyson arched an eyebrow, clearly unconvinced but polite enough not to press further. "I see. Well, I'll take your word for it—for now.

But if something is bothering you, please know that my door is always open. I may not look it, but I'm quite good at listening and I care about all of my students."

His gaze lingered on me for a moment longer, probing for a reaction. My heart raced under the weight of his scrutiny. I wanted to look away, but something about him held me in place.

"Thank you, Mr. Black," I mumbled, grabbing my bag and rising to leave.

"Miss Sady? Greyson," he corrected smoothly, his lips quirking into a faint smile. "You can call me Greyson."

"Uhm… okay," I stammered, backing toward the door. "Thank you, Greyson."

He gave a slight nod, his gaze lingering as I slipped out into the hallway—cheeks burning, pulse unsteady.

And promptly walked straight into Kelsey, whose expression of amusement and curiosity made for the most endearing combination.

Chapter 6

"Hey!" Kelsey chirped, her grin wide. "Everything okay? Was he tough on you?"

I exhaled, feeling oddly relieved to have someone my age checking in on me. "Nah, honestly, just a misunderstanding." Shouldering my backpack, I turned down the corridor. "Got dressed in a rush, and apparently, it raised some concerns."

She nudged me playfully. "Don't sweat it."

Her lighthearted tone pulled me back to reality, and I managed a weak smile.

"I mean, I did notice you looked a bit off today, but I just figured—new school, new town. Or maybe this was all the rage in Paris?" She winked, her amusement contagious, pulling more of my own from seemingly nowhere. "But let's face it, Mr. Black isn't exactly your run-of-the-mill teacher, am I right?"

Before I knew it, we were strolling down the hallway together, sharing smiles and easy banter like we had known each other for years. *How odd.*

"Thanks," I said, appreciating her easy-going nature.

"Anytime, Sady. I got your back."

Her grin was effortless, like it was the most natural thing in the world to offer loyalty to someone she barely knew. Then, just as quickly, she was swept into the current of students filling the hallway.

I stood there for a beat, momentarily dumbfounded that a complete stranger had just told me she had my back. *Does she possess no sense of self-preservation?*

My hesitation to head to my next class shifted from uncertainty into a decision. Instead of joining the throng of students shuffling toward their destinations, I veered left, away from the classroom halls and toward the library. I needed a moment—no, several moments—to think. To breathe. To process whatever weirdness this day was shaping up to be.

Libraries had always been my refuge, no matter the country, no matter the school. There was something familiar about them, as if their hushed aisles held the secrets of every life I could imagine but never live. This one was no different—the scent of old paper and ink curled through the air, warm and familiar. Shelves lined with stories stretched out like quiet, watchful sentinels, offering escape routes in neatly bound volumes.

Here, time slowed. Expectations faded. I could disappear into the stacks and exist only in the turn of a page.

I wandered through the shelves aimlessly, my fingers trailing along the spines of books. Titles blurred together as my thoughts tumbled with images of Greyson. His probing questions, the way he looked at me like he could see straight through my carefully constructed walls—it was unnerving. Worse, it made me feel *exposed.*

Stopping in the mythology section, I pulled a thick, leather-bound book from the shelf. The cover was embossed with a golden labyrinth, its intricate paths gleaming under the dim light.

The Gods Within: Myths of Human Divinity.

"Fitting," I muttered, sinking into the nearest chair.

Flipping through the pages, I let my mind wander. The illustrations were stunning—detailed depictions of ancient deities, their faces ageless yet impossibly expressive. The artist was seriously talented.

One caught my eye: a two-page spread of a goddess with violet eyes that mirrored mine, her hands outstretched as she wielded a sword engulfed in silver flames. Her expression was both serene and fierce, as though she could bring worlds to life with a touch or reduce them to ash with a glance.

Who are you? I whispered, running my fingers over the image.

The caption below read: Hekatari, Keeper of the Everlasting Flame.

Her gaze seemed to follow me, the intensity of her violet eyes almost too much to bear. There was something familiar about her.

*Stop it. T*his is absurd. She's a drawing, a figment of someone else's imagination.

And yet...

Curious, I flipped to the About the Author section in the back. Elira Vasquez, a contemporary visionary artist, had undergone a spiritual pilgrimage deep into the Amazon rainforest, where she participated in ayahuasca ceremonies led by indigenous shamans. According to the blurb, she claimed these visions allowed her to commune with celestial beings, ancient gods, and primordial energies, shaping her work as she sought to translate the divine into paint and ink.

I stared back at the goddess on the page. *Was she one of those visions? Or something more?*

The sound of footsteps pulled me from my reverie. I looked up just as Kelsey rounded the corner, her auburn bob bouncing with every step. She spotted me immediately, her face lighting up with a grin.

"There you are!" she exclaimed, plopping down in the chair across from me. "I thought I saw you sneak in here."

"Needed some quiet," I said, closing the book and offering her a small smile. "Rough start to the day."

"Tell me about it," she replied, pulling a pack of gum from her pocket and offering me a piece. "Greyson can be intense, huh?"

"That's one way to put it," I muttered, unwrapping the gum and popping it into my mouth. "He's... different."

She arched an eyebrow, leaning in with a conspiratorial glint in her eyes. "Different, huh? Is that code for 'hot in a tortured-artist kind of way'?"

My cheeks burned, and I fumbled for a response. "I—no! That's not what I meant."

Kelsey laughed, nudging me lightly. "Relax, I'm kidding. Mostly." Then, with a knowing smirk, she added, "But seriously, you're not the first girl, or boy, to notice. He's got this mysterious vibe that drives people crazy."

I groaned, burying my face in my hands. "Great. Just what I need—more reasons to feel awkward around him."

"Hey," Kelsey said, her tone softening. "You're overthinking this. He's just a teacher. Sure, he's unconventional, but at the end of the day, he's still just as human as the rest of us."

If only she knew how much that distinction mattered.

Easier said than done. But I nodded anyway, grateful for her effort to reassure me. "Thanks, Kelsey."

She grinned. "Anytime. Now, come on—if we don't get to class soon, we're both going to get detention."

I hesitated, glancing toward the hallway that led to my next class. Kelsey was already gathering her things, her movements brisk, like someone who had learned that waiting too long meant being left behind. She had latched onto me without hesitation, as if she'd simply decided we were friends before I even had a say in the matter.

And strangely, I didn't mind.

But the thought of sitting through another hour of forced smiles and pretending I wasn't a tangled mess inside was exhausting.

"I think I'm going to pass," I said, trying to keep my tone casual.

Kelsey froze, one eyebrow arching in surprise. "Pass? On class? Are you sure?"

"Yeah," I said quickly, brushing off her concern. "I just... need some air. No big deal."

Kelsey frowned, her brow creasing with worry. "Sady, you sure that's a good idea? You're new. You don't want to get on the teachers' bad side on your second day."

"Trust me, it's fine," I insisted, shouldering my backpack. "I'll just go for a walk, clear my head. And I'll convince my dad to call into the office for me—I'll tell him I've got cramps."

"Oh, great idea. If your Dad's cool with that kind of stuff. Mine never would be." Kelsey hesitated for a moment longer, her eyes flickering between me and the hallway. Finally, she sighed. "You're lucky I like you, Sady. If anyone asks, I'll say I have no idea where you've gone."

"Thanks, Kelsey," I said, flashing her a grateful smile.

"Don't make me regret it!" Kelsey called over her shoulder as she disappeared into the crowd.

As the hallway emptied, I slipped through the side door and into the open air. The fresh breeze hit me like a balm, cooling my heated skin and easing the tightness in my chest.

The courtyard stretched out in front of me, a small patch of grass dotted with benches and enclosed by a low stone wall. A few students lingered in the shade, scrolling through their phones or chatting in hushed tones. None of them seemed to notice me. For the first time all day, I felt like I could breathe.

A nearby park beckoned. Across the grass, a towering maple tree stood with a thick canopy of leaves—perfect for disappearing into.

Pulling my backpack tighter over my shoulder, I made my way toward it, gauging the distance to the ideal spot. With a fluid motion, I leaped up, catching a low branch and swinging myself into the crook of the trunk, concealed behind a screen of foliage.

The warmth of the sun filtered through the leaves from above, casting shifting patterns of gold and umber across the grass below. It was the kind of day that begged to be savored, yet I sat hidden among the branches, cocooned by nature's embrace. The steady sway of the wind whispered against my skin, carrying the faint, earthy aroma of autumn's approach.

For a brief moment, the world seemed to pause just for me.

I leaned back against the sturdy trunk, letting the rough bark press into my shoulder blades. *Inhale. Exhale. Just breathe.* I mimicked the rhythm of the branches swaying above me, willing my mind to quiet.

But it didn't.

It circled back—relentlessly—to the one thing I didn't want to think about.

Greyson.

His eyes, his voice, the way he had looked at me, as if he were trying to unravel a puzzle. *As if I were the puzzle.*

I disliked it. And yet, I couldn't shake the feeling that he'd seen something in me no one else had. Not even my parents.

Kelsey said he's just a person. *Just a teacher.*

Easy for her to say. She wasn't the one who felt like her entire existence had been peeled back and scrutinized by a single glance.

And yet... she wasn't wrong. Letting myself spiral over a teacher was ridiculous. Even if there was something about him that felt—familiar.

No. That was crazy.

I pressed the heels of my hands against my eyes, sighing loudly.

Reflection is a familiar companion. I had always been like this—too much in my head, always analyzing, dissecting, searching for meaning. My parents called it excessive for my age, but what did they know about teenagers? As far as I knew, their only frame of reference was me. *I blame Dad's genes.* That, and the whole lack-of-friends thing.

They usually shut up about it when I brought that up. Chalk it up to parental guilt.

I don't feel young. But I'm not sure I feel *anything* the way I'm supposed to. Like there's some standard, some expectation I should fit into, but I can't quite grasp it. I don't know if that makes me different or just... disconnected.

Watching my parents, I knew love existed. It was in the way Dad's entire body seemed to settle when Mom entered a room, like she was gravity itself. It was in the quiet way they moved around each other, instinctively attuned—like two parts of a whole that had never been separate to begin with. A bond so effortless, so *undeniable*, it felt almost tangible.

But was what I was feeling now anything close to that? Or just a passing infatuation? A subconscious craving for connection? Or was it part of the storm I had felt coming—that undercurrent in the air I couldn't quite name?

The solitude I had embraced my entire life suddenly felt... lonelier.

Even my parents, for all their warnings about attachment, had each other. They knew what it was like to be *seen*, to have someone who was theirs in a way that went beyond words.

Maybe this is just human nature, I mused, my fingers idly tracing patterns on the bark beside me. *Not that I'd be the best judge.* Maybe even introverts need something. *Someone.*

Time slipped away in a blur as I sat in the tree, my thoughts spiraling up and down. Kelsey had started wedging herself into my life with quiet persistence—never pushing, never demanding, just... there. And somehow, that felt steadying in a way I hadn't expected.

By the time I finally glanced at my watch, the sun had shifted lower in the sky.

A jolt of urgency shot through me.

Crap.

If I didn't show up soon, Dad would come looking. And the last thing I needed was him striding into the school, all six-foot-five of supernatural intimidation, demanding to know where his daughter was.

Reaching out in the way only I could, I sent a quiet thought toward him.

DAD, I'M ON MY WAY. PLEASE DON'T ASK UNTIL I GET HOME.

My words hung in the air like a silent plea. I wasn't just delaying the inevitable—*I was avoiding the truth.*

His response came almost instantly, our telepathic link thrumming with calm certainty.

OKAY, SADY DOLL. I'M HERE.

I sighed, rubbing a hand over my face before gripping the branch above me and swinging down with practiced ease. My feet hit the ground softly, and I brushed stray leaves from my sweater before making my way back to the school's bike rack. The lock clicked open, and within seconds, I was pedaling hard, the cool air stinging my cheeks as I raced home.

Navigating through the quiet streets and parks where I often imagined other people's lives felt strangely comforting. There was something soothing about moving unnoticed, slipping past homes where the lights glowed warmly, where the distant hum of muted television sets drifted through open windows. *Little fragments of an ordinary world.*

A life I would never fully inhabit.

When I reached the front steps, Dad was already there, standing just inside the doorway, framed by the warm glow of the house's interior—a silent sentinel. It almost felt like he'd been waiting there since the moment I contacted him.

His face softened when he saw me, but a quiet concern still lingered in his stance.

I stopped at the last step, my fingers tightening around the strap of my backpack.

For a moment, neither of us moved.

A jagged mix of emotions tangled in my chest—frustration, guilt, exhaustion. *I didn't want to need this.* Didn't want to feel like a child, running home after a bad day.

I should have been stronger.

Dad didn't push. He just waited.

That was the worst part. *He knew I needed the choice.* He wouldn't force me to step forward, wouldn't demand an explanation or pull me into one of his signature bear hugs. He would simply stand there, unwavering, until I decided.

My throat tightened.

I could keep walking, brush past him like none of this mattered. Like I wasn't unraveling inside.

But I was.

And for all my stubbornness, all my resistance, my feet betrayed me, in the best possible way.

I closed the distance between us, colliding into his embrace.

The instant he pulled me close, the tension broke. I exhaled unsteadily, gripping his shirt like it was the only thing keeping me grounded.

His hand cradled the back of my head, fingers threading gently through my hair the way he used to when I was little.

He didn't speak. He didn't need to.

I pressed my forehead against his bicep, eyes squeezed shut, letting myself have this—just for a moment.

The anger I had been nursing all day—the frustration at him, at Mom, at everything, which was nothing to say of the confusion of the past few days—melted away the second he wrapped me in his familiar embrace.

Sometimes, even at eighteen—practically an adult—you just need your dad to hold you and tell you it's going to be okay.

And this was definitely one of those times.

"Let's get you inside," he murmured, his voice calm and steady.

Without hesitation, he bent down and hoisted me onto his back with effortless ease, like we'd done this a thousand times before. I didn't resist—too drained to argue—as he carried me into the kitchen. The familiar scents of home surrounded me—coffee, vanilla, and the lingering warmth of toasted cinnamon.

And there, on the counter, sat a pint-sized tub of my favorite vegan ice cream—coconut cherry chocolate, lid already off, spoon ready.

I let out a half-laugh, half-sigh, shaking my head. "You're not subtle, you know."

He grinned sheepishly, setting me down on the counter. "It's called strategic parenting."

I rolled my eyes but couldn't help smiling. Dad knew better than to bother with a bowl—he'd learned long ago that I'd finish the whole thing straight from the carton. He handed me the spoon, and I dug in, savoring the cool sweetness on my tongue.

For a moment, the world outside didn't matter.

Dad shuffled his feet—a rare occurrence. He only did that when he wasn't sure how to proceed, which was rare.

"Sady doll," he began hesitantly. "I know this morning didn't turn out like any of us thought. I want to apologize for my reaction to your... revelation. And your mother's."

I paused, the spoon halfway to my mouth.

Dad wasn't uncomfortable with apologies, but he didn't offer them lightly—especially when it came to protecting me.

"I know how lonely you are," he admitted, his voice barely above a whisper.

The words hit harder than I expected.

"Before I met your mother, I wandered this earth for eons," he continued, his voice quiet, measured. "Always on the outside looking in, much like I sense you do now. I watched people build lives, forge bonds, fall in love, and break apart. Witnessing their joys and sorrows was the closest I ever came to connection—until her."

He exhaled, a soft sound caught between a sigh and a rueful chuckle. "For a long time, I thought my duty would be company enough. That purpose could replace what I saw in others." His gaze turned distant, lost in some faraway memory, ancient and weighty, as if the past had never quite let go of him.

Then, just as suddenly, he chuckled, shaking his head. "Well, not in a million years did I think I'd know love—until I saw your mother."

The emotion in his eyes caught me off guard. *I didn't know how to respond.*

"Dad, it's okay. Really, I'm fine. It's just—" I couldn't bear to meet his gaze, so I focused on the nearly empty ice cream tub, scraping the remnants with my spoon. "Well, sure I guess I feel something. I just don't know what. And it scares me a little."

Dad cleared his throat awkwardly. "So, uhm... about this boy at school—wait, is it a boy?" His cheeks colored slightly, and he scratched the back of his neck in a rare moment of flustered uncertainty. "We didn't think to ask. Have you talked to him? Her? Them?"

The sudden shift in topic caught me off guard, and I nearly choked on the last of my ice cream. "Dad!" I groaned, feeling my face heat up. "Seriously?"

His attempt at nonchalance was painfully obvious as he fidgeted, his giant frame somehow managing to look small. "What? I'm just trying to understand. It's important to me—important to us—that you feel supported."

And therein lay my dilemma. Do I tell the whole truth, nothing but the truth, or—?

"Well, we have spoken, and on a few occasions, he has even winked at me." Letting Dad know it was a member of the opposite sex seemed safe enough. *For now.*

I thought my response would suffice, but maybe not. Dad got a weird look on his face—like he was holding in a fart or something.

"Winked? That's a bold move. Do you..." He trailed off, clearly out of his depth. "Do you think there's mutual interest?"

I shook my head, eager to end the conversation. "Dad, I have no idea. It's uncharted territory for me too." My voice softened, a hint of weariness creeping in. "Honestly, I wish I could hear him—like I can hear you and Mom. It would make everything so much easier."

The room fell silent for a moment, my words settling like dust between us. Dad's face shifted, his expression unreadable as he processed what I'd said.

"Well, if you ever want to talk about it," he said finally, his tone gentle but firm, "we're here. Always."

"Thanks, Dad." I managed a small smile, grateful for his support even if the conversation had been mildly mortifying. "I'm honestly just tired now."

He patted my shoulder, his usual grin returning. "Alright, go relax. I'll call you when dinner's ready."

I slid off the counter, the pressures of the day pressing down on me again as I headed for the stairs. Pausing in the doorway, I glanced back at him. "And if school calls about me skipping classes after homeroom... can you cover for me? Maybe say I had a doctor's appointment?"

"Wait, what?" His voice came out as a grunt of surprise, but I didn't wait for his response. I simply retreated to my bedroom, shutting the door behind me with a sigh.

Sinking onto my bed, I stared up at the skylight, the faint glow of the evening sky casting shadows across the ceiling. My thoughts drifted to the goddess in the book I'd seen earlier—Hekatari, Keeper of the Everlasting Flame. There was something about her that felt... familiar. But that was impossible, *wasn't it*?

I rolled onto my side, my eyes falling on the family photo on my dresser. In the picture, Mom's violet eyes sparkled with the same intensity I'd seen in Hekatari's. A shiver ran down my spine. *Was it just a coincidence?*

Well, now my mind was a tangled mess of questions with no

answers, a quiet unease threading through me. A lump formed in my throat, hot and heavy, and my vision blurred despite my efforts to hold it back. Frustration, confusion, maybe even a little fear welled up behind my eyes, spilling over in quiet, stinging tears. I blinked hard, but there was no fighting them—not tonight.

Instead, I let exhaustion swallow me whole, dragging me into restless sleep.

Chapter 7

The mouthwatering aroma of sizzling eggs and bacon drifted through the house, pulling me from sleep. For the first time since moving in, uneasy dreams hadn't tangled around me. Dawn had arrived, and somehow, I'd actually slept through the night. My sluggish mind struggled to accept it.

Only briefly wondering which parental unit had checked on me—or if they had at all. Normally, I'd find such intrusions annoying, but not today. Three days without training with Mom, and I was starting to get suspicious.

Bacon meant Mom was home, while Dad may be the one cooking it, she would be the only one eating it. Mom's culinary skills were as limited as her patience, with bacon being her greatest triumph. Anything else she attempted was likely to emerge charred, undercooked, or transformed into something unrecognizable. Her frustration level could be measured by where the remains landed—on the wall or in the garbage. Speaking of throwing, Dad had once tried to eat bacon, but his allergy meant he just threw it up instead.

A creak outside my door signaled Mom's presence. She was waiting, listening for signs of life. *Damn it.*

"Sady baby?" she called softly, an unusual hesitation in her tone. "May I come in?"

"Sure, Mom," I replied, choosing diplomacy over defiance.

She entered tentatively, her cheeks slightly flushed—a rare but endearing sight. "Your dad mentioned your chat yesterday... and your missed classes." She paused, choosing her next words carefully. "I owe you an apology for my outburst."

What is it with my family and turning all shades of red? *We are never like this.*

I was caught off guard, Sera Smith wasn't exactly known for apologies. "It's okay, Mom. I'm fine," I said, offering a half-truth. Rest always has a restorative effect. *Sorta.*

She nodded, preparing to leave, but then, as if struck by a whimsical impulse, she turned back, a mischievous glint in her eyes. Before I could react, she bounded onto my bed, snatching up a pillow and brandishing it like a floppy medieval sword.

"EN GARDE!" she declared gleefully.

"Oh, if this is your idea of an apology, bring it on!" I shouted, grabbing the nearest pillow and launching into battle.

For a glorious few minutes, we weren't mother and daughter navigating the complexities of life—we were just two kids at a sleepover, giggling and letting loose.

Dad eventually intervened, coaxing us downstairs with promises of breakfast. But not before handing me a garbage bag and sighing dramatically at the wreckage. Surveying the battlefield of feathers and fabric, he muttered something about needing to replace *at least* five pillows and possibly the bed frame.

By the time we finished cleaning up and I packed my bag for school, the smell of bacon had fully saturated the house. As we finally descended the stairs, the scent hit me again—stronger this time. Oddly, it made my mouth water uncontrollably. *That's new.* I shook off the strange craving and focused on my vegan breakfast burrito instead, savoring the familiar flavors.

Mom was already at the table, gripping her coffee like a victory mug, as if she'd just conquered a small kingdom and was basking in her triumph. Meanwhile, Dad flipped another batch of bacon with his usual efficiency.

"Sady, you might want to document this moment," he said dryly. "Your mother is actually sitting down for breakfast."

She shot him a look over the rim of her mug. "Watch it, Sam."

"You okay, Mom?" I smirked, sliding into my chair. ""Ya don't usually stop moving long enough to drink your coffee sitting down."

She stretched her legs out, a rare, relaxed smile playing at her lips. "I am, actually. Found this incredible place yesterday—Brass Belles, a pole and aerial fitness studio in Mississauga. And Sady doll, it's not just a studio—it's a whole vibe. The kind of place where people walk in unsure, maybe even a little guarded, and leave standing taller, feeling like they belong in their own skin."

I raised a brow, stabbing my fork into my burrito. "Is this another one of your not-so-subtle efforts to correct my height deficiency? Because I hate to break it to you, Mom, but unless this place teaches aerial genetics, I'm pretty sure I'm stuck down here forever."

Mom snorted, shaking her head. "Oh, never mind that short stack, this has nothing to do with height. Anyways, the owner, Cassandra? She's built something really special. You can tell the moment you step inside—it's not about looking a certain way or being at a certain level. It's about feeling strong, connected. Everyone there, every single person, is just... welcomed. No judgment. No pressure. Just a space where people can move, explore, exist. It reminded me how much I love that—being in my body instead of just... in my head."

Dad took a sip of his coffee, unimpressed. "Let me guess. We're getting a pole in the living room now."

Mom smirked. "Tempting, but no. Though, Sady," she turned to me, eyes bright, "I was thinking we might take a class together. You'd love it."

I raised a skeptical brow. "Me? At a pole fitness class?"

She shrugged, utterly unfazed. "Why not? It's not just the pole, there's aerial silks, hoop, strength training—it's all about feeling powerful in your own skin."

I hesitated, picking at my burrito. But there was something in the way she said it, that gleam in her eye she always had when she talked about dance. Movement. Freedom. And maybe… just maybe, it wasn't the worst idea in the world.

Dad smirked as he set down his plate. "Just promise me neither of you will try to install a rig in the house."

Mom grinned. "No promises."

I laughed, shaking my head. "Alright, Mom. Maybe one class."

Her whole face lit up, and the rest of breakfast felt easy. Like we were finding our rhythm again.

And speaking of rhythms, by the time I arrived at school, the usual hum of chatter and laughter filled the air. Students milled about in groups, their energy buzzing with the kind of carefree excitement I couldn't quite relate to. I slipped through the crowd, keeping my head down and my pace brisk. Blending in had become second nature, but today felt harder.

The morning's peculiarity followed me to school like an unseen shadow.

Standing by my locker, I spotted Kelsey leaning casually against the metal, as if she'd been waiting for me for some time.

"Hi, Sady," she greeted, her genuine smile accompanied by a sheepish shrug as she adjusted her backpack.

"Morning!" I returned, aiming to sound casual, though my mind was already wondering about Mr. Black's attire. "What's up?"

"Oh, nothing much," she replied, offering another shrug. For a fleeting moment, I thought I saw weariness in her expression—a shadow beneath her eyes. *Must be my imagination.* "Just thought we could walk to homeroom together?"

Like a complete idiot, I swiveled around, half-expecting her to be talking to someone else.

"Silly Sady, I meant you!" Her smile took over her whole face.

"Ah, sure, why not?"

Books in hand, we made our way to class. Her constant chatter, once something I might have found grating, had become oddly endearing. But as she spoke, my thoughts kept drifting to Greyson, muffling her voice like background noise.

Homeroom was anything but ordinary.

Greyson Black stood on his desk, resplendent in a medieval costume, complete with gold-pointed shoes. He waved a beret adorned with feathers—including a grand peacock plume—gesturing dramatically and occasionally swatting students in the face. Whether mischievously deliberate or accidental clumsy was anyone's guess.

"Greetings, noble scholars and wayward souls!" he proclaimed. "Step forth into this hallowed hall of learning and folly! Today, we shall venture into the world of the Renaissance and rediscover all things literature, culture, and of course—history!"

Kelsey, my new steadfast companion, rolled her eyes, her lips pressed into a crooked, knowing smile as we made our way to our seats amidst the spectacle.

"Miss Sady, enlighten us about the Renaissance, if you would," Greyson called, singling me out, perhaps hoping to catch me off guard. *Challenge accepted.*

"Well, Mr. Black," I responded, slipping off my jacket and settling into my seat with determination. I had no intention of looking incompetent today. "Which Renaissance are we discussing?" I asked, interlocking my fingers neatly and resting my hands on my desk. "The Carolingian of the eighth century? Or perhaps, the Ottonian in the tenth? By your attire, shall we all assume it will be the one in Florence during the fourteenth to sixteenth centuries?"

All the students whipped their heads around and erupted into murmurs. Suddenly, I was the center of attention. *Crap.* Not what I had intended.

"Well, paint me impressed, Miss Sady!" Mr. Black exclaimed, abandoning his perch on the desk and discarding the ridiculous beret. "Let's journey through the Renaissance of Florence, Italy, shall we?"

Relieved as the focus shifted back to him, I caught the movement at the edge of my vision—Kelsey's silent high-five, just a fraction too late.

Her hand faltered midair before she quickly withdrew, tucking it under the desk as if it had never happened. A faint pink tinged her cheeks, her expression shifting into something I recognized all too well—uncertainty, embarrassment, the quick need to retreat before anyone noticed.

Guilt prickled at my spine.

She was trying. *Trying to be my friend.*

And here I was, too slow, too caught up in my own head, always a step behind in social situations that should have been easy. *Why is this so damn hard for me?*

I turned toward her, ready to say something—anything—but the teacher had already launched into the lecture, his voice cutting through the room like a gavel striking wood. The moment slipped away, buried beneath note-taking, discussions, and the steady tick of the clock.

By the time the bell rang, Kelsey was already gathering her things, her movements swift and practiced. I opened my mouth, scrambling for the right words, but before I could speak, she was gone—swept away by the tide of students pouring into the hall.

A second too long—standing there, rooted to the spot, while the hallway filled and the window of opportunity closed. Chasing after her now would only make things worse. Just another weirdo dodging backpacks and elbows in a crowded corridor.

Maybe it wasn't a big deal. Maybe she'd already brushed it off. *Maybe.*

The next couple of classes passed in a blur, my focus splintered between whatever the teachers were saying and the nagging feeling in my gut that I had messed up—and I cared. By the time the lunch bell rang, I was practically vibrating with impatience.

I almost knocked over another student in my rush to the cafeteria, scanning the crowded space before I spotted Kelsey. She was sitting at a table with three others who looked vaguely familiar.

"Hey, Kelsey!" I called, feeling a twinge of nerves as I approached.

The cafeteria, always a chaotic mix of voices and clattering trays, suddenly felt too loud. Too many moving bodies, too much energy pressing in from all sides. I could navigate a packed street in Paris without breaking stride, yet somehow, walking up to a group of students and inserting myself into their lunch felt infinitely more daunting.

My fingers tightened around my lunch container, palms slightly damp as I forced myself to keep moving. She had been nothing but friendly, and yet, a small part of me braced for an awkward dismissal—like maybe our easy rapport in the hallways didn't translate to cafeteria seating arrangements.

"Hey Kelsey, uhm—about earlier," I said, hesitating just long enough to feel ridiculous. "I kinda missed the moment, but... I saw the high-five. Sorry."

Her head lifted at the sound of my voice, and for a split second, I worried I'd interrupted something. But then—

Her face lit up with an immediate, forgiving smile. *Warm. Uncomplicated.* A stark contrast to the whirlwind still kicking around in my thoughts.

"No problem," she said, waving off my apology like it was unnecessary. Without hesitation, she shifted her tray, making space beside her in an open, wordless invitation.

I exhaled, some of my tension easing, and moved to sit beside her just as she gestured toward the other three at the table. "Sady, these are my friends Linda, Michaela and Jamie."

Scrutinizing the scene before me, trying to recall where I had seen their faces, I studied the trio curiously.

Michaela, with her striking moon-shaped face and cheekbones I'd gladly bribe someone shady for, was nibbling a French fry straight from Jamie's hand. Her blue-grey eyes held an easy sharpness, observant yet playful, and her mouth seemed permanently tilted in a way that made her look like she was always on the verge of a laugh—like the world was just a little more amusing to her than it was to everyone else.

Jamie, the clear source of the French fry supply, watched her with quiet devotion. His short, spiked hair and Superman

T-shirt—stretched over a body teetering on the edge of adulthood—gave him an earnest, almost boyish charm. He seemed utterly smitten with her, like she was the most fascinating person in the room.

Ah yes, young love. Equal parts adorable and mildly nauseating.

Then there was Linda, sitting across from Kelsey, absently flipping through a book as she listened to the conversation around her. Her shoulder-length dark blonde hair—touched with just a hint of ginger when the light hit it right—framed a face that was open, warm, the kind that made people instinctively trust her.

Light brown eyes, soft and thoughtful, flicked across the page before lifting to the conversation, carrying the kind of quiet kindness that put people at ease without trying.

Beside her tray sat another book, not a textbook or novel, but something titled *The Secret Language of Plants.* The worn spine suggested it had been read more than once. She didn't seem distracted, exactly—more like someone who could listen and read at the same time, balancing two worlds without effort.

Something about her immediately put me at ease, though I wasn't sure why. It was an odd feeling—like I should have already known her.

And then it clicked.

The fog lifted, and I finally placed their faces. They were also in our history class. Boy, for someone who had been trained to pay attention to everything, I had been slacking. Badly.

Something else I could blame on Greyson.

Sliding into the seat on the other side of Kelsey, I glanced at them and said, "Right—history class. I knew you looked familiar."

"Yeah, we sit in front of you," Jamie said, leaning forward with a grin. "That was some kind of smackdown you gave Mr. Black earlier. So, what's the deal? Are you secretly some kind of Renaissance expert?"

Shrugging, I tried to downplay the attention. "My family lived in Italy for a while. It's kind of unavoidable to learn about the Renaissance when you're there. It's everywhere—schools, museums, even random statues in the park."

Jamie nodded like he was taking mental notes, then narrowed his eyes in exaggerated analysis. "Yeah, I knew there was something about you."

I shot him a skeptical look. "Something about me?"

His smirk deepened. "Day one, you walked into class rocking those badass bold red Chucks—like you owned the place. The exact same ones as Mr. Black."

Blinking, I barely caught my next breath. "Wait—what?"

Kelsey giggled. "Oh, don't pretend you didn't notice. You and Mr. Black were shoe twins. The moment you walked into class, he clocked them."

Michaela snorted. "Yeah, we all did. It was like a slow-motion showdown. You two locked eyes, and I swear, for a second, it looked like he was trying to figure out if you stole them from his closet."

A scoff escaped me, but Jamie's comment sent a jolt of recognition through me. *The shoes.*

Of course, I'd noticed. *How could I not?* I had just prayed I was the only one who caught it, that it had been some cruel cosmic joke meant just for me.

Apparently not.

They had all noticed. And worse? They were convinced *he* had noticed too.

Jamie leaned back triumphantly, grinning. "So, yeah. Red Converse, matching our weirdly charismatic teacher? That's either fate... or the start of your villain origin story, Converse-Girl."

A huff of exasperation slipped out as I shook my head. "That's what you're going with? Not, like, *History Nerd* or something actually related to my intelligence?"

"Nah," Jamie said, waving me off. "Converse-Girl has a vibe. It's effortless cool, just like the shoes.

Besides, matching sneakers with a teacher on your first day? That's some cosmic-level weirdness."

Rolling my eyes, I fought the amused twitch at the corner of my lips. "Yeah, yeah. Well, let's not make it a thing."

"Oh, it's *already* a thing," Michaela said, smirking. "Better get used to it."

She popped a fry into her mouth, chewing thoughtfully before reaching for a carrot stick and pointing it at me like an accusation. "Anyway, back to this Paris thing—thought you moved here from there?"

Her voice cut through Jamie's laughter, and suddenly, her attention locked onto me with unnerving precision. She snapped the carrot stick in half, her assessing gaze making me feel like I was under a spotlight. The field hockey stick leaning against the cafeteria table left me with the distinct impression that she knew exactly how to use it.

"We did, but we lived in Italy before that," I admitted, cursing myself for not sticking with the simpler *I-am-a-history-nerd* story.

"Oh my God!" Michaela exclaimed, springing up from her seat and startling Jamie enough that he nearly choked on his soda.

I had been right about her height—easily five-nine, maybe even taller—but up close, it was her presence that really filled the space. She had strong legs and full hips, the kind of build that made her impossible to overlook, but there was an ease to the way she moved, like she had long since made peace with taking up space.

But intimidation wasn't what I felt.

She swung her long mahogany hair over her shoulder, her field hockey stick bumping against the bench as she leaned in conspiratorially, both hands banging onto the table in front of me. Oh, she definitely knew how to use that stick—but all I got from her was unshakable confidence and fierce, easy friendship.

"So jealous! I've never been anywhere! Is it true that Italian guys are arrogant jerks with big d—"

"Woah, hey girl," Jamie interrupted, barely recovered from his misadventure with the Coke. And he was so obviously besotted with every facet of her. "I'm sitting right here, you know!"

The look she gave him in return made it obvious that she had no intention of visiting Italy, for the arrogant jerks or any of their body parts for that matter.

Then, without warning, her attention snapped back to me. "Okay, serious question, Converse-Girl. Team Edward or Team Jacob?"

The conversation took a sudden left turn, and I wasn't ready for it. I blinked. "Uhm... what?"

Michaela tilted her head as if I had just revealed a deep personal failing. "Twilight. You have to have an opinion."

Oh. *That.* There had been no escaping the craze—trailers everywhere, posters in every bookstore. But unlike most teenage girls, I hadn't just *watched* the movies with my mom or read the books alongside Dad—I had *dissected* them. What started as normal entertainment turned into a full-blown family analysis of just how *wrong* the portrayal of vampires was.

Because real vampires? They didn't sparkle.

They didn't mope around high schools, pining for human girls.

And they sure as hell weren't tragic, misunderstood loners.

They were relentless. Ruthless. My family knew that better than anyone.

So, no. I had never picked a side. Never debated which fictional vampire was dreamier. For me, *Twilight* had never been about *Edward versus Jacob*—it had been about how absurdly humanized monsters could be when put through the Hollywood filter.

But somehow, I didn't think that was the answer Michaela was looking for.

So, I glanced at Kelsey for backup.

She grinned, utterly unfazed by the sudden shift in interrogation. "Team Stefan, all the way." *Come again, who now?*

Michaela groaned. "Ugh, of course you'd pick the broody one. Damon is such a sexy bad boy."

Still at a loss, I looked to Jamie next.

He smirked. "Team Winchester."

That vaguely rang familiar. *Supernatural*. I was pretty sure Dad had started watching it recently—something about the celestial themes catching his interest. I hadn't paid much attention, but I remembered walking past the living room once to find him watching two guys in flannel debating free will and destiny over a trunk full of weapons.

Michaela shot him an unimpressed glare. "That's not even the same genre."

Across the table, Linda—quiet up until now—shrugged as she absently thumbed through her book. "Team Mulder."

Everyone turned to look at her.

"From X-Files?" Kelsey asked.

Linda nodded, deadpan. "The only answer that matters."

Michaela muttered something under her breath about nerds before rounding back on me, expectant. "Okay, back to you. What's your team?"

I opened my mouth, then closed it. Nothing. Absolutely nothing.

Kelsey must have sensed my slow descent into social ruin because, before Michaela could demand an answer, she leaned forward with a sly grin. "Forget teams, let's talk about Jamie's latest writing project."

Jamie groaned. "Seriously? Betrayed by my own friend?"

Michaela's face lit up with new interest. "Wait—are we finally talking about your novel? Spill, Lover!"

Just like that, the spotlight shifted, and I could breathe again.

Jamie told us about a story he had started to write, hoping to finish it by graduation and submit it to a publishing house. My silence went unnoticed, swallowed by their eager voices sharing their lives with a newcomer.

And that's how we spent the rest of our lunch—sharing some banter and stories. Michaela recounted how she and Jamie met on the first day of high school. She had spotted his baby blues a mile away, and when she saw him wearing his signature Superman T-shirt, she decided *he was hers.* Poor guy didn't have a hope in hell—not that Jamie seemed to mind.

After a while, the conversation shifted. Michaela leaned back, twirling her hair absentmindedly. "So, what's your deal, Converse Girl? You're, like, ridiculously chill for someone who moves so much. Don't you ever miss... I don't know, staying in one place?"

I hesitated, caught off guard again, my gaze drifting to Kelsey, who was watching me with quiet curiosity. "Guess I've just gotten used to it," I said finally. "Moving around, I mean. My parents, and their jobs, are... complicated. Staying in one place hasn't really been an option for us."

Kelsey tilted her head slightly, a flicker of something unreadable passing through her expression.

"I can't relate," she said after a beat, her voice light, but her fingers absently tracing the edge of her tray. "I've lived in the same house my whole life. With my dad and my four brothers—same walls, same rooms, even after Mom... you know."

She let the words drift off, not finishing whatever thought had cast a shadow over her face.

"I can imagine it has a sense of freedom, yeah?"

The way she said it—not quite envy, not quite longing, but something in between—lingered in the air, quiet and unspoken.

Michaela glanced at Kelsey, as if seeking permission, then turned back to me, her tone gentle. "Her mom died when we were all in first grade together. It was... sudden. One day she was there, and then..." She hesitated, her voice trailing off. "It's not something we talk about."

Her words hung in the air, and for a moment, the table fell silent. I blinked, trying to imagine navigating a world without my mom. As much as she drove me insane, I couldn't fathom the loss.

Michaela placed a hand on Kelsey's shoulder, her usual confidence softening into something more careful. "Her mom was incredible," she said, warmth laced through the memory. "She used to take Kelsey to the playground every single day after school and on weekends, rain or shine. No exceptions."

A small, nostalgic smile flickered across Michaela's face. "And she made *the best* chocolate chip cookies. Seriously, it was like magic. She'd always bring them to school events—fundraisers, field days, class parties. And if we were at the playground, she somehow always had a few tucked away, like she knew we'd need a snack before we even realized we were hungry."

Her voice softened. "She just... knew things like that. She made everything feel safe."

Kelsey's lips curved into a faint smile, but her gaze dropped to her hands. "Yeah," she said, her tone wistful. "I'll never forget the playground. There was this one time—it was pouring rain, and we just stayed on the swings, giggling like nothing else mattered. It was... perfect."

The way she said the word *perfect* sent a shiver through me. It was the kind of tone that implied those moments were rare, fleeting, and perhaps never replaced. There was something in her voice, something she wasn't saying outright, but it lingered in the spaces between her words.

My estimation of Kelsey went up several notches that day.

Jamie, who had been quietly listening, leaned forward, elbows resting on the table. His usual easygoing energy was still there, but something about his posture—too still, too deliberate—hinted at something more.

"Those brothers of yours?" he asked, his tone easygoing but edged with something else. "Four of them, huh? That's gotta be... a lot."

Kelsey's smile stiffened, but she quickly masked it with a shrug. "It's... never boring," she said, forcing a lightness into her voice.

The words hung there for a beat, their unspoken weight slipping past but not unnoticed. Michaela's expression tightened briefly—just for a flicker of a second—before she smoothed it over with a practiced ease, masking whatever crossed her mind beneath a light, almost too-easy smile.

"You've been holding your own since first grade," Michaela said with a laugh. "I mean, who else could survive four brothers and still come out tougher than half the guys at this school?"

Kelsey let out a soft laugh, but there was something off about it—too light, too practiced. Like a response she'd given a hundred times before.

The conversation lulled, the usual cafeteria noise fading into the background. None of us rushed to fill the silence. It stretched between us, not exactly uncomfortable, but weighted with something unspoken.

Then, just as the moment threatened to settle too deeply, Kelsey straightened, a flicker of her usual spark returning. "Hey, Sady, want like the rest of my mozzarella sticks? I'm sooo full."

Kelsey had already pulled me in—offering friendship without hesitation, without expectation, like she'd just decided I belonged. Apparently, that generosity extended to food as well.

I glanced at the golden, gooey sticks, the faint aroma of melted cheese wafting up from the tray.

"Thanks, but no," I said with a hesitant smile. *Oh, the joys of navigating the delicate balance of dietary choices in a cheese-loving world.* "I'm vegan."

"Vegan?" Michaela echoed, her eyes widening in mock horror as she reached over to snag a mozzarella stick from Kelsey's tray. "How do you survive? Cheese isn't just food—it's a way of life." She took a big bite, groaning dramatically as she chewed. "Seriously, I tried going vegan once. Lasted twelve hours before I crawled back to the altar of cheddar."

Jamie snorted. "That's generous. I'd say you barely made it to dinner."

"Details," Michaela said with a dismissive wave, finishing off the stick. "Anyway, you're weird for giving it up, but I respect the discipline."

"Honestly, you don't miss something you've never had," I said, a grin breaking through as Michaela clutched her chest like she was personally offended, eyes rolling skyward as if mourning my lack of cheese appreciation.

Laughter bubbled up around the table, and I found myself giggling along with them, the lighthearted banter a welcome reprieve.

But then Kelsey's soft voice cut through the noise, quieter and more thoughtful.

"You don't like the idea of hurting anything, do you?" she asked, her gaze steady and unflinching.

The question caught me off guard, its accuracy landing like a perfectly placed arrow. I blinked, taken aback. "Actually, yeah," I said after a moment, nodding. "Something like that."

Her lips curved into a faint, understanding smile. "I thought so," she said simply, her tone almost wistful. "It suits you."

Jamie tilted his head, his fork pausing mid-air. "Wait, you figured that out just like that?" he asked, his tone a mix of curiosity and admiration.

Kelsey shrugged, a light blush creeping into her cheeks. "You just get a sense about people sometimes, you know? Sady's just not the kind of person who'd be okay with hurting anything—or anyone."

His expression shifted to something thoughtful, and he turned to me. "That's actually kind of cool. One of the characters in the story I'm writing might be vegan. Do you think you could tell me more about what that's like? You know, for research."

"Sure," I said, smiling at the unexpected request. "Anytime."

"Okay, but let's not pretend she's not missing out," Michaela said, stealing another mozzarella stick from Kelsey's tray with enthusiasm.

"Cheese will always be the MVP of food groups."

We all laughed, Michaela's antics effortlessly lifting the mood. But Kelsey's quiet insight lingered with me, her words a gentle affirmation I hadn't realized I needed. It wasn't just the camaraderie of sitting with them—it was the feeling of being seen.

Michaela leaned back in her chair, swiping another mozzarella stick off Kelsey's tray with practiced ease, her eyes glinting with mischief. "Speaking of missing out, you should've been here the first week Mr. Black started teaching."

"Why?" I asked, intrigued despite myself. "What happened?"

"Oh, get this," Michaela said, her tone dripping with intrigue. "He climbed out onto the third-story windowsill in full view of the courtyard. Half the student body thought he'd lost his mind. He stood there for, like, five minutes, waving his arms around like some medieval king surveying his kingdom."

"Why?" I asked, trying to picture the scene.

"To prove a point about perception," Michaela explained, shaking her head with a wry smile. "He wanted to show how people react differently when you change the narrative. From the courtyard, he looked like a crazy person about to jump. Someone even called emergency services, I bet it was the principal. From the classroom, he looked like he was just enjoying the view. And, of course, from his perspective, he was just making a point."

Jamie nodded, chuckling. "He's always doing stuff like that. Remember the time he taught an entire lesson while perched on top of his desk? Said he was 'elevating the discussion.'"

Kelsey snorted. "Don't forget the day he came dressed as Shakespeare and insisted on reciting every instruction in iambic pentameter. Y'all my brain hurt for days after that."

I couldn't help but laugh. "I guess he's... unconventional."

"That's one word for it," Michaela said with a grin. "But you can't deny his methods work. Even the slackers pay attention in his class. And if they don't, he finds a way to make them."

"Like yesterday, when he singled me out?" I said, the memory still fresh.

Kelsey smirked. "Yeah, but you handled it like a pro. He definitely didn't expect you to school him on Renaissance history."

"Miss Sady, the Renaissance expert," Jamie said with a mock bow. "Your reputation precedes you."

"And yet, somehow, he even got me to care about history," Linda chimed in, shaking her head in amusement. "Tying everything back to plants? That's what kept me interested. He made it impossible to ignore how much plants have shaped history—medicine, trade, even war."

Michaela grabbed her field hockey stick, spinning it once before using it to point at Linda like a judge about to make a ruling. "See, *this* is why he's dangerous. He tricks you into learning."

We all burst out laughing again, the warmth of the moment wrapping around me like a protective cocoon. For the first time, like ever, I felt like I belonged—not just in the group, but in the conversation itself.

And for reasons I couldn't quite explain, I felt like Greyson Black had something to do with it.

Chapter 8

By the time I got home, the late-afternoon sunlight was casting golden streaks across the front porch. I paused at the door, taking a deep breath as the faint—and confusing—aroma of pancakes reached me. Sweet and warm, it curled through the air like a quiet invitation. I pushed open the door, stepping into the familiar vibration of home with only a moment to process that today had been... different. *Good, even.* But there was an unfamiliar weight to it, like I was carrying pieces of something I hadn't yet assembled.

Something had changed. I felt it before I could name it, like a shift just beneath my skin, a thread pulling at the edges of my awareness.

"Hey, Sady doll!" Dad's voice carried from the kitchen, loud enough to reach me but laced with unmistakable affection. "How was school?"

"It was great," I said—perhaps a tad too enthusiastically—while slipping off my shoes and heading toward the clatter of pans and plates.

A moment later, his head popped around the corner, eyebrows raised. "Great?" he repeated, staring at me like I'd sprouted a second head. "Not fine or okay? Did I hear that right?"

I shrugged, trying to play it cool, though his reaction made me grin. "Yeah, great. Why?"

He disappeared back into the kitchen, muttering loud enough for me to hear. "I'm calling the newspaper. Sady Smith had a great day at school. Stop the presses."

Rolling my eyes, I followed the sound of his voice and leaned against the doorframe. The scene was pure Dad—flour dusting the counter, batter dripping from the edge of the bowl, and a teetering stack of pancakes growing steadily on a plate. He was mid-flip when I stepped into the room, his back to me.

"Seriously, though," he said, glancing over his shoulder. "What's the occasion? You don't just throw great around like it's no big deal."

"I don't know," I said, grabbing a plate from the cabinet. "It was just... a good day. I sat with some people at lunch. Kelsey, Linda, Michaela, and Jamie. It was nice."

His head whipped around at that, eyes wide with surprise. "You? Sat with people?"

The spatula slipped in his grip, and the pancake launched off the griddle with *way* more force than necessary—flipping end over end like a buttery, syrup-laden UFO.

I saw it coming. Normally, I would've just sidestepped—duh. But for some reason, instead of moving, my brain decided to try to *will* it to stop midair. Time stretched out, comically slow—but not in the cool, supernatural way. More in the *watching-my-own-humiliation-unfold-in-real-time* kind of way.

And then—*smack.*

The pancake hit my chest, sticking for a second before beginning its slow, humiliating slide down my shirt.

"Dad!" I yelped, stumbling back as the freshly cooked, butter-covered pancake slid down my shirt. "That's hot!"

"Oh crap—I mean, ah, I am so sorry!" Dropping the pan, he rushed over with a towel and tried to clean my shirt, only to end up making a bigger mess. To say nothing of the awkwardness of having my dad pat down my barely-there chest.

"Dad, stop!" I laughed, batting his hands away. "You're just smearing it everywhere. And are we seriously having pancakes for dinner?" Not that I was complaining, but having one down the front of my shirt was less than ideal.

Hurrying back to the stove to rescue another pancake before it burned, he managed to flip it just in time. "Yeah, I thought it might be a nice change. Mom won't be home tonight, so it's just you and me, kid."

"I'll go change my shirt."

"And maybe you'll tell me the real reason behind that bounce in your step and squeak in your voice," he called after me. "...when you come back down."

Damn it. My favorite shirt, taken too soon by an airborne food tragedy. Racing up to my room, I mournfully tossed the pancake-soiled top into the sink, mentally lighting a candle in its honor. After swapping it out for a soft gray hoodie, I nearly skidded on my heels from moving too fast back down the stairs.

I found Dad in the living room, balancing two plates piled high with fluffy stacks. He'd already set up on the couch, a bottle of real maple syrup perched precariously on the coffee table next to an open jar of peanut butter and an assortment of random toppings.

"Dinner's ready!" he declared, holding up the plates like a victorious chef.

With a graceful leap, I landed just within reach, careful not to disrupt his pancake-laden equilibrium. "Seriously? We're eating here?"

"Why not?" he said, handing me a plate. "Pancakes are comfort food. And nothing says comfort like the couch. Besides, I know how fond you are of those bar stools your Mom brought into the dining room."

I couldn't argue with that. I took the plate, pouring just enough syrup to cover the top pancake without letting it drip onto the edges. "You're lucky Mom isn't here," I teased. "She'd have a fit if she saw this."

"Well, she's not here," he said with a wink. "Which means we get to eat like rebels."

Shaking my head, I dug into the stack, the sweetness of the syrup and the warmth of the pancakes smoothing out the highs and lows of the day's emotional rollercoaster. For a while, we ate in companionable silence, the only sounds coming from the soft hum of the refrigerator and the occasional clink of forks against plates.

"So," Dad said after a few minutes, leaning back against the cushions. "Are you going to tell me what's really going on? Or am I supposed to guess?"

"What do you mean?" I asked, feigning innocence as I reached for more syrup.

"Oh, come on," he said, his tone teasing but pointed. "You don't just come home looking this... light. Something happened at school. Spill."

There was no way I was going to say a word about Greyson. *Turns out I didn't have to.*

His eyes narrowed suspiciously. "Wait. Is this—" he gasped, clutching his chest like he'd been mortally wounded before dramatically collapsing against the couch cushions. "Is this the crush thing?"

Somebody had been watching too many teen dramas.

I choked on my pancake. "What? No!"

Dad grinned, completely ignoring my reaction. "Oh, this is

definitely the crush thing. Sady doll, is there something you want to tell me?"

"There is absolutely nothing I want to tell you," I shot back, stabbing my fork into my pancake for emphasis.

"Mmhmm," he mused, drumming his fingers against the table, a slow, knowing rhythm that only made his grin widen. He was enjoying this far too much. "Who are they? Should I be sharpening my throwing knives? You know I have excellent aim."

I groaned. "Ugh, Dad! You sound like Mom, it's creepy."

"That's true. Knives are really her thing. I mean, I suppose I could tolerate the idea of you dating. When you're forty."

I rolled my eyes. "This is a deeply concerning level of parental overreaction."

"That's what you signed up for when you picked me as your dad," he said with a satisfied grin.

I sighed, pressing a palm to my forehead. "That's... not how genetics work."

"Debatable," he said. "So, in the meantime, your mother and I could build a fortress."

I scoffed, tossing a piece of pancake at him, which he caught mid-air with alarming reflexes. "Dad, we already live in a fortress."

He paused, considering. "Fair point. But I'm thinking even more fortified—"

"We already have reinforced steel doors, two-way mirrored shatterproof windows, and a security system that could put Fort Knox to shame," I reminded him. "What exactly is missing?"

"A fully retractable drawbridge and a high-powered turret?" he offered. "And a moat! Those never go out of style."

I rolled my eyes, but the laughter bubbled up before I could stop it. "Right. Because that's totally not overkill. I don't think they have suburban building permits for that kind of thing."

"Ha, fair point," he countered, pointing his fork at me. "But one day, when some punk, or punkette, shows up thinking they're worthy of my daughter, you'll be grateful I installed a medieval defense system."

I shook my head, fighting a smirk. "You're impossible."

"That's the spirit," he said, raising his fork in victory.

He had his turn, so I thought I might as well test the waters, while Mother was absent.

"What if—" I tossed the question out casually, testing the waters. "the reason I have a bounce is because of the boy I'm crushing on?"

"Ah, well," he began, mouth full, risking a minor choking incident—but the effect was priceless. "I would—"

"Ha, I'm just kidding!" I interjected, a chuckle slipping out. "Can't have your tombstone reading *'death by pancake,'* now can we? Seriously though, I meant what I said before. I sat with a couple of other students at lunch. And it was good—I mean, really good. Kelsey sits next to me in history class, and it turns out Michaela and Jamie sit in the row in front. Michaela is... well, she's impossible to ignore. Not just because she's loud—she is, by the way—but because she makes everything feel bigger, more alive. She's got this way of pulling people in, like gravity with great hair. And Linda? She's... well, if anyone could figure out how the world works just by studying the roots of a tree, it'd be her. Kelsey lost her mom when she was in first grade, not sure how, but, Dad, she is so full of kindness and hope. And Jamie? He's going to be a famous writer one day. I can feel it."

"Uhm, are you okay, Sady doll?" Dad was looking at me cockeyed, slightly in shock. "That was a lot of words and not a lot of breathing.

You are awfully... bubbly?"

Despite what people assumed about my personality—that I was quiet, observant, maybe even a little detached—I had never been described as bubbly. But the truth was, I didn't actually know what people assumed about me. I'd spent so long avoiding notice, dodging conversations, keeping to the edges of every room, that I had no idea what anyone thought of me. If they even thought of me at all. I had also never cared.

Until now.

I paused, fork hovering over my plate, the realization settling like an unfamiliar weight in my chest. *Bubbly? Me?* That wasn't who I was. I was the girl who blended into the background, who studied people instead of jumping into their conversations. I wasn't the type to light up when talking about my day.

But today, I had.

And surprisingly? It had felt... *good.*

My fingers tightened around the fork, my mind racing to untangle the contradiction. Had I changed, or had I just never been in a place where I could feel this way before?

Was it the people? Kelsey, Linda, Michaela, Jamie—their warmth, their openness—had cracked something in me I hadn't realized was closed off.

Or was it something else?

A shiver ran down my spine, my thoughts inevitably circling back to *Greyson Black.*

Nope. I wasn't going there. Not now. Not when I'd finally found some kind of normal. I clenched my jaw and focused on cutting my pancake into perfect squares, grounding myself in something simple, something controllable. If I didn't acknowledge it, maybe it would just disappear.

Still, the feeling lingered.

I glanced at Dad, who was still watching me like I was an alien that had crash-landed into his living room.

"Relax," I said, forcing a smirk. "I'm not about to start wearing pink or joining pep rallies."

He narrowed his eyes, not buying it. "Are you sure? Because I swear I just saw a sparkle in your eye, and I'm deeply unsettled."

I rolled my eyes, pushing my plate away. "I'm just... happy, okay? Can we just let me have that?"

His face softened immediately, all teasing vanishing. "Of course, doll," he said, his voice gentler.

Hmm, a mischievous thought occurred to me.

"Alright, fine," I relented, feigning exasperation, and seeing if I could trigger one more minor apoplexy. Afterall, rolling my eyes had become a daily thing in this household. So had making my father choke mid-chew. "My crush kissed me, and that's why I'm acting weird, okay?"

The effect was immediate, and far more rewarding than I expected.

"Arrghh, Dad, relax! I'm kidding! Again!"

He coughed, thumping his chest as he glared at me. "Please don't give your poor old man a heart attack."

"Please, that would be like saying Mom will die of old age."

As we neared the end of our pancakes, I set my plate on the coffee table and glanced at Dad. He was lounging back into the couch cushions, looking satisfied with his culinary triumph. But beneath the contented exterior, there was a faraway look in his eyes, a quiet restlessness in the way his fingers tapped idly on the armrest.

I knew that look—something was weighing on him, pulling him

into the depths of his own thoughts. The best way to snap him out of it? A little distraction.

"Hey, Dad," I said, straightening up with a playful smile. "Can you help me with my history homework? We're covering the Renaissance."

His eyes snapped open, and he sat up straighter, mock surprise written all over his face. "Did I accidentally feed you enchanted pancakes?"

I rolled my eyes but couldn't help the amused tug at my lips. "It's just history," I said, pulling out my notebook. "I figured you'd have some... insight into Leonardo da Vinci?"

"Insight?" he repeated, already puffing up with exaggerated importance. "Insight doesn't even begin to cover what I have to offer."

His smile stretched wider, eyes gleaming with the kind of enthusiasm that made it impossible not to get swept up in the moment. He leaned forward slightly, hands already gesturing as if the story was too big to be contained by words alone, and launched into an epic storytelling adventure.

"Ah, let's see now." he mused, leaning back with a thoughtful look. "You cannot have a discussion of any kind about the Renaissance without talking about Leonardo. You know, he wasn't just a genius—he was the ultimate Renaissance man. A painter, inventor, scientist, mathematician... the list goes on. But what made him truly extraordinary was how he saw the world. He looked at everything—art, nature, machines, even the human body—as interconnected. Nothing existed in isolation for him."

As he spoke, I reached for my notebook without thinking, flipping it open as if drawn in by sheer curiosity. Scribbling down notes with one hand, I leaned in slightly. "So, he was curious about everything?"

"Exactly," Dad said, pointing at me like I'd just won a prize.

"And because of that curiosity, he didn't just observe the world—he experimented with it. He dissected bodies to understand anatomy, designed flying machines centuries ahead of his time, and painted works like the *Mona Lisa* that still leave people in awe today."

"Flying machines?" I asked, intrigued. "He really thought humans could fly back then?"

"Oh, he didn't just think it—he believed it," Dad said with a grin. "And he almost figured it out, too. His designs were brilliant, even if the technology to make them work didn't exist yet. Your mom used to tease him about it."

My jaw dropped, pen hovering over the page. "Wait. What?"

Dad froze, his grin faltering for half a second before he covered it with a cough. "Did I say that out loud?"

"Yes," I said, narrowing my eyes. "You just said Mom used to tease da Vinci."

He sighed, rubbing the back of his neck. "Well, I suppose there's no harm in telling you a little. But just a little, okay?"

I nodded, leaning forward eagerly.

This was our thing.

For as long as I could remember, every now and then, in the right mood, at the right time, Dad would let something slip—some offhanded comment, some muttered name from the past. And if I caught it fast enough, if I pressed just the right way, he'd tell me a little more.

It was like uncovering secret puzzle pieces—each revelation adding a layer to history I'd never get from textbooks and learning about my parents all at the same time.

Like the time he casually mentioned that Mom once sat across from Rasputin, met his infamous gaze without flinching—and left him shaken.

He tried, of course. He always tried. The hypnotic charm, the honeyed words wrapped in just enough truth to make the lies go down easy. Most people fell under his spell before they even realized a game was being played.

But Mom? She wasn't most people.

She let him talk, let him weave his illusions, let him think, for the briefest moment, that he had her. And then, with the kind of effortless precision only she possessed, she pulled the ground out from under him. Move by move, layer by layer, she dismantled the power he thought he held—not just on the chessboard between them, but in the charged space where manipulation usually reigned in his favor.

When she placed him in checkmate, he barely noticed.

He was too busy staring at her. For once, Rasputin, the master of control, found himself grasping at someone he couldn't bend to his will.

Dad had smirked when he told me the story, shaking his head. "I think that was the first time he realized he'd met someone who saw him—really saw him. And he hated it."

Then there was the time he grumbled that Napoleon was insufferably dramatic—but, oddly enough, had a surprising talent for baking.

And the day I found out Dad had taught Shakespeare how to throw a proper punch, after the bard nearly got himself killed in a tavern brawl over a terrible sonnet.

And now? Da Vinci.

I fought to keep my expression neutral, but internally, my brain was vibrating with excitement. This was one of the big ones.

Some names carried more weight than others, and Leonardo da

Vinci was practically a historical titan. A man whose mind had been centuries ahead of its time.

And my parents had known him? Had seen him before the world did? Had—if Dad wasn't exaggerating—shaped him in some way?

Yeah, this was going into the mental vault.

I leaned in, my voice barely above a whisper. "Tell me everything."

Dad chuckled, but I didn't miss the way his eyes softened, like he relished these moments too.

"All right," he said, settling into his storyteller's rhythm. "But don't say I didn't warn you."

He stretched his arms out along the back of the couch, tilting his head slightly as if deciding where to begin. I could start to see the memories flickering behind his eyes, moments pulled from a time so distant it shouldn't have been possible. *Telepathy did have its uses.*

For a brief second, I wondered what it was like for him—to carry centuries of stories, moments in time that had been reduced to myths and textbooks for the rest of the world. To have witnessed the rise and fall of empires, to have stood beside people history had only recorded in faded ink. And in moments like this, I got to experience the most interactive storytelling of all times. It was even better than 3D movies.

And now he was just... here. Sitting on a couch. Eating pancakes with his daughter.

The contrast was almost absurd. He'd walked through history, shaped moments that ended up in textbooks, and now his biggest concern was making sure I had enough syrup.

Something about that sat strangely in my mind, like a puzzle piece that didn't quite fit.

Dad exhaled slowly, a ghost of a smile playing on his lips. "Your mother," he began, his voice softening, "saw Leonardo's potential before anyone else did. We met him when he was just a precocious child, many years before he became an apprentice under Verrocchio. She said he had the spark of someone who could change the world—not just with his art, but with his ideas. And she wasn't wrong."

"You guys really knew him when he was kid?" I asked, my voice barely above a whisper.

Dad nodded, a faraway look in his eyes. "Your mom had this way of seeing what people were capable of, even when they couldn't see it themselves. She encouraged him, challenged him. They'd spend hours talking about the stars, about how everything in the universe was connected. It drove him to dream bigger, to push beyond what anyone thought was possible."

"And you?" I asked, my curiosity growing. "What did you do?"

"Well," he said, chuckling, "I ended up as the model for one of his sketches. She terrified the poor man when she initially stripped me down and then tied my hands to the ceiling beams."

My jaw dropped. The pieces clicked together with horrifying clarity—the proportions, the posture, the wild, unkempt hair.

Oh. Oh no.

"You were the *Vitruvian Man*?"

Dad spread his arms wide, grinning. "Guilty as charged."

I stared, my brain short-circuiting as an awful truth settled in. The world had been studying an anatomically correct drawing of my father for centuries.

Ah hell. It was in textbooks. In museums. On posters. I'd seen it in classrooms.

I clapped a hand over my face. "I can never unsee this."

Dad had the audacity to look amused. "Little did I know that one of his 'random sketches,' as he called it, would become one of the most famous works in history."

Rolling my eyes, I pushed my plate onto the coffee table and curled up in his lap. *Enough about that visual.* There were far better stories to focus on.

"Can you tell me more?"

His smile widened, warm and full of mischief. "Oh, I've got stories you wouldn't believe."

"Tell me," I said, leaning in. "I want to hear them. As long as they don't involve either of my parents getting nude, please."

He shifted, settling into the cushions like a storyteller preparing for a long night. "All right," he said, his tone playful. "But don't say I didn't warn you."

And then he began. Tales of faraway places, of people and moments that felt more like legend than history, spilled from his lips, weaving together like threads in an intricate tapestry.

He spoke of Da Vinci's flying machines, of secret notebooks filled with ideas centuries ahead of their time, of paintings layered with hidden codes. Each word pulled me in deeper, but it was more than just his voice—his memories, shared through our telepathic bond, wrapped around me like a living dream. In an instant, I was *there*, standing at the edge of history, watching it unfold through his eyes.

His stories bled into one another, each more vivid than the last, until my thoughts grew hazy, my body sinking deeper into the warmth of the moment. Sleep crept in at the edges of my mind, and before I could fight it, my eyes drifted closed.

Chapter 9

The remnants of a fading dream clung to me as I stirred, my body still tangled in yesterday's clothes. The faint scent of pancakes lingered on my sleeve, mingling with the memory of Dad's stories. His narratives, less brutal than Mom's, carried a peculiar charm—breathing life into his characters with the cadence of his voice.

"Sady baby?" Mom's voice cut through the lingering fog in my mind. "Are you ready?"

I blinked away the haze of sleep and glanced at the clock. Five o'clock. My reprieve from training had officially ended.

"Just a minute," I called, dragging myself from the warm cocoon of my bed. My muscles protested as I stretched, already anticipating the brutal efficiency of Mom's sessions. Stripping off my clothes as I shuffled across the room, I hoped for something aggressive to shift the anxiety coiled tight in my chest—a punching bag, maybe.

Note to self—careful what you wish for because you just might get it.

Rummaging through my drawer, I pulled out a nondescript workout ensemble—yoga pants, a hoodie, and a sports bra. As I dressed, a fleeting thought crossed my mind.

I wonder when Greyson wakes.

Ah, hell. *Seriously?* Of all the things my mind could latch onto, why *this*? Irritation flickered through me as I shoved the thought aside, feeling ridiculous.

Shaking it off, I headed downstairs.

A steady rhythm of soft thuds met me as I approached the basement. Mom was already at it, a blur of motion as she attacked the jump rope with ferocious precision. Her feet barely seemed to touch the ground, spinning and hopping in a sequence so intricate it made me dizzy just watching.

Beside her, two new pairs of sparring gloves rested on the floor—waiting.

"Daughter," she greeted without missing a beat, her precise movements seamlessly transitioning into a flourish of hops. "It's time to try something new today."

I folded my arms, already bracing for whatever 'new' meant in her vocabulary. "Ha. Like there's anything left I haven't suffered through."

Her eyes gleamed. "Oh, ye of little faith."

A grin tugged at my lips. This was our rhythm—challenge, retort, escalate. We both thrived on the energy of slinging playful insults, each exchange sharpening the edge of the next.

"My darling offspring, that's where you're wrong—oh, so very wrong," she shot back with a smirk, clearly enjoying herself. "Warm up and meet me on the mat in five."

That smirk should have been my first clue.

Movement grounded me, restoring a sense of focus. I started with my usual hip-mobility drills, ignoring the fact that Mom would likely shake her head. Admittedly, some of the movements resembled drunken yoga poses, but I'd learned to listen to my body—a lesson many of my peers would never grasp. For all my desire to fit in, there were perks to being me.

"All right, Mother, what's the plan?" I asked as I approached the mat. She was already slipping on a pair of sparring gloves, her stance deceptively relaxed. Tossing a smaller pair to me, she said nothing.

Catching them against my chest, I frowned. "Eh, what? Why do these feel so heavy?"

"Check inside."

Remember when I said that my family has a weird sense of humor, especially when it comes to surprises? Well, I should have mentioned that hers, in particular, comes with a hint of sadism.

Within the confines of those gloves were small, almost imperceptible, razor-sharp pins. I took a count, fingers tracing the barely discernible outline of each one. Ten? No, perhaps fifteen nestled within the seams, meticulously sewn from within.

"Is this a joke?" I inquired, eyebrows furrowing in disbelief.

"You wish, ankle biter," she retorted, flexing her hands inside her matching pair of gloves. "Let's just say this lesson is designed to leave an impression."

"Have I neglected a chore, or is this some new form of torture?" I asked, slipping the gloves on cautiously. *Not at all comforted by the thought that she is also wearing a pair.*

"Sady baby, from the day you could walk, we've honed your skills for combat. For survival."

"Yeah, so? I thought I was already pretty proficient," I protested.

Her smirk, now more of a grimace, deepened. "Oh, sweet offspring of mine, you've yet to truly face a foe. You've yet to grasp the agony of battle—the raw dance of pain and defense."

Her use of *offspring* grated on my nerves, a calculated jab. Pushing my buttons seemed to bring her endless amusement.

"Ah, I beg to differ. You and Dad haven't pulled your punches since

I was eight, so I've felt plenty of pain. Thanks very much."

Her stance shifted, a challenge in her eyes that I knew too well. There was no talking my way out of this.

"Transient pain, yes," she countered. "But prolonged—wounds that worsen with every defensive maneuver? No."

Despite my accelerated healing and heightened pain thresholds, I was not impervious to harm. Admitting it, begrudgingly, felt like swallowing a bitter truth. And if I am willing to admit that first day of school with that biting feeling of doom in the air, then *this is probably not the worst of Mom's ideas.* That didn't mean I had to like it, though.

"Well, let's punch this day in the face, shall we, Sera?"

She wasn't the only one who knew how to push buttons. Addressing her by her first name, not her hard-earned title of Mother, or Mom, earned a subtle twitch of her right eye.

The next thirty minutes were a blur of adrenaline and agony. Each punch I threw forced the pins deeper into my hands, every hold slicing fresh lines into my skin. Blood trickled down my wrists, making my grip slippery, but I refused to give her the satisfaction of seeing me falter.

When we finally collapsed onto the mat, our chests heaving, the gloves lay in a bloody, tattered mess beside us. Mom grinned, her face flushed with exertion. "Well, I must say, that was exhilarating! And it looks like you're finally getting the hang of that bow-and-arrow chokehold."

"Uhm, thanks?" I muttered, my hands screaming with fire. "Can I go get ready for school now?"

I sensed her longing for a tender moment, but I was already up and not waiting for permission. Heading up the stairs, I collided with Dad.

"Whoa, Sady doll!" His grip on my shoulder jolted me, momentarily distracting my attention away from the stinging pain that I knew the shower water would bring to the cuts on my hand. *I heal fast, but not that fast.*

His eyes raked over me, landing on my raw, bloodied hands. "Why in Dad's name are you bleeding? What happened? Where is your mo—?!"

"Relax, Dad, just another *hands-on* lesson courtesy of Mom," I reassured, slipping free from his grasp with a newfound ease, thanks to my startling revelation. "I'm fine."

His hand caught my wrist before I could fully escape, turning my palm upward. The faintest tremor ran through his fingers as he examined the damage.

"This—" He drew in a rough breath, his voice strained. "This isn't training, Sady."

I shrugged, pretending it didn't bother me. "It's just a few cuts. No big deal."

"This—" He swallowed whatever he was about to say, shaking his head. His thumb ghosted over the thin line of crimson still pooling near my knuckles. "Sera has always been extreme, but this is beyond that. This is—"

He stopped himself, pressing his lips into a hard line.

I gently tugged my hand from his grip. "Seriously, Dad. I'll be fine in an hour."

He didn't respond immediately, just studied me like he was looking for some tell I wasn't offering.

Then, with another muttered curse that sounded more like a sigh, he pivoted sharply toward the stairs—

And bellowed, *"SERA!"*

The force of it vibrated through the walls. I cringed as his heavy footsteps pounded downward. I didn't hear Mom's reply, but I could imagine it—her smug grin, his exasperation, the inevitable back-and-forth that would, as always, end in a stalemate.

Shaking my head, I trudged toward the bathroom.

It didn't matter. This had always been our way. Mom's training methods were brutal, but effective. Dad's concern was valid, but it wouldn't change the reality of my life. And we both knew it.

Still, there was something different in the way his jaw had tensed, in the way his fingers had curled around mine like he could will the wounds away.

A sudden pang of guilt crept up my spine. Not for myself. *For him.*

Dad never wanted me to be a fighter, a shield, a constant line of defense. He wanted me to be a kid.

Too bad that had never been an option. Not with *them* after us.

Catching a glimpse of myself in the mirror, I winced. My hoodie was a disaster—splattered and streaked like I'd walked through a crime scene. Blood clung to my hands, smeared along my arms, and left faint red smudges trailing up my neck. *Great.*

Stripping down quickly, I stepped into the shower, letting the warm water cascade over me. The initial rush eased the tension in my shoulders, but as the water hit my hands, the sting flared to life. I hissed through clenched teeth, watching as the faint streaks of blood swirled down the drain. The warmth was soothing, but I needed something stronger to jolt my body into healing.

Reaching for the nozzle, I cranked it to cold in one swift motion. The icy water slammed into me, stealing my breath and making every nerve in my body come alive. The intense contrast sent my circulatory system into overdrive, the cold constricting blood vessels near the surface and driving warmth back to my core. *Welcome to First-Aid 101.*

Supernatural style.

I braced myself against the wall, letting the chill do its work. My shredded palms burned with each pulse of cold water, but I knew the process was already underway. By the time I turned off the shower and toweled off, the worst of the damage was gone. The cuts were now faint lines, pink and tender but healing fast.

Once I had dressed and made my way downstairs, the smell of breakfast had already started to fade. I found Dad in the kitchen, hunched over his plate of leftover frittata. He stabbed at it with the kind of intensity that suggested the earlier confrontation with Mom hadn't gone in his favor.

"Ehr, flmmpf—" He attempted to speak around a mouthful of egg, only to choke halfway through, coughing as he tried—and failed—to swallow properly.

I smirked, slipping onto the stool across from him. "Don't hurt yourself, old man."

"It's *Dad,*" he corrected, glaring at me before sighing. "And I'm fine. Are you?"

"As usual, Mom had a point to make, and one I needed to learn. I'm fine."

"Sady doll, I'm sorry, I wish I knew..." His words trailed off, heavy with regret.

I tensed. The last thing I needed was a deep conversation about why I should or shouldn't be okay with Mom's training methods.

"I don't really want to talk about it right now, okay?" I cut in, sidestepping any impending discussion.

He studied me for a beat, then exhaled through his nose, nodding slightly.

Stepping off the barstool, his long legs carried him into my personal space—a space I wasn't feeling too generous about sharing at the moment. "Here, let me see."

Flipping my palms up so he could inspect the shredded skin already knitting itself back together, I braced myself for what was next. Dad scrutinized my healing hands, a tumult of emotions crossing his face.

Tears welled in his eyes, battling with the fierce resolve that clenched his jaw so hard I swore I heard a crack. For a brief, absurd second, I wondered if he'd just broken a tooth.

"Your mom wanted to apologize, you know," he said as I slung my bag over my shoulder.

"Oh, did she?" I asked, raising an eyebrow. "Has she figured out how to do that yet, or should I brace myself for more quoted song lyrics instead?"

He sighed, his expression softening. "She's harder on you because she knows how strong you are. But that doesn't mean she doesn't feel it too."

I gave him a small smile, not ready to unpack the many layers of Mom's methods. "I'll be fine," I said simply, pulling the door open. "I always am."

As I made my way to the backyard, his reply was lost in the slam of the door.

The cool morning air hit me as I stepped outside, a welcome contrast to the warmth of the kitchen.

The sting in my hands had dulled to a faint ache, though gripping the handlebars of my bike was uncomfortable. Still, the rhythmic motion of pedaling and the fresh bite of the air in my lungs helped push the tension from the morning into the background.

I parked my bike in the back parking lot today and made my way inside, my thoughts preoccupied with the day ahead. The hallways were unusually quiet, but I didn't think much of it—probably just one of those rare moments when the usual chaos hadn't caught up to me yet.

When I pushed open the door to homeroom, I froze.

Greyson Black was there, alone, standing by the window. His back was to the door, one hand resting lightly on the windowsill, the other holding a coffee mug. The soft morning light caught on his dark shirt and the sharp angles of his frame, making him seem almost unreal.

An odd sense of déjà vu hit me—Dad often stood like that at windows.

"Hello, Miss Sady."

I hesitated, gripping the strap of my bag. "How did you—" The words caught in my throat. He hadn't turned around. His gaze was still fixed on the view outside, yet he knew it was me. There was no reflection on the windows that could have shown him who had just entered. *I checked.* "How did you know it was me?"

He didn't answer right away. Instead, he took a deliberate sip, stretching the pause just long enough to make me uneasy.

"You're here before the chaos begins," he said, his tone light but layered. "That's new."

"It's only day four, I hardly think that establishes a pattern." I frowned, stepping farther into the room. "You didn't answer my question."

"Did I need to?" he replied, finally turning to face me. His sky-blue eyes locked onto mine, and for a moment, I forgot what I was going to say. "But I do have a question of my own."

I blinked, caught off guard by the shift in conversation. "What?"

"Are you injured?" he asked, his tone casual, like he was commenting on the weather.

My heart thrummed in panic, and a quick glance down revealed that one of the cuts on my hand hadn't quite healed yet. The tight grip I had on my textbook had pressed the wound open again, and a thin bead of blood smeared faintly against the book's corner.

Greyson tilted his head slightly, his gaze flicking down to where my hands clutched the book against my chest. The corners of his mouth twitched upward—not quite a smile, and definitely a clenched jaw.

I swallowed hard. "You tell me."

His expression didn't change, but something in his eyes darkened—concern, *maybe*. A flicker of tension in his posture.

My breath caught. "It's fine," I said quickly, dropping the textbook onto my desk and tucking both hands into the pocket of my hoodie. "Just a papercut."

Greyson didn't respond right away. Instead, he took a step closer, his eyes scanning my face as though searching for something deeper.

"Careful, Miss Sady," he said quietly, his voice low and measured. "It's easy to hide a wound, but much harder to ignore the pain it causes."

The words sent a chill down my spine. My mouth opened to respond, but the door swung open first, and a group of students filed in, their chatter filling the room with energy.

His attention shifted effortlessly to the board as though the exchange had never happened. I ducked my head, pretending to flip through my notebook, but my thoughts were still spinning.

How had he known about the blood?

And why had it felt like he was speaking to more than just a physical injury?

"Sady!"

Kelsey's voice snapped me out of my daze. She slid into the seat beside me, her glasses slipping down her nose. "Wow, early and looking like you're deep in thought. What's up with that?"

"Nothing," I said quickly, though my tone probably betrayed me. "Just... thinking about the Renaissance."

She snorted, pulling out her own notebook. "That's got to be a first."

"Yeah, well, Mr. Black has a way of making it hard to forget," I muttered, glancing up just as Greyson turned to face the class.

"Good morning, my little architects of intellect," he began, clapping his hands together. The room quieted almost instantly, his presence commanding attention as easily as flipping a switch.

"Yesterday, we ventured further into the labyrinth of the Renaissance. We touched on trade, patronage, and geography. But today, we focus on something far more thrilling—curiosity."

He leaned against the edge of his desk, his gaze sweeping the room. "Curiosity, my friends, is the heartbeat of progress. It's what drives us to explore, to experiment, to create. Without it, the Renaissance would've been nothing more than a whisper of potential."

Kelsey rolled her eyes beside me, her pen hovering over her notebook. "He's really laying it on thick today."

I stifled a laugh, but I couldn't deny that he had a way of drawing you in, even when you didn't want to be. His voice carried a rhythm that made every word feel significant, like a thread weaving a tapestry.

"To illustrate," Greyson continued, reaching into his desk drawer, "let's consider the tools of experimentation. The things that fuel our drive to know more."

He pulled out a small, unassuming object, concealing most of it within his hand. Only glimpses of its metallic surface were visible—brass, most likely, aged and worn. It bore a vague resemblance to an old compass or drafting tool, with subtle, gleaming edges catching the light. Yet, the deliberate precision with which he handled it, as though guarding its significance, sent a ripple of unease through me.

My body moved before my mind could catch up.

Bracing against my seat, I lashed out with a sharp sidekick, striking Kelsey's chair hard enough to send it skidding across the floor—straight into the next row of students. The legs screeched against the tile, but miraculously, the chair stayed perfectly upright. Kelsey remained firmly seated, wide-eyed and frozen, as if she'd just been teleported.

At the same time, I surged to my feet, my fingers snapping closed around the airborne object a split second before it could reach where her head *should* have been. The sharp edges bit into my already tender flesh, but I barely registered the sting.

Silence crashed over the room. Every pair of eyes locked onto me.

I stood there, chest rising and falling, fingers clenched around the object, my pulse pounding in my ears. The weight of the moment pressed in, but the only person who didn't seem fazed was Greyson.

He remained calm, collected—almost amused—as he tilted his head and regarded me. "Impressive reflexes, Miss Sady."

"What the hell was that?" I opened my hand to inspect the object—it was nothing more than a harmless antique nautical compass, its edges slightly dulled by age.

"An example," he said smoothly.

Across the room, he moved with unhurried ease, closing the distance between us in a few measured strides. By the time I registered just how far he had thrown it, he was already in front of me, plucking the compass from my palm. His fingers brushed mine briefly, sending a strange, fleeting jolt up my arm.

"Of how curiosity can sometimes... surprise us."

Kelsey, still half-frozen in her chair—exactly where I'd launched her—stared at me, wide-eyed. Her fingers gripped the edges of the seat like she was afraid moving might set off another chain reaction.

"What just happened?" she breathed.

"I—" I started, but Greyson cut me off.

"Miss Kelsey," he said, addressing her with a smile that was almost disarming. "Your friend here was simply demonstrating the importance of being alert. A valuable lesson for all of us, wouldn't you agree?"

A few nervous chuckles rippled through the room, breaking the charged atmosphere as students exchanged wary glances, clearly unsure whether the whole thing had been planned.

Kelsey shot me a bewildered look as she straightened her chair, her grip lingering on the edges like she wasn't entirely convinced the danger had passed.

Slowly, I sank back into my seat, my pulse still hammering as I tried to process what had just happened.

Greyson turned back to the board, but not before glancing at me over his shoulder, his tone light, almost teasing.

"You can relax now, Miss Sady. The Renaissance is hardly a battleground."

The room slowly settled, the charged atmosphere melting into a ripple of nervous laughter as Greyson turned back to the board. But I couldn't shake the meaning of his words—or the strange feeling that the entire demonstration had been meant for me.

Or for him.

Chapter 10

Kelsey leaned toward me, her voice low. "Sady, are you okay? That was... intense."

"I'm fine," I murmured, though my hands still felt a dull throb from catching that stupid piece of metal.

Greyson, who was now putting up a ginormous poster on the board, his movements calm and deliberate as if nothing had happened.

I glanced up—and immediately regretted it.

There, in all its anatomically unfortunate glory, was the Vitruvian Man by Leonardo da Vinci.

Oh. Oh no.

A snort came from the back of the room, followed by muffled giggles. Someone muttered something about proportions. The snickering spread like wildfire.

Greyson, unfazed, reached into his desk, pulled out an obnoxiously large smiley-face sticker, and—without hesitation—slapped it directly over the most problematic region.

The laughter erupted, then faded almost instantly.

"Better?" he asked dryly, arching an eyebrow at the class.

Quickly averting my eyes, finding the wood grain on my desk and trying not to let the sound of my teeth clench be heard. There was no way I was looking at that sketch again.

"This," he said, stepping back to reveal a rather large detailed sketch of an ancient symbol—a circular design with rays spiraling outward. "Is the *Vitruvian Man* by Leonardo da Vinci. But it's also much more than that. What do you see?"

The class fell into an uneasy silence.

I was too busy trying to stare anywhere but at the board, my body already sinking into my chair as if I could physically remove myself from the situation.

Then, Michaela, completely unbothered, leaned forward, tilting her head like she was analyzing a fine work of art.

"Well," she mused, tapping her chin, "first impression? That is one very naked, very well-proportioned man."

Laughter rippled through the room. I closed my eyes. *Nope*. Absolutely not.

"Also, I guess it kinda looks like a diagram? Maybe a map?" She paused. "But mostly, a very sculpted, very symmetrical dude."

Someone muttered, "She's not wrong." Jamie choked on a laugh. The giggling spread.

I could feel my soul trying to detach from my body as I slid even further into my chair, willing the floor to swallow me whole.

"Interesting interpretation," Mr. Black said, nodding. "Anyone else?"

"Well, It's human anatomy, right?" Linda ventured. "He was obsessed with figuring out how the body worked."

"Correct," Greyson said, his voice laced with approval. "But there's another layer. Something deeper."

He tapped the board lightly with his knuckles. "Da Vinci's work was not just about science or art. It was about understanding the connection between the human and the divine. This drawing, this man stretched within the boundaries of a circle and a square, is a symbol of harmony. It represents the belief that humans are the bridge between earth and the heavens."

I sat up straighter, a strange, familiar tug pulling at me. Greyson's words struck a chord, echoing fragments of things Dad had said the night before—about how Mom saw something in Da Vinci that others missed.

She had recognized his hunger for understanding, his need to make sense of the world through patterns and form. She had coaxed him to explore those ideas further, nudged him toward the questions he had always been on the verge of asking.

Like she had known he was meant for more.

"This idea wasn't unique to da Vinci," Greyson continued. "Many cultures throughout history have believed in higher powers—forces beyond our understanding that shape our world. The Renaissance was a time when science and faith coexisted, intertwining in ways that often seem contradictory to us now. But to them, exploring the mysteries of the human body or designing a machine that could fly was an act of faith. A belief that humans were capable of reaching for the divine."

The room was quiet, his words draping over us, thick with insinuation. Kelsey shot me a quick glance, her brow furrowed as if she could feel the same shift in the air that I did.

Greyson paced slowly in front of the board, his gaze sweeping the room. "And what of today?" he asked, his voice dropping slightly. "Do we still believe in higher powers? Do we still look to the skies and wonder if there's something greater than ourselves? Or have we grown so cynical that we've forgotten how to dream?"

His words felt like a challenge, his eyes flicking briefly to mine before moving on. I tensed slightly, clenching my hands beneath the desk, the sting of my earlier wounds grounding me.

"Miss Hamilton," Greyson said suddenly, pointing at Kelsey. "What do you think?"

She blinked, startled by the sudden attention. "Uhm... I guess some people still believe in that stuff," she said, her voice quiet, almost hesitant. "My mom used to believe in angels. She said they were... guides, I guess? Watching over us, listening to our prayers. She really believed they could hear you."

Greyson nodded thoughtfully. "And you? Do you share her belief?"

Kelsey's gaze dropped to the desk, her fingers tracing a small, invisible circle on the surface. Her voice, when it came, was softer. "I don't know," she admitted. "Maybe. Sometimes it feels like there's something out there... but it's hard to say. Sometimes, I wonder if they're really listening."

"Fair enough," Greyson said, his tone gentle but probing. "Belief is often shaped by experience. And experience is the lens through which we see the world."

Jamie raised his hand, his usual relaxed manner giving way to a spark of mischief. "What about aliens?" he asked, a grin tugging at the corners of his mouth. "If we're talking higher powers, doesn't it make sense to include, you know, advanced civilizations watching us from some distant galaxy?"

A ripple of laughter moved through the room, but Greyson's expression didn't waver. He tilted his head slightly, his eyes narrowing as if he were genuinely considering the bald question. "An interesting proposition," he said finally, his voice measured. "After all, belief in extraterrestrial life could be seen as a modern iteration of ancient myths—gods descending from the heavens, beings with knowledge beyond our comprehension."

Jamie's grin widened. "So, you're saying aliens are basically the Renaissance version of angels?"

The class laughed again, and I forced myself to join in, but a faint unease settled in my limbs, restless and lingering. Jamie's offhand comment hit far closer to home than he—or anyone else in the room—could have guessed. *Angels.* The word lingered in my mind, a weight I didn't want to carry. I clenched my hands beneath the desk, igniting fresh flashes of pain—*damn it*—willing my expression to remain neutral as Greyson continued.

"Whether we call them angels, aliens, or gods, the concept reflects humanity's desire to understand the unknown," Greyson said, his voice calm but deliberate. "These beliefs shaped civilizations, inspiring art, literature, and even scientific discovery. Which brings us to your homework."

He stepped behind his desk, lifting a neat stack of cue cards. The class groaned in unison, already sensing trouble. Greyson's smirk deepened as he walked around the room, holding the cards like a magician about to perform a trick.

"You'll each be writing a 5,000-word essay," he announced, pausing to let the collective gasp settle. "Your topic, assigned randomly, will be a belief from an ancient culture—something rooted in the supernatural, the divine, or the unexplained. I want you to explore how it influenced their worldview and how it might still resonate today. Simply draw a card when I pass by, and the fates will decide."

"Fates?" Jamie asked with a laugh. "What if I don't like my topic? Can I trade with the person next to me?"

Greyson's eyes gleamed with mock severity as he leaned forward, his voice taking on an almost theatrical flair. "Do you think the ancient

Greeks negotiated with the Moirai?" he said, pausing for effect. "No trades, Jamie. The Fates weave the threads of destiny, and once they've spun their design, there is no turning back."

The murmurs grew louder as he began moving through the rows, holding the cards out like offerings. One by one, students drew their assignments, their reactions ranging from groans of despair to quiet excitement.

His presence loomed beside my desk, holding that small piece of paper like it was a bribe—or a threat. It was hard to tell with him. I refused to look up, keeping my focus fixed on the worn corner of my desk. With swift fingers, he placed the paper directly on my textbook. I grabbed it too quickly, and our fingers brushed for just a second—but it was enough to send a warm flush across my skin, my heart beating a little faster than it should have.

Unperturbed, he turned around and gave Kelsey her paper. My senses were on overdrive, so when I gingerly turned that paper over and read the words, I had to practice some serious control—both in my breathing and in resisting the urge to leave the class before the bell rang.

When Greyson moved on to the next row, I stared at the cue card in my hand:

Ancient Greece, the God Ares and Goddess Artemis, and Queen Otrera.

The pit in my stomach deepened as I glanced at Kelsey, who was flipping her cue card over with a resigned sigh. Honestly, both of these could have been pulled straight from my mother's autobiography.

"Hatshepsut," she muttered, frowning. "The Egyptian pharaoh and the God Amun?"

Greyson nodded approvingly from the next row. "A fascinating subject. Hatshepsut was a woman who defied the norms of her time, ascending to power in a patriarchal society. A testament to belief—not just in gods, but in oneself."

Kelsey groaned, shoving the card into her notebook. "Great. Now I get to spend two weeks on someone I can't even spell."

"You've got this," I said, my voice steadier than I felt. *What are the chances of two cue cards being so closely linked to my mom?* My gaze flicked around the room, taking in the furrowed brows and murmurs as other students read their topics. *What other strange cue cards were out there?*

"Sady?" Kelsey's voice snapped me out of my spiraling thoughts. "You good?"

"Yeah," I said quickly, slipping my card into my notebook. "Just... thinking about my topic."

"What'd you get?" she asked, curiosity brightening her expression.

"Ancient Greece," I replied, keeping my tone casual. "Ares, Artemis, and the Amazon queen who started it all."

Her eyes widened. "Lucky. That sounds like something straight out of a fantasy novel. Meanwhile, I'm stuck with Egypt's ultimate workaholic."

Greyson continued through the rows, handing out the remaining cards, his movements deliberate but fluid. When he finished, he turned back to the board, tapping the word BELIEF he'd written earlier.

"Remember," he said, his tone turning firm, "this assignment isn't just about summarizing history. It's about understanding how belief shaped these cultures. Push past the surface. Dig deep. The deadline is two weeks from today."

The bell rang, releasing the frustration in the room as students began packing up their things. Kelsey groaned, shoving her card into her bag. "Two weeks for five thousand words? He's delusional or deranged."

"It's not that bad," I said, though it wasn't the length of the essay that made my head shake—it was the topic itself. "Just start with the basics."

Kelsey rolled her eyes but grinned. "Spoken like someone who hasn't tried to spell Hatshepsut yet."

I hesitated before blurting, "Actually, I think I can help if you want. I've got some notes from my last school where I had to research ancient Egypt." *Not like I could tell her about mom's involvement.*

Kelsey's smile widened. "Okay, show-off. But I might actually take you up on that. I was planning to just google her and hope for the best. Want to be Facebook friends? You know, make it official?"

"Oh, uhm." *Hell.* The whole social media thing was something my family avoided at all costs. *At all costs.* Dad had been known to hack into accounts just to make sure there were no accidental photos of any of us. "Can we do phone numbers instead?"

Her jaw dropped slightly, her eyes glimmering with something that looked suspiciously like disappointment mixed with confusion. *Ah hell.*

"Kelsey, oh, please don't..." I hadn't had nearly enough interaction with people my own age to know how to handle this. "It's my parents. Their jobs. We can't be on social media. It's not personal, I swear—please."

She swiped at the corners of her eyes, like she wasn't quite sure why they were watery in the first place, then rolled her shoulders in something between puzzlement and reluctant amusement.

"Well, Sady, since your family has you living in another decade, I suppose we can go through the whole ordeal of exchanging phone numbers."

This girl must have descended from saints. Maybe I should ask Dad to dig into her ancestry, *just to be sure.*

But then Kelsey did something that, despite all my years of preparation, training and vigilance, caught me completely off guard.

She hugged me.

"Thanks, Sady," she said, her voice softer than usual. "For offering to help. I appreciate it."

I blinked, still processing what had just happened. "Uhm, yeah," I stammered, recovering quickly. "Of course. Anytime."

Since day one, Kelsey had always carried herself with a quiet sort of certainty, like she had already decided we were friends before I even had a say in it. But this... this was different. There was something unspoken beneath the surface. A hesitation. A vulnerability she hadn't let slip before.

And for some reason, it made me feel like I'd wandered into uncharted territory—because, well, I kind of had.

The rest of the day passed in a blur. Classes came and went, and by the time the final bell rang, I was practically sprinting to my bike. The pressure of Greyson's assignment, Kelsey's unexpected hug, and the endless questions whirling in my mind all pressed down on me as I pedaled home. The rhythmic motion of cycling helped clear my head, though it did little to settle the nagging feeling in my gut.

When I rounded the last corner, a prickle of unease ran through me at the sight of Mom's SUV parked in the driveway. *If I were Spider-Man, my spidey-senses would be tingling.*

I retreated to the backyard with my bike, granting myself a moment to steady my breathing and conjure up some feeble defenses—just in case she broached the topic of moving again. As I leaned down to secure the chain, I heard the faint crunch of footsteps behind me, and my body went rigid.

"Rough day, Sady doll?"

I spun around, the bike chain slipping from my hands, to find Dad standing just behind me, his broad frame silhouetted against the fading light.

"Ack Dad! seriously? Can you *not* sneak up on me like that?"

He remained still. And silent.

Uh-oh. *Something's up.*

I shook my head, securing the bike chain with more force than necessary. "What are you doing out here? Aren't you supposed to be inside doing... Dad things?"

"Thought I'd wait for you," he said, his tone softer now. "We need to talk."

The seriousness in his voice made me pause. "What's going on?" I asked cautiously, standing up and brushing my hands off on my jeans.

"Let's head inside," he said, gesturing toward the door.

I followed him in, setting my bag down by the door as Dad made his way to the living room. Hesitating, the knot in my stomach tightened as I dropped onto the couch while he remained standing.

"Where's Mo—"

"Your mother is going away on a training exercise for a few days," he informed me, his tone grave.

I was already gearing up to make a joke about giving them space when she returned, sparing myself the trauma of overhearing their inevitable post-mission reunion. But then the words lingered, pressing into my mind like an itch I couldn't quite scratch.

Training exercise.

A shudder traced its way up my spine, my breath faltering as the truth settled in. "It's *them*."

Dad's expression darkened, his voice dropping to a grave whisper. "One of her contacts at the UN told her about a small village. The media's calling it the work of a rebel faction, but..." He hesitated, his eyes flicking away before meeting mine again. "The damage is... extensive. No one really knows the full extent yet, but it's bad. Women, children, the elderly—it's like they were wiped out."

"Where?" *Something tells me I already know.*

"Just outside Pemba, Cabo Delgado."

Ah hell.

"How did *they* find us?"

"Sady doll," he murmured, lowering himself to one knee, a gesture designed to meet my gaze without making me look up at his nose hairs. *And it also happens to be how he makes sure I don't have a total shit fit.* "It's been ten years since we lived there. *They* haven't found us. We are safe."

"To hell with that! Tell that to the families we knew! And we both know *they* don't ask—they extract."

Somewhere in my conscious brain, I knew it wasn't Dad's fault, and he didn't deserve me yelling at him. He knew it too. But he still let me dish it out. Didn't even reprimand my use of the word *hell*.

"Your mother is upstairs packing her bags. She only plans to be away for three days. Every precaution is being taken ahead of her arrival. We have someone on the ground who will meet her on the tarmac and take her straight there. She knows how to be safe."

Okay, he had a point. Mom wasn't the type of woman whose safety you had to worry about. *Like, ever.* If anything you would want to worry for the safety of the place.

"Before she leaves, I think she wants to apologize for this morning."

Dad's tone softened, a quiet plea hidden beneath the words. "Would you please go up and give her a chance?"

So there was another reason behind this ambush of his.

"Sure, Dad. But let's be real—she still apologizes like it's a strategic maneuver, not an actual feeling."

"Let her try. Please. For my sake?"

An eye roll conveyed my reluctant agreement, met with his grateful grin. As I ascended the stairs, I really hoped he was listening. The muffled sound of a suitcase zipper reached me before I knocked lightly. The door creaked open under the force of my knuckles, revealing Mom perched on the edge of her bed, a sleek black duffel bag resting beside her. Her back was to me, her posture as straight as a ruler.

"Hey, Mom."

And there it was.

A blade, held less than an inch from my navel.

"Oh, for Tartarus' sake! Don't sneak up on me like that, Sady baby!"

"Yeah, because clearly, I was tiptoeing!" I shot back, exasperation laced with amusement. *She's already on high alert, and she hasn't even left yet.* This must be more serious than Dad let on. "So, anyway, Dad said you wanted to talk."

If you can't tell, this isn't the first time my mother has *accidentally* brandished a blade at me. Mother is rarely—and I mean rarely—ever surprised. Don't ask what happened to Dad the three times he did it. It involved stitches. I guess I should be grateful for small favors, and her uncanny ability to halt abruptly.

"Oh, right, uhm, yeah, about that." She cleared her throat, avoiding eye contact. "About this morning."

At least she paused in her packing and sat on the edge of the bed to look at me. It always took her a few minutes to build up to it.

"Uh-huh." I crossed my arms. No way was I making this easy for her.

"So, I was thinking about it, and you know—love means never having to say you're sorry."

Oh no, she didn't.

"Came up with that all by yourself, did ya, Mom?" I deadpanned. Even *I* recognized that line from *Love Story*, despite it being well before my time.

"Sady baby, you know that everything I do..." She hesitated, then rushed the rest, as if saying it quickly would make it land better. "I do it for you."

I stared at her. "Try again, Mom."

Now she's moved on to song lyrics. Bryan Adams. *Seriously?*

She groaned, rubbing her temples. "Ugh, you know I have a hard time with this kind of stuff!"

"And I have a hard time with razor-sharp pins shredding my hands to bloody bits and having to explain to my teacher at school that it's just a damn papercut!"

The dull thud on the stairs indicated Dad's silent vigilance, poised to intervene if needed. The dismay etched on her face suggested today wasn't one of those days, and I almost—*almost*—felt a flicker of pity.

"I'll be back by Sunday night, okay? And this time, you get to choose what we train on Monday morning. Deal?"

This was her peace offering. Her long arms reached out to me, and I grudgingly let her pull my hand—and then my whole body—into her lap, where she hugged me close. Not the gentle, snugly kind of hugs Dad gives. This was *fiercer*, enough that my right shoulder gave a crunching sound.

"Ooof, Mom! Breathing is still a requirement!"

Dad had been hovering long enough to know we were fine and headed back downstairs. I was quick to follow, leaving her to finish her packing. Besides, I was starving.

I flung open the fridge, scanning the shelves for something that seemed remotely appealing.

The leftovers, snacks, and even the usual easy-to-make options failed to hold any interest.

For the first time, I *couldn't figure out what I wanted to eat.*

That was new.

Is this what other teenagers deal with? Do they stand in front of the fridge, waffling over whether they want something salty or sweet, only to lose their appetite entirely?

Or maybe they're stuck agonizing over things like late growth spurts at eighteen, or why they can never decide what show to watch. Or wondering if the annoying hunger they felt five minutes ago has *suddenly* turned into this hollow indecisiveness that doesn't make sense.

Normal problems. Simple ones.

Things I probably wouldn't even notice if I weren't already swimming in my own strange mix of unease and distraction.

I wondered if they ever realized how lucky they were.

Chapter 11

When I was startled out of a deep slumber by a persistent beeping from my phone, my hand instinctively clenched into a tight fist, poised to obliterate the offensive device. Then realization dawned on me: *I'd given Kelsey my phone number.*

Kelsey: Morning, sleepyhead!

It took me a moment to process the message and another to notice that it was nearly noon. I'd slept far later than my routine ever allowed. *Damn.* My rhythm seemed completely off these days, and if *I* had noticed, it wouldn't be long before Dad did too. For once, I wished it was Mom who had stayed behind instead of him. At least I could distract her with a song or a workout whenever she got too observant.

Me: Ha, morning Kelsey, can you spell Hatshepsut yet?

I'd spent most of Friday night organizing my assignment and brainstorming ways to circumvent Mom's involvement completely. *Luckily, the internet is brimming with resources.* But honestly, when you know the truth behind the myths and legends, sticking with the lies becomes an arduous endeavor.

Kelsey: Googled her—info overload. My brain tapped out. Stopped. YELP!

Me: Do you mean HELP? ;)

Kelsey: YES! Wanna get coffee & head to the downtown

library?

I was about to yell down the stairs to ask Dad when his voice echoed in my mind.

WHAT'S UP, SADY DOLL?

I startled for a moment. I wasn't used to him initiating telepathic conversations out of the blue.

I'M GOING TO HEAD TO THE LIBRARY TO MEET KELSEY. SHE'S HAVING A MINOR HOMEWORK MELTDOWN.

SCHOOL WORK ON THE WEEKEND? WITH A FELLOW STUDENT NO LESS?

His tone carried the familiar teasing edge, even in my mind.

DON'T MAKE IT WEIRD, OKAY?

WEIRD? ME?

His amusement was practically tangible.

GO AHEAD. BUT DON'T FORGET, WE'RE TAKING THAT RIDE TONIGHT. CATCH SOME STARS.

GOT IT.

And then, just as I thought the conversation was over, his voice dropped to something quieter, more deliberate—inside my mind.

AND, SADY DOLL... TRY TO ENJOY YOURSELF?

That last comment made me pause, my fingers curling gently around my phone. Dad always had a knack for knowing exactly what I was feeling, even when I wasn't entirely sure myself.

My phone pinged a second before I could hit reply.

Kelsey: U still there?

Me: Yeah, just checked w/my Dad. How's in 30 min?

Kelsey: Perfect. See u soon.

I sighed, setting my phone down as my stomach growled, the hollow ache demanding attention. Glancing at the clock. I saw that there was time to grab something before I left, but getting ready first felt like the priority—especially if Kelsey's boundless energy was going to test my patience today.

Grabbing my go-to weekend outfit—a pair of slightly faded jeans, my favorite vintage band tee, and an oversized flannel shirt, for me that is, I'd swiped from Dad ages ago—I started dressing quickly. The soft fabric of the shirt was a small comfort, even if my hunger was making me irritable. My fingers fumbled slightly with the buttons, and I muttered, *Calm down, stomach. Food's coming. Just... chill for a minute, will you?*

I caught sight of my reflection in the mirror. My dark hair was an untamed mess, curling slightly at the ends. With a sigh, I grabbed a scrunchie off my nightstand and pulled it back into a loose, messy bun.

Then it rumbled so loud that even Dad heard it. All the way down the stairs.

"Wow, kiddo, was that your stomach or are you hiding a bear up there?" he shouted up the stairs.

Hilarious.

"What can I say, maybe I'm having a growth spurt?" I muttered under my breath, rolling my eyes at no one in particular as I fastened my shoelaces and headed down the stairs, fully prepared to silence my belly before it staged a full-blown rebellion.

The sizzling of the pan and the warm scent of Dad's omelet were not helping the situation. I was starting to comprehend what other teenagers meant when they used the word *hangry*. Frankly, I was on the verge of snapping at Dad when he stuck a steaming bowl of hot oatmeal under my nose, the sweet scent of apple and cinnamon instantly making me more agreeable.

"Ohhh, Dad, you're a lifesaver!" He'd even added some vegan

protein, blueberries, pumpkin, and hemp seeds—ensuring this wasn't just breakfast, but a *strategic meal plan*.

But as I dug in, he turned pensive, studying me with an intensity that felt a little too close.

"Were you serious about the growth spurt?"

Of course, he had heard me. Damn it. The Watcher. The eyes and ears that never missed a thing, even when I desperately wished they would. In that moment, I was certain those eyes were burning a hole straight through me.

"Nah, I think that's what teenagers call sarcasm or a joke?" I offered, attempting to diffuse the tension. But I was met with silence—a brooding, knowing kind.

Arms crossed over his broad chest, his forearms looked even more massive than usual. His mouth pressed into a firm line.

I shoved another spoonful of oatmeal into my mouth, hoping food would serve as both a distraction and a shield.

"Let's not joke about that particular topic when your mother is around, alright?"

Considering how Mom felt about my height—something she termed as *abnormal* and *defective*—this advice was undoubtedly prudent.

"Yeah, no problem. And on that cheerful note, I'm gonna go now."

The sun struggled to break through the thick gray clouds, casting the streets in a muted, silvery light as I made my way downtown. The cool autumn air nipped at my cheeks, but there was a lingering warmth in the breeze, a reminder that summer hadn't quite let go. My flannel shirt felt just right against the chill, and my shoes crunched softly against the damp pavement, the occasional gust carrying the scent of wet leaves and wood-burning chimneys.

Strolling along the busy main street, I noticed that traffic moved at a more leisurely pace than usual. *Weekend mode activated.* People wandered in and out of shops, couples strolled through the park, and children played in front of Rose Theatre while their parents idly sipped coffee, soaking in the last remnants of summer.

Maybe I could give this town a chance to grow on me. *Maybe.*

The library wasn't far, but the walk gave me just enough time to clear my head—or at least try to. The weight of Mom leaving, Greyson's cryptic comments, and this strange hunger all churned in my mind, vying for space. I shoved my hands into my jacket pockets, trying to push them aside and focus on the here and now.

The first school weekend was here, and for once, I had something resembling a social plan. Not that studying at the library with Kelsey counted as groundbreaking, but it was a step away from my usual routine of training and trying *not* to think about the weight of everything I didn't understand yet.

By the time I reached the library, the tall glass facade reflected the shifting clouds above, its sleek modern design at odds with the semi-historic buildings surrounding it. The scent of coffee from the café next door mingled with the warm aroma of fresh baked goods, made my hunger pangs flare up again.

I spotted Kelsey instantly. She was perched on a bench outside, a half-empty coffee cup in one hand and her phone in the other. When she saw me, she waved enthusiastically, her energy radiating even from this distance.

"Hey, Sady! Over here!"

She practically bounced off the bench to get my attention, and I couldn't help but grin at her enthusiasm for tackling our assignments.

"Oh my god, so I kinda googled that queen last night, and I had *no* idea that Egypt ever even had a female pharaoh. Okay, well, I mean I knew about Cleopatra, but she was way later, and let's face it, it sounds like she got a lot of help from those Roman guys, right? But this Hatshepsut? I think she might be like the first real feminist or something."

She spoke so fast I wondered how many cups of coffee she'd already consumed.

"Uhm, hey Kelsey, and a good morning to you too!" I shot a glance toward the café next door. *Do they have something tolerable, preferably vegan?* My stomach was already making some pretty odd rumbling noises, the kind that *probably* weren't just gas ready to exit my body. "Do you mind if I grab something quick to eat before we head inside?"

"Oh, sure, no problem!"

She hooked her arm into mine, pulling me toward the entrance as she continued rambling about her admiration for an Egyptian queen who also happened to be a protégé of my mother's. *That was weird to think, let alone say out loud—not that I would.*

Armed with a vegan bagel slathered in peanut butter and spiced cherry jam, I did my best to follow Kelsey's train of thought as she elaborated on her late-night deep dive into Egyptian history.

Kelsey tugged me toward the entrance, her coffee cup bouncing precariously in her hand as she gestured wildly with the other. "Okay, so I found this video last night—don't laugh—it's this historian guy who was ranting about how Hatshepsut had to basically rebrand herself to trick people into letting her rule. He said it was genius, like the ancient version of a PR campaign."

I raised an eyebrow as she pushed the library door open. "So, Hatshepsut was the original influencer?"

"Exactly!" she said, laughing as we stepped inside. "I mean, minus the selfies and hashtags. Though, come to think of it, hieroglyphs were basically the first emojis, right?"

I snorted. "Sure. Big Eye, Bird, Squiggly Line totally screams #QueenVibes."

We dissolved into laughter but had to stifle it quickly as we stepped inside, silenced by a severe glare from the librarian that could have turned us to stone.

The library's warmth wrapped around me like a blanket, the quiet hum of activity a sharp contrast to the bustling energy outside. The faint smell of paper, ink, and a hint of lemon cleaner filled the space. Rows of tall shelves stretched out in neat, endless lines, punctuated by clusters of tables and study nooks. The large windows let in the gray light from outside, casting the space in a soft glow.

We found a table near the back, away from the small groups of students scattered across the room. Kelsey immediately plopped down, her bag hitting the floor with a dull thud as she pulled out her notebook.

"Alright," she said, flipping to a blank page. "Where do we start? Research? Brainstorming? Existential dread?"

I sat down across from her, setting my bag carefully on the chair beside me. "Let's start with some research and outlines. Dread can come later."

She groaned but nodded, typing quickly on her laptop. "Fine, but you better spill all your secrets about Hatshepsut. You were way too confident yesterday."

I hesitated, my fingers grazing the edge of my notebook. "Well... she was a pioneer," I said carefully. "She took on roles that no one thought a woman could. She wasn't just a placeholder—she made Egypt stronger. Richer. And she did it without starting wars."

As I spoke, memories of bedtime stories came flooding back—Mom's voice weaving tales of clever queens and fearless leaders, always emphasizing the power of strategy over brute force. The irony was *never* lost on me, given the infamous Sera Smith temper. Back then, they felt like just fantastical stories meant to lull me to sleep. Now, they felt like something more.

Kelsey's eyes lit up, her earlier dread melting into curiosity. "That's actually... really cool," she said, her tone shifting. "Like, genius-level cool. No wars? Just ruling like a boss babe?" She shook her head, clearly impressed.

"Yeah, sounds about right."

"Alright," Kelsey said, breaking my thoughts. "Your turn. What do you know about this Amazon queen of yours? What was her name again? Ostara? Wait, isn't that Easter?"

I couldn't help it—a genuine laugh escaped me. "Otrera," I corrected, shaking my head. "And no, she's not Easter. But nice try. And, actually, more than I should."

Kelsey raised an eyebrow, leaning forward. "Care to elaborate? Because unless *Xena: Warrior Princess* counts as a credible source, I'm not going to be much help with your topic."

I laughed despite myself, shaking my head. "As much as I'd love a dissertation on Xena's battle cries, I think we're stuck with actual history on this one."

"Ugh, fine," she said, rolling her eyes but grinning. "So, what's the deal with her? Was she like, Wonder Woman's great-great-great-grandmother or something?"

"Close enough," I said, flipping open my notebook and sketching a quick outline to center my thoughts. "Otrera was the first queen of the Amazons, and depending on the myth, she either founded the tribe or shaped it into what it became. She's tied to Ares, the god of war, and Artemis, the goddess of the hunt—both of whom had... let's call them conflicting influences on her."

"Conflicting how?" Kelsey asked, resting her chin in her hand.

"Well, Ares was all about brute force and conquest. He saw the Amazons as an extension of his own thirst for war. Artemis, on the other hand, valued discipline and independence. She wanted them to be strong, but not just for the sake of war—she pushed for balance. It's like they were constantly tugging Otrera in two directions—one wild, one calculated."

Kelsey nodded slowly, jotting something in her notebook. "So, let me get this straight. She had to deal with a bloodthirsty war god on one side and a perfectionist goddess on the other. And she still managed to run an entire tribe of warrior women?"

"Exactly," I said, a small smile tugging at my lips. "She didn't just survive—she thrived. She carved out a space for her people in a world that was constantly trying to erase them."

Kelsey sat back, looking impressed. "Okay, that's officially badass. If you don't turn that into your thesis, you're wasting your potential."

"I'll keep that in mind," I said dryly, though Otrera's name still pressed against my thoughts. The connection between her and my family history felt too close for comfort, but Kelsey didn't need to know that.

"Alright," she said, tapping her pen against the table. "I've got my feminist pharaoh, and you've got your Amazonian queen. I say we crush these essays and make our history teacher question his life choices."

"Deal," I said, laughing softly. "But no emojis, okay?"

"No promises," she shot back with a grin. "And you better not sneak in any *Xena* quotes."

My mouth quirked sideways. "Fair trade. You keep it emoji-free, and I'll keep it *Xena*-free. Let's see who cracks first."

The next few hours passed in hushed whispers, interrupted only by the occasional muffled laughter, as we talked about formidable women in history. I found myself wishing—maybe for once—that I could tell someone my mom was the OG of them all. But I couldn't. So I didn't.

The textbook I unearthed on the Amazons contained one of the scant accounts of Otrera, hailed as one of the earliest Amazon queens. Most tales depicted her as either the consort or the daughter of Ares. Her daughters, Hippolyta and Penthesilea, had made their own headlines in history, carving their names into legend.

But even queens answer to greater forces. Otrera had been pulled between gods, her daughters left to shape what remained of her legacy. It made me think about my own mother—not just the stories about her, but the choices that had rewritten history, the war she'd fought in that still echoed in whispers. Maybe power always came with a cost. Maybe daughters were always left trying to make sense of what came before them, whether it was myth, war, or something far more personal.

The quiet hum of the library surrounded us as we buried ourselves in research. Kelsey was fully engrossed in an article about Hatshepsut's trade expeditions, muttering under her breath as she scribbled notes. Meanwhile, I stared at the same paragraph in my book for what felt like the hundredth time, my focus slipping with every passing minute.

The faint smell of leftover coffee from Kelsey's cup wasn't helping. Neither was the fact that my breakfast and bagel from earlier had officially worn off.

"Did you hear that? Did someone sneak a cat into the library?"

She caught me off guard, having heard my stomach before I did. *What the hell is going on in my body?* My appetite had always been healthy, but this was verging on the absurd.

"Uhm, Kelsey, I'm pretty sure that's my belly."

Kelsey's lips twitched, and before I could stop her, she burst into muffled laughter. "Sady, that sounded like something out of a wildlife documentary. Like, 'And here we have the ravenous predator, desperate for sustenance in the wild.'"

"Ha-ha," I said dryly, though a reluctant smile tugged at the corners of my mouth. "Glad my suffering is so entertaining."

Her grin faded slightly, replaced by a flicker of concern. "Wait, you're not, like, hypoglycemic or anything, are you? Do we need to find you some juice? One of my brothers has diabetes, and whenever he gets low, he gets all shaky and super cranky—it's scary."

The casual mention of her brother held something in her tone that wasn't there before, choosing her words with more care. I glanced away, forcing my expression to stay neutral. "I'm fine," I said quickly. "I don't have any health conditions, let alone diabetes. Just a bottomless pit of a stomach."

She studied me for a moment, then relaxed, her playful smile returning. "Okay, but I'm officially calling it. Snack break. Let's find something before your belly decides to eat your notes."

I hesitated, glancing down at the jumble of words on the page in front of me. "But we haven't even—"

"Sady, come on," she interrupted, standing and grabbing her bag. "I've seen what happens when my brother gets hangry. It's not pretty. Let's find you something to eat, and then we'll crush this research."

The mention of her brother again made me pause, but the faint lightheadedness creeping in from my growing hunger overrode my reluctance. With a sigh, I stood and started toward the vending machines at the back of the library.

"Nah, Sady, that will not do," Kelsey said, looping her arm through mine. "You're not surviving on vending machine snacks when there's an actual restaurant two blocks away. My treat."

"Kelsey, I—"

"Nope," she interrupted, her determination evident. "No arguments. You need real food, and I'm not letting your stomach growl through our research session. Let's go. Besides, who can concentrate on Egypt when there's a wild beast, also known as your belly, roaring under the table?"

With that, she tugged me outside, and I let her lead, the crisp autumn air hitting us as soon as we stepped into the open. The sun, which had been shy all morning, suddenly burst through the clouds, casting a golden hue over the street. For a moment, the warmth on my face and the vibrant light made me wish we hadn't spent most of the day indoors, tucked away in the library's quiet corridors.

Kelsey was already chattering, waving her coffee cup for emphasis as she talked about her strategy for tackling Hatshepsut's trade policies. I smiled, half-listening, my thoughts drifting briefly to Mom and her bedtime stories. With her away for the weekend, I'd have to rely solely on memory—or the somewhat dubious accounts of historians written centuries, if not millennia, after the fact—for my own research on the Amazons.

That was when I felt it.

It was subtle at first, a faint shift in the breeze that prickled the edge of my senses. My shoulders tensed as my surroundings seemed to sharpen. The steady hum of the street filled my ears—footsteps on the sidewalk, distant laughter, and the low rumble of engines idling at a nearby light. My eyes darted to the intersection just ahead, where a line of cars waited patiently for the light to turn green.

All except for one.

The driver of a dark sedan, seemingly in a hurry, began creeping forward, the sun's sudden glare obscuring their view. At the same moment, Kelsey, noticing the walk signal had changed, took the first eager steps off the curb, still chattering and glancing back at me to make sure I was keeping up.

Time seemed to slow.

The sedan's front fender edged closer, the driver squinting against the blinding sunlight. Kelsey's stride was light and carefree, her left leg already stretched toward the asphalt. Two more steps, and the car would strike her—her leg, her hip, maybe worse.

There was no time for doubt.

Chapter 12

In a single fluid motion, I closed the distance between us, my hand gripping her elbow firmly. I yanked her back onto the curb with controlled force, careful not to pull too hard, knowing my strength could easily send her tumbling. The car rushed past, the whoosh of displaced air whipping around us, a blinding blur of metal and speed. I felt the heat of it as it swept by, just inches away. Kelsey stumbled slightly but caught herself, her breath coming in sharp gasps, her wide eyes locked on the spot where the car had been.

"Whoa!" Kelsey exclaimed, her voice high-pitched with adrenaline, buzzing from the narrow escape. Her body shifted as if trying to shake off the shock, her feet moving restlessly, like her energy couldn't quite find a place to settle. She looked at me, wide-eyed and breathless, her chest rising and falling in quick, uneven breaths. "Sady! Damn, that was a close call!" She ran a shaky hand through her hair, her gaze darting back to the spot where the car had been, as though trying to make sense of what had just happened. Her hands trembled slightly, and I could see the lingering shock in the way she held herself, as if she still hadn't quite realized how close she'd come to disaster.

Kelsey's wide-eyed look slowly softened as the adrenaline began to fade, but I could feel the tension still hanging between us. I took a deep breath, forcing my muscles to loosen, though my pulse still hammered in my ears like a warning bell. "Meh, just paying attention," I said, trying to sound casual. "You know, finding my bearings in this new place. People drive differently in every town I've lived in, and most of the time, it doesn't make sense. So I just have this habit of being on alert around vehicles, I guess."

Her lips twitched, the initial shock giving way to a bubbling smile. It started as small giggles, but soon she was laughing fully, the sound warm and genuine.

I found myself wondering—was this a normal teen girl reaction to almost getting hit by a car? Or was it some weird post-traumatic stress thing? Either way, the laughter felt oddly comforting, even if it didn't make sense.

"Guess I owe you more than lunch," Kelsey said, her voice a mix of breathless relief and nervous laughter. "Twice now, actually. First that compass in class, and now this? What are you, my guardian angel or something?"

I smirked, shaking my head as we stepped back onto the sidewalk. *If only she knew.* "I think that's a stretch. I just have good reflexes."

"Good reflexes?" she echoed, giving me an incredulous look. "Sady, you caught that thing midair like some kind of ninja. And now this? I'm starting to think you've got superpowers or something. Like Spider-Man, only—" she gestured vaguely at me, "—girlier."

I glanced down at myself, taking in my well-worn jeans, scuffed boots, and a hoodie that had seen better days. Hardly the uniform of a superhero, unless Spider-Woman was rocking this look. Not exactly "girly" either. More like "don't mess with me, I'm probably carrying snacks and a book or two."

"Not Spider-Girl," I said casually, though her choice of words triggered a flicker of unease. "But I'd need a much better suit, and possibly a tragic backstory. Besides, it's nothing, I've just learned to pay attention. You know, new town, unfamiliar drivers, that sort of thing."

"Right, you said that already," she said, giving me a skeptical look. Then her lips twitched, and she broke into a grin. "Well, whatever it is, I appreciate it. Seriously. That car—" She shivered slightly, the adrenaline clearly still working through her system. "I didn't even see it coming."

"Neither did the driver," I said, nodding toward the now-distant sedan. "The sun blinded them. It wasn't your fault."

"Still," she said, bumping my shoulder lightly with hers, "if this keeps up, I might start thinking you were put in my life for a reason."

I laughed, the sound feeling lighter than it had in weeks. "Let's just call it good timing and leave it at that."

After the near-miss, Kelsey was back to her usual self in no time, her energy undeterred as we settled into a cozy diner a few doors down. The food was simple but satisfying—just enough to keep my stomach from growling for the rest of the afternoon. *I hoped.*

Between bites, Kelsey peppered me with questions about my topic, her curiosity spilling over as she shared bits of what she'd uncovered about Hatshepsut. I nodded along, offering what I knew—how Hatshepsut had built temples that rivaled her male predecessors and rebranded herself as a king to secure her rule. In return, I told her about Otrera, the Amazon queen who supposedly founded an empire of warrior women and left her mark on mythology, and possibly history if you consider the Trojan wars. By the end of lunch, we were trading facts and theories like we were solving a mystery, both a little more excited about tackling our essays. Her enthusiasm was infectious, and for a while, I forgot about everything else.

As we left the restaurant, Kelsey looped her arm through mine, pulling me toward the bus stop. "Okay, so I've been thinking," she said, her voice teeming with excitement. "I need a break from all this ancient history tomorrow. How do you feel about thrift shopping? There's this place on Queen Street that's supposed to have amazing vintage stuff."

I smiled faintly, warmed by her excitement. This would mark the most time I'd spent with anyone my age outside of school, and she already wanted more? *Huh.* "I mean, it sounds great, but I'll have to check with my dad first. He's got this whole stargazing thing planned for tonight, so I don't know what tomorrow looks like yet."

"Fair enough," she said, her grin undiminished, though there was a flicker of something in her eyes—curiosity, maybe a little envy. "You're lucky, you know," she added after a pause. "My dad and I... well, let's just say stargazing isn't really his thing."

Her words weren't bitter, just matter-of-fact, but they hit me anyway. I hadn't thought much about how unusual nights like this were.

"Yeah," I said softly, a little more aware of how much I took for granted. "I'll let you know if I can make it. Noon work?"

"Yes! Awesome!" she exclaimed, skipping ahead a few steps. "This is going to be great."

The bus whisked her away, leaving me standing there, feeling a bit puzzled. And hungry. *Again.* This was becoming beyond absurd. I was starting to think my stomach was possessed.

The streets were quieter now, the golden hues of the afternoon fading into the softer tones of twilight. My steps slowed as I took in the calm, the distant hum of the town settling into its weekend rhythm.

At least the hunger was distracting me from thinking about Greyson.

Wait—never mind, there he was again.

As I stepped into the house, warmth enveloped me, carrying the familiar scent of something savory lingering in the air. The roasted richness of whatever Dad was making in the oven should have been comforting, but it barely scratched the itch gnawing at the edges of my senses.

I kicked off my shoes by the door, letting out a soft sigh as the day's weight began to settle. The quiet hum of the refrigerator drew me towards the kitchen, and my stomach gave an almost desperate growl.

This was getting ridiculous.

Dad had left me a note letting me know that his latest project would require his concentration but that he'd come out of his cave as soon as the sun started to go down. *Catching stars is still on the agenda, as promised.*

Dad was always good for that. If he promised something, he kept it. Mom, on the other hand, could be a bit more volatile—but not intentionally. At least, I don't think so. One time, she promised we'd go to a festival, only to disappear on a 'last-minute work trip' an hour before. Dad covered for her, as always, but even then, I knew the difference.

Perusing the contents of the fridge, I spotted Dad's leftover frittata from yesterday wrapped up in tinfoil. My stomach demonstrated its enthusiasm by releasing a tiger-sized growl.

It's made with eggs. I don't eat eggs. I never have. I'm not supposed to.

Except today.

Today, however, I let my stomach dictate my next actions.

The frittata was promptly deposited into the microwave, sans tinfoil, while I nibbled on celery sticks, zoning out with daydreams of Greyson and what he might be doing on weekends. My thoughts were rudely interrupted by the ping of the microwave. Bowl in hand, backpack slung over my shoulder, I headed upstairs to my bedroom to finish up this assignment.

Greyson.

The name had been looping in my mind since the first day of class. His cryptic comments, his unnervingly accurate insights, and the way he seemed to know things he shouldn't—it all felt too deliberate, too specific.

If I was going to write about the Amazons, Ares, and Artemis, I couldn't ignore the strange feeling that Greyson somehow fit into this puzzle, whether he realized it or not.

Taking a bite of the frittata, I opened a search engine and typed his name into the bar:

Greyson Black.

The results were underwhelming to say the least. A few social media profiles popped up, but none of them were him. No photos, no links to anything useful. Just a name in the void.

Frowning, I refined the search: Greyson Black + history teacher. That turned up a little more. Three tangible hits.

2009 New history teacher welcomed to the local high school.

2010 History class unearths ancient burial site in abandoned quarry under the guidance of Mr. Black, a local history teacher.

2011 Local history teacher forges alliance with Royal Ontario Museum for graduating class.

No Facebook. No Instagram. No Twitter. No social media to be found. Only three images, each of them from the aforementioned local papers. Blurry, black and white, barely recognizable.

Well, that was a waste of time.

I chewed slowly, my thoughts tangling as I stared at the search results. It was like trying to search for a family member of mine. Just as impossible. If Greyson was hiding something, he was doing an excellent job of it. But the more I thought about it, the more I realized that I wasn't just curious about him—I was *suspicious*. He'd picked up on things about me that no one else had, not even Kelsey. And then there was that antique brass compass.

Looking down at my meal, I figured it was wise to also look into my unusual, constant state of hunger and the questionable choice of food. I typed:

Persistent hunger, unusual appetite causes

The screen filled with an avalanche of medical conditions.

Polyphagia. Prader-Willi syndrome. Leptin resistance. Stomach cancer. Intestinal cancer.

Note to self—do not google medical crap. It will turn even the most stoic individual into a hypochondriac.

"Hey, Sady doll!" Dad's booming voice shattered my concentration and momentarily drowned out the sound of my belly. "How about grabbing a burrito-to-go for our bike ride?"

"Oh yeah!"

"Then grab your jacket and come on down!" His loud footsteps suggested he had already laced up in his boots, which meant he was planning for a long ride. *Excellent.*

"I heard about this place called the Badlands, near Caledon. Thought we could check it out."

"Sure thing, Dad. That sounds like the perfect distraction!"

"What exactly do you need a distraction from?" *Damn it.* I should have kept my mouth shut.

"Uhm, homework, obviously!"

"Oh right, because teenagers are renowned for their adoration of homework."

With an exaggerated eye roll, I turned just in time for my dad to lob my helmet at my face. No warning, of course. I barely caught it before impact. Irony at its finest: the thing meant to protect my head nearly gave me a concussion. Clearly, this was going to become a pattern.

Dad swung his leg over the Harley and settled into the seat, patting the spot behind him. "Hop on."

I climbed on, wrapping my arms around his waist as the engine hummed to life beneath us. The vibrations traveled through me, grounding me in the moment. This wasn't new for us—Dad and I had been "chasing the stars" for as long as I could remember.

When I was little, he'd carry me in one of those child carriers strapped to his chest. As I grew, he'd hoist me onto the back of his motorcycle—first in a seat designed for kids, and later on my own—and we'd pick a direction and simply ride. Eventually, he would pull over, and we would seek out a cozy spot, drop a blanket on the ground, and turn skyward to admire the stars.

The way he tells it, I was a colicky mess as a newborn—red-faced, wailing, and absolutely relentless. Mom couldn't take it, so Dad bundled me up and stepped into the backyard, desperate for anything to quiet me. The second I saw the night sky, though, I went silent. Just... staring. He swears my tiny fingers reached up, grasping for something I'd never even seen before. *Catching stars,* he called it. That was the night he knew—this would be our thing.

And so, this became our cherished daddy-daughter ritual, especially when Mom was away on one of her trips.

It wasn't until we were outside the city limits, with the cool wind whipping past, that I tilted my head back and caught a glimpse of the first stars appearing in the darkening sky. The hum of the engine and the rhythmic thrum of the tires on the road were familiar and comforting, the perfect soundtrack for our shared tradition.

But this year was going to be different. I was eighteen now—old enough to finally get my own bike. We'd started to talk about it a month ago, the plan was going to be set in motion: I'd be learning to assemble and tune my own motorcycle with Dad's help. A rite of passage, as he liked to call it.

Tonight was no different. We meandered through the darkness of the Badlands for a little while before getting back on his bike, venturing further north until he discovered the perfect spot.

Dad cut the engine, and the silence that followed was vast, wrapping around us like the endless sky above. He stretched out the blanket, patting the ground beside him as he leaned back on his elbows. I followed, settling beside him, the cool earth pressing against me. The blanket offered some comfort against the cold ground, but it was nothing compared to the warmth radiating from Dad, his body temperature naturally high, a heat that seeped into me the moment I sat next to him. There was no risk of me getting cold, not with the warmth of the blanket and the heat from him spilling over, making everything feel cozy despite the chill of the night.

"Hey kiddo," he said, his voice barely above a whisper. "You would tell me if anything was wrong, wouldn't you?"

His otherworldly senses seemed to have kicked in—or were those just standard Dad abilities? Yet another topic to google. *Or perhaps not.*

"Honestly, Dad?"

"When have we ever not wanted honesty?"

"Do I need to bring up that time Mom—"

"Alright, alright. Fair point. Yes, I would very much like honesty, daughter of mine."

I took a breath, rolling my gaze from the stars to him. "I think I made a friend."

"And—that is a positive development, I presume?" His massive shoulder nudged mine ever so slightly, prompting me to shift on the grass to avoid getting squashed.

"Yeah, of course. Just feels... odd."

"Well, admittedly, that is a first." His large, warm hand enveloped mine, giving it a gentle squeeze. Lying side by side, I could feel the rise and fall of his breath, steady and unhurried.

There was something calming about the quiet rhythm of it, the solid presence of him next to me.

For a breath or two, neither of us spoke. That's one thing I loved about talking with Dad—he was never in a hurry, never pressed me to fill the silence. He just let it stretch, giving me the space to think. And somehow, that always made everything feel a little less overwhelming.

"The usual, I suppose," I admitted. "When we move, I have to say goodbye. And, well, ya know, worst-case scenario, she could find herself caught in some kind of crossfire and get hurt."

"Oh, right. That."

A shimmering silver star streaked across the midnight blue sky.

"Quick, Sady doll, make a wish."

I scoffed. "Why bother? None of my other wishes ever came true."

The words left my mouth before I could stop them, the bitterness in my own voice surprising me. A beat of silence stretched between us, and regret immediately followed.

"Dad, I'm sorry," I murmured, shifting to look at him. "I didn't mean it like that."

"Don't you know that we see how hard this life is for you?"

Dad's voice was quiet, the kind of quiet that carried weight. The sudden intake of breath, followed by a slow and somewhat unsteady exhale, betrayed emotions he rarely let surface.

"Sera longed to be a mother so badly she would have destroyed heaven and hell to make it happen. And I have always yearned to be a father. I don't even remember a time when I didn't. But, if I'm being honest—we were selfish in our desires. We never truly considered the kind of life that our child would have."

I swallowed, unsure how to respond.

"Well, in your defense, I don't think anyone could have foreseen..."

"Hey, I'm the parent here," he interrupted, his tone lighter. "I'm supposed to be doling out comfort and sage advice, remember?"

A chuckle escaped him, breaking whatever emotion had been stuck in his throat, and with it, the strain between us loosened. We lapsed into a comfortable silence, gazing up at the sky.

Catching stars.

For a little while, time stopped.

Then, a deep, unmistakable rumble shattered the peace.

Dad's head snapped toward me with exaggerated horror. "Whoa, please tell me that was your stomach and not your butt!"

I choked on a laugh, doubling over as he recoiled in mock disgust. Leave it to Dad to accuse *my* rear end of making that kind of noise.

"Ahem, no?" I gasped between giggles. "I believe you are the record holder of loudest backside noises in this family."

"Oh, I'm not so sure about that, Sady!" He pushed himself up from the ground, dusting off his clothes. "You weren't born yet when your mother and I lived in Morocco. Let me tell you, some of the dishes there did not sit well with her. Not at all."

"No way! Mom? She acts like she's physically incapable of farting or burping. Like it's some kind of superpower she has to maintain her dignity at all costs."

"Nah, but don't tell her I told you. It would take me years to get out of the doghouse on that one." He retrieved his helmet and zipped up his jacket. Then, more seriously, "But for real, kid—was that your stomach?"

My shoulders sagged as I averted my gaze. "Yeah, it was. Been having some issues with it all day. Just feeling hungry. Like, every few hours. I had your apple and cinnamon porridge for breakfast—still the best. Then a vegan bagel with peanut butter and jam. After that, Kelsey and I grabbed tofu stew with two of those fresh-baked buns at the café. And I—"

He wasn't just *listening* now—he was *assessing*.

"So... you did eat my frittata? The one I was saving for a snack before dinner?"

I winced. "Yeah, and I know. You don't have to remind me. It has eggs. I know. But, Dad, it's my choice, okay?"

He sighed, running a gloved hand over his jaw. "Sady doll, making changes to your diet is something we should discuss as a family."

He wasn't wrong. But now I was in a mood, and I didn't want to give him the satisfaction of admitting it.

"You know, I bet every teenager on this planet can eat whatever the hell they want without having the whole family chime in on their decision."

Dad's brow furrowed, his voice dipping into that calm-but-dangerous tone. "First of all, please watch your language. You know I don't like you using that word. And second, you're not every teenager. And you know that too."

I clenched my jaw, taking a steadying breath. *Right.* Because I'm not normal.

"Ugh, fine, Dad, but can we just wait until Mom gets home before getting into this? I would really like to have one more drama-free day. Please."

He studied me for a long moment before nodding. "I suppose that's fair."

He extended his gloved hand toward me, pulling me up behind him on the bike.

The ride home was silent, but not totally uncomfortable.

When we arrived, I headed straight to my bedroom without so much as saying goodnight. The guilt hit me instantly, thick and heavy. I knew he was only looking out for me. He always was. And I hated that my first instinct was to snap at him. Was it the hunger? The stress? Or just hormones screwing with my mood?

I buried my face under my pillow, willing the frustration to fade.

Downstairs, I could hear him lingering at the foot of the stairs.

Watching over me. Like he always did.

Chapter 13

A steady vibration rattled against my headboard, dragging me out of sleep. For a second, I thought it was my stomach again—because, lately, that seemed to be a theme—but no. This time, it was my phone.

Kelsey: Wakie wakie, Sady! Ready to thrift?

Oh, right. I'd almost forgotten I made plans with Kelsey.

Me: Duh! Yeah! Where and when?

I shoved off the covers, stretching until my joints popped, my brain still sluggish from sleep. My phone buzzed again just as another sensation hit me—the unmistakable smell of frittata. My stomach gave a low, insistent growl. *Here we go again.*

Kelsey: Value Village on Queen Street. 11 a.m.?

The clock read ten. Plenty of time to shower, eat, and cycle over.

Me: Deal. See you then.

The heat from the shower was exactly what I needed. The agitation running down my spine wasn't just from my usual bizarre hunger battle. Between my mind's near-constant pull toward anything involving Greyson and my stomach's relentless demands, I hadn't considered what—or *who*—Mom might find. She was coming back tonight.

I knew she'd be fine. She always was. If anything, I should be more concerned about whoever—or whatever—was on the receiving end of her… well, *her*.

"Sady, doll?"

Whoa. I hadn't even noticed Dad climbing the stairs. *Not good.* Distractions are becoming a real problem.

"I come bearing a peace offering," he said.

Opening the door, towel wrapped around my damp hair but fully dressed, I found Dad holding a plate piled high with steaming, delicious-smelling frittata. Spinach, beetroot, sweet potatoes, and that unmistakable aroma of Cajun spices wafted through the air. My mouth involuntarily salivated. Like, literally and *excessively*.

"Uhm?" Dad tilted his head, a curious smile tugging at his lips. "I haven't seen you drool like that since you were a teething one-year-old."

"Dad, I'm hungry. It's normal to salivate, isn't it?"

His barely contained laugh escaped through his nose.

I snatched the plate from his hand and slammed the door in his face in what I *hoped* was a dramatic, point emphatically made kind of way. My mood did not improve when, between bites, I could still hear Dad laughing to himself all the way down the stairs.

I stomped down to the front door, heels thudding against the floorboards, determined to be loud enough for him to notice. *Childish*? Maybe. Ask me if I cared.

"Dad, I'm heading out to meet Kelsey!" I shouted.

"Whoa, wait!"

He was so engrossed in whatever he was reading, my entire production of stomping had gone completely unnoticed. What a waste of energy.

"Mom's coming back tonight, so can you please be home by seven?"

Ah yes, the family tradition.

Sunday nights, seven o'clock—family time was non-negotiable. It had been that way for as long as I could remember. Board games sprawled across the coffee table, a mismatched deck of cards that somehow still held its shape despite years of use, and an array of snacks that always included something salty, something sweet, and something vaguely questionable that Dad insisted on trying at least once. A rare piece of normalcy in a life that had never really been normal.

Tonight would be anything but normal. It wasn't just game night—Mom would have something to report.

Her trip—the investigation—would cast its shadow over everything. Whether she came back with good news, bad news, or nothing at all, it would hang in the air, waiting.

"Sure, Dad, no problem. I'm just heading out with Kelsey to do some thrift shopping. Maybe grab lunch?"

"Here, take this." He handed me a glass container filled with still-warm frittata. The scent alone was enough to make me reconsider my earlier sulking. "I'll have dinner ready by the time Mom gets home."

I shoved the container into my backpack, nodding absently. Outside, a faint chill hinted at the changing season, just enough to justify my flannel-lined jean jacket. Swapping out my usual red high-top Chucks for my trusty oxblood Solovair boots from London, I secured the backpack straps and hopped on my bike.

Mom had picked them out. At the time, I'd resisted—hard. The color was too intense, too much like her. But somehow, over time, they'd grown on me. Maybe it was the way the leather softened, molding to my feet. Or maybe it was the way the deep, dark red caught the light, shifting like something alive beneath the surface. Either way, they had earned their place in my rotation.

Second place, anyway. My Chucks would always be first.

With the warm frittata tucked in the glass container, a couple of vegan protein bars—*damn, gotta love Dad's foresight*—and my notebook, I was well prepared for just about anything.

As I pedaled down the quiet streets, the rhythmic click of my tires on pavement matched the buzz in my head. The morning was fresh, and my mind wasn't entirely consumed by tangled thoughts. Today was about something simple. Something *normal.*

A school friend.

Of course, the minute anything related to school entered my mind, it got hijacked by thoughts of Greyson. *Damn it.*

Arriving at the shopping complex's huge parking lot, I scanned for a bike rack where I could safely lock mine. Sadly, this town didn't have the best reputation for keeping bicycles safe, and I had no intention of losing mine to some nondescript thief.

"Sady!"

A voice rang out across the lot.

"Over here!"

Kelsey was standing near the entrance, waving with both hands like she was signaling a rescue helicopter. *Does she have a caffeine habit I don't know about?*

"Heya," I said as I dismounted and locked my bike. "Where's yours?"

"Oh, I don't have one. My dad says I'd break every bone in my body if I tried. He's not wrong," she said with a shrug, holding out her arm to reveal a fresh bruise on her wrist in the shape of what might have been a coffee table corner. "I'm just really good at running into things."

"Besides, the bus works just fine."

"Fair point." I tightened the straps on my backpack. "Ready?"

She nodded enthusiastically, and we stepped into the thrift store, greeted immediately by the mixed smells of old fabric, faint detergent, and the indescribable scent of... *vintage?*

"This place is amazing," Kelsey said, already beelining for a rack of oversized sweaters. "I found a whole bag of clothes here last month for under twenty bucks."

As we wandered through the aisles, she took the lead, pulling out everything from neon windbreakers to a denim jacket lined with what *might* have been faux-sheep's wool. Meanwhile, I stuck to browsing, amused by her relentless enthusiasm.

"This one screams you," she said, holding up a graphic tee that read: *I'm just here for the snacks.*

I smirked. "Not inaccurate."

She laughed, tossing it over her arm. "You have to get it. It's too perfect."

A familiar voice cut through the thrift store's low hum of activity, before I could retort.

"Is that you laughing like a hyena, Miss Kelsey Hamilton?"

We turned to see Michaela and Jamie strolling toward us. Michaela's long, dark hair swished dramatically over her shoulders, as if she were making an entrance on a runway. Jamie, ever the dutiful boyfriend, trailed a step behind her, holding a shopping bag from the store next door.

"Wait, I think there are two hyenas," Michaela teased, stepping around a rack of coats to join us. "Kelsey, do I even want to know what's so funny this time?"

Kelsey stuck out her tongue. "Just showing Sady the wonders of thrift-store fashion. What are you guys doing here?"

"Halloween shopping, of course," Michaela said with an exaggerated air of importance. "I'd never trust a store-bought costume, and besides, everyone knows the best pieces are found at thrift shops."

I raised an eyebrow. "You sound like an expert."

"Well, duh." Michaela flipped her hair back with a flourish. "Halloween is my holiday, after all."

Jamie let out a low hum of amusement, pulling her close and nuzzling her cheek in a way that sent a quiet flutter through my stomach—not from hunger this time. "You forgot to mention your birthday," he reminded her.

Michaela beamed. "Right! Born on October thirty-first. The queen of Halloween parties. I don't just celebrate it—I am it."

"Not a bad day to be born," I said, genuinely impressed. "Better than sharing it with baby Jesus on Christmas, right?"

"Exactly!" Michaela said, tossing a feather boa around her neck with theatrical flair. "And it's the one night of the year everyone can pretend to be someone else."

For a moment, I let my mind wander. *Who would I be, if I could be someone else?* The answer came too easily: someone Greyson's age. Someone who didn't feel like an awkward kid every time he looked my way.

Michaela's voice snapped me out of my thoughts. "You should totally come to my party, Sady. It's gonna be amazing."

"Thanks. I'll think about it," I said noncommittally. I'd never been to a party before—never even been invited to one—but the idea of blending in, even just for a night, held a certain curiosity. It wasn't entirely unappealing.

Jamie, clearly trying to keep the mood light, glanced between us. "So, what's next on the agenda? You guys want to do lunch and then go rollerskating after this?"

"Sure, as long as I'm home by seven," I said, shifting my backpack to one shoulder. "Kelsey, you in?"

She hesitated, glancing at her watch. "Yeah, I think so. I'll probably have to leave a little earlier than you, though. My dad's strict about curfews."

"Fair enough," I said, offering her a reassuring smile. Her hesitant shrug was in stark contrast to her bubbly nature from the morning, but I chalked it up to caffeine deficiency.

"Perfect!" Michaela declared, already leading the way to the checkout. "Let's grab lunch and then hit the rink. I need fuel if I'm going to roll circles around y'all."

Leaving the thrift store, our backpacks protected our thrift purchases and Kelsey's had tucked something wrapped in newspaper in the front of hers. Michaela and Jamie's finds were especially eye-catching: Michaela held up a long, elegant black gown with lace sleeves that trailed down to her wrists, paired with a statement silver necklace that gleamed like moonlight. Jamie, on the other hand, had managed to find a pinstripe suit complete with a vintage pocket watch and a snazzy black bow tie.

"Morticia and Gomez?" I asked, tilting my head as I eyed the ensemble. "Very on-brand."

Michaela grinned wickedly, draping the gown over her arm. "You caught me. We're going for classic spooky couple vibes this year. What do you think?"

"You're going to crush it," I said honestly. "That's a classic Halloween power-duo look."

Jamie beamed happily. "As if I had a choice. Michaela decides, and I just go along for the ride."

"Oh, please," Michaela said, rolling her eyes affectionately. "You're practically Gomez already."

"Minus the mustache," he added with mock solemnity, running a hand over his smooth upper lip.

We found a spot on the curb outside to sit and eat burritos while waiting for the rink to open. The conversation flowed easily, and I realized... I felt... *normal.* Like this was what being a teenager was supposed to feel like. *I think.*

"So," I began, glancing between Michaela and Jamie, "you guys really been together since the first day of grade nine, huh?"

I couldn't help but wonder how these two had found what, by all accounts, appeared to be genuine love so early in their life.

"Yup, one look at his baby blues and I knew he would be mine." Michaela looped her arm through Jamie's, giving him a quick kiss on the cheek. "What about you? Any mysterious lover in your well-traveled past?"

I nearly choked on my burrito. "Umh, that would be a nope."

"What? Like none you keep in touch with or...?"

"Michaela, how can I say this delicately?" Eye rolling is definitely a teenage communication technique. "I've never dated. So, when I say a solid nope. Total blank slate."

Jamie looked genuinely shocked. "What kind of idiot guys are you hanging around? They must be blind. Or wait, should we be asking about girls instead?"

I didn't respond right away. The truth was, so far, it hadn't been either. The idea of dating—whether guys or girls—hadn't really crossed my mind. With all the moving around, with keeping my head down, I'd never exactly had the luxury to think about it. And honestly? It felt like one more thing I couldn't quite figure out.

Kelsey shifted uncomfortably, noticing the hesitation in my silence. Her voice was quiet but firm as she added, "She's not the only one, you know." She gave a small shrug, as if offering her own experience to fill the gap I hadn't yet voiced. "It's not always that easy."

Michaela shot him a glare but seemed to soften as Kelsey's words hung in the air. I could see her pause, thinking about how to respond, but instead, she turned her focus to Kelsey, a gentle understanding crossing her face.

Kelsey shifted in her seat, her gaze drifting as if to avoid the weight of their attention. "It's not that easy for me," she murmured, voice quieter now. "With… everything at home. My dad, my four brothers… dating just feels like something that's… not on the table right now, you know?" Her words trailed off, leaving the air heavy with the unspoken realities of her situation.

Jamie's grin faded for a moment, his usual playful energy quieting as he took in Kelsey's words. Then, with a deep breath, he leaned back in his chair, eyes softening. "You both deserve someone who's not blind, or clueless, or… whatever. Someone who'll see how amazing you are. You're both incredible, and anyone who can't see that, well… they're just idiots."

"Thanks," I said dryly, grateful I didn't have to answer, though I could feel a faint blush creeping up my neck. "Glad you think so."

The conversation shifted as we finished our burritos, the wrappers crinkling as they were stuffed into the nearest trash can. Michaela stretched her legs out in front of her, the hem of her black jeans brushing against Jamie's, who sat closer now, absently tracing circles on the curb with his finger.

"So," Michaela started, her voice taking on that familiar teasing lilt, "if you've been living this romance-free life, what do you do for fun?

What's your thing?"

I hesitated, glancing at Kelsey, who immediately filled the silence.

"Oh, Sady?" Kelsey said, leaning forward, her tone carrying an easy confidence. "She's the kind of person who's always there before you even know you need them." She shot me a knowing look. "Like a human safety net."

I groaned. "Kelsey—"

"What? It's true." She shrugged. "You guys, remember when Mr. Black randomly chucked that antique compass across the room? Everyone else was still processing what was happening, and Sady just—caught it, while sidekicking me to safety. No hesitation. Like she knew it was coming before it even left his hand."

Michaela's eyebrows lifted. "Ohhh, yeah. That was kind of insane."

Kelsey nodded. "And that's not even the weirdest part."

Jamie frowned. "There's more?"

"Oh yeah." Kelsey leaned in, her voice taking on a mix of teasing and intrigue. "Yesterday? She saved my life."

Michaela blinked. "Wait, what?"

"I mean, maybe I wouldn't have died, but I sure as hell would've been in the hospital." Kelsey's face turned serious. "We were walking downtown, just talking, when this car came out of nowhere. I didn't even see it. But Sady? She grabbed me before it even hit the brakes. Yanked me back like it was nothing."

Jamie sat on the curb, arms stretched out behind him for support, a smirk tugging at his lips. "Alright, let's break this down. Lightning-fast reflexes, disaster-predicting abilities, mysterious past..." He tapped his chin thoughtfully. "Yup. I'm calling it now—Sady's actually a Teenage Mutant Ninja Angel."

Michaela burst out laughing. "Oh my God. Please let that be your secret hobby."

I groaned. "You guys are so dramatic. Seriously, it was nothing."

Please let us change topics. Those words were hitting far too close to home.

He leaned forward, his brow furrowing. "Fine, Converse-girl, what's the deal then? Do you have some wild secret hobby, like, I don't know, competitive knitting or urban beekeeping?"

Michaela giggled, nudging him with her shoulder. "Urban beekeeping? Really?"

"What? It's a thing," he said, throwing his hands up.

I rolled my eyes but couldn't stop the small smile tugging at my lips. "Sorry to disappoint, but no beekeeping here. I guess I just like being outside. Hiking, cycling—stuff like that."

"Hmm, outdoorsy and mysterious," Michaela mused, tapping her chin. "I can work with that."

"Oh, please don't," I said, trying to suppress a laugh.

Interrupting spotlight, Kelsey perked up. "Hey, the rink's open!"

Sure enough, the neon sign on the building's façade flickered to life, the words *Skate-A-Rama* glowing in bold dark neon pink letters. A steady stream of families and teenagers had already begun trickling through the doors.

"Let's go!" Michaela declared, grabbing Jamie's hand and practically dragging him to his feet. "I haven't been skating in forever."

He snorted, brushing off his jeans as he stood. "Forever? Are you kidding me? We're here at least four times a month because someone takes advantage of my part-time job to skate for free."

Michaela shot him a playful glare. "Okay, maybe not forever, but it's been at least two weeks."

"Two weeks," Jamie repeated, shaking his head with mock

exasperation. "You're such a liar."

She turned back to us with an unbothered shrug. "Anyway, I haven't skated in forever," she said again, sticking to her story. "Let's just go."

Kelsey grinned, nudging me as we trailed behind them. "They're like an old married couple," she whispered.

"No kidding," I said, watching as Michaela dramatically gestured for Jamie to hurry up, her every movement exaggerated for effect. He rolled his eyes but followed close behind, clearly not as annoyed as he pretended to be.

The rink was already buzzing with activity by the time we reached the counter. The familiar scent of popcorn and waxed floors mingled with the hum of chatter and the steady beat of 1980s pop music blasting from the speakers.

The older woman behind the counter greeted Jamie with a warm smile. "Hey, kid. Working today?"

"Nope, just skating," he said, leaning casually on the counter. "Hook us up with some rentals?"

"Of course," she said, already pulling skates from the shelves. "Michaela keeping you busy?"

"Always," he said, smiling as he handed her our sizes.

Michaela rolled her eyes but smiled as she leaned on the counter beside him. "He lives for it. Don't let him fool you."

With our skates laced up and lockers secured, Michaela was already halfway onto the rink, her movements smooth and effortless. Her confident strides and graceful twirl in the center commanded attention, celebrating every inch of her broad, curvy frame as she turned to wait for us, a triumphant grin on her face.

"Hurry up, slowpokes!" she called, her voice carrying over the music.

Jamie groaned as he wobbled his way to the rink's edge, gripping the barrier for support. "Some of us don't have the grace of a figure skater, you know." He glanced toward Michaela, his expression softening as she spun effortlessly across the rink. "And don't let anyone tell you that bigger girls are lazy or slow or clumsy, because they are dead wrong. Michaela could skate circles around all of us, and she knows it."

"Good thing you've got charm to make up for it," Michaela teased, blowing him a kiss before skating backward in a wide circle.

Kelsey stepped onto the rink next, her arms stretched out like a tightrope walker. "Why is this harder than it looks?" she muttered, glancing nervously at the flashing lights spinning across the floor.

"You're doing fine," I said, offering a reassuring smile as I followed her onto the smooth surface. Meanwhile, I had to consciously adjust my movements to stay deliberately unremarkable.

Michaela glided past us, her laughter light and carefree. "You guys are too cute. Just relax—skating's supposed to be fun!"

Kelsey grumbled under her breath but managed to keep her balance, skating closer to me for reassurance. "If I fall, promise you'll catch me. You're my guardian angel, remember?"

"I promise," I said, though I wasn't sure she needed the help. Despite her initial hesitation, Kelsey was adapting quickly, her confidence growing with each lap.

Jamie, meanwhile, had finally ventured off the wall, his movements stiff but improving. "I swear, Michaela's only making me do this so she can laugh at me," he muttered as he passed us.

"Obviously," Michaela called back, effortlessly skating circles around him. "But you love me anyway."

Jamie sighed, shaking his head as a grin spread across his face. "Can't argue with that."

Kelsey leaned closer to me, her voice low. "See? Old married couple. I'm telling you."

I giggled softly, focusing on keeping my pace steady and measured. The temptation to pick up speed or try something flashy was constant, but I held back, reminding myself to stay inconspicuous. Be *normal.*

As the music shifted to a faster track, the rink seemed to come alive with energy. A group of kids darted past us, their laughter echoing as they wove through the other skaters. Kelsey wobbled but caught herself, letting out a relieved laugh.

"Okay, I may be getting the hang of not falling on my ass," she said, her enthusiasm growing.

"You've got this," I said, nudging her lightly. "Next thing you know, you'll be showing up Michaela."

Michaela overheard and laughed as she skated up beside us, her hair whipping behind her. "In her dreams! There's only one queen of the rink, and you're looking at her."

Kelsey rolled her eyes but smiled. "I'm not here to dethrone you, don't worry."

The four of us continued skating, falling into an easy rhythm as the afternoon wore on. Michaela kept showing off, Jamie kept grumbling, and Kelsey and I found ourselves laughing more than I'd expected. Laughter, as it turns out, helped alleviate my hunger pangs. For a time.

It almost felt like I belonged here.

Like I could forget about everything else and just enjoy the moment.

Like a normal teenager.

But as I caught a glimpse of my reflection in the rink's mirrored wall, the feeling faltered. The face staring back wasn't just a teenage girl having fun with her friends. It was someone carrying secrets they couldn't see.

By the time we finished skating, the four of us were a sweaty, giggling mess. Michaela declared herself the undisputed queen of the rink—again—while Jamie pretended to bow dramatically at her feet.

"Your Majesty," he said, offering her an imaginary crown.

"Oh, stop," she said, grinning ear to ear. "Actually, don't stop. I like this."

Kelsey and I rolled our eyes in unison as we packed our things. Outside, the air had cooled even more, and the sky glowed in deep shades of orange and purple as the sun dipped below the horizon.

"That was fun," Kelsey said, falling into step beside me as we walked toward the parking lot, where my bike was thankfully still waiting for me. Her energy had mellowed slightly, though her usual enthusiasm still sparkled in her eyes. "I'm glad you came."

"Me too," I admitted, feeling a strange warmth at the thought. For all my hesitations, today had been… *normal.* Good, even.

As we reached the bike rack, Kelsey suddenly stopped and fumbled with her bag, pulling out something wrapped in old newspaper.

"Here," she said, holding it out to me with a shy smile. "I got this for you."

I blinked, caught off guard. "What is it?"

"Open it and find out, silly."

I hesitated but took the bundle, carefully peeling back the crinkled newspaper to reveal a small, fabric-bound journal. The cover was embossed with a crescent moon and stars, the soft texture warm under my fingertips.

"Kelsey…" I stared at it, unsure of how to respond. "You didn't have to—"

"I know," she said quickly, cutting me off. "But I wanted to. You said you didn't have a diary, which, to me, is like a horrendous crime for a teenage girl. Besides, I wanted to say thank you for being my teenage-mutant-ninja angel!"

There was that word again. I didn't know what to say. The truth—that keeping a diary was about as safe as shouting my secrets from the rooftops—stuck in my throat. But so did something else: the realization that Kelsey had been paying attention. She'd noticed something so small, something I hadn't even thought much about, and turned it into this.

She stepped closer, leaning in to give me what could only be called a rib-crushing hug. *Well, rib-crushing for a human, that is.*

"I just knew when you walked into class that we were going to be best friends," she said, her voice muffled against my shoulder. "Something about you makes me feel—I don't know, normal? Safe. Weird, I know. Just go with it, okay?"

I made *her* feel normal? A pang of guilt tickled my throat. Who was I to convince her that being friends with me was anything but safe?

When she pulled back, her eyes were bright, a mix of excitement and nervousness. "So... you like it?"

I clutched the journal a little tighter, nodding. "Yeah. I love it. Thank you, Kelsey."

Her smile widened, and in that moment, I knew I couldn't tell her the truth. I couldn't tell her about the risks or the secrets or the danger. Besides, whiny Elena or brooding Stefan from *The Vampire Diaries* weren't exactly shining examples in my humble opinion of devout journaling habits. Not now. Instead, I tucked the journal into my bag as carefully as if it were made of glass.

"You're full of surprises, you know that?" I said, slinging my backpack over one shoulder.

"Right back at you," she said with a wink. "See you tomorrow?"

"For sure."

As we parted ways, the weight of the journal in my bag felt heavier than it should have—like it carried more than just blank pages.

Kelsey's voice echoed back as she walked off, calling out to Michaela, "Five bucks says Greyson shows up in a toga tomorrow!"

Michaela laughed. "No way, it's going to be Napoleon. Cane, hat, the works!"

I couldn't help but smile at their antics, their laughter trailing behind me like the last notes of a favorite song. It stayed with me as I biked home, settling into the quiet spaces I usually kept guarded. I felt something I hadn't dared to before—the start of some type of comradery maybe.

Chapter 14

The familiar glow of our porch light came into view as I cycled past the driveway, veering toward the side entrance. The cool evening air brushed against my cheeks as I slipped through the gate and into the back garden, heading straight for the shed.

My stomach growled loudly—again. The hunger had been gnawing at me on and off all day, annoying really, despite the frittata snack, protein bars and the burrito I'd devoured hours earlier. Thankfully, the music at the roller rink had masked the noise, but no distraction could silence the ache for long. No matter how much I tried to ignore it, it always returned, stronger and more insistent than before.

Pausing for a moment, I had noticed Mom's SUV parked out front, but the house felt eerily quiet. *Too quiet.* The kind of quiet that prickled at the edges of my thoughts, making me wonder if I'd overlooked something.

"Sady baby."

Speak of the devil. She came bolting out of the back door, and I barely had enough time to lean my bike against the shed wall before I was tangled in her arms.

"Where have you been?"

I checked my watch to make sure I wasn't late: 6:57.

Nope.

"Out with friends," I said, trying to keep my voice light. "Dad didn't tell you?"

At this point, I couldn't shake the growing sense of unease. Mom was always intense after a mission, but this was different. She wasn't just on edge—she was *unsettled*. And where was Dad? He should have been here by now, grounding her with his usual calm, reassuring presence.

Instead, she stood alone, weariness written into every line of her body.

My stomach tightened.

I'd expected bad news. We all had. But the way she carried it—like it was heavier than she'd prepared for, heavier than *we* had prepared for—made my skin prickle.

Something had changed.

And whatever it was, it was worse than we thought.

"Friends? Since when do you have friends?"

Harsh, but fair.

There was something in her tone—a mix of curiosity and something protective. I met her stare head-on, forcing myself to hold steady. "We went thrift shopping, ran into some other kids from class, had lunch, and then roller-skated."

"Friends," she repeated, her words softening slightly as if she were testing the word. "I guess I should've known this day would come."

I furrowed my brow. "What day?"

"The day you'd start getting attached to people," she said, her tone even but weighted. "It's not a bad thing, Sady. But it does make things... harder."

A stubborn, and likely snarky, reply got stuck in my throat, as her words settled over me.

"I know, but you don't have to make it sound like Doomsday."

"Do you?" She stepped closer, her shrewd eyes catching the light from the streetlamp just across from our yard. "The more attached you get, the harder it is to leave. To protect yourself if you have to."

"I know," I repeated, quieter this time, gripping the strap of my backpack tighter and clenching my free hand into a fist. *Deep breaths, Sady.*

"Sera, enough," Dad's voice cut through the night as he joined us outside. His tone was firm but calm, the dish towel slung over his shoulder a clear sign he'd just come from the kitchen. "We talked about this. Be gentle."

"For Tartarus's sake, Sam, she's not that fragile."

"Sera, you promised."

"Fine, but I still need to understand what is happening."

"Guys, I'm standing right here."

"Dinner's on the table. Why don't we take it inside and get all caught up?" Leave it to Dad to inject some normalcy into the situation.

I nodded, relieved to have the conversation steered toward neutral ground. As I moved to follow him, my stomach let out an ungodly growl, loud enough to echo in the stillness of the backyard.

Mom's head snapped around, her instincts taking over before I could blink. Her hand shot to the hilt of the blade strapped beneath her right rib, a move so smooth it seemed like second nature. In one fluid motion, she shoved me to the ground, her voice sharp and commanding. "Get down!" The command cut through the still night air like a whip crack.

Before I could process what was happening, the blade was out, gleaming ominously in the dim light from the porch. Its edge caught the faint glow, reflecting a cold, calculated sharpness.

"Whoa! Mom!" I scrambled to the side, rolling out of her path. My arms instinctively wrapped around my torso, protecting the one spot she'd obviously thought was in danger. "It's just my belly!"

Dad froze mid-step, caught somewhere between concern and amusement. Then, as the absurdity of the situation settled in, his shoulders started shaking with barely contained laughter.

"Sam," Mom warned, the weapon still poised. "What exactly are you laughing at?"

"Nothing," Dad managed, though a deep chuckle escaped him. He wiped a hand over his mouth, failing miserably at hiding his grin. "Just... do you really think someone's sneaking up on us with a tactical plan to impersonate a stomach growl?"

Mom's eyes darted between us, her grip on the blade loosening slightly. "It could've been something else. You can't be too careful."

"Oh, come on, Sera," Dad said, stepping closer and gently plucking the blade from her hand. "It's dinner time, not an ambush."

The culprit growled again, quieter this time but no less insistent. Mom's posture finally relaxed, though her piercing stare didn't soften completely. By this point, I just rolled my eyes and walked past her into the house. *To eat.*

She followed close behind, muttering about vigilance and complacency. It might've been intimidating if I hadn't caught the faintest twitch of a smile at the corner of her mouth. Oh goody, I have a feeling this will be added to her *"how to annoy the hell out of Sady"* repertoire.

Inside, the kitchen was warm and inviting, filled with the scent of roasted vegetables and spices. Dad handed me a plate piled high with lentil loaf and caramelized carrots, while Mom grabbed a glass of water and sat across from me, her perceptive gaze settling like a hawk.

"Eat up," Dad said, settling into his chair with his own plate. "And no growling this time. Your mom might think the lentils are attacking."

Mom shot him a look, but her silence was sharper than any words. Her focus remained on her plate—medium-rare steak, roasted sweet potatoes, and thick slices of portobello mushrooms, the savory aroma mingling in the air.

I dug in, the gnawing hunger in my stomach gradually subsiding with each bite. But even as the food eased the emptiness inside, I couldn't help but feel the lingering sting from the scent of her meal—the rich, smoky scent of meat and earth. I shoved the thought aside, pushing forward with my own meal, trying to ignore how much it made me ache.

Slowly, the tension from earlier unraveled, fading into the background as the quiet comfort of our surroundings settled in. Here, at the table, with the hum of normalcy wrapping around me, it almost felt like nothing was wrong. Almost.

Except the conversation itself was anything but normal.

"So, Sady," Mom began, her fork poised midair. "Has anything else happened? Anything that could explain this... unusual hunger?"

Her tone was measured, but her eyes were focused, watching for any tell. This wasn't casual small talk. This was an interrogation disguised as concern.

"No," I said quickly. *Too* quickly. "I mean, nothing out of the ordinary."

She arched an eyebrow, unconvinced. "Nothing? No strange feelings, no unusual instincts?"

"Nope," I said, shoving another bite into my mouth to avoid saying more. It wasn't a total lie. Sure, there had been moments. Like when

I'd grabbed Kelsey and yanked her out of the path of that speeding car without thinking, or when I caught the compass Greyson had thrown at her way faster than I probably should have.

But those weren't unusual, were they? At least, not if you didn't look too closely. Kelsey hadn't seemed to notice anything unusual about how fast I'd moved—or if she had, she hadn't said a word. That was what mattered, right? Besides, those moments didn't explain the hunger clawing at me like it had its own agenda.

"All I know is that Dad's frittatas are the only thing that seem to keep me satiated for any length of time. I've been snacking on vegan protein bars, eating celery like it's going out of style, and doing my damndest to keep my stomach from growling at people."

"And don't you think we should discuss this as a family?" Mom speared another slab of steak with her fork, her voice deceptively casual.

"Nope. My stomach. My body. End of discussion, Mom."

"Sera, I think it's important that Sady listens to her body on this one. We can't control everything, after all." Leave it to Dad to be the voice of reason.

"Uhm, thanks, Dad." I exhaled, relieved. "Now, can we talk about Mom's trip? I would think that is more important than my digestive system."

Mom set her fork down neatly, her scrutiny sharpening just a fraction. "Fine."

For the next hour, neither Dad nor I spoke a word.

Mom had touched down in the belly of a cargo plane, slipping seamlessly into a meeting with one of her many connections. That woman had a contact in every corner of the world, and slipping past security was just one of her many talents. With little time to spare, they set off, navigating rugged dirt roads in an old military surplus vehicle—its reinforced frame built for handling the unforgiving terrain. They avoided checkpoints, steering clear of any scattered villages along the way, moving with the kind of precision that only came from experience.

Mom's destination had never been in question. It was the kind of place we had long since left behind, one of many we had distanced ourselves from in the name of safety. I hadn't been there since I was eight, but the memories still clung to me—faded snapshots of quiet streets, familiar faces, and a life that felt distant now.

Her voice was steady as she recounted the details, but the gravity behind her words made the room feel smaller.

"I started on the outskirts," she said, the unspoken meaning settling over the table like a shadow.

She had moved methodically, like she always did. The roads leading in were eerily quiet, the usual signs of life long gone. No wandering livestock. No merchants setting up their stalls. Just empty space where a thriving village should have been.

As she made her way deeper, the first signs of destruction appeared. Homes scorched beyond recognition, doorways caved in, personal belongings scattered like ghosts of the lives that had once filled them. The village itself had been reduced to a shell, the air thick with the acrid scent of burned wood and something far worse.

By now, the devastation had been blamed on insurgent rebels or some other faction that was always causing trouble in that part of the world. Most of the bodies had been burned, making it nearly impossible to identify who—or what—had caused the massacre.

But Mom's not the type to stop at the obvious.

She had combed through the ruins, studying every detail the way she always did—looking for the truth hidden in what others had already deemed unsalvageable. She found traces—scattered belongings, marks on walls, disturbed earth. And then, when she got into the trenches, when she really looked, the truth revealed itself.

The bite marks confirmed her suspicions. And when she discovered the black, oily substance hardened under the heat of the fire, she knew.

We all knew. It was *them*, and *they* had committed this massacre.

It wasn't until she reached the remains of our old house that she found the only sign of life.

The walls were scorched, the roof partially collapsed, and what little remained of our belongings had been reduced to ash. And yet—someone had survived.

A girl. No older than twelve, which meant she would've been a toddler when we lived there. Her parents, knowing the danger, had hidden her beneath the steel-plated floorboards before they were killed—a safeguard that shouldn't have existed, but did.

Because my dad had built it.

Not for them, but for *us*, back when this house had been ours.

Whoever had taken over our old home had been trusted enough to know about some of the security measures he'd put in place. Not all of them—Dad had always been careful—but enough. Enough to know that beneath the ordinary wooden floor lay something stronger, something meant to withstand more than just time.

And when the moment came, they had remembered.

They had used what little advantage they had left and made the only choice that mattered—keeping their daughter safe.

She had been alone for two days.

When Mom found her, she was trembling, wide-eyed, her voice hoarse from smoke and grief. Her courage had come from her parents, who had told her that if Mom found her, she should spare no detail.

Between sobs, she described shadowy figures that moved too fast to be human, their eyes faintly glowing in the dark. She spoke of low growls that didn't sound like any animal she had ever heard—and of the screams. Screams that cut off too abruptly.

Her parents had told her to stay hidden, no matter what, but before she had found safety under the steel-floorboards, she had seen enough to haunt her dreams forever.

Mom made sure the girl received the medical attention she needed to heal from the burns. In addition, she ensured her future would be secure—immediate therapy for emotional support and nipping PTSD in the proverbial bud, private education, a safe home, full financial support. It was the least she could do in the wake of such unimaginable loss. But no amount of care could erase the terror in her eyes as she recounted what she had seen that night.

I swallowed hard, gripping the edges of the table as Mom's words settled over me like fog.

"But Mom," I asked slowly, "how did they even find the village? I thought we were careful."

She exhaled, shaking her head. "We obviously missed something." A pause. Then, "Do you remember that small bakery that opened a few months before we left?"

I furrowed my brow, trying to recall. "Vaguely. You mean the one Dad helped build the chimney for?"

"The very one."

"What happened?"

Mom pulled something from her pocket and tossed it onto the table. "This. One stupid, blurry photo."

I stared down at the faded image, my fingers tightening around the edges.

The terracotta and sienna of the dirt around the base of the chimney did nothing to distract from the very tall figure standing at the back. Towering over most of the other people in the photo, even though his back was turned, it was obvious that it was Dad.

White-blond hair, standing out like a beacon among a sea of dark brown afros. The scars across his back visible, thanks to his habit of going shirtless in the heat. Even in the grainy, smudged print, there was no mistaking him.

The photo looked like something straight out of the 1970s, the kind you'd expect to see in a faded print shop on the outskirts of a small town. It must have been printed at the village's tiny shop back then, but somehow, a digital file had made its way through the ether—into the wrong hands.

The physical copy, poor and smudged, had been deliberately nailed to the doorframe of our old house. Waiting for Mom to find it.

"Sam," Mom said, her game face firmly in place. "They left five of their soldiers behind—concealed, well-armed, and ready for an ambush."

Dad inhaled slowly, his fingers curling around the edge of the table. "And?"

"I neutralized the threat."

She meant *she killed them.*

I didn't feel bad about it. Not even a little.

Silence stretched between us, thick and heavy.

The casual way she said it didn't change the fact that she had walked into a death trap, knowing full well what she was up against. *And she still won.*

A chill worked its way down my spine.

I had never doubted Mom's abilities. I had seen her take down people twice her size without batting an eyelash. *Literally*. But this wasn't a bar fight or some roadside skirmish. This was *five* of *them*—hunting us since before I was born.

And she had walked away without a scratch.

Across the table, Dad exhaled slowly, rubbing a hand down his face. "Five of them... Like in New York. Sera, we haven't had to face more than one at a time in nearly two millennia." His voice was steady, but the seriousness of those words pressed into the silence.

Mom didn't flinch.

It was me who was caught up in questions and turmoil, but I knew better than to pipe up. She looked both fierce and fragile, like any word might cause her to fracture. So, I stayed silent.

A few moments passed, and then she reached for the deck of cards in the middle of the table.

"Now," she said, glancing up at us, her expression unreadable—not quite a smile, not quite a challenge, but something colder. Something edged with the weight of everything left unsaid.

"Shall we play Uno?"

The cards snapped as she shuffled, the sound sharp in the silence. A distraction. A moment of normalcy forced into a night that was anything but.

Dad sighed loudly, rubbing his temples as he muttered about '*Only our family could follow up a massacre with a game of Uno*' but reached for his hand of cards anyway.

It wasn't until later, when the game had ended and Dad wandered off to clean up, that Mom and I were left alone at the table.

She was still shuffling the deck, her fingers moving in smooth, practiced motions. Not out of distraction. Not out of boredom. Just...

something to do.

I traced the rim of my water glass, letting the quiet settle between us. The clatter of dishes from the kitchen filled the space Dad had left, but neither of us moved.

The game was over. But the dread wasn't.

That was close.

I didn't realize I'd spoken the words aloud until they hung between us, quiet but solid.

Mom didn't answer right away.

She just exhaled, shifting slightly in her chair, the tense set of her shoulders softening for the first time all night.

She set the deck down, face-up.

"I don't like close," she admitted.

She didn't say *I was scared* or *it was dangerous.* She didn't need to.

It was rare for her to give me anything unpolished, anything raw. Sera Smith was a force, unshaken by storms, untouchable by doubt. But here, in this small, stolen moment, she gave me something real.

I studied her face, searching for the edges of whatever emotion she wasn't saying. But her violet eyes remained focused, steady.

Still, I noticed the small things.

The way she sat back slightly, shifting her weight like some unseen tension had only just started to unravel. The way her fingers—always steady, always sure—hovered over the cards instead of moving through them.

A rare hesitation. The tiniest twitch under her left eye.

A whisper of exhaustion.

I nodded once, accepting the moment for what it was.

Then, I nudged the deck back toward her. "Best two out of three?"

The corner of her mouth lifted slightly, the closest thing to a smile she had given all night.

And just like that, the moment passed.

She picked up the cards and started to shuffle.

I watched her hands move—smooth, precise, like the shuffling was just as much muscle memory as breathing. She wasn't looking at the cards, wasn't even really thinking about them.

She was processing.

Just like I was.

The faint clatter of dishes had stopped in the kitchen. A moment later, Dad reappeared, drying his hands on the dish towel still slung over his shoulder. He hesitated just long enough to scan the room, taking in the subtle disquiet still lingering in the air, before pulling out his chair and dropping back into it with a quiet sigh.

For a while, he just sat there, watching as Mom absentmindedly shuffled the deck. He didn't speak right away, didn't push. But after a beat, he leaned back, exhaling like he was finally letting go of the weight pressing down on his chest.

Then, he smirked. "You know, if you keep shuffling those cards like that, Sera, we're gonna start thinking you're plotting something."

Mom snorted softly, but she didn't stop.

Dad sat for another minute, then finally stood with a stretch, rolling his shoulders before clapping a hand against the back of my chair.

"Call it a night, kiddo," Dad said, nudging my shoulder lightly. "Get some sleep while your mother convinces herself this wasn't a big deal."

The tense edges of our conversation lingered under the surface, disguised beneath a game of Uno and forced casualness.

I wasn't fooled.

I don't think any of us were.

Mom shot him a look but didn't argue.

I took that as my cue.

By the time I made it upstairs, exhaustion didn't hit the way I expected it to. I was tired, but my body didn't feel like shutting down. My muscles ached from skating, my brain from thinking, but instead of feeling heavy, I felt... wound too tight.

I went through my usual nighttime routine—brushed my teeth, changed into pajamas, climbed into bed—but it felt forced, like I was just checking off steps instead of actually preparing to sleep.

Every time I closed my eyes, I saw the grainy photo of Dad, nailed to the ruins of our old home. I saw the scorched earth, the blackened walls. I imagined the girl hiding beneath the floorboards, her hands clasped over her mouth as she tried not to make a sound.

I imagined what would've happened if Mom hadn't been the one to find her.

I flipped onto my other side, yanking the blankets higher, but my mind wouldn't stop.

This wasn't the first time.

It wasn't the first time a place we had lived had been discovered after we left. It had happened only a couple of times over the years. My parents had always followed up—always investigated.

But this?

This was worse.

The last time it had happened, I had been twelve. The village had been ransacked, a few homes burned, but no casualties. It had all been blamed on a gas leak. The investigation had revealed that whatever had come for us had arrived too late—like a hound sniffing at the scent of a long-gone trail. *They* had searched, hunted, but whatever they were looking for had already slipped through their fingers.

All they found were whispers.

Faint traces.

Rumors carried like the wind—always just out of reach. Precisely how my parents always planned.

It was terrifying, sure. But it hadn't been… this.

Not a massacre.

Not five of them.

Not a coordinated attack. With a message posted for Mom to find.

Kicking the blankets off completely, I let out a frustrated sigh. *Why does it feel like something is shifting?*

Frustration curled inside me like a coiled spring. *I should have told them.*

Not about the hunger—that was just some weird body thing, right? Maybe a growth spurt or something else that made my body feel out of sync. That wasn't the issue.

But the other stuff—the moments that seemed small at first, but now felt too big to ignore.

The moment with Kelsey.

The compass in class.

Both times, I had moved too fast. Reacted too fast. It hadn't been noticeable at the time—not to them, not to anyone else—but now, in the dim glow of my bedroom, I wasn't so sure.

Now, I didn't know if these small things even compared to when I thought about everything else. I groaned and rolled onto my belly, pressing my forehead into my pillow. I wasn't ready for another conversation tonight.

I didn't know what scared me more.

The fact that our past had caught up to us again. Or the fact that, deep down, I knew something was off about me too.

It was going to be a long night.

Chapter 15

Monday morning came far too soon, dragging autumn in its wake. The trees had transformed seemingly overnight into a tapestry of fiery orange, golden yellow, deep garnet, and muted purple. A brisk breeze now hung in the air, whispering away the lingering warmth of the sun. Fallen leaves blanketed the ground, muffling the crunch of footsteps as the days of the week seemed to tumble down as quickly as the foliage.

Lunches with Kelsey had settled into a routine—a surprising one, but not unwelcome. We had found a quiet nook at the end of the hallway near the drama room. Today, the smells wafting from the cafeteria gnawed at my self-control, but Kelsey didn't seem to mind the privacy or the hushed space. Michaela and Jamie occasionally joined us—when they weren't making out under the gym bleachers. I couldn't decide if I was happy for them or jealous.

No, scratch that. I didn't envy them exactly. I just wasn't used to this—being part of something, even something small. They weren't quite friends in the way people toss the word around so easily, but they were more than I'd ever had before.

This week, I had resolved to avoid anything that might draw attention, embarrassment, or suspicion. My arsenal included a near-endless supply of snacks to stave off hunger pangs at inconvenient times. Mr. Black—Greyson—remained frustratingly drool-worthy, but I'd convinced myself my infatuation was just a passing phase. Totally manageable. *Probably.*

Mom and I trained every morning, but thankfully, she'd abandoned her attempts to incorporate new techniques into our regimen. I needed stability—a steady rhythm, even if my *normal* wasn't like anyone else's. Dad, meanwhile, was buried under work. I suspected he was digging for answers about *them.*

And then it was Friday.

"Hark, ye wandering souls!" Greyson's voice boomed, adopting an almost theatrical tone, his words dripping with the cadence of old British English. "Prepare thyself to tread the shadowed paths of Paradise, where the lost and the seeking find their tales entwined."

The classroom erupted into chatter, students tossing out guesses about Hawaii, Jamaica, or other tropical destinations. Suspicion tugged at me, especially as he started handing out books. From my vantage point at the back, I squinted to make out the titles on the covers. The words were faint, almost blurred, and for a moment, I questioned if I was imagining them. If I'd had spidey senses, they'd be tingling. Again.

The hardcover book landed on my desk, and Greyson's trademark wink and exaggerated brow wiggle were already seared into my memory. My face betrayed me with an embarrassing blush, and I clenched my hands between my thighs, determined to avoid further humiliation—heaven forbid our hands touch, even accidentally.

The book itself seemed innocuous enough, its midnight-blue cover unassuming but for the elegant gold foil lettering:

Paradise Lost by John Milton.

This was history class, not English lit. My eyes darted around the room, searching for anyone else who found this odd. No one seemed fazed. Sure, the book had historical merit—first published in 1667—but its themes leaned heavily into theology and allegory, not history.

As if that wasn't enough to make me question the logic, this book also happened to be one of the few written works published in history that contained some very peculiar insights about my parents' origins. And ironically, it's got some dirt on Mom's ex. I'd read it at least twenty times since I was five.

Mom had sought out Milton about a decade after it was published but was too late. He had already passed away. She did, however, find his daughter, Deborah, who served as one of his amanuensis, along with her sister, a scribe who helped write the book. His interpretation of the Bible's version of the rebellion in heaven and the fall of man had too many grains of truth for our family to ignore. Mom was pretty sure that someone gave Milton, or maybe even his daughter, the inside scoop. There was just no other way for those details to have made their way onto the pages. They never found out who though. Thankfully, there was still enough hidden or perhaps deliberately distorted to keep the full truth a secret.

Caught up in my thoughts, it wasn't until too late that I realized I'd completely tuned out Greyson's instructions. Blinking, I tried to piece together what little I had caught, but the words slipped through my mind like smoke, elusive and impossible to hold onto.

"Students, please be prepared to bring your proposed exploration for Monday's class so that I can approve it." His voice cut through my haze, and I froze, scrambling to pretend I'd been paying attention. He scanned the room, his gaze lingering just long enough on each student to ensure they were listening—or at least pretending to.

And then his stare landed on me. His mouth twisted slightly, as though trying to suppress a smile. "—before you move on to the next part of the assignment."

Neither of us blinked. My lungs forgot how to function. The bell broke the moment, shattering the tension.

I hurriedly gathered my things, stuffing Paradise Lost into my bag as quickly as I could. Kelsey was already slinging her backpack over her shoulder, her movements casual and unhurried.

"Kelsey," I hissed, leaning closer as I shoved my notebook into my bag. "What's the assignment? I... totally zoned out and missed it."

She raised an eyebrow, her lips curling into an amused smirk. "Zoned? You mean while you were busy having a staring contest with Mr. Black?"

I flushed, glaring at her. "Please, just tell me."

She exhaled softly, patience shining through yet again as she zipped up her bag. "We're supposed to write a thesis on how Paradise Lost either reflects the time it was written in or if it has modern merit."

"Modern merit?" I echoed, frowning. "What's that supposed to mean?"

"You know, how it might still be relevant today. Like, does it say anything about society now, or does it just belong in history books?" She shrugged, slinging her bag over her shoulder. "I guess it's one of those 'make-you-think' assignments. Honestly, I'm just gonna google it later."

I nodded, her explanation jogging just enough of my memory to reassure me. "Thanks."

"No problem," she said, grinning. "Just try not to let Greyson fry your brain next time, okay?"

"Noted," I muttered, ducking my head as we headed out of the classroom.

Outside, the crisp autumn air had turned downright chilly, and I silently congratulated myself for leaving my bike at home that morning. The thought of pedaling against the wind, my fingers stiff with cold, had been enough to make me opt for the bus instead.

As I pulled my jacket tighter around me, I spotted Kelsey, Michaela, and Jamie standing near the bus stop. Jamie was animated, his hands gesturing wildly as he talked.

"Paradise Lost, huh?" Jamie said, his voice carrying above the din of passing students. "It's actually kind of cool. A war in heaven? Angels versus demons? That's some epic superhero stuff right there."

Michaela rolled her eyes but smiled. "You would find a way to make Milton a Marvel spin-off."

"Why not?" Jamie grinned, undeterred. "It's practically built for it. Think about it: Lucifer as the anti-hero, the ultimate rebellion story. And the stakes? Heaven and hell. It's perfect."

"Whatever you say, Stan Lee," Michaela teased, adjusting the strap of her bag. She turned to me, softening. "What about you, Sady? Any grand thesis ideas yet?"

"Not yet," I admitted, tucking my hands deeper into my jacket pockets. The motion brought a faint, awkward prickle of unease—probably because my mind was still tangled in things I didn't want to dwell on. Things about my family that didn't belong in casual conversation. "I'm still trying to figure out how Milton connects to modern merit, or whatever Greyson was talking about."

"Jamie's got the modern merit down," Kelsey quipped, grinning. "Superheroes are so twenty-first century."

We laughed, our breath curling in the early fall air as the buses began pulling up to the curb. Kelsey's bus came first, a short route heading in the opposite direction of mine. She gave a quick wave, her bright smile lingering as she disappeared up the steps.

Michaela and Jamie walked with me to the next stop, their route home passing through the nearby neighborhood. "We figured we'd keep you company for the walk," Michaela said, shrugging off her bag as Jamie kept pace beside her. "You know, for morale or whatever."

"Sure," I said, grateful for the gesture, even if I didn't know how to say it. We reached the stop just as my bus rolled in, its brakes hissing against the cold air.

"Well, good luck with Milton," Jamie said, giving me a thumbs-up as Michaela rolled her eyes and tugged him along. "And don't overthink it! Epic battles—that's the way to go!"

I climbed the steps to the bus, smiling faintly at their banter. As I took my seat, I realized I hadn't taken this route before. My bike was my usual escape—a faster, quieter ride that let me clear my head. But today, the cold had won, and now I was stuck with the noise and chaos of public transit.

Settling into a seat near the back, I let my head fall against the window, the vibrations of the engine thrumming through me. My breath fogged up the glass as I stared out at the blur of red and gold leaves whipping past. The bus ride should've felt mundane, ordinary, but a restless energy hummed beneath my skin, refusing to let me relax.

The bus groaned to a halt at my stop, and I stepped off into the sharp autumn breeze. My fingers tightened around the strap of my bag as I turned onto my street, willing the day's disquiet to stay behind me. The streets were quiet, save for the occasional rustle of leaves skittering across the pavement. As I walked the last few blocks to the house, my mind churned with the day's events.

Greyson's assignment still nagged at me. *Paradise Lost.* Milton's words weren't just literature in our house; they were practically a mirror to my parents' past, a whispered warning that echoed through generations.

What did he know? Or worse, what was he trying to figure out?

I should've told Mom and Dad about all the odd history assignments by now. Normally, I didn't hesitate to share details about school—especially when an assignment danced too close to the family's hidden history. But this wasn't just one assignment. It was a pattern, and all of it tied back to Greyson.

And that was the problem.

All week, I'd been dodging any mention of my crush, and ergo all things history teacher, in conversations with my parents. When Mom casually asked how history class was going, I'd mumbled something vague—*"It's fine, same as always"*—before quickly steering the topic elsewhere. When Dad, always more observant than I gave him credit for, had nudged me for details about my teachers, I'd managed to deflect with a laugh and a noncommittal shrug.

Careful. I'd been so careful. Deflecting had become second nature, and so far, they hadn't pushed. Not even about the crush I'd been awkwardly wrestling with. They'd noticed—of course they had—but to their credit, they'd given me space and privacy instead of prying. For that, I was grateful. I wasn't ready for questions I wasn't sure I could answer. Not yet.

But now, with this assignment hanging over me, I wasn't sure how much longer I could keep up the act. If I so much as mentioned Paradise Lost, Mom would zero in on the connection in an instant. She'd start asking questions—pointed ones I couldn't answer without admitting that Greyson wasn't just another teacher to me.

I wasn't ready for that conversation. Not when I didn't even understand what his deal was, let alone my own tangled feelings about him.

All I knew was that the last thing I wanted was Mom analyzing every word he said or dissecting every glance I imagined in class. Given her over-protective nature, I would be lucky not to end up in the Arctic living in an igloo as far and remote as humanly possible.

So, for now, I kept it to myself. It wasn't a lie, exactly. Just... a delay.

I kicked a stray rock down the street, watching it bounce away into the shadows. The wind tugged at my hair, and I shivered, though I wasn't sure if it was from the cold or the unease crawling under my skin.

Greyson's assignments had been nagging at the edges of my mind for a while now. At first, they had seemed quirky, sure—maybe even a little unconventional—but I'd dismissed them as the eccentricities of a passionate teacher.

However, the pattern emerging now was too glaring to ignore, especially with this latest project in the mix.

It started innocently enough with the first assignment about cultural belief systems—exploring how ancient civilizations worshiped deities or, as some theories suggested, beings they mistook for gods. We were tasked with analyzing myths of powerful entities appearing in geographically disconnected societies, cross-referencing legends of divine messengers that bore striking similarities. The overlaps were uncanny. *Too* uncanny.

Greyson had us dig into figures like Hatshepsut, the pharaoh who claimed divine descent from Amun, and study stories like those of the Queen of the Amazons—a warrior and ruler many believed to be pure myth. And yet both connected to Mom. *I made a mental note to ask Jamie, Michaela and Linda about theirs another time.*

Back then, I'd chalked it up to coincidence. After all, Greyson wasn't shy about embracing unusual angles.

But now? Now, I wasn't so sure.

The next assignment had taken an apocalyptic turn. Greyson had us dissect the history of doomsday prophecies, pulling threads from myths of serpents devouring the world, fire raining from the skies, and eternal darkness. I'd been assigned the Mayan prediction of December 2012—the same year I turned eighteen. This year to be precise. The parallels between the assignment and the stories Mom or Dad sometimes let slip about our family had set my nerves on edge.

Coincidence? It didn't feel like one, especially only being two weeks into the school semester?

There was the compass toss. The class had laughed, chalking it up to another one of his quirks. But Greyson? He hadn't laughed. Not surprised but expecting. Like he had known exactly what I would do.

Then came the Vitruvian Man. Staring at the very detailed, very nude depiction of my father in front of my entire class? *Yeah*. New trauma unlocked. And through my spiraling horror, Greyson's gaze had lingered.

And then there was yesterday. The strangest lesson yet. Greyson had us rearrange our desks into a circle—a "roundtable discussion," he'd called it, the phrase itself evoking the camaraderie and spirit of King Arthur's knights. Except instead of nobility and honor, we were tasked with dissecting civilizations whose belief in deities had fueled violence. From ancient crusades to sacrifices offered in the name of divine favor, the discussion spiraled into what Greyson described as the eternal war of good versus evil.

At first, it felt like the usual philosophical exercise he favored. But then, his tone shifted, and he hit us with the kind of questions that linger long after the bell rings.

"Who decides?" he had asked, his scrutiny sweeping over the room. "Who is god and who is good?"

The questions hung in the air, resonant and unanswerable, as if the circle itself demanded truth. The rest of the class stumbled through vague attempts to sound profound—murmurs of justice, morality, and the power of belief—but I kept my mouth shut.

What was I supposed to say?

In my world, the line between *god* and *good* was a blurred, shifting thing. And it wasn't a line I wanted to cross in front of anyone.

Now, with Paradise Lost added to the pile, the pattern was impossible to ignore. This wasn't any ordinary history class or history teacher. This was something else entirely—something deliberate.

Greyson wasn't just teaching us; he was searching for something. Or maybe *someone*.

By the time I reached the house, the sky had deepened to slate gray, the last streaks of sunlight hiding behind clouds. The porch light flickered faintly, a warm beacon against the gathering dusk. The sight of home should've been grounding—predictable, safe—but as I climbed the front steps, the familiar quiet felt different.

Not just the usual stillness of late afternoon. Too quiet.

The air felt heavy, like the house itself was holding its breath.

I set my bag down carefully by the door, every sound amplified in the stillness.

"Hello?" I called, my voice hesitant.

Silence.

The kitchen was empty, and the rest of the house was just as still. That could only mean one thing: Dad was in his workshop.

He normally asked me to stay away, insisting it wasn't a place for me. *Too much classified work.* But tonight, something felt... different. Something felt *wrong*.

I grabbed an apple from the counter as I passed through the kitchen, its cool weight steady in my hand. I took a slow breath, trying to steady the uneasy tension creeping through me. No need to startle the old man.

DAD?

I called out telepathically, the familiar connection between us fluttering to life like a faint echo.

Not even five steps into the backyard, and I could sense him moving.

His protective shield—normally steady and impenetrable, like a fortress—was flickering weakly, as if cracks had begun to form in its foundation.

Dad was never not calm.

It would take a cataclysm to rattle him. His control over his presence was nearly absolute, his stealth almost eerie for a man of his size.

But not today.

Today, something had slipped past that ironclad composure.

A quiet hum rippled against my instincts. It wasn't loud or obvious, but it didn't have to be. The tiniest break in his control was enough to set me on edge. Something *was* wrong.

He stepped out of the workshop, his shoulders tensed, his head tilting upward to scan the sky. The look on his face stopped me cold.

Dad was always looking up—toward the sky, the stars, the past. His expression was usually wistful, like he was chasing fragments of some private memory he never shared.

But not today.

Today, he was fixed on the present, on something much heavier. His green eyes were clouded, weighed down by grief, worry, confusion—all tangled together in a way that made him look worn in a way I wasn't used to seeing. Like he was searching for answers he wasn't sure he wanted to find.

There was no longing in his eyes today.

Only something raw. Something unspoken. *Something was very wrong.*

I held my breath, my own shield instinctively tightening around me. Years of training with Mom and Dad had ingrained the importance of keeping it flawless. The telepathic shield wasn't just personal—it was a safeguard for everyone. It cloaked our powers, shielding us from others like us, and protecting humans from any accidental energy leaks.

Without it, stray thoughts or emotions might spill out, triggering unintended consequences—or worse, exposing us.

Maintaining the shield was delicate work. It wasn't just about locking away my thoughts—it was about controlling the ebb and flow of my energy, keeping it invisible and contained. With enough focus, it could even ripple outward, influencing those nearby. A subtle nudge here, a calming presence there.

But it took precision. Constant vigilance.

When we slept, the shield didn't vanish—it became passive, a quiet hum beneath our awareness, still protective but not as strong as when we were conscious. And right now, Dad's shield—normally seamless and unshakable—was faltering.

What the hell could have caused that?

"Dad?" I voiced softly, taking another step forward. The ground beneath my feet felt colder than it should, the air too still.

He didn't turn right away, his eyes still fixed on something I couldn't see. When he finally looked at me, his expression shifted just enough to let a flicker of his usual calm through.

But the edges of his shield were still trembling.

"Sady doll, what time is it?" he asked, his voice quieter now, like he was holding something back—subduing an edge of worry or something darker. His eyes locked onto mine, and for a moment, that fierce fatherly love was there, shining through the worry, and it hit me like it always did—right in the *feels*.

He and Mom had tried for so long to have a child, and I think he'd given up at some point, though he kept going to humor her. And then I happened. I don't think he's ever recovered from the shock, as pleasant as it was. He doesn't talk about it much, but the way he looks at me—like I'm some impossible miracle—says everything.

Right now, though, that fierce love was tangled with something heavier. His shoulders were rigid, his fists clenched—held tight like he was bracing for impact. But it was his eyes that struck me most. Glassier than usual. Too full.

I knew these signs immediately. *Grief. Worry.* The weight of something unspoken.

I was observant like that. Afterall, I was my father's daughter.

After eons of being still, his body rarely showed anything but calm, and not much fazed him—except Mom's temper.

So when I saw him like this—fists tight, posture coiled—I knew it was big.

And probably bad.

Chapter 16

"It's just a bit past four o'clock?" I said, stepping closer. His shield fluttered again, sending faint ripples against my own, but I pushed the unease aside and walked straight into his arms.

He stiffened for a second, caught off guard, before his arm wrapped around me, pulling me close. The next thing I knew, I was at serious risk of having a rib—or maybe two—cracked. He was hugging me back that hard.

"Ah, Dad?" I mumbled into his chest, tapping his shoulder.

When he finally let me go, his eyes met mine—softened yet distant, as though his mind was still somewhere else entirely.

"Sady..." he began, but stopped, his gaze darting briefly back toward the workshop. The tautness in his shoulders hadn't eased, and something unreadable flickered across his face.

"You're scaring me," I said quietly, trying to catch his eye. "What's going on?"

He hesitated, his hand falling from my shoulder as he shifted his weight, clearly wrestling with whatever had happened before I arrived. For a moment, I thought he might deflect, the way he and Mom always did when things got too close to dangerous. But then he sighed, the sound dulled and full of unspoken weight.

"Well..." he said finally, his jaw tightening, "you know my work doesn't usually hit this close to home. But what I just saw—"

He didn't finish. His knees buckled, and he crumpled right in front of me.

"Uh-oh," I muttered, my heart rate spiking. "How bad is it?"

The words had barely left my mouth when he pulled me back into his arms, holding me so tight his head pressed against my chest. His breathing was unsteady, and the tension radiated off him in waves. He only did this when it involved *them.* Whatever had him shaken was bigger than I'd imagined. *How could it be worse than what Mom had found on her trip?*

His workshop door was wide open. That alone was enough to send a ripple of discomfort through me. Dad never left his workstation accessible—not to me, not to anyone. Whatever he worked on back there, it was locked away for a reason. But now the door was ajar, and I could see the monitor inside, its screen glowing faintly as it replayed a video on a loop.

He finally let go of me, standing up shakily. His voice wavered as he spoke. "A new client hired me to investigate a security video that was found in New York."

"New York?" I echoed, confused. "Why are you—"

"Sady doll," he interrupted, his tone low but insistent. "You need to see this."

Not *important*. Not *urgent*.

Just need—like this was something fundamental. Something that would change things.

I didn't get the chance to argue. His hand closed firmly around mine, his touch steady, guiding, but not forceful. Before I even registered the shift in his stance, I was already at his workstation.

The grainy footage on the monitor looped endlessly, its flickering light casting shadows across the room. Dad nudged me closer to the screen, his hands settling on my shoulders. His grip was gentle, yet it grounded me, as though trying to keep me tethered in the midst of everything that was unraveling. A soft, trembling sigh escaped him, filling the small space between us.

A screen could be dismissed. It was just pixels, something I could disconnect from if it got too heavy.

But his hands on my shoulders said something different—something I couldn't shake. They weren't holding me back; they were holding me together, anchoring me to this moment. His breath, unsteady and thick, curled around the edges of my thoughts, leaving a knot in my stomach that I couldn't untangle.

Whatever I was about to see wasn't just violence.

It was something more.

The video showed a tall man, at least six foot seven—huge even by Dad's standards. I calculated his height quickly when he stood next to a signpost in what looked like an abandoned subway station. Don't ask why I know the height of subway signposts. Mom says I'm an encyclopedia of useless knowledge. *Thanks, Mom.*

The station looked straight out of New York's early subway days—pre-1920s, maybe—with ornate columns and remnants of gas lighting, the kind of underground design that screamed turn-of-the-century grandeur. The footage was grainy, but I could still make out the man's broad frame and steady stance. For lack of anything better, I mentally dubbed him *The Sentinel.*

He wore a long sable trench coat—leather or suede, maybe—and matching biker boots. His black trousers looked worn, almost threadbare along the hems near the ankles. Like he walked barefoot in nature, a lot.

For a few seconds, The Sentinel just stood there, shifting his weight from foot to foot, like he was waiting for someone who was already late. Then he started to pace—back and forth, his movements deliberate but taut, like a spring wound just a little too far. Every now and then, his attention flicked toward the clock on the wall, the faint crease in his brow deepening.

When he passed directly under the light, I finally got a clear look at him. He had short, dark hair, and a scar that ran from the corner of his left eye, cutting across his temple and vanishing into his hairline. The wound was old, a thin line that somehow added to his rugged charm rather than detracting from it. Even through the grainy video, his healthy, sun-warmed glow was obvious—like someone who spent just as much time outdoors as he did looking camera-ready. The Sentinel was Hollywood-star handsome. *Familiar, too, though I couldn't pin down why.*

Suddenly, he froze mid-step.

Something startled him—maybe a sound, though the video had no audio. The lights flickered, and the screen went dark for two seconds—I counted. When the picture returned, he wasn't alone.

Five men surrounded him now. Compared to The Sentinel, they were unremarkable in size, but their presence sent a chill racing down my spine. They were dressed identically—steel-toed black boots, faded denim, leather jackets of varying styles, and Aviator sunglasses, despite the clock on the wall showing it was nine in the evening. They looked like a cheesy boy band... if a boy band could make your stomach drop with dread.

Compared to The Sentinel, these guys were ghosts—pale, washed-out, almost unreal. Their very presence in the grainy footage made my skin crawl.

"It's *them,*" I whispered, my voice barely audible.

"It's *them,*" Dad confirmed, his voice as unsteady as his shield.

The Sentinel studied the newcomers, his eyes darting between the men as they fanned out, encircling him with deliberate precision. My stomach sank when I noticed the pattern beneath his feet—a pentagram.

He adjusted his stance slightly, lowering into a Krav Maga position—defensive but balanced, steady and confident. Even as the ghostly men grinned those sharp, predatory smiles, he didn't flinch. Their dominant canines gleamed, and that was all I needed to see.

"Vampires," I whispered, the word curling off my tongue like a curse.

Not the sparkly kind. Not the mysterious, seductive, or even tortured soul kind you might find in a teen novel or TV show. These vampires didn't radiate charm or allure. They looked like predators, pure and simple, and their presence made the grainy footage feel even darker.

I snuck a glance back up at Dad. Even though this wasn't the first time he'd watched the video, it was still making him shudder. His hands on my shoulders tightened slightly, the emotions rippling through him like a warning.

Turning back to the screen, I watched as the Sentinel flinched ever so slightly. Despite that, his stance remained self-assured, his movements controlled. Confident. Until the moment the ghostly men reached under their jackets and pulled out narrow, sharp-looking daggers.

The blades caught the dim light of the subway, their surfaces gleaming unnaturally. I estimated them to be around nine inches long—slender but lethal. *Inherited Dad's observation skills,* I thought wryly. *Sometimes it's a pain in the butt, but not today.*

These daggers weren't anything you could pick up on eBay or Amazon. They were unique, almost ceremonial in appearance, their black obsidian surfaces streaked with swirling, oxblood-red patterns. A shiver traced its way up my spine as realization hit. I'd only ever seen one other blade like that—because, of course, someone in my family would casually own a murder weapon that looks straight out of a vampire's starter pack.

The Sentinel tried to smile, but even through the grainy footage, I could see the unease shadowing his face. His posture shifted slightly, and then his lips moved. I leaned closer, focusing on the shape of each word—clear, deliberate. *Did I mention I know how to read lips?*

I don't know where she is, and even if I did, I'd die before I told you.

Everything around me faded, leaving only those words echoing in my mind, if only but for a moment.

What happened next was so fast it might as well have been a blur. That's where Dad's handiwork came in—he'd built a special program to slow down footage like this, letting us see every detail that would otherwise be impossible to catch. As the slowed footage began to play, the scene unfolded with an almost surreal clarity, like something straight out of a Marvel or DC movie.

When the Sentinel shrugged off his trench coat, I blinked, questioning what I was seeing. Beneath the worn leather, his bare chest was tanned and powerfully built, broad shoulders tapering into solid lines of muscle. A leather harness crisscrossed his torso, its clean, geometric design drawing even more attention to his imposing frame.

But what really caught my eye was his left wrist.

Encased in a bronze-hued metal cuff, streaked with veins of shimmering gold, it extended nearly to his elbow. At first, it looked like a piece of ornate armor, something decorative—but then he moved. The cuff shifted with him, the metal catching the dim light, revealing its true nature.

It wasn't just for show.

It was a shield—compact, functional, and anything but ordinary.

In his other hand, he held a blade forged from the same rich, earthen metal, its surface streaked with those same luminous gold veins. The patterns swirled as if alive, twisting beneath the metal like something waiting, breathing, watching.

My jaw dropped.

I'd only ever seen one other blade like that.

And I knew exactly what it meant.

Dad's.

"Oh, hell," I muttered, my breath hitching. The man's brash grin, faintly visible in the slowed footage, revealed deep dimples in his cheeks. Dimples that looked far too familiar. Despite his darker coloring, the resemblance was undeniable.

"Dad," I whispered, my voice shaking. "He's—"

As if seeing vampires caught on candid camera wasn't surreal enough, I watched in stunned amazement as the footage revealed a lengthening shadow behind him that reached past his fingertips. At first, I thought it was a trick of the flickering subway lights, but that idea was quickly discarded as the shadow continued to grow, unfurling behind him. My jaw dropped as I realized what I was seeing.

Wings.

Rich, velvety bronze-touched wings, each spanning at least two or three meters, unfurled from the man's back like something out of a dream—impossible and yet right there. Even with the grainy video, I could see a faint glow along their edges, like they were lit from within.

Not blinding, but just enough to give them this eerie, halo-like vibe. It was subtle, almost like the wings were alive with their own energy, and it made the whole thing feel bigger—heavier—than it should've been. Their sheer presence swallowed the dim subway platform whole, commanding every inch of space.

"Holy hell, Dad, is that—?" The words tumbled out before I could stop them, but this time, Dad didn't even flinch. Normally, the use of *hell* would earn me a stern look or a quick reprimand. Now? Nothing. His silence said everything.

I glanced at him, but his eyes were glued to the screen, his jaw tight, the tension radiating off him in waves. My heart pounded in my chest as I turned back to the footage. This wasn't just some stranger caught on security cameras.

This was family.

"Shhh, pay attention kiddo," Dad murmured, his voice thick with something I couldn't place—grief, maybe, or dread.

This was the first time I saw what my parents once were. They had long ago lost their wings. But that is a story for another time.

Back to the scene that was unfolding, one of the vampires—Nephilim, as the Bible calls them—sneered through gritted teeth, his expression twisted with fury and shock. They looked as stunned as I felt, seeing an angel who still had his wings.

The next five minutes were a blur of movement but I knew it had to be longer than that. Much longer.

Dad's program had slowed the footage down, stretching out the details, giving me time to see what most human eyes never could. What played out in front of me, clear and precise, had likely unfolded in real time with blinding speed.

The vampires attacked him with a ferocity that was terrifying to witness. Each of them moved like a flash, striking with a coordinated, predatory determination. The angel held his ground, using his left wrist cuff to block their attacks. But for every strike he managed to deflect, two more broke through his defenses.

Seconds on the screen—minutes in reality.

And he was running out of both.

His wings moved with lethal grace, acting as both shield and weapon. They slammed into the vampires like battering rams, sending bodies careening into the subway station columns, or swept through the air like giant fly swatters, knocking attackers off balance.

One of the vampires got in close, and the angel's wings folded around him, trapping him. In one swift motion, the angel drove his blade into the vampire's torso. The vampire staggered and crumpled to the ground, his body convulsing as it began to disintegrate.

The sight was horrifying. His flesh shriveled, peeling away in layers, revealing dried muscles and brittle bones that turned to dust. It was like watching a mummy being slowly unwrapped—grotesque, deliberate, agonizing. I'd always known that vampire anatomy differed from humans, but knowing was different from witnessing. My stomach twisted into knots, a sickening pressure building as nausea clawed at the back of my throat.

That move cost the angel precious time. The remaining four vampires swarmed him, their coordinated attacks overwhelming. They kicked his legs out from under him, bringing him to his knees. Each one grabbed hold of an arm or a wing, immobilizing him.

Then they struck.

The angel's scream, even muted by the video's lack of sound, was excruciating. The vampires drove their daggers into the bases of his wings, blood sprayed from the jagged wounds as they worked, severing his wings from his body. My breath hitched, terror washing over me in waves, freezing the blood in my veins.

Would they kill him?

Even maimed and bleeding, the angel kept fighting. He struggled against them, dragging one of the vampires down with him and preparing to drive his blade into the creature's chest. But another vampire advanced from behind, his movements swift and calculated. He smashed the handle of his dagger against the angel's skull with a sickening *whomp*.

The angel collapsed, his body hitting the concrete hard. Unconscious.

Two of the vampires were barely standing, their injuries severe enough that they might need help from their comrades. The others divided the weight of the unconscious angel between them, their movements cold and efficient. Without hesitation, they stuffed the severed wings into a massive black burlap sack. Then, one by one, they jumped off the platform and disappeared into the shadows of the subway tunnels.

The video fizzled and cut out.

The silence in the workshop was deafening. I couldn't speak. I couldn't think. My mind reeled as I tried to process what I'd just seen.

Dad was heartbroken. Shattered. His shield, so steady even in moments of danger, crumbled completely. He dropped to his knees, again, his entire body shaking, the sobs wracking through him like aftershocks of an earthquake.

"The angel said 'she,'" I whispered, the realization hitting me like a freight train. "They were looking for me. And they found him instead."

"Sady doll," Dad choked out, his voice breaking. "That

is—was—Cassiel."

The name landed in the air, brimming with pain and memories I couldn't fully understand.

"I haven't seen any of my brothers in over a millennium," he continued, his sobs unrelenting. "I thought they were all gone."

His hands gripped the edge of the workbench, his knuckles white, his breath coming in shallow gasps. "I don't even know if Father sent him. Why didn't he try to contact me first?"

With his massive frame trembling, as though the burden of everything he had seen had finally proven too much, I stepped closer. At once, unsure of how to comfort him, unsure of how to process my own emotions, but seeing my father like this—broken, raw—was almost as jarring as the video itself.

In that moment, I truly understood just how much we had lost. And just how much we still stood to lose.

To hell with it. This called for desperate measures.

MOM?! DAD NEEDS YOU NOW!

Her reply came immediately, calm but pointed.

HOLD ON, I'M ON MY WAY HOME ALREADY. TEN MINUTES OUT.

I shot back, the urgency thick in my tone.

MAKE IT TWO!

I turned back to Dad, who was still trembling, his head in his hands. "Dad, I'm here." My voice softened, and I knelt beside him. It's not often a daughter has to comfort her parent. "Mom will be here in two minutes. Take a deep breath. Please."

His response was a faint nod, but his breathing was shallow, uneven. I wasn't sure what else to say or do—my thoughts were reeling, so I just closed in and hugged him. *Surprise, even supernatural beings can have panic attacks.*

First, *they* were close. Physically that is.

But New York had been a couple of years before Pemba, which likely meant *they* were not on our trail.

Second, that meant they had been on his trail, and they had fought other angels. How many, and had any of them survived?

Third, *they* were moving in packs now. Mom had faced five in Pemba, and now these five?

Five, I thought, stunned. *How the hell had Mom neutralized five of them without wings?*

And finally, they hadn't killed the angel—Cassiel. They took him. And his wings. Somewhere, they had taken him.

But why?

The questions kept looping in my mind, colliding with one another. How old was the footage? Who had sent it? I felt like I was running out of time before I even knew what to do.

I didn't have to look up to know Mom was close. The air shifted, her presence pressing against my senses. Dad was too upset to notice, even though her shielding was haphazard, the edges frayed. She swept in behind him, wrapping her arms gently around his hunched form and kissing each shoulder blade—where his wings used to be.

My parents' scars always struck me in moments like this. Dad's were deep slash marks, gaping and raw-looking, while Mom's were puckered burns, uneven and jagged. They were the only marks on their otherwise flawless bodies. Despite hundreds—possibly thousands—of battles, no weapon had ever left a scar except for the loss of their wings.

"Shamsiel, my love, my heart, what happened?" Mom's voice was soft, steady, yet edged with a quiet protectiveness that gathered the air around her. She held his gaze as he turned, searching his face for answers, for something unspoken. Concern flickered beneath her calm exterior, a steady force as he slowly rose to his feet.

The raw anguish in Dad's expression made her flinch. She hadn't flinched in Mozambique. Trust me, my mom doesn't scare easily, but this? This terrified her.

"It was Cassiel," Dad said, his voice breaking. "Alive. *They* found him."

He leaned forward, and she rose onto her toes, their foreheads meeting in a gentle, desperate touch. It only took seconds for Dad to share what he had seen and felt, the memories flooding into her mind as their connection flared to life.

Mom's reaction was immediate and primal. A low growl started deep in her throat, growing into a full-throated snarl that vibrated through the air, dangerous and raw. She wanted to fight. She wanted to kill. But more than anything, she wanted to inflict the kind of pain they write about in the darkest pits of hell.

All because the love of her life—Dad—was hurting.

Dad's hand came up to her cheek, his touch steady despite the turmoil in his own body. It took him a few moments, but he soothed her rage, pulling her back from the brink before she could take off and rain hell down on New York herself. Slowly, her breathing steadied, though her hands were still clenched into fists at her sides.

Then, as if moving with the same unspoken command, they both reached for me, pulling me into their arms. Mom's grip was iron-tight, her body trembling with barely restrained fury, like a storm ready to break. Dad's arms were steady but heavy, his grief palpable, sinking into me like a weight I wasn't sure I could carry.

And me? I stood frozen between them, my mind a tangled mess of confusion and dread.

The silence around us wasn't empty; it roared with everything unsaid—pain, rage, and questions I didn't even know how to ask.

Mom was the first to recover, as always. She stepped back, her expression fierce and determined. "Sady baby, put your big girl panties on because you are going hunting," she barked, her tone firm and commanding.

"Hunting?" I repeated, my heart racing.

Chapter 17

"Time to use that new feather technique we talked about," Mom continued, her voice leaving no room for argument. "Go as far as your reach will allow. Make sure you do not linger or touch any of them, no matter what."

Normally, I would have rebelled at being bossed around like that. And frankly, any reference by a parent to their teenager's underwear should be outlawed.

I swallowed hard, her order crystal clear and sinking in. *Hunting*. I knew exactly what she was asking me to do—something she and Dad couldn't. Despite our size difference, I was stronger than they were, at least in this particular way. So, I stopped, dropped, and sat.

Settling into a lotus pose, palms pressing into the cool grass, the connection to the earth felt grounding. The closer to the ground, the better—less distance to fall if fainting happened. Slowing my breath, I focused on the rhythm until it evened out, steadying both mind and body.

This was critical. I'd never done this before—not like this. Like one of my favourite movie characters, Flynn from Tron Legacy, I had 'knocked on the sky, and listened to the sound'.

Never deliberately sought them.

If *they* were in New York, that was only a twelve-hour car ride away—less for one of us. Closing my eyes, I inhaled deeply and let my senses reach outward. It felt a bit like I imagined Professor X using Cerebro, only without the dorky helmet.

I began.

Auras.

Most humans were muted, their colors washed out like sun-bleached sand—warm pastel shades, their presence barely more than a faint hum on my radar. Their auras flickered softly, a low heat, gentle and fuzzy around the edges, like the warmth of a fading sunset.

Vampires, though, were different. Their aura hit like a blast of arctic air, sharp and merciless. It wasn't just cold—it was below freezing, the kind of chill that crept into your bones and made you feel brittle. Their colors burned violently against the darkness: a deep crimson, raw and unrelenting, threaded through with tendrils of smoky gray that pulsed like poison.

New York. That's where I needed to start.

Focusing my senses southward, I swept across the miles, keeping my touch light and delicate. A feather, not a net. If they felt me, everything would go to hell.

There! Gotcha!

"Still in New York," I said aloud, my voice steady despite the growing pressure in my chest. "Deep in an old subway system no longer on the grid. Bloody hell, there are at least twenty of them, maybe more. Oh, crap!"

The metallic, coppery tang of my own blood filled my mouth as I bit my lip, breaking my concentration.

"Sady baby, pull back now!" Mom's hands gripped my shoulders, too tight.

"What happened?!" Dad's tone was protective, urgent.

"They can't feel me," I said, though my voice wavered. "They're too busy feeding. At least seventeen humans... but they're fading. Fast." The words stuttered out, fractured and uneven, as tears burned behind my eyes. Helplessness clawed at my throat, choking me. "I can't save them."

Mom's grip softened, but her voice cut through my frustration with the precision of a blade. "Focus, Sady. Any sign of movement beyond the perimeter?"

She wasn't just asking. She was redirecting me, pulling me out of the helpless spiral I was teetering on and back to the task at hand. Mom knew exactly how to anchor me when the grief became too much—*keep searching, keep moving, keep going.*

"Hold on," I muttered, redirecting my senses. I let my reach flow further, sweeping southward across the cities and towns. The winds seemed to guide me, tugging at the edges of my awareness.

"Got one more," I said, my voice tight. "Alone. Wait, he's different—hold on."

I reached deeper, trying to make sense of what I was feeling. Colder than a human, but not like the others. The temperature wasn't the icy void I'd come to associate with vampires—it was lukewarm, distant but not lifeless. Like embers buried beneath ash.

And his aura—it was wrong. Faded. Watered down, like something vibrant that had been left too long in the rain.

Crimson, but washed out muted into something softer—mauve, maybe. Not the violent, pulsing red of vampires, thick with hunger and need. Like old bruises instead of fresh wounds. The dark gray swirled around it, familiar yet dulled, as if someone had taken what he was supposed to be and bled the saturation from it, leaving only a ghost of what should have been.

I swallowed, uneasy. He was close enough to the others to be connected—like a thread pulled loose from the same fabric. But whatever had touched him, changed him, had left him something... in between.

I pulled them in to show them. There was a beat of silence.

"And guess where?" I added, unable to stop my mouth from curling up in mirth, despite the conflict still thrumming under my skin.

"New Orleans," Mom said, her voice part menace, part amusement. I could practically hear her eye roll, the low rasp of her chuckle curling through the silence like smoke. The cliché wasn't lost on any of us.

The sound broke my focus too abruptly. I pulled back, but not before I felt it—him.

New Orleans boy had felt me.

"Ah, hell!" I snapped, fumbling to sever the connection. It only took a second, but it was long enough to leave me stumbling. Somewhere between here and there, I had sensed something—or someone.

It shimmered like sunlight tangled in moss, bright and lush, a green so full of life it felt like breath itself, like the essence of something vast and unbroken. Gold threaded through it in rippling streaks, shifting like dappled light through leaves, a warmth that didn't burn but embraced.

The sensation curled through me—soft but insistent, as if it had always been there, just waiting to be noticed. It tugged gently at my senses, subtle yet undeniable, like a breeze carrying the scent of blooming flowers, of damp earth after rain.

Feminine. Inviting.

Unlike anything I'd ever felt before.

My eyes flew open too quickly, the jarring release slamming through me. Mom's face was mere inches from mine, her etched features taut with concern. The shock knocked me backward, my body hitting the grass. Exhaustion swept over me, leaving me gasping.

Mom's hands were already on my shoulders, her grip firm but not forceful. "Sady baby, breathe. Slow it down," she instructed, her voice even, though her eyes flickered with something else—worry, calculation.

I struggled to ground myself, my body still trembling from the exertion. "I—I'm okay," I panted, blinking rapidly to clear the spots in my vision. "Just... give me a second."

Dad crouched beside me, his expression grim, his watchful gaze shadowed with something I couldn't quite place. "What in Dad's name happened?" His voice was quieter than usual, but there was no mistaking the strain woven into every syllable.

I swallowed hard, trying to slow the frantic beat of my heart. "I felt them," I rasped. "The vampires. They're still in New York, and they're... feeding. But I didn't linger—I swear."

Mom nodded, but her eyes narrowed slightly, like she wasn't sure she believed me yet. "You said that. And?"

And.

And New Orleans.

And the moss-green I had never encountered before. *Her.*

I hesitated, the words catching in my throat. "New Orleans Boy," I admitted, while sharing a telepathic glimpse so they could see what I felt.

WONDER WHAT HAPPENED TO HIM, IS HE THE RUNT OF THE LITTER OR SOMETHING?

Leave it to Mom to accuse Vampires of having litters.

"He was alone, and I think—" I let out a quick breath."I think he sensed me."

Dad's entire posture stiffened. "Are you sure?"

"No," I said honestly. "But maybe. It wasn't direct. I didn't pull straight back home, you taught me better than that. I—" I frowned, struggling to explain. "I sort of... veered. I didn't want to make a straight retreat in case someone was tracking me, so I let my pull drift before breaking the connection. That's when I—tripped over her."

Mom tilted her head. "Her?"

I let out a slow breath, staring up at the sky. "She sure as hell felt like a her," I admitted. "Definitely nothing like them, or the New Orleans guy. The opposite in every way, actually. Like standing in a sun-dappled clearing, all moss-green and gold, something vibrant and breathing."

Silence hung thick in the air. I sat upright, every muscle tense, watching as both my parents stared at each other—neither offering a single glance, nor rushing to explain. It wasn't often that they were stumped.

Mom broke the silence first. "Describe her. Devil is in the details."

Dad groaned, pinching the bridge of his nose. "Sera, please don't bring him into this conversation." He nudged her shoulder with an exasperated sigh. "Last thing we need right now is his name floating around."

Mom smirked. "I didn't say his name."

"You didn't have to," Dad muttered.

I blinked between them, feeling like I'd just walked into a conversation that was way above my clearance level.

Mom turned back to me, her teasing slipping away as she refocused. "Describe her, Sady. Exactly."

I took a breath and let my mind drift back to the sensation and pulled them with me, to the strange, impossible vibrancy of that presence. "She was warm," I said slowly. "Not just in color but in feel. Young. Vital. Not just alive, but... thrumming." I struggled for the right word, shaking my head. "She felt like motion, like something waking up."

Mom's lips parted slightly, but she didn't speak.

Dad frowned. "Not ancient, like your mom or me?"

I shook my head. "Definitely not. Steadier than me, maybe a little older? Or possibly just more assured? Nothing that says 'I've been here for centuries and have seen things.' She was... becoming**?**"

Something in Mom shifted. Just a flicker, but enough that I caught it.

Dad tapped his fingers against his knee, considering. "You tripped over her, but she wasn't waiting for you?"

"I don't think so." I hesitated. "I don't know. I didn't get intent, just presence. I'm certain, she did not sense me. Although I"m not sure exactly where I veered to."

Mom and Dad shared another look, and I could tell they were running through a mental checklist of things I wasn't privy to.

Dad exhaled through his nose, leaning back slightly. "Ramira might have some insight."

Mom nodded, though her jaw was tight. "Agreed."

I took a hopeful breath. "Aunt Ramira?"

Mom snorted but kept her focus on her phone. "I'll message her now. Who knows? We may see her before our Christmas trip if she knows something about this new presence."

I exhaled, my shoulders relaxing just a little. I *loved* Ramira. A visit with her was always equal parts chaos and fun, and if she had answers, even better.

But something still gnawed at me, lingering like an itch in the back of my mind.

I let myself fall back onto the grass again, throwing an arm over my eyes. "I'm starving," I muttered weakly, staring up at my concerned parents' faces. "Can we please get takeout? Thai?"

Mom's expression softened, though the tension never fully left her. "Sure, I'll grab takeout. We'll focus on reconnaissance and investigating for now, until we can sort out what's going on."

Her tone was overly chipper, the kind of forced cheer she used when trying to keep me calm. But her body betrayed her. Her shoulders were too straight, her movements too precise, like she was holding herself together by sheer will. The way her fingers tapped rhythmically against her leg—too quick, too deliberate—told me she was already strategizing, mentally running through plans.

I tried to push myself up, but my legs felt shaky, unsteady, like the weight of the telepathic work still lingered in my bones. Dad noticed before I could even ask for help. He reached over, his hand steady on my arm, guiding me to my feet.

"Easy there," he murmured, his grip gentle but firm, steadying me as I took a slow step forward. I wobbled slightly but regained my balance, feeling the aftershocks of the energy surge still buzzing faintly at the edges of my consciousness.

As we moved toward the living room, Dad's eyes flicked toward the workshop. His work wasn't done—I could feel the pull it had on him, though he said nothing. He followed us in, sitting quietly by my side as I sank into the couch. The cushions felt like they might swallow me whole, but I didn't resist. My limbs were heavy, my head still slightly buzzing from the mental strain.

Mom disappeared into the kitchen and returned moments later

with a gel ice pack. She pressed it to my forehead with a no-nonsense pat, as if the cold might somehow soothe away the strain that had left me sprawled there.

Dad stayed next to me in silence, unspoken worries resting gently between us. He didn't ask questions—he never did until he thought he had answers of his own. I closed my eyes for a while, giving the ice pack a chance to do its job. while letting the faint ticking of the clock and the hum of the refrigerator fill the space between breaths.

When Mom returned from the Thai restaurant, the scent of lemongrass, coconut, and chili entered the house with her, mingling with the brighter notes of fresh basil and roasted peanuts. It should have been comforting, but the silence around the table was anything but. Unrest clung to the air between us like a shadow—dense, unyielding, and charged.

It was clear, even before the plates were cleared, that Mom and Dad were headed straight for the workshop. Strategizing next moves, figuring out who this new client was, who knows.

I might as well have been invisible. *Honestly?* That was fine by me. Let them strategize and plot the next move; I could barely sit upright without feeling like I'd been run over by a truck. Battle plans and war rooms could wait.

Having the house to myself was nothing new. I trudged upstairs, intending to figure out my homework, but the moment I sat down at my desk, my mind rebelled. The words on the page blurred together, the shapes of letters and numbers refusing to arrange themselves into anything meaningful. My head throbbed, the aftereffects of the mind excursion still lingering like an unwelcome shadow.

I tossed the textbook aside with a frustrated sigh, leaning back in my chair. My gaze wandered to the ceiling as I tried to untangle my thoughts. I'd been so ready to tell Mom and Dad about Greyson's strange assignments—ready to lay it all out and let them piece together what I couldn't. But then the video happened. And the vampires. And the angel, *Cassiel*.

And suddenly, Greyson felt so... small. Insignificant in the face of everything else we were dealing with.

At least, that's what I told myself.

Still, I couldn't shake the relief that came with avoiding the topic entirely. If Mom or Dad knew how much space Greyson occupied in my brain—how his assignments seemed deliberately tailored to poke at the edges of our secrets—I wasn't sure how they'd react. *For now*, at least, that could stay my secret.

I glanced at my homework again, the pages mocking me with their neat rows of problems and prompts. My thoughts were too tangled, my energy too spent. Closing my eyes, I rested my head against the back of the chair and let the silence of the house settle over me.

I wasn't ready for sleep yet, but I wasn't ready to face the chaos in my head, either. For now, I'd sit here, letting the quiet soak in, and try to find some semblance of calm.

My body felt too heavy for the chair, every limb weighed down by the strain of the day. With effort, I shifted my focus to the clock—long past when I'd usually hear Mom moving around or Dad humming to himself. Tonight, the house felt hollow, like it was holding its breath. The textbook lay forgotten on the floor, its pages splayed in silent accusation, but I ignored it.

With a groan, I pushed myself up from the chair, the motion slower than it should've been. My body protested, every muscle tight and aching, but I forced myself to move.

Stumbling toward my dresser, I flicked off the desk lamp, plunging the room into soft shadows. Tugging my hoodie over my head, I let it fall to the floor, then reached for something clean to sleep in. The simple act of pulling on fresh clothes—a quiet, automatic ritual—helped settle the restless buzz in my mind. It was a signal to my body, a wordless reminder that the day was done.

I peeled back the blanket and sank into the mattress, the soft sheets wrapping around me like a gentle nudge toward sleep. Only, I ended up staring at the skylight, the shadows dancing faintly with the movement of the trees outside.

Whatever comes next, I thought hazily, *we'll face it together.*

I shifted onto my side, hugging my pillow closer, but sleep didn't come.

The stillness of the house should have been comforting, but it wasn't. The silence wasn't peaceful—it was waiting. And beneath it, my thoughts churned, unwilling to let go of the night's events.

The footage of Cassiel wouldn't leave my head. The way the vampires moved together, calculated and methodical. The efficiency in how they brought him down, the slow, agonizing way they sawed through his wings. It wasn't just about removing them—it was meant to maim. To capture him. Alive. *I think.*

I'd seen violence before. Up close and personal.

Christmas in New York.

I had been six years old, bundled up in layers against the winter chill, my tiny mittened hand wrapped in Dad's as we wove through the crowds in Times Square. The city looked like something out of a Hallmark movie—twinkling lights, towering Christmas trees, the scent of roasted chestnuts and hot chocolate mixing with the frosty December air. We had just finished ice skating, my laughter still breathless from where I'd slipped and slid my way across the rink.

Then I felt *them*.

Even now, I could still remember it—that creeping, unnatural cold curling around my spine. Like a strong gust of wind had sliced through my layers, a chill so deep it felt like it had settled in my bones. It had been the first time I'd ever sensed an aura like that.

And my parents? Zero hesitation.

Mom had scooped me up mid-step, her grip like iron, her heartbeat rock steady against my cheek. Dad was already moving, weaving through the masses faster than a human should have been able to. They didn't care who saw them—the priority was getting away.

By the time I realized what was happening, we were running.

The festive music, the laughter, the jingle of bells—all of it blurred together as my world tilted, the city flashing by in streaks of color. The further we got, the fiercer the cold became, like a storm brewing behind us.

Then came the fight for our lives.

I didn't remember how we got there, only that we had ended up in an abandoned high-rise, a helicopter waiting for us on the rooftop.

What I did remember?

Being passed back and forth between my parents like a damn game of hot potato.

One moment I was clinging to Dad's jacket as he sprinted up a stairwell, his breath ragged but controlled. The next, I was in Mom's arms, my face buried against her shoulder as she twisted mid-air, the sound of metal slicing through flesh filling my ears.

Steel meeting bone. A pained, inhuman shriek. Blood splattering against the walls.

Back to Dad.

He moved like a ghost, too fast, too silent, my tiny frame tucked against him as something huge slammed into the railing behind us, sending chunks of concrete flying.

Back to Mom.

The scent of copper was thick, metallic and cloying. I peeked over her shoulder, my heart hammering as I caught sight of one of them—his black eyes locked on us, his lips curled back over elongated teeth, the corner of his mouth slick with blood. *I didn't scream.*

Fear is funny like that.

When we reached the rooftop, the three of us were covered in blood. Theirs mostly, but some of my parents. My hands were stained crimson where they had gripped my parents' clothes, my small mittens drenched in the evidence of their fight.

Dad had turned, standing between us and the stairwell, his shoulders heaving, his knuckles white around his blade.

Mom had practically shoved me into the helicopter, strapping me in with precision while her violet eyes blazed with intensity. She spun toward the pilot's seat, her movements sharp and purposeful. Just before the doors slammed shut, I caught one last glimpse of Dad, standing there, his expression unreadable as he watched us take off.

He had barricaded the stairwell, shoving a thick steel pipe through the handles, buying himself mere seconds. Then he was running, full speed across the rooftop, his boots pounding against the concrete as the gap between him and the helicopter widened.

I barely had time to register what was happening before he launched himself into the air. A leap no human would have been able to make.

The rotor blades whipped the air into a frenzy, sending loose debris skittering across the rooftop below. My breath caught as Dad's fingers closed around the landing skids, his body swinging wildly from the force of the aircraft's ascent.

For a single, heart-stopping second, he dangled there, muscles tense as he fought against gravity. Then, with a grunt of effort, he pulled himself up, gripping the edge of the open cabin and hauling himself inside, landing in a crouch beside Mom.

Only then did the helicopter doors slam shut.

All I could do was press my face against the glass, watching the building shrink beneath us, the barricaded door already splintering under the force of whatever—*whoever*—was behind it.

And worse—I learned what it meant to be the reason we were found.

Even at six years old, I had known that it wasn't just bad luck. It wasn't random. It wasn't some unstoppable fate catching up with us.

It was *me*.

I had broken a rule.

I knew which one.

It had taken less than a week for them to find us. So, when Mom's grip tightened around me and Dad's face went blank with calculation, I knew instantly what was happening. He pivoted, adjusting, strategizing—fixing my mistake before it could get us killed.

They never said it. Not once.

But I felt it in every hurried glance, every extra layer of security after we escaped, in the way we left New York mid-year, no warning, no goodbyes, no chance to say I'm sorry.

One day, I was in the heart of the city, skating at Rockefeller Center, watching the Christmas lights twinkle against the night sky.

The next, I was on an island in the middle of the North Atlantic, where the wind howled through the cliffs and the only lights at night came from the stars.

I never asked them if they blamed me.

I never had to.

Because I blamed myself enough for all of us.

I had been the reason we ran then.

And now, I was the reason for this.

The video. The way Cassiel fought after acknowledging that he knew of my existence, yet swore my location would remain hidden, even though, in the end, he didn't know where I was. How he had lost.

A fresh wave of nausea coiled in my body, but there was nothing left to do with it. No way to fix it. No way to undo what had already happened.

My body felt like lead as I rolled onto my other side, pressing my forehead into the pillow, willing my thoughts to quiet. *Enough. Just stop thinking.*

To my surprise, my mind listened.

Sleep hit hard and fast, pulling me under in an instant.

No dreams. No nightmares.

Just silence.

Thankfully.

Like my brain had finally decided to protect me from myself.

Chapter 18

Mom's SUV peeling out of the driveway pulled me from a dreamless slumber.

My body felt like it had been wrung out and left to dry—exhausted, sore in ways that logic told me were emotional but felt undeniably physical. Every limb ached, my movements sluggish, like I was still dragging pieces of sleep with me.

I blinked, the last remnants of sleep dissolving as a rich, savory scent curled up the staircase, coaxing a low, insistent growl from my stomach. Eggs. Herbs. Potatoes. Dad was making frittatas—one of the few things that actually kept me full these days.

Not bothering to change out of my Harley Quinn pajamas (*don't judge me)*, I trudged down the stairs, each step landing with the grace of a sleep-deprived zombie, drawn forward by the irresistible scent of food.

"Hey, kiddo," Dad greeted, his voice softer than usual. He cradled a mug of coffee in his hands, his face lined with exhaustion, as if the kitchen counter was the only thing keeping him upright. "How're you feeling after yesterday?"

I sighed, leaning against the other side of the counter, and shot him a half-grin. "I'll let you know as soon as you pour me some coffee."

He complied without a word, sliding a steaming cup my way. But his silence lingered a beat too long. I glanced up, and there it was—that look. The one that meant he was overthinking, second-guessing himself. His brow furrowed as he stared into the dark liquid, fingers tightening slightly around the ceramic, knuckles pale.

"Sady doll," Dad said finally, his voice low, measured—not hesitant, but careful. "Did I make a mistake showing you that video?"

His eyes searched mine, not just for an answer but for something deeper—a sign of regret, of anger, of something I wasn't even sure I felt yet.

Blinking, caught off guard. The hesitation in his voice, the flicker of guilt in his eyes—it wasn't like him. Not Dad. He wasn't supposed to doubt. That was my job.

Dismissing it would've been easier—an eye roll, a quick wave off. But the worry, the genuine search in his eyes, cut through my usual sarcasm.

A slow exhale. A reassuring shake of the head. "No, Dad. You didn't make a mistake." A humorless chuckle slipped out. "If anything, this was easier. A screen is still a barrier. It's not the same as being there."

I met his eyes, steady and unflinching. "Remember when I was six? Christmas. New York"

His fingers tightened around his coffee mug, the muscle in his jaw flexing.

"After I felt that Surge—the very first time—before you and Mom carried me through a war zone." My voice wavered, but I pushed forward. "I've smelled their blood before I even understood what that meant. Heard their bones break. Felt you both get hurt as you passed me between you."

My throat tightened, but I didn't stop. "And by the time we reached the helicopter, we were all covered in it."

Dad let out a slow breath, his fingers tapping once against the mug before going still.

"Take a breath, Dad," I said, my voice quiet but steady. "While that video was without a doubt gruesome, was that really any worse than what I've already lived through?"

He didn't answer.

I shook my head. "You didn't show me anything I haven't already lived through. And you didn't traumatize me any more than I already was."

His gaze snapped back to mine, weary, but still assessing.

I sighed, dragging a hand through my hair, trying to put the feeling into words. "But you did show me something else." My throat tightened, but I forced myself to keep going. "For the first time, I saw what you were. What Mom was. Not just in stories or careful explanations—or an artist's rendering—but standing there, real, undeniable. An angel. You let me see the truth."

His shoulders dipped, as if the invisible burden had lightened.

"I just don't want you to lose what's left of your childhood," he murmured, his voice rough. "I know I can't shield you forever. I just wish—" He cut himself off, shaking his head. "I just wish you didn't have to carry this."

I gave a small, crooked smile. "Too little late for that, eh Pops?"

I THOUGHT WE AGREED I WOULD ACCEPT ANY FATHERLY NICKNAME EXCEPT THE ONE THAT MAKES ME SOUND LIKE A POPSICLE?

A rough chuckle escaped him, but it didn't quite reach his eyes.

The silence stretched between us, thick with words neither of us knew how to say. Then, with a sigh, I took another sip, breaking whatever serious moment we had slipped into.

"You're good father, Dad." I wrapped my hands around my coffee mug, letting the warmth seep into my fingers. "You've been preparing me, not coddling me."

His brow lifted slightly. "Yeah?"

I swallowed and held his stare, the honesty settling in my body like a quiet truth. "Yeah."

He nodded slowly, as if he were letting my words sink in. Then, without a word, he reached over—not to ruffle my hair, not to tease—but to cup the back of my head, his fingers threading gently through my hair in a quiet, steady gesture.

I exhaled, leaning into it just slightly, just enough to let him know I didn't mind.

"You're stronger than you think, Sady doll," he murmured. "And I'm so damn proud of you."

My throat tightened, and for a second, I couldn't find my voice.

So I just nodded.

For a moment, neither of us spoke. The silence stretched with a fullness of everything we'd said and everything we didn't need to.

Eventually, I slid onto the kitchen stool next to him, blinking away the lingering fog of sleep. My eyes finally focused on him, and... oof. He looked like hell. I'd bet a hundred bucks he hadn't slept a wink. Was this just worry? His jogging pants were the same ones he wore yesterday, and I had no qualms about pointing that out.

"Dude, you look like ass," I said, a smirk tugging at my lips.

"Don't let your mother hear you talk like that!" His chortle softened the threat, making it about as intimidating as gummy bears. "Speaking of your mother, she got a possible lead on that subway station location. Lets you off the hook for any training today."

"Ah, so that's why I heard her tires screeching instead of her voice this morning."

"Sady, can we ease up on the grumpy attitude toward Mom for a second?" He took on a pleading edge. "You know she's doing what she's best at, right?"

"Yeah, I know." My voice wavered, frustration threading through the exhaustion still clinging to me.

I sighed, running a hand through my hair again. "It's not just the violence, Dad—it's who it's happening to and where." I looked at him, searching for the right words. "We always knew they would never stop searching for me, but now it's hitting places we left behind. People who have nothing to do with this. It feels like it's escalating, even if they aren't getting any closer to finding us."

I rubbed my arms, a chill creeping up my spine, making the hairs on the back of my neck stand on end.

"Maybe I just wanted a hug from Mom," I admitted quietly. "Some kind of... I don't know, reminder that I'm still a kid in all this. That I'm not just a mission to be handled."

Running a hand through my hair, I tried to shake off the weight pressing down on me. "I know this isn't just about me. Cassiel was your brother, and I wouldn't wish what happened to him on anyone. But my worst enemy did this, right?" My gaze met his, steady now. "So, yeah. For once, can we just... sit with that?"

The regret hit instantly. My words, gentle as I had tried to make them, had lashed out at the wrong person.

"Sady, I—." *Ah hell,* please don't cry.

"Dad, I'm sorry." My voice cracked as I stumbled off the stool and wrapped my arms around his waist. "I'm just tired, and hungry, and scared. Oh, and really sore for some reason."

We stood there for what felt like forever, holding each other as the tears came. His long arm reached over my head to open the freezer. A second later, he handed me a pint of ice cream. Breakfast of champions—coffee for the caffeine, frittata to fill up my bottomless pit of a stomach, and ice cream to soothe the savage beast.

Guess this was just more of that strategic parenting?

"Hey kiddo," he said softly, "I'm sorry we weren't there for you last night. Seeing Cassiel after all these years—it was a lot. The attack was a shock, and your mom and I went into defensive mode, trying to strategize every possible outcome to protect you. But you do know that you could have come to us anytime, right? And, well, we talked about moving—"

Ah hell, I knew it. This was going too smoothly, too well. I knew I couldn't trust this to last.

"Dad, can we please talk about this as a family before you guys uproot me again?" I bit my lip, not able to hold back the words I didn't want to admit. "I like it here."

I let out a frustrated breath, shaking my head. "They're in New York, which for us was 12 years ago. Mozambique was 10 years ago. They don't even know where we are. They have no clue."

I paused, the weight of what I was saying sinking in. The idea of moving again set my teeth on edge. I couldn't—wouldn't—say it out loud, but the friends I'd made were a vulnerability, one my mom would never understand. I wasn't sure where Dad stood on it, but I needed to know he didn't see it as something to erase.

"Don't worry, kid. That's actually why your mom peeled out of here this morning. She's mildly perturbed with me."

"Oh? What did you do, or say?"

"I told her it was time to stop reacting, to slow down just enough to make decisions from a more stable base." He shrugged his shoulders at me. "And I told her that going forward you would be an active part of all our planning."

My jaw dropped, and I promptly missed my mouth with the spoon, letting a freezing dollop of ice cream slide down the front of my top. "Ah crap, that's cold!"

Dad grinned. "I hate to admit it, but you've grown into a capable young woman. Still not sure how I feel about you dating, but when it comes to them, I know we can handle anything—together."

"Wow," I said, blinking in surprise. "Didn't see that one coming."

"It might not make sense now, but one of my brothers once said, 'The past is a lesson, not a sentence.'" He tapped his spoon against his jaw, his eyes distant, like he was seeing something far away. "Took me a long time to understand what he meant. Your mom's past... it's harder for her to let go of. Mine was different, but it doesn't make it any easier. Just... please be patient with her, okay?"

"Hey, as long as we're not moving, I can do that."

"Good." Dad smiled. "Now, can I ask one more favor?"

"Sure, I've got ice cream in my belly and I don't have to pack any boxes." I grinned like the Cheshire Cat. "Whatcha want?"

"My client's data was fake—completely fraudulent. I want to know where that video came from and why it was sent to me. Something about this feels off."

"You're like a dog with a bone." Tossing the empty tub into the recycling bin, I smirked. "Go do your thing. I'm going to head out for a bike ride, okay?"

"Sure, just check in once in a while, will ya?" His voice carried that familiar mix of warmth and caution.

"You got it, Pops!" I called back, already taking the stairs two at a time.

"Hey, don't call me that! I'm not a popsicle!" he shouted after me, but I could hear the faint guffaw in his voice.

It took no time at all to make my way to the edge of town using the interconnecting bike paths. The crisp air filled my lungs, and with each pedal stroke, the tension of the past few days unraveled with every movement.

To my right, construction sites and bustling crowds created a chaotic contrast to the quiet rhythm of my ride, so I veered left, drawn toward what looked like a forest or a nature reserve I hadn't explored yet.

The noise of the city faded, replaced by the soothing rustle of leaves and the occasional birdsong. Tall trees loomed above me, their branches stretching out like a protective canopy. The deeper I went, the more I felt the woods' quiet strength settle around me, the dirt path beneath my tires soft and forgiving.

I slipped into the zone. This was freedom for me.

The vampires, the video, my parents—it all faded into a distant blur. It was just me and the rhythm of my bike, the steady hum of the wheels grounding me in the moment. My breath synced with my movement, my body flowing effortlessly with each turn of the pedals.

There was nothing but this—the trail, the air, the simple act of moving. It was like breathing with the earth itself, finally free from the weight of everything that had been pressing down on me.

That is, until I had to come to a screeching halt.

Out of nowhere, someone stepped directly into my path.

Barely managing to stop in time, I wrenched the handlebars to the side. The sudden motion sent me careening over a small ledge. My bike and I tumbled together, bouncing off rocks and loose dirt. The world spun in a blur of foliage and snapping twigs before I landed flat on my back, my legs tangled in the bike's spokes, my skull connecting with a particularly unforgiving rock.

I lay there, momentarily stunned, my vision swimming as I swore in Latin.

"That is not a very ladylike thing to say, although points for creativity, Miss Sady."

You have *got* to be kidding me.

Gingerly opening my eyes, I found myself staring up at none other than Greyson Black. Worry creased his brow, his sky-blue eyes scanning my tangled mess of limbs and twisted bike with alarming intensity.

And like clockwork, heat crept up my neck, settling in my cheeks with a betrayal I couldn't control.

Seriously, what was it with this guy and finding me at my absolute worst? Of course, *this* was how fate—or maybe just my cursed luck—decided to throw us together. I could practically hear the universe snickering in the background.

"Please don't move, Miss Sady." He said, his tone calm but firm. Not giving me a chance to protest, he reached down, his hands surprisingly gentle as he lifted the warped frame off me. "Let's get this bike off you carefully and inspect you for damage"

I rolled my eyes, already shifting my legs around so I could sit up. "You don't have to worry about me. I'm fine."

He didn't know that I'd never had a serious injury in my life. Bruises, scrapes—they all healed in minutes, if that. I might be small, but I was unnaturally sturdy. Practically unbreakable, thanks to a lucky draw in the genetic lottery.

He hesitated, his brow creasing slightly, doubt flickering in his eyes. "Well, I could've sworn I heard your skull crack against that rock, but there's not a single cut or even a bump."

His fingers brushed over my scalp, sending tiny shivers down my spine. I let out a girlish giggle that lasted maybe two seconds before I clamped my mouth shut.

No. Absolutely not. *Get it together, Sady.*

His hands continued their careful inspection, and I allowed myself the guilty pleasure of his undivided attention. His sky-blue eyes traveled over me, and I realized too late that while I was probably blushing a pomegranate shade of red, it was going to be awkward to explain my lack of scrapes, bruises, and blood after that fall.

Still, the last thing I needed was for him to start asking questions I couldn't answer. *Crap, how the hell am I going to explain this?*

"You seem intact," he finally said, leaning back with a small smile. "The same cannot be said for your bike, I'm afraid."

Having managed to my feet, I was already brushing dirt and leaves from my clothes, determinedly avoiding eye contact. "Told you I was fine."

Greyson's hand, half-extended to help me, hesitated before retreating into his jeans pocket, the movement as awkward as the moment itself.

"Fine, sure—but I can't help wondering how someone with reflexes fast enough to catch a flying compass midair managed to miss a whole person standing right in front of them."

My face burned hotter. "Maybe I was too distracted wondering what kind of person just stands in the middle of a bike path for no apparent reason at all."

"Touché," he said, his grin widening. "Still, I expected more from you, Miss Sady."

And then we both seemed to hold our breath.

I could swear I felt tingles of electricity between us, a faint, buzzing charge in the air. I looked up into his eyes, not expecting to see—annoyance? Or was that disgust?

The moment shattered as quickly as it formed. He abruptly stepped back, putting space between us.

I ducked my head, now brushing imaginary remnants of grass, weeds, and dried leaves from my clothes just to avoid eye contact. My outfit might be tough enough to avoid injury, but it wasn't nature-proof, and I desperately hoped it didn't look like I was just trying to cover up how much I'd wanted...

No. *Hoped* was not the word I was going to use. Definitely not.

"I don't suppose you are aware—," he said, his voice cutting through my spiraling thoughts, "that you're trespassing."

My head snapped up, eyes wide with surprise. "Trespassing?"

"This area," he said, gesturing around us with an easy sweep of his hand, "is private property. The reserve you entered is owned by a private foundation."

"Oh, great," I muttered, glancing around at the trees like they'd betrayed me. "So I'm not just a mess—I'm an *illegal*mess."

He actually looked entertained by my sarcasm, like he appreciated the humor in it. Well, at least someone gets me.

I crossed my arms, leveling him with a glare. "And let me guess—this foundation has your name on it?"

He inclined his head slightly, his lips twitching into a smirk. "As a matter of fact, yes. And I don't normally take lightly to trespassers."

"Well, you're just full of surprises," I shot back. "What are you doing out here anyway? Surveying your vast empire?"

Greyson arched an eyebrow, his lips curving into an infuriating smirk. "Perhaps. But the more pressing question is, what are you doing out here?"

I shuffled my feet, glancing down at my ruined bike. "Uhm... bike ride. Needed to clear my head. Found this forest but didn't see any signs."

Nodding towards the trees, his smirk softened into a half-smile. "Well, if you're willing to trust me, my house is just a short walk northwest. We can see about fixing your bike. And perhaps," he added, his voice lowering slightly, "we can discuss how you've managed to survive so unscathed after that fall."

He winked, and my stomach flipped in a way that had nothing to do with the crash. He lifted my bike effortlessly, like it weighed no more than a loaf of bread. With the bent handlebars and twisted tires, it was impressive—and infuriating. He glanced back at me with a grin, then extended his left hand.

The gesture was clear. An invitation.

My heart hammered as I stared at his hand. Somehow, I knew that if I took it, there would be no turning back. It wasn't just a hand to steady me—it felt like a step onto a path I couldn't veer off of, no matter where it led.

To hell with it. I took a deep breath and placed my hand in his.

His grin widened, boyish and utterly disarming, as his fingers closed around mine. The instant we touched, a strange warmth bloomed in the center of my palm, spreading upward, an invisible thread weaving between us. I saw the flicker of recognition in his eyes—he felt it too.

This was all shades of wrong. Not the screaming danger I'd been trained to recognize. No, this was different. *What made it wrong?* He was my teacher.

Distracted, I barely noticed the rock in my path before I stumbled over it. Clumsy. Not something I was used to being. Greyson steadied me with a light touch, and before I could fully regain my bearings, we turned a corner in the path, and there it was.

His house—or should I say cabin—was nestled among the trees, so seamlessly integrated into the landscape that it was almost invisible. Made of weathered wood and old stone, with greenery climbing its walls, it looked like it had been plucked straight from the pages of a fairytale.

Beside the cabin was an equally whimsical shed, its roof moss-covered, as though the forest had claimed it as its own. The door was slightly ajar, creaking ever so softly with the breeze, inviting curiosity. Inside, tools hung in precise rows, each one carefully arranged as if someone had a very particular way of keeping order. Leaning against one wall was a bike—the exact same make as mine. Of course, it was.

Greyson released my hand as we approached the shed, and I bit back the ridiculous urge to protest.

"Please, sit," he said, gesturing toward a weathered chestnut leather chair that looked as out of place in the rustic shed setting as I felt. "Let's take a look at your bike."

I sank into the cushions with a sigh, grateful for the chance to catch my breath. Being that close to him was hazardous to my health. More than tumbling down a ledge, anyway.

As he inspected the twisted metal, bent handlebars, and ruined tire, he began to hum softly—a tune I didn't recognize. I found myself watching him out of the corner of my eye, trying not to stare but failing miserably. His movements were precise, practiced, and oddly soothing. Slowly, the tension I hadn't realized I was holding began to unravel.

"Okay, uhm, Mr. Black, do you and your wife live here?" The question slipped out unfiltered, and I winced internally. *Smooth, Sady.*

Real smooth.

He straightened, a slight smile tugging at the corner of his lips. "No," he said quietly. "As a matter of fact, I live here by myself. Not met anyone with the patience to handle my... let's call them eccentricities."

He reached into the front pocket of his shirt, pulling something out. A single daisy.

"Now, I believe it's time for me to ask a few questions," Greyson said, his voice low and steady. "Let's start with an easy one. Why did you need to clear your head, and as a result, end up tearing through the woods on my property?"

I barely registered his words. He had completely invaded my personal space, reaching out to tuck that same daisy behind my ear. His finger brushed the bare skin of my ear as his hand lingered there, the warmth of his touch sending sparks skittering across my skin, making my breath hitch.

"Uhm—." My brain stalled, time grinding to a halt. That was such a chick-flick moment, and I don't *do* chick-flicks. Or rom-coms. And yet, here I was, a freakin' daisy tucked behind my ear courtesy of my history teacher—*my teacher*—who I happened to have a *very inconvenient* crush on. Which to be fair, wasn't a rom-com either. *Yikes.*

I turned away quickly, needing space to breathe. As I did, I thought I heard him exhale—a quiet, measured breath—before turning back to tinker with my ruined bike. With his back to me, a semblance of my composure returned, though my mind was still whirring with possibilities.

This was insane. Everything about this situation was breaking every rule my parents had drilled into me. Not to mention society. And yet, despite everything, I made a bold decision.

I would trust him.

I wouldn't tell him everything, of course. But I could tell him enough. "We," I began hesitantly, "my parents and I, found out yesterday that one of my father's closest friends was attacked."

Glancing up through my lashes, I tried to gauge his reaction.

"That must have indeed been terrible news," Greyson said after a pause, his voice quieter. He didn't look up from the bike, but I caught the slight pressure in his jaw. "How are your parents holding up?"

"Oh, they're upset, but they have each other," I replied, shrugging one shoulder.

"That leaves you to try and sort things out on your own, does it?" he asked, glancing at me briefly before returning to his work.

"Sort of," I admitted. "I guess."

"Do you know how or why this person was attacked?"

I hesitated, my fingers twisting in my lap, knotting around the truth. "Well, I think my parents have a pretty good idea about the motives. What's been so disturbing is that they were given a security tape to view. The whole incident was recorded, and the authorities needed help identifying the victim."

Greyson straightened, his focus narrowing in on me. "Could they not ask next of kin to identify the body?"

I shook my head, my voice dropping to a whisper. "There was no body. The attackers took him."

The pliers in his hand slipped from his fingers, clattering against the floor with a loud metallic ring. The sound cut through the quiet like a blade, sending a shiver down my spine.

His back stiffened. He turned toward the wall of tools, his hand gripping the edge of the workbench, steadying himself.

That small, involuntary movement made me painfully aware of my own trembling—the quivering I'd been holding back finally breaking through as the weight of the past twenty-four hours crashed over me.

Greyson turned back to me, his piercing gaze softening as he took in the tremor in my lips, the way my chest rose and fell in uneven breaths. He saw it—the way I was barely holding myself together, the terror bubbling just beneath the surface, ready to spill over.

Slowly, he took a few cautious steps toward me, his movements careful, deliberate. He reached out, his hand resting lightly on my wrist—a steady, grounding touch. It wasn't intrusive, just there, offering quiet reassurance. When I didn't pull away, his grip shifted, settling on my shoulder with the kind of warmth that said *I'm here. You don't have to hold this alone.*

That was it. The dam broke.

A sob wrenched its way free from my chest, and I slumped forward into his arms, unable to hold myself back. The tears came fast, unrelenting, soaking into his shirt as I finally let everything out.

He didn't say a word. Didn't try to hush me.

He just held me.

His grip was solid, reassuring—like an anchor against the storm.

I didn't know how long we stayed like that. Minutes? Hours? It didn't matter.

Somewhere my mind registered this could very well be a delayed trauma response. *Yeah, no kidding.*

Eventually, my sobs began to ebb, my breathing evened out as the last of the storm passed.

Greyson pulled back slightly, his hands still resting gently on my shoulders, his eyes searching mine. His voice, when he spoke, was quiet. Steady.

"Now then," he murmured, "I do believe that's what you really needed."

His bright, sky-blue eyes locked onto mine, and I felt the heat rise in my cheeks, spreading across my skin.

I didn't want to pull away.

Instead, I found myself caught in the moment, drawn to something in him I couldn't quite define.

And then, with startling clarity, I realized exactly what I wanted.

I wanted him to kiss me.

Well, crap, that was a first.

As if he could read my mind, he leaned down...

And kissed me—.

Chapter 19

On the top of my head. *Seriously*? What was I, a kid?

A mix of warmth and disappointment settled over me, tangled in a way I couldn't quite unravel. The affectionate gesture, which from a family member, would have been comforting—but instead, it left me feeling strangely adrift.

I barely had time to process the frustration bubbling beneath the surface before Greyson's voice broke through the moment—gentle, but deliberate. Like he had been waiting for the right time to speak.

"At the risk of turning your tears to stares of wrath, there is only one question I'd like to hear your answer to."

His tone was light, but his eyes watched, and waited—studying me like he was trying to map out the pieces I wasn't showing him.

I sucked in a slow breath, forcing my mind to shut the hell up and function. "And what question would that be?"

"Miss Sady, may I escort you home? I'm afraid your means of transport is unusable, and my bike-fixing skills are woefully inadequate."

Greyson stepped back, flashing that half-crooked smile, followed by his signature wink, and finished it off with a flourishing bow and bike wrench still in hand.

I couldn't help it. A laugh burst from me, snorting into full-blown hysterical giggles. It was impossible to stop, and his bemused expression only made it worse. He held out his hand, still smiling, and I let him guide me outside.

Around the house stood his car, tucked neatly away. Just as the giggles subsided, I halted mid-step, my breath catching as I took in the sight. Of all the vehicles I could have imagined Greyson Black driving, I never saw this one coming.

A graphite-coloured Smart car.

The irony wasn't lost on me, and once again, the snorting giggles escaped before I could help myself.

"Mr. Black," I asked, struggling to hold back another laugh, "that's your car?"

"And pray tell, Miss Sady," he said, a mischievous glint in his eyes, "what is wrong with driving an eco-conscious vehicle?"

"Oh, absolutely nothing," I replied, grinning ear to ear. "When you meet my parents next month during parent teacher night, ask them to tell you about my dad's birthday gift."

He raised a single eyebrow at that, his grin widening before opening the passenger door with a slight flourish. "I'll look forward to it," he said as I climbed in.

I shared my address, then spent the rest of the ride willing my pulse to calm down.

Greyson tapped the screen of his dashboard, and soft instrumental music filtered through the speakers. It was something classical—low, slow, and soothing. A melody that felt like it belonged to the woods we'd just left behind, stretching and winding through the trees like something timeless.

I barely registered it.

My mind was too tangled, the last twenty-four hours a relentless loop I couldn't escape. The video. The missing body. The feeling of those monsters still out there, still hunting. The way Greyson had held me—how his warmth had felt safe in a way I hadn't expected. In a way that it shouldn't.

The road blurred beyond the windshield. He was saying something, his voice low and measured, but the words barely touched the surface of my thoughts.

"... always better to replace the inner tubes than the whole frame. Most people assume if the wheel bends, it's a lost cause, but with a little patience..."

I blinked, dragging myself back to reality just in time to see his fingers drum idly against the steering wheel.

"... but I suppose it depends on how attached you are to the bike."

It took me a second to realize he was talking about my ruined bicycle. He hadn't asked anything. No prying questions, no push for explanations. Just filling the silence.

It was strangely thoughtful.

"I'll probably need a new one," I said, my voice quiet but steadier than I felt.

Greyson hummed in acknowledgment, eyes on the road, hands steady on the wheel. He didn't glance at me. Didn't press for anything more.

And somehow, that made the silence between us feel safer. Back to normal again.

The Smart car purred quietly, small but strangely comfortable. The quiet engine, the soft music, the rhythmic motion of the tires against the road—it was grounding in a way I didn't expect, but appreciated given the events of only minutes before.

All too soon, we pulled up in front of my house.

Well, that drive was too damned short.

Mom and Dad's presence brushed gently against my senses before I even saw them. They weren't worried, just curious—watchful.

"Miss Sady," Greyson said, his tone shifting back to casual. "I shall see you Monday in class. Speaking of school, have you thought about your strategy for the Milton project?"

Oh, right. That.

"Well," I began, carefully choosing my words, "I was thinking about exploring how Milton's daughter, Anne, transcribed his works, especially considering that women in her time were excluded from most theological discussions and literacy."

I carefully avoided the rest—that my mom had known Milton's daughter personally. Some truths were too tangled to explain.

Greyson nodded thoughtfully. "A fascinating angle. I look forward to hearing more."

Dad was standing in the doorway as I stepped out of the car, his eyes scanning the driveway. He couldn't quite make out who was behind the wheel, but I knew he was trying.

Turning back to Greyson quickly, I forced a casual tone. "I'll, uhm, need to come by for my bike. One of my parents will drive me."

He glanced toward the garage before returning his focus to me. "Of course. We can make the proper arrangements tomorrow."

An unreadable expression crossed his face, a hesitation lingering on the tip of his tongue. But I wasn't about to stick around long enough to find out.

"Thanks for the ride," I said, already moving. "And sorry about the whole trespassing thing. See ya."

Shutting the door behind me, I turned toward the house, my heart thudding against my ribs. Dad was still watching, his stance easy—but quietly assessing.

Bolting up the steps, I waved over my shoulder as if this was no big deal. Maybe if I played it cool, he wouldn't ask—

Nope.

Dad intercepted me at the top, his hand catching my elbow before I could slip past.

"Everything okay?" he asked, his eyes narrowing as he studied my face.

"Yeah, Dad. I'm fine."

Funny how often I said that. And how often it wasn't entirely true.

Dad's scrutiny shifted past me, lingering on the Smart car still idling in the driveway. I resisted the urge to physically block his view.

"And that was?" he said slowly.

I knew he would ask, but the slight shift in his tone sent a prickle down my spine.

I forced a nonchalant shrug. "Oh yeah, my history teacher. He lives nearby."

Dad's eyes didn't waver.

Mom's presence slid into my awareness before her voice followed, her figure appearing behind Dad. "What happened to your bike?"

"Oh, uhm, I kind of crashed it by accident," I admitted, stumbling over the words. "It's at Mr. Black's house. He said to arrange pick up tomorrow. We'll need to use your vehicle though—can't picture my mangled bicycle on the back of Dad's Harley."

"Sady doll," Dad said, his voice firm but gentle. "That's a lot of words, and none of them are telling us what actually happened."

"I went for that bike ride, like I told you. Something startled me, I veered away to avoid a collision, and ended up in a small ravine. That was one of my teachers, Mr. Black, who happens to live nearby. My bike is in his shed. Not even sure if it's worth trying to repair or just get a new one." I blurted it all out so fast my breath hitched, my lungs struggling to catch up.

Sending a quiet prayer to the skies, that neither of my overly observant parents would clue in that this was not just a teacher. Not for me.

"Sure, Sady baby," Mom remained neutral, as far as I could tell. "We can sort that out tomorrow."

"With one of us," Dad clarified, his voice edged with something unreadable.

I rolled my eyes. "Obviously."

Mom and Dad exchanged a look. The kind that sent a ripple of unease through me.

Oh, fantastic. We're already at the parental telepathic conference stage.

Dad sighed, scrubbing a hand down his face. "He drove you home."

Again, not a question.

"He offered to drive me home," I corrected. "And considering my alternative was limping back on foot, it seemed like a better option."

Crap, I never limped. Was I laying it on too thick?

Mom's head tilted slightly, and I knew that look well. She was now assessing. *Calculating.*

Dad exhaled slowly, but to my surprise, he let it drop. For now.

Mom, however, wasn't finished. "This is the same teacher who made you stand up in front of class on your first day?"

I sighed dramatically. "Yes, Mother."

"And now he's driving you home."

I crossed my arms, fixing her with a dry stare. "He's also the same teacher who gave me homework, but you're not making a conspiracy out of that."

Dad huffed out a reluctant laugh. Mom's lips twitched.

For now, they let it go.

I didn't know whether to be relieved or worried.

I could feel Dad still watching me, his posture relaxed, but his mind clearly working through something. He wasn't entirely letting this go—I knew that much.

Mom, meanwhile, turned toward the kitchen, her fingers already reaching to tie back her hair like she was gearing up for something. "Did you eat yet?"

I opened my mouth, but Dad cut in first. "Sera."

She paused, glancing over her shoulder, seeing both of our worried faces.

"Oh, both of you, relax. I'm not cooking, Sam, that's all you darling. I can help chop ingredients. Just give me a knife and point me where ya need me. "

I scowled. "Maybe I am hungry."

Mom smirked, but her gaze flicked toward the garage again. The unspoken question between them passed easily, and I braced for impact.

Dad exhaled through his nose but let it slide, shaking his head as he moved toward the kitchen. "Fine. But if you're helping," he said, glancing at Mom pointedly, "no getting creative with the knives."

Mom pressed a hand to her heart in mock offense. "Sam, please. When have I ever—"

"The London incident," Dad cut in dryly.

"The cabin in Iceland," I added.

"That one time in James Town," Dad finished, side-eyeing her as he started pulling ingredients from the fridge.

Mom sighed, rolling her eyes as she selected a knife from the block—her favorite, the one with the Damascus steel blade and the handle worn smooth from years of use.

"Fine," she muttered. "I'll try to keep things simple."

Dad didn't look convinced, but he was already focused on measuring out ingredients, his movements precise, methodical—completely opposite to Mom, who sliced through vegetables with the kind of speed and accuracy that could probably rival a professional, but lethal, chef.

While he carefully scooped out exact teaspoons of spices, she made quick work of several bell peppers, her blade flashing as she diced them with effortless precision. Within minutes, there was a pile of neatly cubed vegetables on the cutting board, separated into three distinct sections—one for her, one for Dad, and one for me.

"Alright, here's what we've got," Dad said, scanning their combined prep work. "For you, Sady, we'll do a chickpea and spinach frittata. This still work for you?"

I nodded. "Yep. No complaints."

"For me, I'll do a lentil and vegetable stir-fry. And for her—" he shot Mom a look "—I assume you'll want steak, since you never eat anything leafy willingly."

Mom smirked. "Correct. But I'll take some of those caramelized onions you're making, too. And don't skimp on the mushrooms, and don't forget my peppers."

He muttered something about *carnivores* under his breath, but he was already moving, heating the cast iron pan while Mom kept chopping, switching effortlessly from peppers to mushrooms to herbs.

It was a familiar rhythm, one I had watched my entire life—Dad working with patience and precision, Mom wielding her knife like an extension of her hand, carving through ingredients with speed and confidence.

And me?

I just sat on the counter, snagging pieces of food before they even made it to the stove.

"This is how we starve," Dad sighed as I popped a slice of red pepper into my mouth.

Mom grinned. "It's how we test for poison. A time-honored tradition."

He just shook his head, but the warmth was unmistakable.

For a little while, it felt like a normal Sunday night.

When they offered to do all the cleaning up, knowing my loathing for doing dishes, I took the easy out and bolted up the stairs. In my room, I collapsed onto the bed, staring at the ceiling as the last twenty-four hours replayed in my mind.

First, *they* were still after me. That was never a question they would stop—but the scale of it? That was something else entirely. Twenty of them gathering in one place—by far the largest group we'd ever known about? Someone out there knew about Dad. Not just who he was now, but who he had been. Otherwise, why send it to him?

Second, the daggers. Celestial metal. Both the vampires and the angel had carried them—ceremonial, but deadly, blades, identical in design, but I knew firsthand why the metals and colors were different. The connection between those blades and my family wasn't just coincidental.

Third, there was the angel. Cassiel. Angels were still on Earth, or at least they had been. One of them knew about me. And that meant something I didn't fully understand.

Finally, there was Greyson.

Teenage crush on highschool teacher trumps supernatural crisis. *Or does it?*

My teacher, who had kissed me on the top of my head. Off-limits, yet I had trusted him in a way I never had with anyone outside my family. That strange warmth I felt with him still lingered—unnerving and unexpected all at once.

I worried I wouldn't be able to sleep with so much drifting in my head, but my body had other plans. Exhaustion won out, and I fell into a deep sleep.

It wasn't peaceful.

My dreams were vivid, and suffocating. A world shrouded in shadows, where every movement felt too heavy, too slow. I drifted through the dark, weightless yet sinking, like I was caught between two places—one I couldn't escape, and one I couldn't reach.

Figures surrounded me, shifting, stretching, writhing just beyond clarity. Faceless. Formless. Not quite human. But they were watching. I felt it in the marrow of my bones, in the prickle at the base of my skull.

Waiting.

A whisper threaded through the void, so faint it barely reached my ears. It wasn't a voice exactly—more like an exhale of something alluring. A breath curling along my skin, dragging ice in its wake.

I turned, trying to find the source, but the figures only shifted, moving with me. No matter which way I looked, they were always just out of reach, flickering like candlelight about to be snuffed out.

And then, I saw it. Correction, I felt it.

A presence more than a light, its warmth curling through the cold like the first touch of sunlight after a long winter. Moss-green, threaded rich with gold, the color of deep forest glades bathed in morning light. It didn't just exist—it breathed.

And so did I.

Somewhere between one breath and the next, I felt it—the rise and fall of something unseen, a rhythm that matched my own. A soft inhale, an exhale, a pause. Again. And again. It wasn't just pulsing; it was responding. Meeting me where I was, adapting, waiting.

Welcoming.

A sensation curled through my chest—not just warmth, but presence, something unmistakably familiar, inexplicably *feminine.* There was a grace in the way it moved, a gentle, fluid certainty, like laughter shared in the dark or hands smoothing the edges of a fraying thread. Not soft, not weak—no, this was something steady, something knowing.

I took another breath, and the light flickered—not with hesitation, but something almost expectant, like a hand outstretched in invitation.

She shimmered with an almost playful confidence, flickering like laughter caught in the wind. Yet, beneath that warmth, there was something deeper—an unshaken steadiness, as if it knew me. As if she knew me.

She hovered in the void, delicate yet unyielding, untouched by the shadows pressing in.

Hope.

My muscles tensed, coiled tight, every fiber of me straining toward her—but before I could move, something else rose from below.

Cold. Gray. Crimson.

It surged through the dreamscape like a tide, relentless and all-consuming, swallowing everything in its path. The air thickened, brittle with ice, the ground fracturing beneath me as jagged frost slithered outward like veins of rot. The warmth above remained, pulsing, steady—but now there was something clawing against it, trying to smother it.

The moss-green glow intensified, her radiance spilling over the figures around me, carving them out of the void, sharpening their edges until they weren't just shadows anymore. They stood, not quite solid, not quite spectral—half-formed things caught between light and darkness.

A weight crushed against my chest, tightening, pressing, suffocating. My breath hitched, sharp and ragged, clawing against my ribs as panic coiled deep in my gut. Run. Every instinct screamed it, but I was trapped—the warmth above and the ice curling below, both pulling, both refusing to let go.

Then—

A warning.

The ground fractured beneath me, splintering like glass, cracks racing outward like veins of ice. For one breathless second, I hung there, suspended between forces—caught in the space between light and shadow. Then I fell.

I fought against it, but the darkness swallowed everything, pulling me into its freezing embrace—

I woke up gasping with a sharp inhale, lungs seizing like I'd been holding my breath too long. My skin tingled, not with heat, but with the eerie sensation of something just out of reach—like waking up mid-fall, gravity struggling to remember its claim on me. My throat ached with a thirst so intense it felt like my mouth had turned to sandpaper. The air felt too thick, the room tilting slightly, as if the world hadn't quite settled back into place.

Get a grip, Sady. Not real.

The thought barely settled before a violent shiver raked down my spine. *It had felt real.*

I stumbled out of bed, the room tilting slightly as I made my way to the bathroom. Peeling off the sweat-soaked clothes clinging to my skin, I twisted the shower knob, cranking it to cold. The icy spray hit me like a shock to the system, but I stayed under, letting the water hammer down, willing the fire inside me to stop.

It took nearly thirty minutes before I felt even remotely normal—well, as normal as someone like me could feel. My body wasn't made for normal, not entirely.

Dressed in fresh clothes, I towel-dried my hair and headed downstairs, hoping for a calm, drama-free day before school started again tomorrow. A lazy, mundane, Sunday would be fantastic.

The smell hit me as soon as I reached the bottom step. My stomach growled loudly in response. Something rich and savory was cooking in the kitchen. I followed the scent like a cartoon character chasing the animated wisp of a pie, my steps quickening.

Mom stood at the stove, a pan of bacon sizzling in front of her. She glanced over her shoulder as I entered, warmth flickering in her eyes. "Sady baby, I'll pick you up from school tomorrow, so we can grab your bike from Mr. Black's. We can before dinner, alright?"

I didn't answer right away. Instead, I reached into the pan with quick fingers, snagging a piece of bacon before she could protest. The heat didn't bother me—I popped the slice into my mouth and chewed, savoring the rich, salty flavor. It was perfectly cooked, crispy and succulent, and I couldn't stop the involuntary moan of pleasure that escaped.

Mom's lips tightened, her eyes narrowing with alarm as they darted between me and the sizzling pan. "S A M! Get in here now!"

Chapter 20

Mom screamed so loudly that I winced. Before I could react, her hand closed around my throat, and I was slammed against the fridge, my toes dangling off the ground.

The metallic copper taste of blood filled my mouth—I'd bitten my tongue in the process. Panic froze me in place, my body rigid, my breath locked inside my chest.

Dad burst into the kitchen, instincts honed for danger, but this was not what he'd expected to see.

"Sera?!" he barked, sliding beneath her arm and clutching her wrist. His voice was edged with both authority and fear.

"Let go of our daughter. Now!"

Her grip released abruptly. I collapsed onto the floor, landing hard on my knees. Gasping for air, I rubbed my sore throat, the shock of what I had just done sinking in. *What I had done.* Not her.

"Dad, it's okay," I croaked, my voice rasping. "Let go of Mom."

Dad hesitated, his knuckles still white around Mom's wrist.

"Would one of you please tell me what in the bloody heavens is going on?" His voice was hoarse, his eyes flickering between the two of us, wild with alarm.

Mom's glare was icy and unrelenting. "Our daughter just ate my bacon."

In any other family, that would've been so minor it wouldn't even be worth mentioning. Comical even. But our family was different.

I never ate meat—never.

It wasn't just a moral choice. It was a biological imperative.

Dad was allergic to meat, while Mom thrived on it. Ramira had warned them when I was born that I should grow up vegan, or at the very least, vegetarian. By age three, the choice had been my own.

Until now.

Dad's face paled. His shoulders stiffened. "Sera, it's happening." His voice was quiet, but heavy. "We need Ramira. And soon."

Mom moved before he finished speaking, snatching her phone off the counter with inhuman speed. She swiped open an app that looked more like a black-and-white code matrix than anything designed for casual users.

Her fingers flew over the virtual keyboard, entering what looked like gibberish at first glance. It wasn't *gibberish*—I recognized it as the family cipher, a layered encryption code that required both sequence memory and context.

"What are you doing?" I asked, still struggling to make sense of what had just happened.

"Sending a message," Mom said, her tone clipped, her focus unshaken. "This can't wait."

"To Ramira?" I guessed, still on my knees, my voice hoarse and unsteady.

"To those we trust," she corrected, her words laced with urgency. "And to make sure they know exactly what's happening."

Dad knelt in front of me, his expression softening slightly. "Sady doll, listen to me. Your mom and I knew this day might come, but we hoped it wouldn't. You're going to be okay, but we need to move fast."

The phone pinged, and Mom's focus snapped back to us. "It's done," she announced, though the strain on her face didn't ease. "Sam, we need to talk before we make any decisions."

I didn't like the sound of that. *Not at all.*

Dad helped me to my feet, his grip firm but steady. "Let's go, kiddo. The living room. Now."

"Can someone please tell me what's going on?" I demanded, my throat still tender. I followed them to the couch, sinking into the armchair across from them. A cold prickle ran down my spine at the anxiety tightening their features.

Mom placed her phone on the coffee table, the screen dimmed but still active. She didn't look at it—her focus was now entirely on me. Dad sat next to her, his hand resting lightly on her knee.

"Sady," Mom began, her voice unusually gentle, "it's time we told you something. We've been waiting until... well, until we were certain the time was right."

I crossed my arms, trying to ignore the heavy thud of my heartbeat in my ears. "You mean something you didn't think I could handle?" My tone came out more belligerent than I intended.

"Not exactly," Dad said carefully. "You've always known you were different. You know why we have to move every year after your birthday, and why we've spent your life being cautious."

"Yeah, no kidding," I muttered, shifting in my seat. "Every year, my birthday comes with a free, uncontrollable shockwave package. You know, the one that lights me up like a beacon and screams, *Hey, come hunt me down!* to anyone out there looking. What of it?"

Mom exchanged a glance with Dad before nodding. "And because of that, we've done everything we can to protect you. To prepare you. But what we haven't told you—what we didn't know how to tell you—is why you're different."

That made me sit up straighter. "I thought I already knew. You two lovebirds made me, and that makes me... I don't know, a cosmic miscalculation or something? Like if celestial Romeo and Juliet having a baby?"

"Yes, but there's more to it," Dad said, his voice steady but threaded with something else. Regret? Hesitation? "You've heard the story before, but not all of it."

"The story of—"

"Of you, our Everlasting." And he began recounting the tale of my birth—a story I thought I knew by heart.

Only this time, it was the special *Director's Extended Cut* or something.

I frowned, leaning forward slightly as Dad shifted in his seat. He always did this when he was gearing up to tell a story—gathering his thoughts, piecing together every detail to perfection. Unlike Mom, who favored directness and efficiency, Dad had a knack for turning even the driest tale into something vivid and unforgettable.

But this story wasn't dry.

Not even close.

"What you've always known," he began, his tone softening, "is that after nearly two thousand years together, we'd given up all hope of having a child. And then, in 1994, we miraculously found out we were pregnant. You can't imagine how ecstatic we were, but..." He trailed off, his gaze dropping to his hands. "We were also terrified."

This part wasn't new to me, even the terrified part. I nodded, urging him to continue.

"You already know how *they* came into existence," he stated, his eyes flicking up to meet mine.

He meant the Vampires. The Nephilim.

I nodded, the information ingrained in me from years of careful lessons.

This wasn't the kind of story you'd find in books or movies.

The truth was far darker—far more twisted.

Vampires were the result of an unholy union: the progeny of a Fallen one, their father, and a human mother. Beings caught between two worlds, neither human nor divine, with an unquenchable thirst for blood and violence. And obedient to Mom's ex.

Dad cleared his throat, his shoulders tensing under an invisible weight. "That's exactly why we were so afraid, Sady. The only offspring we've ever known from our kind—angels, Fallen or not—have been Nephilim."

A new, unsettling thought took hold—*what exactly did that make me?*

My stomach twisted at his words, but I stayed silent, letting him continue.

"For as long as we've existed," Dad said, his voice weighted with centuries of sorrow, "any attempt to create life has ended in tragedy. The mothers—human women—always died. Violently. And the children... they were monsters. Bloodthirsty creatures who became the very vampires hunting you now. No one, Sady, has ever known an offspring of our kind to be anything else."

I swallowed hard and glanced at Mom. Her posture was rigid, her hands clasped so tightly that her knuckles had turned white. She gave nothing away, but the pressure in the room pressed down on me like a weight.

My brow furrowing as I tried to piece it together. "I mean, Dad, you're Grigori. Doesn't that matter? Shouldn't it, I don't know, balance things out or something?"

"Yes," Dad said softly, his voice almost reverent. "That's what gave us hope. But even then, Sady..." He hesitated, his eyes dropping. "Even then, we didn't know if you would survive. Or if you would..."

"Be like them," I finished, my throat tightening around the words.

He nodded gravely. "Exactly."

The silence stretched until Mom finally spoke. Her voice was low, steady, but there was a bluntness beneath it that reminded me she wasn't always maternal. "Sady, we didn't know what you would be. We didn't know if it was even possible for someone like me to bring a child into this world without..." She faltered, her lips pressing into a thin line. "Without creating a monster."

Right, she was once one of the Fallen, that much I knew but until this moment hadn't considered what the truly meant. *Crap, now what?*

"So, you both knew there was this risk?"

And they still chose to bring me into this world. *That's gonna need some therapy.*

When she reached for Dad's hand, her voice was quiet but unwavering. "And yet, with you, for the first time, both parents came from the sky... which makes you the child of prophecy."

A child of what now?

"As soon as we knew the pregnancy was real, we went in search of the only person we knew who could help us," Mom said. "My sister-in-arms—Ramira."

"We found her in Romania," Dad added, picking up the thread. "Living in isolation in a fortified old castle, tucked away in the shadows of the Carpathian Mountains near the Danube River. She's the only healer of our kind left, and the only other Seraphim that we know of to have survived the flood with Sera. Her loyalty has always been with your mother, even before the rebellion."

"You mean Lu—"

"When I decided to fight alongside Luke," Mom cut in sharply, her voice marked with both pride and regret, "my entire battalion followed me. Every last one."

Dad nodded, his gaze fixed on her. "She commanded the fiercest and strongest of the Seraphim. So greatly respected for her wisdom and judgment, many chose to follow her without question or hesitation."

"Not one of my finer moments, my love," Mom said, rolling her eyes. But her expression softened, as if the memories were pulling her back to another time. "Fast forward to when the battle was lost. Luke was in chains, on his knees in front of *Him*."

Her voice faltered, but Dad continued. "Instead of ordering death, *He* cast them out—all of them. Anyone who fought on the losing side was banished."

"To hell?" I couldn't help myself, I knew the Bible didn't have it all right, but the parents had always skirted this topic when I tried to go digging.

Mom's lips curved into a bitter smile, her tone laced with an edge of old contempt. "Not hell. The Almighty's favorite playground for *His* precious humans. The ones we were told to adore, to serve. Do you have any idea what it felt like, to be cast down here? To be forced to live alongside them?" She paused, her voice softening but still carrying a trace of scorn. "It wasn't punishment. It was humiliation."

"Earth," I murmured, finishing the thought.

"Yes," Mom said, curling her knees up to her chest.

Dad, seeing her discomfort, immediately wrapped his arms around her, drawing her close. "And that is when the gates of Heaven were closed to our kind forever."

"*He* told us that none of us would ever be strong enough to break through the gates," Mom added, his voice carrying an edge of something unreadable. "Just as we were cast out, and felt the celestial fire start to singe and burn away our wings, did *He* send us with his final words—'A child, born of both blood and hope, shall possess the power to tear open the gates of Heaven and Hell, unraveling the divide.'"

A chill ran down my spine, their words hanging in the air, slippery and hard to grasp. "So... is that it?" I swallowed hard, my nerves jangling. "Blood and hope? *He* doesn't sound very smart. Everyone has blood in their veins."

Dad gave a small, mirthless laugh. "Not everyone has hope, Sady. Not like you."

I raised an eyebrow, leaning back slightly. "Wow, no pressure or anything. Just me and my overachieving veins, apparently."

"None of us fully understood what *He* meant," Dad continued, his voice thoughtful. "But Ramira not only grasped the hidden meaning, she, as a seeress, saw glimpses of the future threads *He* spoke of. It was she who unraveled the layers of *His* words for Luke and your mother, long before I ever laid eyes on Sera."

Mom spoke through clenched teeth. "For Luke, that meant a power capable of bringing the Fallen back... and unleashing chaos beyond anything we could imagine."

"Wait," I interrupted, holding up a hand as I frowned, the pieces refusing to fit. "You're telling me that Ramira—my mysterious healer-seer aunt who loves living in fortresses around the world—just, what? Magically decoded this prophecy-declaration-thing like it was a crossword puzzle? Did she have a vision or something? Or are we talking some cosmic cheat sheet we've never heard about?"

"Not exactly a vision," Dad clarified. "Decoding it like a crossword puzzle isn't too far off, actually. Ramira doesn't see visions the way you might imagine. It's not flashes of the future or voices from the beyond. For her, it's like looking at tangled threads and suddenly knowing how to unravel them. She doesn't just read words; she understands the intentions beneath them, the truths hidden in plain sight."

Mom's fingers curled into fists in her lap, a shadow crossing her features. "Ramira stood by my side—and Luke's—during the rebellion, and just before the gates were opened and our chained bodies were thrown out." Her voice wavered slightly, a rare crack in her armor. "When I tell you that her voice shook with a celestial vibration, when she told us what she had seen, please understand the significance."

I shifted in my seat, leaning forward. Whatever Mom was remembering, it was obviously painful, but I could sense we were getting closer to the root of why my parents were panicking now.

"A Seraphim was, and still is, a Fallen." She looked over at Dad, her eyes softening with something unspoken, but her voice turned bitter. "*He* denied us the gift of procreation. Saving that for *His* precious humans."

Mom was allowing her millennia-long resentment to surface, which meant another violent outburst might not be far away.

Dad placed a calming hand on her arm before continuing. "But Ramira said *His* words—about blood and hope—were a metaphor, or perhaps a riddle. One with many layers."

I rolled my eyes. "Of course, it's a riddle. Why are they always riddles? Seriously, would it kill the universe, or *God*, or whoever, to make a prophecy that's—oh, I don't know—a straightforward memo? And while we're at it, why does the *chosen one* always have to be some traumatized kid? Can't it, just once, be a forty-something divorcee with grown kids and zero fucks to give? They'd probably handle this whole thing way better than me."

Dad shot me a look, one that might've passed for amusement if the situation weren't so dire. "Language, Sady doll. Language."

Mom, who usually would've added to Dad's scolding, didn't even glance my way. Instead, she stared at her hands, her jaw tight as if she were bracing for something.

"She said the child would have to learn what nature versus nurture truly meant," Dad continued. "That this child would have to understand that fate is both a choice and a curse."

"And with it," Mom added, her voice softer, more uncertain, "a promise that love would find a way."

The words hung in the air, thick with something fragile.

Mom's expression was unreadable, but something about it felt... raw. Dad's hand tightened on hers, a silent gesture of reassurance, but I couldn't ignore the way his jaw clenched, the flicker of something dark behind his eyes.

Dad glanced at her, drawing strength from her words. "Because love and hope... they aren't different things, Sady. They're the same. Hope is the seed, and love is what lets it grow. Without one, the other dies."

I leaned back, their words sinking in despite my skepticism.

"Uhm, okay, so... I'm that child?" I asked, my voice unsteady and yet, I am my father's daughter, I could tell they were holding something else back. "What else are you not saying?"

They exchanged a glance—a fleeting moment of silent communication that only deepened my frustration.

"Seriously? Like, am I going to sprout wings or something?" I pressed, frustration lacing my words. "Why do I have to drag this out of you two? Just tell me."

Mom inhaled deeply. "Well, you know I've got history with Lucifer."

I stilled.

She had never called him that before.

Always *Luke*. Now, she dropped his full name like a nuclear bomb, causing Dad to wince.

Mom's voice was quieter, almost hesitant. "I wasn't just his first-in-command and lover. We led the rebellion. Together. He and I were... of one mind. And for a time, I thought... of one heart. In the heavens, and on earth... for a time."

Damn.

This was more than just admitting he was her ex.

I'd always known Mom and Lucifer had a complicated history—her loyalty to him, the way she refused to speak his name unless absolutely necessary. But this... this was different.

This felt *dangerous*.

"Sady baby," she said, her voice faltering in a way I had never heard before, "you need to know that I was just as responsible for the rebellion as he was. As Lucifer. From the beginning, he and I were... entangled."

A cold weight settled in my stomach.

"So what are you telling me, Mom? That you weren't just some tragic exile but... something worse? That the risk of me turning into one of those bloodthirsty monsters is because of you?"

She let out a shaky breath, her fingers curling slightly as if resisting the urge to reach for me. "When we first arrived on Earth, we were furious. Furious at *Him*, at the gates that had closed our home to us forever. Lucifer was enraged—completely obsessed. And so was I. Together, we wreaked havoc among *His* hum—" She paused, correcting herself. "The people of this world. We slaughtered thousands upon thousands, hoping that *He* would intervene, that we might have a chance at retaliation. Or a way to get back home."

A grave silence settled over the room. I knew her past held proverbial demons, but this?

The quiet stretched too long, my frustration along with it.

"Uhm," I started hesitantly, unsure I wanted the answer. "How bad are we talking?"

"Please don't ask your mother to relive everything," Dad cut in, his voice laced with a rare irritation.

"No, it's okay, Sam," Mom said, her gaze locking onto mine, wary but resolute. "She has a right to know. And it's time."

She shifted in her seat, her hands clenching and unclenching. "Let me put it this way, Sady. Many of the stories you've read in the Bible? The ones about the wrath of God? Most, if not all, weren't *Him*. They were us. Lucifer and I, side by side, destroying the Earth little by little, always hoping to provoke *Him* into a confrontation."

Her voice grew harder. "Sodom and Gomorrah fell under our swords. I taught Cain how to kill. We created so much conflict in the days of the Old Testament—brothers fighting brothers, kingdoms warring with each other, blood spilled over nothing. I could give you a list longer than the entirety of the 401 highway."

I stared at her, unable to speak, my pulse hammering in my ears.

"During the pregnancy, Ramira shared with us everything she knew," Dad finally said, stepping closer. His hand lifted slightly, hesitating, before he finally placed it gently on my arm. "Because of who your mother was—who she *is*—there was always a risk of you being born like the others. But listen, kiddo..."

For a brief moment, a vision of my mother—wearing battle armor, covered in blood, surrounded by the dead—flashed through my mind.

I couldn't help myself.

I stood up and took a step back.

Distance.

I suddenly *needed* distance.

"*He* never came down, did *He*?" My voice was almost expressionless, but my throat burned as I pictured all those lives, all the devastation.

"Please," Dad said, stepping toward me, his arms open, palms up. His eyes were full of a desperate plea. "Your mother has spent millennia making reparations, working tirelessly to atone for her past. You have no idea how much good she has done in the world since the Flood."

Out of the corner of my eye, I saw Mom's muscles tense, her jaw tightening. She never liked it when Dad used words like *sin* or *atonement.* It was as if those words scratched at a wound she refused to let heal.

"So," I practically choked on the words. "How many rights fix a wrong?"

A long pause.

"Wait... what does the Flood have to do with anything?"

Dad hesitated, exchanging a look with Mom, who remained silent, her expression unreadable.

His fingers curled slightly, his voice steady but thick with something heavy.

"There's one more thing we haven't told you."

CHAPTER 21

A rising pressure built in my ears, a steady beat matching the rush of adrenaline flooding my system, my body caught in the space between fight and flight. My fingers curled into the fabric of my sleeves, gripping tight, bracing for whatever came next.

There's one more thing we haven't told you.

Mom cut in, her words biting with warning and love all tangled together. "Sam, can't you see we're overloading her?"

Dad didn't waver. "My love, she has to know." His voice was firm, but not unkind.

The room felt too small. The air, too still.

"Know. What?"I swallowed hard.

And then... silence.

The kind that stretches too long, where the answer is right there, just out of reach—where you already know it's going to change everything.

"Fine." Her voice was cold, mechanical—more like a soldier reciting orders than a mother sharing something personal. She turned to me, her expression unreadable, though something flickered behind her eyes—a shadow of the past, a flicker of pain. "The Nephilim you know today, are not the first. Let's call them the second generation."

"Pardon me?" This took a left turn somewhere, and my mind was reeling to catch up.

"For a time, before the Flood, the Seraphim took human lovers. We still don't know how or why, but despite our Father's punishment, some of them conceived. Not because of the men they chose, but because they were the mothers. Their children—the first Nephilim—weren't like the ones you know today. They were stronger, purer, more like us than the humans who bore them. And for a time, they walked this world as something wholly unique."

A shadow of dread slithered over me, thick and paralyzing. The air felt tighter, pressing in, like the walls themselves were listening.

"So—" I asked carefully, my voice barely above a whisper. "These original Nephilim were... different?"

Mom's gaze turned steely. "They were stronger—three times the size of any human. More powerful than anything else that walked the earth." She drew in a breath, her jaw tightening for the briefest second before she continued. "And they were never meant to exist, and nothing that defies divine law is ever left unchecked."

Her next words came quieter, but no less brutal.

"That's why *He* decided to destroy them."

Something flickered across her face—grief, maybe, or something too deep to name. Her voice wavered, just for a second, before she forced it back into control.

"*He* sent the Flood. Every last child drowned, and their mothers—my sisters—chose to die with them. They would not abandon them for their own safety."

She went still, her breath steady but too controlled, too measured.

"It was Ramira who saved me, by secreting us both away on Noah's Arc."

Silence filled the room, thick and suffocating. The echo of history—of loss—settling into every unspoken word.

Mom's hand trembled as she brushed it over her face, a rare break in her composure. Then, without another word, she got up and left the room, her footsteps echoing down the hall.

I stayed put. So did Dad.

I blinked, my mind scrambling to process what I had just heard. My entire life, I had been taught to fear the vampires—the cursed offspring of Fallen angels. *But now?* Now, the history had become disturbingly more personal.

I was connected to *them*.

They were never meant to exist. *Neither was I.*

We don't fully understand how Luke has managed to create so many of these new Nephilim—the vampires—or why they have the powers they do," Dad admitted, his voice tinged with something I couldn't quite place.

"Nearly two thousand years ago, and a few hundred before I met your mother," he continued. "That was the first time the Grigori encountered them—the first time we realized there was a second generation."

He ran a hand down his face, exhaling slowly. "Back then, we thought it was an anomaly. A handful of them, nothing more. We had no idea what Luke had done, what he had discovered. By the time we fully understood, it was too late to stop it."

My brain was still processing, and it was a minor miracle smoke wasn't coming out of my ears.

"This time, *He* hasn't intervened. There's been no flood, no divine retribution." He shook his head. "For two millennia, we've been waiting for a reckoning that never came. And that means... whatever is happening now? It's different."

He leaned against the counter, rubbing his temple, as if the weight of it all had settled into his bones.

"Why would *He* not do something, if *He* knows?" I demanded. My voice was shriller than I intended. "These Nephilim can't be any less dangerous than the first ones, so why hasn't *He* done anything?"

"That's the question we've been asking ourselves for years." Dad's voice was low, weighted with something I couldn't quite name. "Maybe *He* doesn't care anymore. Maybe *He's* waiting for something—or someone."

A chill crawled up my spine at his words, *stupid child of prophecy probably*, but I stayed silent.

"While these vampires aren't like the original Nephilim," Dad continued, his tone measured, like he was piecing together a puzzle even as he spoke. "There's a connection we can't ignore."

Choosing his words carefully, he hesitated. "The first Nephilim were born of Seraphim mothers—Sera's kind. They weren't supposed to exist, and yet they did, defying every law of creation." His fingers tapped absently against the counter before he went on. "But the second generation... they are different."

His gaze met mine, steady but heavy. "This time, the fathers were the Fallen. And their mothers? Human."

He let that reminder sink in before adding, "We don't know how it changed them, only that it did. That it had to. Whatever made them what they are—whatever gave them their abilities—we have to assume it came from the Fallen."

I stiffened. "Wait, what?" A sense of unease coiled tightly within me as I wrapped my arms around myself, fingers gripping my elbows as if bracing against something I couldn't control. "You mean to say that I have something in common with them?"

Dad exhaled, rubbing a hand over his jaw. "Sera's past... was in her blood. And her blood was, is, in you."

"Sady baby." Mom's voice cut through the air from the doorway, steady but weighted.

I turned to face her. She stood tall, not really composed—but I could see it, the tension coiled beneath the surface, the way her hands curled into loose fists at her sides.

"You need to understand something," she said, stepping forward. "Yes, I am Seraphim. But I am also Fallen."

She let that sit between us, like a boundary I hadn't known was there until now.

I turned, my breath catching. She stood there, tension had turned to trembling, tears streaming silently down her face.

Mom never cried.

Seeing her like this—crumbling under the weight of her past, the fear of the growing rift between us—was beyond disturbing.

Dad stepped closer, his voice quiet but firm. "We knew what bringing you into this world meant, Sady. You were the first of your kind—at least, as far as we know. A child of both Seraphim and Grigori blood. We had no way of knowing what that would make you, what it would mean for you."

His jaw tightened, fingers curling at his sides. "But we knew one thing for certain. If Lucifer ever found out about you, he'd want you."

A chill ran through me.

Mom inhaled shakily, forcing the emotion from her face, replacing it with something steadier—something fierce.

"We swore to keep you safe," she said, her voice firm despite the raw edge beneath it. "From the moment we knew you existed, we knew what you would mean to him—what he would try to do if he ever found out."

Her fingers curled into fists, not in anger, but in resolve. "So we did the only thing we could. We disappeared. Ramira, your father, and I—we erased every trace of where we had been, covered our tracks so thoroughly that even your father's brothers couldn't find us."

She fixed me with an unwavering stare. "And we kept the pregnancy a secret. No one could know. Not Heaven, not Hell, not anyone. Because if they did, we knew we'd never get the chance to raise you before someone tried to take you from us."

She took slow, deliberate steps forward, as if each one carried centuries of weight. "We stayed in Ramira's fortress while she ventured out, searching for answers to questions we didn't even know how to ask." She reached Dad's side, looking up at him briefly before continuing. "She promised to return in time for your birth. To this day, we don't know where she went or what she saw. Only that, almost as soon as the labor pains began, she arrived. And at 11:11 p.m., you took your first breath in this world."

I stared at her, my pulse pounding in my ears.

Memories that shouldn't have been mine stirred at the edges of my mind.

Ramira had been the first voice I heard inside my mother's womb—not just a presence, but a pull, a whisper in my mind, calling me forward. It was her voice that coaxed me from the quiet, that told me it was time and that it was safe. It was her hands that reached for me, pulling me from the darkness and into the light.

I remembered. *Everything.*

It was how I knew—my body had released a Surge so powerful, it had knocked Dad off his feet.

Ramira had only just barely been able to withstand it in order to bring me into this world without dropping me.

Dad's voice was softer now, but no less urgent. "Sady doll, when you reached up with your tiny hands and grasped Ramira's finger, it triggered a vision of the future. The year 2012. Your eighteenth birthday. This year."

A lump formed in my throat. "What did she see?"

Dad hesitated. "The future was hazy, blanketed in a strange mist. That meant what she saw wasn't absolute. It could change."

"Dad. What exactly did she see?" I clenched my fists.

"She saw that your life has three intertwining but distinctly different paths," he said, his voice thick with something unreadable. "Each one showing you at its center."

"So that's what's freaking you guys out?" I shook my head. The words didn't quite connect. *What was I missing?* "Three paths? That's a maze, not a future. What are we supposed to do with that? It's another damn riddle"

Dad exhaled slowly, his gaze meeting mine, weighted with something deeper than just concern.

"No, everlasting love of our hearts," he murmured, his voice quieter now, more careful. "That's just the beginning."

He reached for my hands, his touch hesitant, almost as if he expected me to pull away.

I let him take my fingertips.

A cold sense of foreboding settled over me.

I wasn't going to like what came next.

"She saw that no matter which path you choose..." He swallowed, then forced the words out. "You will change."

"What do you mean, I change?" My voice wavered, fear with frustration growing by the minute. The vibes they were giving me right now were all wrong. "Can we cut to the chase, please?"

"Sady baby," Mom's voice trembled, fragile in a way I had never heard before. "One of the paths she saw you walking showed you transforming—into one of *them*."

The words hit like a bullet, ricocheting through my mind, lodging deep, refusing to fade.

One of them.

One of them.

That was a sucker punch if there ever was one.

I slumped back into the armchair, my limbs suddenly weightless, my mind blank. The edges of the room blurred, like the walls had stretched further away, leaving me floating in some vast, empty space where nothing made sense anymore.

"So, I just don't choose that path, problem solved, right?"

The only sound was the slow, rhythmic ticking of the hallway clock. Each second dragged, stretched, pressed down on me, a reminder that time hadn't stopped even though it felt like it should have.

My parents said nothing. They just sat there, giving me space, waiting. Not pushing, not explaining. Just watching, their silence heavier than words ever could be.

Their truth pressed against my chest, thick and suffocating, like a vise slowly tightening.

I couldn't think.

Couldn't *breathe.*

All this time we were running from them. Hiding from them. And they had known this would happen—that one day, I might turn into the very thing we had been running from? The very things they'd trained me to fight?

"Sady," Dad murmured, his voice gentle but steady. "Please, say something."

I blinked, barely registering the sound of his voice.

What was there to say?

That I was suddenly, absolutely terrified? That every second of my life now felt like a countdown to something I couldn't control?

I swallowed hard, my throat tight, dry. "So... what now?"

Dad and Mom exchanged a look.

I hated when they did that—the telepathic conversation, the things left unsaid. It made me feel like a bystander in my own life, and right now, more than anything, I needed to feel like I was part of this.

Mom exhaled, slow and measured, her shoulders stiff. "Now, we wait."

The words landed like a stone in my gut.

"Wait for what?"

For something to change? For me to wake up one day and realize I wasn't *me* anymore?

I didn't like the sound of that.

Not one bit.

Dad was perched on the edge of his seat, his knuckles white where they gripped his knees. Mom had slipped to the floor at his feet, her head resting against his leg. Her usual fierce presence was subdued, replaced by something gentler, more vulnerable and tired. They were both waiting for me to react, the air thick with apprehension and... something else I couldn't name.

I was the first to break the silence.

"Nah, I'm not waiting." I said, my voice flat and resolute. "I want to talk to Ramira."

"Sady baby, I've already texted Ramira," Mom said, her voice taut but composed. "All we can do now is wait for her to respond."

"Wait?" I echoed, incredulous. "You want me to just sit around while you wait for a text message? Really?"

I was already getting to my feet, heading for the garden with purpose. Kicking off my shoes and pulling off my socks, I let the cool kitchen floors connect with my bare feet. "Finding Ramira with technology could take weeks. Do you two even know what timelines we're dealing with?"

Their quick glance at each other was all the confirmation I needed. They were worried, but they didn't have answers. Fine. If they couldn't act, I would.

To hell with waiting.

I was going to find Ramira *my way*.

I stormed outside, crossing the lawn to the large white oak tree that stood solemnly in the corner of our backyard. The chilled grass gave way to cool earth under my feet. I could hear their footsteps behind me, and I didn't need to turn around to know they were following. As I sat down cross-legged on the grass, they stopped short, knowing what I was about to do.

Dad's voice was measured, but firm. "Sady doll, please, you don't have to do this." He stepped forward, his hand reaching toward me like he thought he could stop me with words. "You're not strong enough for this."

THE HELL I'M NOT.

A low hum of energy pulsed outward as I powered up my shield. Dad barely had time to stumble back, startled by the force of it.

I crossed my arms, arching a brow. "Oh, I'm *sorry*, did either of you wake up with my powers this morning? No? Then maybe take a seat and let the child of a stupid prophecy handle this."

Seeing my determination and knowing I had inherited Mom's stubbornness, they sat down a few paces away, observant and tense.

My emotional state gave me strength, but it also made it harder to focus. I closed my eyes, centering myself, reaching out cautiously at first. My focus was clumsy, but it grew steadier with each breath. I pushed farther than I ever had before, feeling my senses stretch beyond the limits I thought possible.

I wanted to tell Mom to take notes, but before the words could form, I felt the soft air stir. Peeking through one eye, I saw her already sitting with pen and paper in hand. Dad was crouched nearby, poised to catch me if I fainted.

I closed my eyes again and pushed harder.

"There's more now. I count twenty-eight vampires in New York," I murmured, feeling the energy signatures of each.

I paused, tilting my head as I pushed my senses farther, stretching into the unseen.

Clusters of vampires flickered across my awareness—scattered, moving, most in small groups of one to three. Their presence felt prickling, restless, like embers waiting to ignite. But one stood apart.

The lone one in New Orleans burned like a fading beacon, isolated yet distinct, as if his muted mauves wanted to be found.

Then—something else.

A presence unlike the others, tugging across my awareness like a comet. It was *her* again.

"That strange moss-green with gold flecks... near somewhere in Mexico," I murmured, my focus locking onto it. "Bloody hell, she feels so much more elegant than anything I've ever sensed before, and she's moving fast. Something's changed about her, but I can't figure out what."

Neither of them interrupted. They didn't ask questions.

They just listened.

As I expanded my focus farther south, the strain started to creep in, but there were fewer humans to distract me. This was the farthest I'd ever reached, and I could feel the edges of my awareness fraying.

Still, I pressed on.

Reaching into South America, I almost missed it.

Buried deep in the Amazon was a cluster of those strange, luscious moss-green auras—similar to the one in Mexico, but not quite the same. There were dozens, at least fifty, each distinct yet muffled, as if wrapped in layers of something impenetrable.

Then, I felt it.

Something else.

A force so immense, so deliberate, it made my breath hitch. It wasn't just shielding them—it was concealing them, wrapping the entire area in something dense and unyielding.

I could sense them—faint, distant, just out of reach—but whenever I tried to push deeper, the presence pushed *back*.

And whoever it belonged to... was powerful enough to keep me out.

"Dad, I think I found another Grigori!" I blurted, my voice taut with strain.

Dad snapped into focus. "Slow down. What do you feel?" His tone was calm but insistent, his presence grounding me.

"He's hot," I said, brow furrowing as I tried to focus. Sweat beaded on my forehead. "Like, *really* hot."

Mom, who had been silent until now, let out a dry hum. "Hot, huh?"

I groaned. "Not *hot* hot, *temperature* hot. Can we *not* do this right now?"

Dad shot Mom a look, but she just shrugged, unimpressed.

"Alright," Dad said, refocusing. "Keep going."

It's like he's oozing sunshine. His color is a bronze-gold flecked with deep brown. But seriously, this dude is just radiating power."

I drew in a quick breath, forcing down the sting of embarrassment. The energy around me pulsed, a drumbeat in my veins that threatened to shake me apart. But I held steady, pushing my senses outward, feeling along the edges of the invisible world.

I inched forward, testing the boundaries of my reach, every step a quiet defiance against the fear clawing at my composure.

"Careful. Feather-touch only." Mom's voice cut through the mental haze, grounding me just enough to keep control.

Then, it happened.

That golden-bronze presence, so distinct, so overwhelmingly powerful, nearly jolted me out of my focus. The warmth, the depth of it—it *had* to be Grigori. Unlike anything else I'd ever sensed but felt like Dad. Only amplified by like a thousand.

A sudden rush of heat rippled through me.

My breath caught.

He had sensed me.

I tried to pull back—fast and smooth—but I wasn't fast enough.

The presence shifted, locking onto me, and before I could retreat completely, a single word slipped through the connection.

Like he already knew me.

My lips parted, the name escaping in a whisper.

"Remi."

The sharp intake of breath from both my parents nearly shattered my concentration, but I gritted my teeth and pushed forward. *I couldn't stop now.* There was too much at stake.

For nearly an hour, I stretched my awareness farther and farther, the strain building until my temples throbbed. The edges of my focus began to blur, but then, at last, I felt her.

Far north, in Scotland, on a small island in the Orkneys of all places.

The sensation of her presence tangling with mine was like a long-forgotten melody. Her oxblood aura had softened over the years, no trace of the obsidian, and now mingling with luminous turquoise veins that swirled through it—just like her piercing eyes.

RAMIRA?

My voice, the telepathic one that is trembled, both in relief and exhaustion. The moment my words reached her, there was silence—so complete, so unnatural, it felt like the world itself had frozen.

Then, chaos.

SADY?!

Her reaction was visceral. I could feel the urgency rolling off her, thick and unrestrained. Ramira—the one who always had answers, who always seemed one step ahead—sounded unprepared.

HOW DID YOU—WHERE ARE YOU?! WHAT'S HAPPENING?!

Her voice lashed through my mind like a whip, and yet unsteady, brimming with something I'd never heard from her before—curiosity laced with fear.

I wasn't sure what shocked me more—her panic or the fact that I could feel it through the tether we'd just formed. *I've never been able to feel her emotions before.*

RAMIRA, THIS WHOLE CHILD OF PROPHECY CRAP, THAT'S HAPPENING. OR AT LEAST THAT IS WHAT MY PARENTS ARE FEARING. THEY ONLY JUST TOLD ME. SURPRISE.

A sudden crash echoed through the connection, followed by a hissed curse. She'd dropped something—a glass, maybe? Whatever it was, I caught a brief flash of light, reflecting off what looked like dark stone walls and the deep red of wine splattering across heather blue tiles.

She was moving fast now, her presence flickering in and out like static interference.

WHAT DO YOU MEAN? EXPLAIN. NOW.

Her tone was ragged, uneven—completely unlike the aunt I knew.

I hesitated.

Even with everything we'd been through tonight, I hadn't expected this. Hadn't expected to rattle her, to catch her this off guard.

Ramira had been my mother's rock. She was the cool-headed but always kind, the healer of our family. No matter how bad things got, she never panicked. *Until now.*

TELL ME EVERYTHING.

I did.

I let it all pour out, unfiltered. I told her about what my parents had revealed, about the vampires gathering in New York, about the tepid temperature and mauve vibes from New Orleans Boy, the massacre in Mozambique, and about the elegant moss-green aura moving fast in Mexico. And finally, about the other presence. *The Grigori.*

The one buried deep in the Amazon.

At that, Ramira stilled.

I felt it in the way her energy shifted, like a thread pulled too tight.

THAT IS NOT POSSIBLE.

Her voice was barely a whisper, while my heart kicked into a sprint.

WHAT'S NOT POSSIBLE? YA WANNA BE MORE SPECIFIC OUT OF ALL OF THOSE OPTIONS?

Another beat of silence.

I WILL LEAVE RIGHT NOW. HEADING SOUTH FIRST, TO CONFIRM WHAT YOU FOUND IN THE SOUTH.

I quickly gave Ramira the information and retreated, when the strain became unbearable. But the moment I started to pull back, something new slammed into my awareness.

New Orleans boy.

Wait—he shouldn't be able to do that.

The intrusion was laughably clumsy, his effort like a child fumbling for a light switch in the dark. I easily sidestepped his probing, only to stumble straight into something far more unnerving.

H*er.*

She brushed against me, and a shiver rolled through my being—unsettlingly familiar. A resonance, rich with gold and moss-green, like hearing the echo of a song I should have known the words to. It pulsed through me, deep and insistent, sinking into my bones like she was trying to give me a boost home.

For a moment, I almost reached back. *Almost.*

Then the connection slipped, dissolving like mist between my fingers.

But the feeling remained. Like a name on the tip of my tongue. Like a promise waiting to be kept.

It was fast. *Too fast.*

A warning flared in the back of my mind, and I had no choice but to retreat, throwing out a false trail to mislead it. My senses reeled, the sheer force of the interaction leaving me breathless.

The moment my focus snapped, the light-headedness hit like a freight train. My blood pressure plummeted, and the edges of my vision went dark. A relentless thudding overtook my senses, drowning out everything but the ragged, uneven breaths I couldn't seem to control.

Was I crying?

I lifted my shaking fingers to my cheek, staring in disbelief at the crimson streak staining my skin. *Well, that wasn't—normal.*

"Sera, her eyes!"

Dad's strangled cry cut through the static in my brain, but I couldn't react. Couldn't move.

A slow, sickening dread coiled in my stomach as I rubbed at my face again, in disbelief, as if I could scrub away whatever *wrongness* was happening to me. But all I managed to do was smear the blood further, the crimson staining my fingertips, my palm, streaking down my wrist.

I felt the warmth of it, the way it clung, slick and unrelenting.

My body wasn't supposed to do this.

The world around me tilted.

My vision warped, and then my body swayed, struggling to keep up with the disorienting shift in my senses.

My body ached.

Not just from exhaustion, but from something deeper, something wrong. My veins felt too tight, like something was threading itself through me, coiling around my ribs, burrowing beneath my skin.

A low, distant hum crawled through my skull, an unnatural vibration just beneath the surface of my thoughts. Not a voice, not a presence—just pressure, like something waiting.

I shuddered violently.

I needed—

A new wave of nausea slammed into me, cutting off the thought, and tumbled backwards.

"Sady!"

Steady hands caught me just before I hit the ground.

The last thing I saw before the darkness swallowed me whole was my mother's face—wide-eyed, her lips parted in horror—she was never scared.

Chapter 22

Waking up in my own bed, still in the same clothes, the worst headache of my life hit me like a freight train.

Seriously, someone please surgically remove the proverbial axe lodged in my skull—thanks.

Mom? Dad?

Ouch. Even reaching hurts. *What fresh hell is this?* My throat ached. I couldn't even croak out to call for them. Not that it mattered—I could hear them—they were at my bedside in seconds.

Through my wincing eyes, I caught sight of them, and the state they were in shocked me. They looked like gods who'd wandered too close to humanity and emerged looking like extras from a disaster movie. Still otherworldly, but in a hungover sort of way.

Dad looked like a train wreck—and his face... his face looked different. The angles of his cheekbones stood out more than usual, his skin paler, stretched tight with exhaustion. Had he... lost weight?

Mom wasn't much better. Her normally sleek, glossy hair was tangled, strands escaping the loose braid over her shoulder like she hadn't bothered to fix it in days. The deep glow she always carried, that quiet, effortless radiance, was gone—her skin dull, almost gray, like the exhaustion had drained the color right out of her. Her eyes were swollen and puffy, which means that unless she had developed an allergy I didn't know about, she had been crying.

"Here, drink some water."

Didn't have to tell me twice. I drained the glass in record time, the cool liquid soothing my raw throat.

"How long have I been—?" I hesitated, unsure if I even wanted to hear the answer.

"Sady baby," Mom's voice was barely a whisper. "It's been four days."

Four. Days.

I blinked, my sluggish brain struggling to catch up. Had I really been out for that long? It felt like I had just closed my eyes, yet my body ached like I hadn't moved in days.

Before I could piece it together, Dad's voice cut through the haze.

"You barely moved," he murmured, his tone uncharacteristically grim. "Four days, Sady. You slept like the dead."

Something flickered across his face—something raw.

"We kept checking," Mom admitted, her voice quieter, rougher than usual. "Making sure you were still breathing."

A chill ran through me.

No tossing, no turning. No dreams. Just an all-consuming blackness that I was only now clawing my way out of. I had slept through *everything*.

I pushed through the fog in my brain. "Ramira?" My head throbbed at the effort.

"She's on her way," Dad said. "But she's taking a detour through South America to check out something you showed her."

A detour? Ah yes, memory was fuzzy but that I did remember.

I squeezed my eyes shut, trying to grab onto something—anything—concrete in my mind. But everything was fragmented, slipping through my fingers like grains of sand.

"Uhm, I don't remember much... My mind is still super foggy. Can you fill me in a little? And before you ask—no, I don't want to rest first."

They exchanged a glance, hesitant but resigned.

Dad leaned forward slightly. "You said the word *Remi.* Do you recall anything?"

The name sent a ripple through my mind, stirring something just beneath the surface.

"Sort of. Maybe." I struggled to piece it together, my voice sluggish. "I felt... bronze-gold, deep velvety browns—powerful, steady. And I think—no, I'm sure—he was shielding something. A whole tangle of those odd moss greens, tucked beneath everything else. He felt... a little like you, Dad. Only way more powerful. Sorry."

Dad didn't flinch at that, but Mom reached for his hand, the strain in her posture unmistakable.

"Mom, he sensed me. I was careful, but he knew I was there. He chose to send that one word. *Remi.*"

Silence.

The kind that made my skin prickle.

I swallowed hard. "Dad, who is Remi?" My voice wavered as a disquieting apprehension filled the room. I didn't like it—any of it. "Wait, I remember... blood. Who was bleeding?"

"You," Mom said, holding up a small, blood-soaked towel. "The strain of your search took its toll and triggered a minor ocular hemorrhage."

"Wow, Mom," I half-giggled before a bolt of pain shot through my skull with pinpoint precision, right behind my eyelids. "Glad you're making it sound so casual."

"From what we can tell, your eyes have already healed," She continued, walking to the window. "But they might still be tender for a few more hours. Maybe longer."

"Oh, well, in that case..." I muttered, trying to sound exasperated, though even moving slightly triggered more pinpricks of pain. I gave up and tried to lay as still as possible. "So, who is Remi, and why are you both so surprised to hear his name?"

Dad began to speak, and Mom became very still.

That... wasn't like her.

Mom was a flurry of movement and energy, always. Seeing her frozen in place sent a ripple of unease through me. It struck me—*not for the first time*—how much I didn't know about my parents. They had been on this earth since Adam and Eve, their lives stretching across millennia even before then. The sheer magnitude of their stories could fill volumes, and even then, it would likely take decades to tell them all.

"Nearly a hundred years after we met, still trying to keep off Luke's radar, our travels took us to what is now called Russia," Dad said, his voice calm and measured, as though recounting a memory from someone else's life. "We built a small cottage in a very remote part toward the northeast—what must be Siberia now. It was the kind of place where winters felt eternal, but the summers, brief as they were, seemed almost magical."

I could almost see it as he spoke—the isolation, the endless snow-covered expanse, and then, fleeting bursts of nature when the world thawed. Having had enough telepathic bedtime stories, my imagination was above average, but this time, the pain of trying to reach made me flinch.

"We started a small farm there," he continued. "Nothing grand, but it was enough. A vegetable garden to see us through the seasons, a few horses for roaming around the hills and fields, goats for milk, a few cows and some chickens for eggs. After years of running, hiding, and living in shadows, it gave us something tangible to hold onto. Something that was ours."

Mom nodded, a faint smile playing at her lips, though her eyes held a distant, almost wistful look. "We learned to till the soil by hand, to coax life from the frozen earth. It wasn't easy, but it kept us grounded. The goats were endlessly stubborn, the chickens constantly tried to escape, and the horses acted like they were above it all—like they were doing us a favor by letting us ride them. But it was worth it."

She paused, then cast Dad a knowing look. "Though I still don't forgive you for the great dietary experiment."

Dad smirked, completely unrepentant. "I maintain that it was a noble endeavor."

I raised an eyebrow. "What, exactly, was this *noble endeavor*?"

Mom sighed dramatically. "Your father had this brilliant idea that if I just cut meat out of my diet, I'd feel 'lighter, healthier, more in tune with nature.'" She made air quotes with her fingers. "Like some kind of angelic detox, which, for the record, is easy for him to say, considering he's been a vegetarian since before it was trendy."

Dad shrugged. "Look, we both came to earth from the same place. You'd think what worked for one of us would work for the other."

Mom shot him a flat look. "That logic is flawed, Sam."

"Well, technically, we never tested it long enough to be sure," Dad muttered.

Mom's eyes narrowed. "I almost ate one of the horses."

I choked on my laugh. "Wait. Almost?"

She smirked. "Let's just say the chickens weren't the only ones trying to escape the farm."

Dad groaned. "One bad night, and suddenly I'm the villain."

I shook my head, "I love that you two turned a quiet farm life into complete chaos."

Mom grinned. "Oh, darling daughter, that was just the beginning."

A strange pang stirred in my chest—longing for something I'd never experienced. I imagined them there, two supernatural beings pretending to be mortals, tending to a farm, chasing stubborn goats, and arguing over dietary experiments. Not having to move every year. The image was oddly peaceful, despite the absurdity of it all.

"Okay, but what does this have to do with Remi?" My patience was wearing thin. My head still throbbed, and the slow, cryptic storytelling wasn't helping. "Seriously, Dad. Get to the point."

He arched a brow, clearly unimpressed with my tone. "I'm getting to it, kiddo. But forgive me if my memory's a little rusty—this isn't exactly a story I've had to tell in the last two thousand years. Or ever for that matter."

Mom still hadn't moved. Her arms were wrapped tightly around herself, her posture unusually rigid. The tension in her stance made me uneasy. Whatever this story was, it clearly didn't have a happy ending.

"Honestly, it was a quiet life," Dad said, a faint smile playing at his lips.

Mom snorted. "Sure. If you ignore all the attempted murder."

Dad sighed. "Well, relatively quiet."

Mom's snort grew more pronounced.

"Uhm, well..." He shot her a pointed look before continuing. "We were still in the honeymoon phase, so maybe quiet is the wrong word. Anyway, one day, while I was out in the field with the horses, I felt it—the air changed. A SURGE in the wind. I knew immediately what it meant."

My breath hitched. I already knew the answer, but I asked anyway. "A Grigori?"

He nodded. "A Watcher was descending."

The Grigori. The Watchers. My father's kind. The name alone gave me goosebumps.

I knew of them, though Dad rarely spoke about his past in detail. He had once been a Watcher himself before he met my mother. The Grigori were volunteers, chosen to descend to Earth and act as God's eyes and ears. They were meant to *watch*—never interfere, never take sides. Even when they witnessed horrors, injustice, or suffering, they remained unmoved. Uninvolved. They were also the only angels who kept their wings upon arrival.

I thought about that—what it meant to be forced into a role of eternal inaction, to observe but never intervene. To hold yourself above the world while watching it crumble.

Mom's voice cut through my thoughts. "In other words, they've always thought they were better than everyone else," she said dryly, as if plucking the words straight from my mind.

Dad shot her an exasperated look but didn't argue.

"The moment he started descending, blocking out the sun with his wings, I knew it was him," Dad continued, his voice quieter now. "I reached out to Sera, warning her not to move. Not to attack. She was—" he hesitated, casting Mom a wary glance. "Well, let's just say that not only was her temper was worse back then, but she was on constant alert. It's a miracle she didn't fry her nervous system."

Mom rolled her eyes. "I wasn't that bad."

Dad ignored her. "His shadow grew larger as he descended, and when he finally landed, the ground trembled slightly beneath his weight. I looked up, and as he stepped into the light, I recognized him instantly." He swallowed, his voice thickening with emotion. "It was Remiel. My closest friend. My brother-in-faith. We were inseparable once—our bond stronger than blood or belief."

I stayed silent, sensing there was more.

"Remiel was shocked to find me alive," Dad went on, his voice tight. "The Grigori believed I had died in battle. Blood had been found at the site. The bodies of a few Vampires. And two shredded, almost beyond recognition wings. My wings."

I sucked in a breath, my mind conjuring a gruesome image of two bloodied wings torn from his back despite my best efforts not to. "So, that's why they thought you were—?"

"Dead," Dad confirmed. "The others assumed my body had been taken. Or worse—eaten."

I grimaced. "Ugh. Gross. Are you serious?"

Dad's lips twitched, but he didn't laugh. "Remiel had been amongst those who found them. He knew immediately they were mine."

Silence settled between us.

"When he saw me standing there, alive, we were both stunned," Dad said. "We embraced—overwhelmed, relieved—but I didn't have time to explain before he sensed your mother in the cottage. His reaction was instant. He leapt into the air and took off toward the house, shoving me behind him. Protecting me."

Mom's body tensed. I could feel the shift in her energy, cutting as a blade.

"Watchers aren't supposed to interfere with humans," Dad explained. "But there were no divine laws preventing them from engaging with the Fallen. And Remiel—" he hesitated, choosing his words carefully. "Remiel had no love for them. Especially after what he thought happened to me."

I already knew where this was going.

"He didn't hesitate," Dad said grimly.

Mom's arms tightened around herself, her jaw set like stone. "Good thing I'm always combat-ready," she muttered. "He announced his hostile, albeit protective, intentions."

"It took me a moment to catch up," Dad admitted, rubbing his jaw.

"Just in time too," Mom said flatly. "Another second, and I would have taken his wings."

Dad winced. "Yeah. That would've been the worst possible outcome."

"He was trying to kill me," Mom shot back, her tone steely. "I defended myself. And, for the record, I was very measured."

Dad snorted. "Measured? You broke two of his ribs, dislocated his shoulder, and nearly crushed his windpipe."

Mom shrugged. "That's measured for me."

Glancing between them, I tried to fully grasp the magnitude of what they were saying.

"I knew who he was the moment I laid eyes on him," Mom said, her voice quieter now. "Even in his anger, I felt it—love. Not for me. But for you, Sam."

Something in Dad's demeanor softened.

"That's why I didn't kill him," she admitted. "Not because I was merciful, not because I couldn't. But because I knew you loved him."

The air between them shifted. Something unspoken passed in that glance, something ancient and deep and far beyond me.

"And you didn't," Dad said with a sigh, running a hand through his hair. "By the time I intervened, you'd both done enough damage to leave a lasting impression—on each other."

I exhaled slowly. "So... what happened after that?"

Mom's features tightened, her tone dipping into something darker. "That, my dearest offspring, is where the real story begins."

I blinked, trying to picture the scene: my mother and a powerful Grigori locked in combat, a deadly misunderstanding that could've ended in disaster. I knew all too well how fast our kind—well, their kind, plus my weird hybrid self—could move. There wouldn't have been time for words to stop them.

"I managed to calm him down," Dad said, his voice softening, though something dark flickered in his expression. "But not with words. I knew they wouldn't be enough—not in that state."

I tilted my head, intrigued. "What do you mean?"

His gaze turned distant, as though he were reliving it. "He was too locked into his instincts," Dad said. "Too certain that Sera was a threat. So, I did the only thing I could think of. I reached out and, in the strongest, most focused blast I could manage, I showed him the last hundred years of my life with your mother."

I frowned. "You mean telepathically?"

He nodded. "The way we communicate with our minds... it was an ability we thought we'd lost when we left Heaven. It was only through your mother that I rediscovered how to use it. Our bond reignited something I thought was gone forever. To this day I'm convinced that love was the key to unlocking that lost power."

"And that actually worked?" I asked, skeptical but fascinated.

Dad's smile was small, almost wry. "More than I expected. Remiel staggered back, completely overwhelmed—not just by the flood of information but by the emotions. The love your mother and I shared, the life we'd built together... it shook him. He saw the battle where Sera and I fought side by side against Luke, the moment my wings were damaged beyond what even an angel could endure. I could've kept them—broken, useless reminders of what I once was—but instead, your mother helped me let them go. In that moment, Remiel understood why I had chosen this path. Why I had chosen her."

I glanced at Mom, who had been uncharacteristically quiet for the last few minutes. A slight flush colored her cheeks, but whether it was from embarrassment, frustration, or something else, I couldn't tell—but it was rare to see her anything less than composed.

"And then?" I prompted, leaning forward.

"He stood down," Dad said evenly. "But not before giving your mother a look I still remember to this day."

"What kind of look?" I asked, caught between fascination and disbelief.

Mom finally broke her silence, a smirk tugging at her lips. "The kind that says, I underestimated you, and now I'm annoyed about it."

Dad chuckled. "That sounds about right. But that moment wasn't just about understanding—it was the beginning of something deeper. He stayed with us after that. For a while."

"We shared food, stories, and enjoyed each other's company," Mom added, her voice softening at the memory. "On Remi's last night with us, he agreed to keep our life—and our love—a secret. No other Grigori would know."

Dad's hand found hers instinctively, their fingers intertwining. The touch seemed to steady them both. The history between them was so palpable it felt almost intrusive to witness.

"Okay, but then why were you surprised to hear Remi's name?" I asked, breaking the silence. "By all accounts, he sounds like a good guy. So, what is with all the angst?

Dad's jaw tightened, the memory flickering across his face. "Moments after Remi took to the air, he spotted movement in the woods. At first, it was subtle—branches shifting, shadows darting—but then he realized what it was. The Fallen. And their offspring. The moment he understood, he didn't hesitate. He turned mid-flight and shot straight back toward our home."

A chill ran down my spine. The story had shifted, taking on a darker, more foreboding tone. Without realizing it, I pulled the blanket tighter around myself, as if that could shield me from the past.

"Remiel landed just outside the front steps, hoping he had arrived in time to warn us," Dad continued. "But he was too late. We had already been surrounded. Nearly twenty of the damned offspring, led by five Fallen." His voice hardened. "It was the first and only time we'd seen them gather in such large numbers. At least until more recent years. Our Fallen brothers, standing alongside their monstrous creations."

Mom's jaw tightened. "And with your father still adjusting to a body without wings, we were not equipped for that fight. We were outnumbered. Vulnerable."

The admission grated on her, and I could tell she hated saying it.

"It was Remi who turned the tide in our favor," Dad said, his attention shifting to the window, as if he could still see it. "He leapt back into the air, hovering above the cottage. I only had seconds to react—just enough time to grab Sera and hit the ground."

"He used an old technique your father had taught him," Mom added, her tone grim and laced with a touch of envy. "One I had never seen before."

Dad nodded. "A pulse—the ability to focus a blast of energy through the force of our wings. Modern science would call it a sonic boom."

I sucked in a breath. "You mean—"

"The sheer force of it blew the roof clean off the cottage," Dad interrupted. "Shattered the windows. Splintered the wood. Sent debris flying."

Mom's smile was thin with memories of frustration. "It didn't kill them. But it did hurt them."

"The surprise alone gave us an advantage," Dad added.

I could picture it—the battle unfolding in a ruined cottage, the air thick with dust and power, wings spread against the sky.

"You should have seen it," Dad murmured, almost to himself. "The moment Remiel descended with his wings unfurled, the sun behind him... for a brief second, it was as if he carried the light of our *Father Himself*."

Awe and terror curled through my chest. I imagined it—this celestial warrior, radiating divine fury, striking down the creatures that had come to kill them.

And yet, despite the sound of victory, I already knew—this was not where the story ended.

"Abbadon and Dumah were in charge—," Mom said, her tone carrying that signature backhanded compliment. "I knew them from before, and they were none too pleased to find me alive. But they didn't waste time dwelling on the past. The moment they recovered from their surprise, they pressed the attack—only this time, their focus shifted to the strongest threat. The Grigori."

Dad nodded solemnly. "Remiel held the line, using every ounce of his strength to shield us from the onslaught."

Mom's posture shifted, her fingers unconsciously brushing the space just above her shoulder blades—where her wings had once been. Her voice softened, tinged with something I couldn't quite place. "I still feel them sometimes, Sady baby. The weight of them, the heat. They weren't just for flight."

She exhaled slowly, her eyes distant. "As a Seraphim, my wings were weapons. Six of them. Each one with a purpose. The upper pair—pure force, able to cut through the wind like blades. The middle, a shield, strong enough to withstand the strongest blows. And the lower?" She let out a breath that wasn't quite a sigh. "Fire. Pure, unrelenting flame."

She looked at me then, something unreadable in her expression. "Each strike was a burst of fire, each beat of air laced with searing heat. I led with flame, carving through our enemies, shielding those behind me."

Her fingers curled slightly at her sides. "And when I Fell, I lost more than just my place in Heaven."

Dad's expression darkened. "With his wings on our side, our enemies lost their advantage. He had already cut down two of the Fallen. And for a moment, it seemed like we might survive."

A flicker of pain crossed his face, his hands clenching as if his body still remembered the fight. "But just as hope returned, Dumah raised a horn—a strange, ancient thing, unlike anything we'd ever seen on Earth—and blew into it."

He paused, his gaze distant, haunted. "We hadn't heard a horn like that since *Heaven*, when we stood together, preparing for battle. We didn't know it had survived the Fall."

A cold ripple spread through me. "What kind of sound?"

Dad's jaw tightened. "One that echoed across the entire valley."

A beat of silence stretched between us.

"And then?" I asked, my voice barely above a whisper.

"Sera was wounded," Dad continued, his tone taut with controlled emotion. "Barely standing."

"And you," Mom cut in, her gaze flashing with annoyance, "were fool enough to let your guard down protecting my weakened side."

Dad didn't argue. The grim set of his mouth said enough.

"We could've held our own," he admitted, "until—"

"He appeared." Mom spat the words, her voice thick with rage. "On the steps of our house."

A chill ran down my spine at the venom in her tone.

I blinked. "*He*? Like—as in *God*?"

Chapter 23

Dad let out a soft, almost incredulous chuckle, his lips tugging into a strained smile. "No, Sady doll. Not our *Father*. If it had been, trust me, this would be a very different story."

"Then who?" I asked, my thoughts spinning as I tried to piece it together. "Who was it?"

Mom's fists clenched at her sides. "Someone I hoped never to see again." Her voice was ice, and unyielding. "His power over the Fallen was suffocating. The moment he appeared, it was as if the very air on the battlefield froze."

"Was it Luci—"

"No, but his presence was immense," Dad admitted, his shoulders tightening.

Mom rolled her eyes, though the bravado didn't quite hide the underlying tremor in her voice. "That wasn't presence. That was his overinflated ego, radiating across the field like a damn thundercloud."

I groaned, exasperation bubbling over. "So, who the hell was it? Why do you two always have to be so cryptic?"

When he spoke again, almost reluctant, to say the name out loud. "It was Azazel."

"His hunting party had actually been tracking Grigori," Dad muttered, his words dripping with loathing. "He had come for

Remiel."

A pause, thick and heavy.

"But he was delighted to find us. It was like a three-for-one special for him"

I blinked. "Delighted?"

Mom nodded grimly. "There's much I could say about Azazel, but for now, let it be enough that he never saw our Father's punishment as banishment—only as an opportunity for more violence. He had always been cruel, loving nothing more than unsettling his enemies... taunting them."

Dad's features contorted into something entirely unpleasant, the likes of which I had never seen. "And taunt, he did."

Her voice dropped into a venomous imitation. "'Well, if it isn't my little errant sister... and who does she have with her but two of our Grigori cousins? My, oh my.'"

I froze, the pieces locking into place. "He called you sister?"

Mom's lip curled. "Only in the loosest sense. We were of the same rank once—long before the Rebellion. Each of us had our own battalions to lead. But his loyalty to Luke came from a much darker place than mine. When the gates of Heaven closed to us, he delighted in tormenting humans, enacting Luke's twisted form of justice."

Dad's grip tightened on Mom's shoulder—a silent anchor. "When Azazel appeared, I stepped in front of your mother instinctively. So did Remiel. We all felt the balance of power shift."

"And the loudmouth," Mom spat, "wasted no time with his games."

Dad's voice dropped into a menacing impression. "'Don't you think it's time to come home, sweet Seraphina?'" His lips twisted. "'He misses you. Says all will be forgiven.'"

Mom's eyes burned, her sneer deepening. "Azazel," she said, voice flat and lethal, "I have never been sweet, and you damn well know it. And Luke doesn't even know how to spell the word forgiven. The only way I'll return to him is if you drag my dead body back to him in a thousand pieces." A pause. "And for that, you'll have to work a lot harder."

The air in the room thickened. Even now, centuries later, the memory alone was enough to reignite her fury.

"Azazel had only laughed." Mom's fingers curled into fists. "When he bowed with that ridiculous flourish, arms spread wide, I knew he was up to something." Her voice was clipped, bitter. "'*As you wish,*'" she mimicked, dripping with sarcasm.

The fact that this took place thousands of years before the classic movie Princess Bride which made that line infamously romantic, not deadly, was not lost on me.

Dad let out a weary sigh. "He always was a sarcastic schmuck."

Mom's lips twitched, but the rage didn't subside. "What we didn't realize was that his bow was a distraction. He was already drawing his weapons—those wickedly curved blades from the scabbards on his back—while his horde of vampires circled behind us."

Dad picked up where she left off, his voice steady but grim. "Those blades weren't just any weapons. They weren't the ones we Fell with. Azazel had stolen them—ripped them from the hands of other Fallen, those he had cut down himself. He reforged them, shaping something larger, deadlier. A twisted evolution of what we once carried. Our celestial daggers gifted to us by our *Father*."

"Remiel surveyed from above, and knew the odds were against us. So, he sent a tight burst to me, trusting that the others wouldn't know we had rediscovered this power."

My heart pounded. “What did he send?”

Dad’s jaw clenched. “To take your mother and run. To stop for nothing.”

I turned to Mom, but she was already shaking her head. “I sensed Sam’s hesitation. His loyalty to his brother and his love for me—both were tearing him apart.” Her voice wavered, just slightly. “Remiel saw it too. So he sent me a message of my own.”

A breath. A single beat.

“Your love must survive. Hope must live.” Her voice broke slightly on the words.

Dad took over, his tone quieter, heavier. “Then Remiel leapt—landed between us and Azazel, wings spread wide. That’s when I grabbed your mother and pulled her back, even as she fought me every step of the way.”

“I wasn’t going to let him fight alone,” Mom whispered. “Even if it meant my death.”

Wow. And they think teenagers are dramatic?

I rubbed my temples. No, wait. This probably was *dramatic.* If it hadn’t been for Remi, I wouldn’t be here. Their story pressed against my chest, thick and suffocating, but I couldn’t look away. I needed to hear the rest.

Dad’s voice shifted, dropping into another imitation. “‘And so, the Angel of Death meets the Angel of Hope. Tell me, Remiel, do you still believe *Daddy* will open the gates for you? Do you still think your pathetic little watcher reports and prayers matter?’”

Mom snorted, shaking her head. “The Grigori were never ones for idle banter. Remiel wasn’t about to waste his breath on Azazel’s theatrics. He just stepped forward and said, ‘Hope must live.’”

Dad’s voice softened, barely above a whisper. “That was the

moment your mother finally relented. She let me pull her away."

I swallowed, the gravity of his words sinking in. 'But you looked back, didn't you?"

Dad's hands clenched into fists. "I had to."

A deep, steadying breath.

"What I saw..." His voice faltered. "It almost made me regret my promise to him."

Beside him, Mom went still, her body tensing like she was bracing for impact.

Dad's jaw tightened. "Azazel—" his voice broke slightly, the name cutting through the air like a wound, "—had embedded his blade into Remiel's chest."

The breath I was holding shattered.

"It looked like it had pierced his heart." Dad, a haunted look in his eyes, turned his face etched with something deeper than grief towards me.

"So, you see, Sady... your mother and I don't just owe Remiel our lives." His voice dropped to something quieter, heavier. "We've been honouring his sacrifice ever since."

The words barely had time to settle before he stepped closer to Mom, wrapping his arms around her. Her face crumpled, her shoulders shaking with raw, unfiltered grief.

And then, just like that—she was sobbing.

Hysterically.

"Uhm... Mom?" My voice wavered between panic and helplessness. I wanted to get up, to go to her, to do something—but my body refused to cooperate. The weakness pinning me to the bed was unfamiliar, and I hated it.

"Sady baby, stay in bed." Her voice cracked as she wiped her face roughly with the back of her hand. Without another word, she turned and strode toward the stairs, her movements brisk and determined despite the silent tears still streaking her face. "Let me get you some soup."

I blinked. *Soup?*

I glanced at Dad, expecting him to follow after her, to stop whatever emotional breakdown masquerading as a culinary endeavor was about to unfold. Normally, he was the one who hovered, offering comfort food if I so much as sniffled, which had been almost never. But now? He just stood there, staring after her, his expression an unsettling mix of sorrow and concern.

"She's…" I hesitated, searching for the right words. "She's not okay, is she?"

Dad sighed, his shoulders slumping. "No. She's not."

His voice slipped into my mind, carefully.

SADY DOLL, BE NICE TO YOUR MOTHER RIGHT NOW. SHE'S NEAR A CRACKING POINT. AND… WELL… SHE COOKED. BE GENTLE WITH HER, PLEASE?

I groaned internally, frustration bubbling beneath the surface.

SHE COOKED?

That explained the look on his face. *Mom cannot cook.* Everything she has ever attempted has ended in disaster—and I'm not just talking about the food. The kitchen itself never walked away unscathed. Once, she managed to poison Dad so thoroughly he had to drink liquefied activated charcoal for an entire day.

Still, I couldn't exactly argue with him.

FINE. BUT IF I DIE FROM FOOD POISONING, THAT'S ON YOU.

A flicker of amusement softened his features, but he didn't reply. Instead, he stepped aside as Mom reentered, balancing a tray in her hands with surprising precision. A steaming bowl of soup—something vaguely mushroom-scented—sat in the center. She placed it on the nightstand before pulling up a chair beside my bed.

She settled in, a rare softness easing across her face. "Here," she said, picking up the spoon. "Let me help you."

I froze. "Uhm..."

There was no universe in which this ended well. The last time she spoon-fed me, I'd been a toddler. It hadn't gone great then, and I highly doubted it had improved now.

Realizing the same thing at the same time, she gave me an almost sheepish grin. "Right. You're too old for that, aren't you?"

"Yeah." I let out a breathy laugh. "I think I can manage."

She relinquished the spoon, and we shared a brief smile before I dipped it into the bowl. Bracing myself, I brought the first spoonful to my lips and took a cautious sip.

It wasn't *terrible*—which, by Mom's standards, was basically a culinary miracle. But the moment the warm liquid slid down my throat, a new problem arose. My thirst, already simmering beneath the surface, flared to life with a sudden, blistering intensity. My hands trembled slightly. *Had she used every grain of salt in the house? Or maybe the entire neighborhood block?*

"Well?" she asked, leaning forward, hope shining in her eyes. "How is it?"

I swallowed, forcing my voice into careful neutrality. "Oh, uhm... it's okay."

Technically *not* a lie.

Her hopeful expression wavered, and then—under her breath—she muttered, "I think I'd rather lick one of those salt blocks they give to goats."

I paused.

Then the absurdity of the statement hit me, and a startled laugh burst out, bright and unfiltered.

The moment it escaped, pain knifed through my skull—quick, blinding, and sharp enough to make me wince.

Mom followed a beat later, her laughter brittle and uneven, frayed at the edges with exhaustion. It wasn't easy, natural laughter. It was the kind that bubbled up when everything felt too heavy, too impossible—the kind that fought to keep the cracks from deepening. Like our nervous systems resetting.

Dad, who had been leaning against the doorway, finally stepped forward, his hands tucked into his pockets. His presence grounded the moment, a steady counterweight to the unraveling tension. Concern flickered across his face, tempered by something quieter—something like cautious relief.

"Hey, kiddo," he began, his voice gentle but probing. "Do you think you'll be up for going to school tomorrow? Your teacher, Mr. Black, has been calling twice a day to check on you. He also dropped off your bike, which, by the way, I've already repaired."

I groaned, the thought of school settling over me like an unwelcome guest. "Ugh, right—I have two projects due." Still, I scanned myself internally, assessing. The pounding headache was dulling to a faint throb, and my limbs no longer felt like lead. My body was already repairing itself. "Yeah, I think I do feel better. I'll just work on them from my bed today."

Mom perked up slightly. "Maybe I could help? I took some time off work to stay home with you." A pause. "What are the projects?"

I hesitated, picking at the edge of my blanket. "Well, the first one is basically done. Remember? Ancient Greece—Ares, Artemis, and

Queen Otrera. It's a 5,000-word essay." I shot her a look. "If you could read through it for edits—but please don't add anything only you would know, okay? Just... stick to what's in the history books."

A knowing smirk ghosted across her lips, but she nodded. "Fine. And the second one?"

I took a deep breath. "Paradise Lost."

Dad's eyebrow arched slightly, but Mom was the first to react. "That's... an odd project for high school, and history. Most teachers steer clear of religious content."

Something in her tone made me wary. I shrugged, keeping my voice casual. "Mr. Black is a little unorthodox. But his students have some of the highest averages—not just in his subject, but for the entire school."

Mom didn't look convinced. "So, what's the angle of the project?"

Apparently, I'd been *too* vague.

"He wants us to analyze the story behind the story—kind of a who's history is history approach. I was thinking about how Milton's daughter did a lot of the writing because he was going blind. It was an era when women were excluded from most theological discussions and literacy, so I thought I'd explore that."

Mom's eyebrows lifted, a small approving smile creeping across her face. "Oh, that's brilliant! Anne never got the credit she deserved. History always found ways to put a wedge between her and John. He barely had any people in his employ—the poor man was broke most of the time." A pause. "Let me know if you want me to look it over."

I nodded, grateful. "Thanks, Mom. I might take you up on that."

The rest of the day passed quietly, me curled up in bed, my laptop balanced on a pillow tray as I worked. I kept my analysis straightforward—focusing on the philosophical and historical context while steering clear of anything too esoteric. The angle on gender inequality gave me plenty to work with, and it felt... safer.

It only occurred to me that my phone had been off this entire time. Wondering if Kelsey might have reached out, I turned it on and almost immediately regretted it. No less than 20 texts, all of them increasing in urgency. I scrolled to the latest one.

Kesley: Mr. Black assured me today that you are fine, just home with the flu. I wish you would reply to let me know you're ok. Can't have my super ninja-mutant-angel on the fritz now, can I?

Time for damage control, this time of the mundane kind, for which I was oddly relieved.

Me: Hey Kelsey, sorry for being MIA, got a super-mutant flu. Had turned phone off night before I got sick, and just wasn't in any condition to even look at a screen. Major headache and fever. Back to school tomorrow.

Normally, my messages were more concise, but I felt she deserved more. Reaching back to my headboard, the phone pinged before I could set it down.

Kelsey: Thank God!!! I was going to send out the search & rescue team soon. We will talk about this tomorrow, you are never to go radio silent on me again, you hear me bestie?

Me: Ok, I promise. See u tomorrow.

Kelsey: I really am glad you're ok. Prepare for hugs.

With everything going on, I really hoped I could keep that promise to her. Wait, she had called me bestie? What happened in four days?

By mid-afternoon, my headache crept back in, a slow, dull pressure settling behind my eyes. My concentration wavered, the words on my screen blurring together.

"Sady baby?" Mom's voice was soft. I looked up to find her standing in the doorway, watching me with that quiet, assessing gaze. "You're pushing yourself too hard. Put it away for now."

"I'm fine," I muttered, though even I didn't sound convincing.

Her expression hardened into that no-nonsense look—the one that meant she wasn't taking arguments. "Rest. Now. The essay will still be there later."

Dad appeared behind her, nodding in agreement. "She's right, Sady doll. You need to give yourself a break."

I sighed but didn't argue, reluctantly closing my laptop and sinking back into the pillows. But rest didn't come easily. Despite the dull throbbing in my skull, my thoughts refused to settle. It felt like I'd lived a thousand lifetimes in the past few days. The weight of everything pressed down on me.

The attack on Cassiel. The revelations about my parents' past. The horrifying truth of who my mother used to be. And now... the promise of my own transformation.

It was too much.

Mom had always been my rock, my best friend. But today, something felt different—like I was seeing her through a cracked lens, the image no longer as whole as I once believed.

I'd always known she and Dad came from different factions—Seraphim and Grigori. And I'd understood, at least in a vague, secondhand way, that her past had been darker than his. That while Dad had been a Watcher, an observer, Mom had been something else entirely.

But *this*?

Oof.

She—the woman who carried me, birthed me, raised me, protected me—had once slaughtered entire cities just to provoke *Him*. My mother. Not just a warrior, not just a soldier, but a villain of mythic proportions.

How was I supposed to reconcile that with the person who'd just made me salty soup?

And then there was me.

This supposed child of prophecy. A future I never asked for, written in stone or the stars before I even existed. Was I really so powerless? The idea that I didn't have a choice, that this change or any change for that matter was inevitable, filled me with a slow, simmering rage that sat in my chest.

Grandpa Almighty sure had a lot to answer for.

I tried to redirect my thoughts—grasping for anything less overwhelming. But instead, my mind drifted to him. *Greyson.*

The last time I'd seen him, his touch had sparked something strange, something unfamiliar. A warmth that still lingered beneath my skin. Had I imagined it? Was it just a crush, a teenager's misguided fascination with her teacher? Or had he felt it too?

The thought only frustrated me more. As if being a teenager wasn't hard enough, I now had to contend with prophecies, supernatural transformations, and an unrelenting thirst.

My body demanded water constantly—four liters down and I still felt parched. At this rate, I was single-handedly keeping the bathroom in business, and I half-expected my bladder to stage a protest. Even the sandwich Dad had brought me earlier tasted off, though it had helped dull the edge of my hunger.

Everything felt wrong, like the world had tilted off balance and left me scrambling to find my footing.

Exhaustion finally won.

Sleep pulled me under, drowning any chance to make sense of

anything.

My nights of dreamless sleep were at an end, and I found myself floating in an endless ocean, gazing up at a sky so vast it stretched beyond reality. The water was cool and soothing, the sun's warmth a golden embrace. For a moment, everything felt calm.

Then, it changed.

The ocean stirred, shifting beneath me, its colors bleeding like living ink unraveling into the current.

To my left, sapphire wove with streaks of brushed silver—warm, tranquil, a steady presence that moved with the ease of an unhurried tide.

To my right, moss-green laced with gold surfaced, its motion deliberate, measured, as if it was waiting. It didn't move forward like the others—it simply existed, constant and steady, a presence that felt both new and impossibly familiar. It hovered just beyond reach, close enough to sense, but not yet touch—like a hand lingering at the edge of an unspoken promise.

Then, from below, soft dark gray marbled with muted mauve began to rise, brushing against my legs. It didn't feel threatening—more like it had always been part of the ocean, waiting just beneath the surface.

It lingered, shifting uncertainty around me, neither pulling me down nor pushing me forward. Not hesitant, exactly—more like uncertain, testing, feeling out its place in the currents. It curled around my ankle, then slipped away, only to drift back again, an awkward presence unsure of what it was meant to do.

I floated amidst these swirling, living colors, cradled by their currents.

Then the sun vanished.

A shadow swallowed the sky, and the wind howled. The ocean

bucked beneath me, its currents twisting, thrashing, no longer a cradle but a force wild and untethered.

Floating was no longer an option.

The ocean thrashed, twisting, dragging, tossing me like a rag doll caught in a storm. A wave slammed over me, forcing salt into my lungs, burning, choking. I coughed, gasped—but there was no air. Just water. Just the pull of something deep and unrelenting.

The colors around me reacted—no longer just drifting—their movements frantic, desperate. To keep my head above water.

The sapphire blue, moss-green, and muted mauve wrapped around me like lifelines, their tendrils holding me just above the surface.

Then the cold hit.

Obsidian black surged up from below, thick and suffocating, like an oil slick creeping over my skin. Tendrils of oxblood red wove through it, dark and pulsing, like veins carrying something old and restless beneath the surface.

For a fleeting second, I thought of Venom—that Marvel anti-hero.

But this wasn't an origin story.

This was wrong.

Cold. Malevolent. Hungry.

The vibrant colors surrounding me fought back, swirling into a chaotic whirlpool, their currents clashing against the black. Sapphire, moss-green, and muted mauve wrapped around my arms and torso, anchoring me against the pull of the dark.

The pressure was unbearable—as if I was being torn apart between them.

Then, I looked up—and saw it.

A shadow above me, a luminous helix of gold and deep brown, structured and controlled, a presence that felt both infinite and grounded.

It reached down, its strands wrapping around my hands and arms, pulling me upward.

Hope flickered. *Escape*. But my body was caught in the middle.

The obsidian black pulled from below.

The helix of light pulled from above.

My entire being stretched to its breaking point, while other colours tightened around my torso.

Saltwater burned in my throat. I tried to scream, but my voice was stolen, drowned in the chaos.

And then—

I woke with a gasp.

Drenched in cold sweat.

My throat ached, raw as if I had swallowed seawater. My body screamed for relief, thirst clawing at me with an intensity that bordered on desperation.

My hand shot out, fumbling for the pitcher of water on my nightstand. I drained it in seconds.

Still. Not enough.

CHAPTER 24

Dad's quick, determined footsteps echoed up the stairs before the door even opened. I knew what he was going to say before he even opened the door.

"Sady doll, are you alright? I heard you scream."

"Yeah, Dad, I'm fine. Just a bad dream, that's all," I replied, my voice hoarse from the lingering panic of the dreamscape. And boy, I bet Freud would have a field day with my subconscious. *Didn't Dad say he knew him?* I made a mental note to ask for tips another time.

He hovered for a moment, his brow furrowed, before nodding. "Well, if you're sure you're okay, I've got breakfast waiting for you downstairs. Come down when you're ready."

Retreating back down the hallway, it gave me a chance to shake loose the proverbial cobwebs. I tumbled out of bed, the remnants of my dream still clinging to me like a second skin.

Somehow, I managed to shower, dress, and sit through a quiet breakfast with Dad. Mom had gone into the office—so much for taking time off work. As I stood to leave, Dad swooped in behind me, wrapping me in a hug with his impossibly large arms.

"Would you please come straight home after school?" he asked, his tone softer than usual. "There's something I want to give you."

Mildly curious, I nodded. "Sure."

Stepping outside, I took a deep breath of crisp morning air. Even with the sun breaking through the clouds, a chill lingered. The bus ride to school felt interminably long, though that might've been because I was still bone-tired from the night before.

Butterflies stirred in my stomach as the bus pulled up to school. I bolted to the bathroom—not because I was sick *(which, now that I thought about it, would have been a first)*, but to check my reflection. I grimaced. My skin was almost ghostly white, a stark contrast to my usual warm complexion. Oh well, no one would question my absence due to illness. I still looked sick as a dog.

Making my way down the hallway, I spotted Kelsey bounding toward me from the opposite corner, her expression a mix of relief and panic.

"Oh my God, where the hell have you been?" she cried, nearly tackling me in a hug. Just further proof that I was not fully recovered—no human could have accomplished this prior to today.

I stumbled, laughing softly as I tried to regain my footing. "Hi, miss me?"

"Sady, don't even joke about that!" Her voice cracked slightly, emotions clearly on edge. Something in her tone tugged at my already-frayed nerves.

"Whoa, Kelsey, it's okay. I'm fine," I reassured her, even as my own nerves jittered like live wires. "I'm better now."

"Well, I absolutely forbid you from ever getting sick again, okay?" She fluttered her lashes at me, attempting humor but failing to mask the worry beneath.

"Don't worry. I hardly ever get sick, so this should be it for the next ten years."

She looped her arm through mine and didn't let go until we were inside homeroom.

"Welcome back, Miss Sady," Mr. Black said from his seat behind the desk, his tone as smooth and playful as ever. "We are pleased to see the rumors of your demise have been greatly exaggerated."

I tried to avoid eye contact, desperate to stop the inevitable heat from rising to my cheeks. But my eyes betrayed me. When I lifted them, everything in me went still.

Dressed entirely in black, his piercing cerulean-blue eyes seemed even more vivid than usual. But that wasn't what had me tongue-tied. His hair—his cobalt hair—was the showstopper. Gone was the pomegranate mohawk, and what was left was a striking, electric hue.

The stunned silence in the room broke with a burst of giggles when a student blurted, "Ogle the teacher on your own time."

And there it was. The dreaded blush bloomed across my cheeks, lighting me up like a Christmas tree. Making a mental note to plot revenge on the commenter, I all but stumbled to my desk. My one hope was to stay under the radar for the rest of the class—or, better yet, the entire day.

As the class settled in, Mr. Black stood and moved toward the front of the room, a leather-bound folder tucked under one arm. He clapped his hands together, the loud crack cutting through the chatter.

"All right, everyone, let's get started. I hope you've all brought your Ancient Beliefs essays and your Paradise Lost theories, as today is the due date for both. If you haven't"—he arched a brow, his cobalt hair catching the light—"well, let's just say, you'll find yourselves starring in an impromptu interpretive dance performance of your incomplete assignment after class."

A groan rippled through the room, followed by nervous laughter. After all, this was Mr. Greyson Black we were talking about. He could be dead serious or just pranking us. As students fumbled through their bags and folders, Mr. Black moved between desks, collecting papers with his usual air of amused detachment.

Beside me, Kelsey whispered furiously under her breath as she dug through her oversized tote bag. "Ugh, I swear, if I can't find this damn thing..."

"What, the essay?" I asked, keeping my voice low as Mr. Black approached.

She nodded, her curls bouncing as she rifled through a chaotic pile of papers. "Yeah, and my *Paradise Lost* thing. I stayed up until, like, three a.m. finishing them. I think I might've actually hallucinated Milton standing in my living room at one point."

I bit back a laugh, glancing toward the middle of the room where Mr. Black stopped to collect a particularly messy sheaf of papers from one of our classmates. "I'm sure they're in there somewhere. You're practically the queen of overachieving."

"Overachieving?" she huffed, finally producing two slightly crumpled documents. "If by 'overachieving,' you mean being a complete basket case who survives on caffeine and sheer panic, then sure."

I smiled faintly, grateful for her usual brand of dramatic honesty. "At least it's over now."

Kelsey sighed, slumping in her chair as Mr. Black neared our row. "Yeah, but for what? Another B+ because I didn't write something groundbreaking? He's so hard to read. Like, what does he even want?"

"Maybe just honesty?" I suggested, though even I wasn't sure if that was the right answer.

Kelsey snorted softly, shaking her head, her voice dropping so low I almost didn't catch the words. "Honesty. Right. Yeah, honesty's great—until it's not."

Something about the way she said it gave me pause. The forced edge in her voice, the way she quickly busied herself smoothing imaginary creases in her essay..

"Maybe," I said quietly, but encouragingly, "honesty works better on paper."

Her lips twitched into a shadow of her usual smile, but her eyes didn't quite meet mine. "Yeah. Paper doesn't hit back."

The words were mumbled out so fast I almost didn't process them, and by the time I did, she had already leaned back in her chair, the moment had slipped away.

Mr. Black reached our desks, his eyes moving between us, halting any further attempt I had to press Kelsey. She stiffened, quickly handing over her papers with an almost sheepish smile. I followed suit, placing my neatly stapled essay and theory onto the growing pile in his hands.

"Thank you, Miss Sady," he said, his tone polite but carrying something unreadable.

I nodded, feeling the blush creep up my neck again. As he moved on to the next row, I turned back to Kelsey, who gave me a knowing smirk.

"Honesty, huh?" she whispered. "I think he's more interested in whether or not you noticed his hair."

I rolled my eyes, grateful for the distraction. "Don't you have something else to stress about?"

"Not anymore," she said with a grin, leaning back in her chair. "Oh wait, now I just get to stress about how bad they are."

Mr. Black returned to his desk after collecting the last of the assignments and launched into an animated—if not slightly macabre—lecture on death and immortality, a topic cultures around the world had been obsessed with for millennia. Kelsey nudged me once or twice, whispering comments about his new look and earning muffled giggles from me. It was easier to fall into her rhythm, to let her chatter fill the space where my thoughts would otherwise spiral.

When the bell rang, signaling the end of first period, Kelsey grabbed her bag and shot me a grin. "Catch you at lunch?"

I nodded. "Sure."

She hesitated for a second, her grip tightening on the strap of her bag, before forcing a bright smile and disappearing into the crowded hallway. I watched her go, still replaying the unease in her voice when Mr. Black's voice reached me, low and careful.

"Miss Sady, if you're feeling recovered enough, could I interest you in a woodland trail biking adventure? Only this time, no trespassing required. After dinner, perhaps?"

I blinked, certain I'd misheard. But when I turned around, he was already at the door, adjusting his sleeves, his back to me. For a moment, time felt suspended, the question hanging in the air, unanswered.

My heart raced, thoughts crashing into each other like waves. Had he really just said that? Or had my exhausted brain conjured it out of thin air? I held my breath as if pausing the world might somehow make it clearer. I opened my mouth to speak, but the words never came. He was already gone, stepping into the hallway without a backward glance.

Strange. Did I hold my breath that long?

The classroom was empty now, and I realized I wouldn't get any answers standing there. The questions ricocheted in my mind, relentless and unyielding. Dare I go? Would I be putting him at risk? How fast is this change supposed to happen? Was it already happening? And were hallucinations part of this transformation? The uncertainty created more questions than providing answers.

But as pointless as the questions felt, I couldn't stop them. My life had taken so many twists, turns, and unexpected dives that I was beginning to lose my grip on what even mattered anymore. A part of me—the part stubbornly clinging to normalcy—wanted to say yes. To go. To pretend, just for a while, that everything wasn't unraveling.

Even though I suspected that going for a bike ride with the teacher you're crushing on wasn't exactly listed on the teenage normal menu.

It was pointless to wonder, because at this point—and yes, I was aware of how many times I'd used that word—it was anybody's guess. *And honestly?* I was reaching a point where I was dangerously close to not giving a shit.

The rest of the morning passed in a blur of half-listened-to lectures and the scratch of pencils against paper. In English, I found myself doodling in the margins of my notebook while Mr. Simmonds droned on about Shakespearean tragedy. Chemistry wasn't much better—just a haze of formulas and numbers that refused to stick in my tired brain.

When the lunch bell rang, I was more than ready for a break. My stomach growled in agreement as I slung my bag over my shoulder and headed for the cafeteria. It was hard to focus on anything when my thoughts kept circling back to the chaos of the past few days—and the unanswered question from homeroom.

"Can we just grab our food and go sit in our spot today?" Kelsey asked, her voice tight. She grabbed my hand fiercely, as though holding on to our friendship depended on this one gesture. My reply never had a chance—she was already leading me toward the cafeteria.

The students had staked their usual claims on the tables, chairs rearranged to form unofficial territories for each group. Cliques held court in their respective arenas, the leaders surrounded by their loyal subjects. It was one of the things I wouldn't miss about high school—the forced separation, the boundaries that some people carried into adulthood as if they were gospel.

Kelsey let go of my hand to rush ahead, flagging Michaela and Jamie near the hallway closest to the drama room. She gestured animatedly, clearly explaining that we'd meet them there after grabbing food. I lingered behind, heading toward the cafeteria line, distracted by the sea of noise and movement.

I would miss this though. Her, and the others.

I didn't even see Bethany until I collided with her.

The tray she was holding wobbled, tilting at a precarious angle before everything—soup, salad, and whatever questionable side dish the cafeteria had conjured up that day—came crashing down.

Right onto her shoes. And her pants. And her blouse.

For a second, there was only stunned silence. Then, she whirled around, her face twisted in fury.

"You stupid, clumsy bitch!" she screeched, loud enough to turn heads across the cafeteria.

Heat rose to my cheeks. "I'm sorry. Here, let me grab you a new lunch." I bent down, already reaching for a napkin, hoping to diffuse rather than ignite. The murmurs of our growing audience prickled at my back, but I focused on the mess in front of me.

Bethany, however, stood firm, fists planted on her hips like she was commanding the field at halftime. Her voice, shrill and practiced, cut through the room—the kind that demanded attention, that thrived in moments like this. Because of course she did. Captain of the cheer squad, reigning queen of popularity—Bethany fed off an audience like a fire starved for oxygen.

She gave me a slow, smug once-over before tossing her hair over her shoulder. "Guess cleaning up other people's messes is in your blood. Must be nice, though—having a mommy who can't stick around long enough to deal with them herself."

I stilled.

The words landed with a dull, sinking weight—not because they were clever, not because they were cutting, but because they hit in just the wrong way. Like she had thrown a match onto embers that were already smoldering.

Logically, I knew her taunts were childish and uninspired, the kind of insult you'd expect from someone who equated volume with strength. *Mommy* felt like a weak jab, a lazy attempt to poke at something vulnerable. But something about this one... hit differently.

I inhaled slowly, lifting my gaze to meet hers.

"Listen, Bethany," I said, keeping my tone calm but firm. "I'm helping clean up, and I'll pay for a new lunch. That's it. Deal with it."

I resumed picking up the tray, ignoring her glare. The air shifted—just slightly—and I should have paid attention to that warning. But then her heel slammed down on my right hand, grinding it into the floor as her knee came up toward my face.

She connected. Pain exploded across my nose, tears springing to my eyes. Not from injury—it was superficial—but from the sheer fact that she'd landed a blow. My reflexes should've kicked in. My training should've stopped her slow, clumsy attack.

And what happened next, should also have never happened.

My left hand moved on its own, grabbing behind her raised knee, locking it in place. I stood, throwing her backward with far too much force. She hit the ground with a loud thud, and I planted my right foot firmly on her sternum, pinning her down. My other hand gripped her ankle, pulling her leg just enough to make her panic.

"If I stomp as hard as you did, I could crush your lungs and likely crack your rib cage." The words hissed through my clenched jaw, my voice low and venomous. "Would you like me to stomp?"

Bethany's eyes widened, her bravado crumbling into fear. "Please, no," she whimpered. "I'm sorry."

Her trembling voice barely registered over the roaring in my ears. My pulse pounded, drowning out the cafeteria noise, the murmurs of the crowd, and even my own thoughts. For a moment, it was just me and her—this strange, dangerous moment of power that felt foreign and frightening.

Then I looked up.

Kelsey stood by Michaela and Jamie near the edge of the cafeteria, her face pale and frozen in shock. Her wide eyes weren't filled with admiration or support. They were filled with fear. *Of me.*

That was exactly the reality check I needed to put a lid on my rage. My hands loosened, and I released Bethany abruptly, stepping back as she gasped and scrambled to her feet. The spell was broken, and the cafeteria came rushing back into focus—tables and chairs, trays of food, and dozens of eyes all glued to me.

Too many eyes.

The whispers started immediately, growing louder with every step I took away from Bethany. Words I couldn't make out at first, jumbled and overlapping, then one that cut through the noise like a blade.

"Freak."

Tears burned at the corners of my eyes as I shoved past the crowd, my hands trembling uncontrollably. I needed to get out. Now.

I burst into the hallway, the hum of fluorescent lights doing little to drown out the echoes of the cafeteria. My breath hitched as I stumbled toward the office, forcing the lump in my throat down long enough to speak.

"I'm not feeling well," I said, my voice barely above a whisper. "Can you please call home for me?"

The secretary gave me a concerned look, but I didn't care. My parents would wonder why I hadn't just reached out telepathically, but right now, I didn't want them in my head. I didn't want anything that reminded me of what I was.

I just needed to go home. To breathe. To figure out what the hell was happening to me.

Ten minutes later, Mom showed up in the SUV, looking every bit the part of a normal mother picking up her daughter—if you ignored the way her presence turned heads. Her sleek sunglasses masked any emotion, but her flawless beauty and commanding air had the office receptionist scrambling to greet her.

A quick glance at the clock made me suspect she broke a few traffic laws on the way here. *Not normal.*

"Hello, I'm here to pick up my daughter, Sady Smith," Mom said, her voice smooth but clipped.

The receptionist blinked, clearly flustered. "Oh, yes, of course. She's just over there." She gestured toward me, where I'd been sitting quietly, trying not to draw attention. "Poor thing seems quite ill. She's so pale. Perhaps some hot broth would—"

"I thank you not to advise me on how to care for my daughter," Mom interjected sharply, cutting off the well-meaning comment.

The receptionist's mouth opened and closed like a fish gasping for air. Meanwhile, Mom turned on her heel, snatched my backpack from beside me, and walked toward the door without checking to see if I was following.

Dragging myself to my feet, I mumbled a faint thank-you to the receptionist before trailing behind Mom. No words were exchanged as we walked to the car, and the drive home was equally silent. I could feel her curiosity, her need to ask questions, buzzing beneath the surface.

At least I hoped it was curiosity and not irritation.

Chapter 25

When we arrived home, Mom dropped my backpack by the door with a dull thud. The house looked the same as always—neat, calm, and ordinary. But nothing felt normal anymore.

Frustration bubbled up inside me, and I stomped into the living room, flopping onto the couch with a graceless thud. My hands clenched into fists as the events of the day replayed over and over in my mind. I couldn't decide if I wanted to cry or scream.

Dad emerged from the kitchen, his eyes already narrowing as he took in my tense posture. Without a word, he crossed the room and pulled Mom into a quiet, knowing embrace. She stayed silent, wisely choosing not to press me for answers.

Dad, though, didn't need to ask. He knew I had called her from school. He knew something was wrong.

"Take your time," Dad said gently, his voice low and calming. "Inhale slowly, deeply. Pause. Exhale gently. Breathe. Release."

The tautness in my shoulders didn't loosen right away, but his steady tone gave me something to hold onto. Following his instructions, I focused on my breathing until the storm in my chest began to settle. I was too tired to talk, and frankly, even though I craved normalcy, I didn't trust my voice. Finally, I closed my eyes and let the memories of the day flow, sending them telepathically to my parents in a series of fragmented scenes. The cafeteria. Bethany. The rage. Kelsey's terrified expression. The whispers.

When I opened my eyes, Mom was sitting on Dad's lap, and they were exchanging puzzled glances.

"And here I was starting to hope you'd inherited some of my restraint," Dad teased, the corners of his mouth twitching with amusement.

Mom's eyes narrowed, clearly taking offense. "Excuse me?"

Dad only grinned, unbothered, and shared a few mental flashes with me—memories of Mom in moments eerily similar to my own. Each scene played out like a highlight reel of righteous fury: her knocking someone flat, pressing a foot to their chest, a snide smirk on her lips as she delivered some scathing, rhetorical question.

The parallels were undeniable.

Mom scoffed, crossing her arms. "I was nothing like that."

Dad arched a brow. "Oh? Want me to replay the time you took down three Watchers in under a minute because they 'looked at you funny'?"

I blinked. "Wait, what?"

Mom sighed, pinching the bridge of her nose. "Sam, I swear to—"

"See? Exactly like her," Dad said with a smirk.

It was too much. A strangled laugh escaped me, followed by another, until the three of us were laughing so hard that tears streamed down our faces.

The laughter felt cathartic, but as the mood settled, Dad turned serious again. "Sady doll, I'm afraid this change is happening faster than we thought," he said, his tone measured. "And it's so much worse than we expected. It seems you're not turning into a *them*, but..."

He paused dramatically, his mouth twitching ever so slightly before delivering the punchline. "...you're turning into your mother!"

Mom burst out laughing, and Dad couldn't hold back his chuckles. Their ridiculousness dragged me into another fit of laughter, breaking the pressure for a few blissful moments.

Several minutes later, we managed to collect ourselves. Mom, always quick to take charge, decided to call the school about Bethany.

"Hello, this is Sady Smith's mother," she said smoothly. "I'm calling to ask about the incident that took place in the cafeteria at lunchtime."

There was a pause, her expression shifting from curiosity to mild annoyance as the silence stretched. I fidgeted with the hem of my shirt.

"Oh, I see. Well, my mistake. Sorry for bothering you." Her voice was clipped, betraying her confusion as she hung up the phone.

"Sera, what did they say?" Dad asked, his brow furrowing as he stepped closer.

"They had no idea what I was talking about. Not a single student reported anything about a fight or even a disturbance."

"What?" I blurted, my heart racing. "That's not possible. I swear, I'm not making it up!"

Mom's voice remained neutral, but the slight clench of her jaw told me she wasn't as unaffected as she wanted to appear.

She exhaled, rubbing her temple before waving a hand dismissively. "Don't worry, Sady baby, I'll dig into it more later." A beat of silence, then, almost too casually, she added, "For now, let's eat. I'm starving."

I glanced between them, expecting Dad to protest, to push back against the abrupt shift, but he only studied her for a moment before nodding.

Something about the way she brushed it off felt *off*. Like she already had a theory, one she wasn't ready to share.

Pondering it further was interrupted because my appetite flared with a new flush of intensity I wasn't used to. Dad had made his amazing veggie lasagna with cashew cheese, and Mom had grilled a steak for herself—rare, of course. Dinner passed in relative quiet, but something about the aroma of her steak made me uneasy. Even after three hearty portions of lasagna, the scent of the meat lingered, stirring a hunger I didn't want to acknowledge. By the time Mom finished her meal, I let out a breath of relief, glad the temptation was gone.

Well, that was a new one I would have to watch out for, I thought grimly. And I wasn't looking forward to finding out what this development meant.

Dad excused himself before the dishes were cleared, heading toward his workshop. Something clicked in my memory.

"Hey, Dad!" I called out just as he reached the outside door. "What is it you wanted to give me?"

He paused, turning back with a look that was both solemn and slightly distracted. "Oh, right," he said, slipping a hand into his pocket. "Your mother and I had been waiting until your graduation to give you these. With everything happening, well, we felt like you should have them now."

He pulled out a small mocha satchel, the dark fabric soft and worn. Tugging the strings open, he revealed a pair of earrings. Delicate silver hooks held tiny white feathers, their edges shimmering with a subtle bronze-gold hue in the light.

"Dad?" My voice barely came out, a whisper carried on breath I hadn't realized I was holding.

I reached for them, fingertips grazing the delicate strands. They radiated a gentle warmth—not hot, but like sunlight against bare skin on a perfect summer day. A warmth that felt *alive.*

"Are these…?"

"Yes."

He stepped closer, wrapping an arm around my shoulders, pulling me in with the kind of warmth that only a father could provide. His voice softened, almost reverent. "Your mother saved them after I..."

He didn't need to finish the sentence.

The image of my father—bleeding, broken, his wings severed and lying in a pool of blood beside him—flashed through my mind. It wasn't just some imagined horror. Thanks to that surveillance footage, I had seen what it might have looked like. Witnessed it in a way I never wanted to.

And now, I held them in my hands.

A piece of him that had once carried him through and from the heavens, now small enough to fit in the palm of my hand.

I wrapped my arms around his waist, holding on as though that could undo the memory.

The feathers felt impossibly light against my skin—the irony of *light as a feather* was not lost on me. But their warmth seeped through my fingers, thrumming softly, a vibration wrapping around my entire body.

Then, all at once, *it hit me.*

Not like a slow realization, but like a bolt of lightning, crackling and electric.

I was holding actual angel-wing feathers.

My father's feathers.

"Sady doll," Dad said softly, his voice thick with emotion. "I wish I could tell you that everything is going to be okay, but the truth is, we're in completely uncharted territory. In all my years of watching over this earth, you are so incredibly unique. And I'm not just saying that because I'm a besotted-with-the-miracle-that-is-his-daughter kinda dad."

"Yeah, so you both keep telling me," I muttered, my attempt at sarcasm falling flat as the intensity of the moment closed in around me. "Do you think these can help me... not turn into Mom? Or... *them*?"

"Honestly? We don't know," he admitted. "But I have faith."

"In what? Your *father*?" I couldn't hold back the sarcasm or the accompanying eye roll. "*God*, also known as *Grandpa*?"

"No, my darling everlasting." His gaze softened. "In you."

The air around me seemed warmer, making it harder to focus. I rubbed my temples, trying to ignore the buzzing in my head. "Dad?" I asked hesitantly. "Do you think it'd be okay if I went for a bike ride? You know, just to clear my head a little and get rid of this anxious energy?"

He studied me for a moment, concern flickering across his face. But then he nodded. "Alright, kiddo. Check in with us? Please?"

"Of course," I said quickly, clutching the feathers tightly as. I hurried to my room, my heart still hammering from what I was holding in my hands. Slipping inside, I carefully set the precious feather earrings on my dresser, my fingers lingering on them for just a second longer than necessary.

A deep breath. A moment to steady myself.

Grabbing my jacket, I headed toward the backyard, where my bike leaned against the shed. The cool metal frame felt solid and familiar under my hand—a reminder of the ordinary life I was trying to hold onto.

"Sady baby, wait up a minute!" Mom called, practically skipping out of the house with her helmet in hand. The sight would have been amusing—neither of us actually needed one for protection, our skulls being supernaturally sturdy—if it didn't send a small jolt of dread through me. "Do you want some company?"

"Oh, Mom, I—uhm, it's okay." What could I tell her? That I was about to meet up with my teacher for what could be the most inappropriate and possible awkward adventure of my life?

"This wouldn't have anything to do with your crush, would it?" She gave me a sly smile, walking toward me so quietly that I realized she was shielding our conversation from Dad.

Before I could come up with a denial, she took my hand, her fingers warm and firm. In a tightly controlled burst of thought, she shared glimpses of her early days with Dad—soft, playful memories. Thankfully, the *PG* version. My sanity was spared that at least. Overlapping them, she layered observations of me, like tiny puzzle pieces falling into place.

I KNOW HOW YOU FEEL, SADY.

Her voice slipped into my mind like a whisper—soft yet undeniable, threading through my thoughts like a current beneath still water. It wasn't intrusive, wasn't forceful. Just *there*, wrapping around the edges of my mind with quiet understanding.

JUST PLEASE, BE CAREFUL. YOU KNOW I COULDN'T BEAR IT IF SOME BOY BROKE YOUR HEART.

Her frown softened, the concern lingering in her eyes for just a moment longer before something more playful took its place. Slowly, her lips curled into a wicked smirk—the kind that meant she was already thinking of all the ways she'd personally make someone pay if they hurt me.

I'D HATE TO HAVE TO REMOVE HIS HEART FROM HIS CHEST AND FEED IT TO HIM OFF A GRILL.

It was a joke. Mostly.

But beneath the teasing lilt of her voice, there was something else—something threatening. A quiet, unshakable promise woven between the words. Because if someone did break my heart, if they hurt me in a way she couldn't fix, she wouldn't just stand by.

She wasn't the type to sit on the sidelines, to offer hollow comforts or say I told you so. No, Mom was the kind of person who acted. Who did something about it.

And the glint in her eyes told me that whoever dared to cross that line would regret it.

Deeply.

I hugged her tightly, burying my face in her hair, which smelled like rosemary and wind. For a moment, I forgot that it was her blood coursing through my veins that was turning my world upside down.

"Thanks, Mom. I love you," I murmured. "I promise I'll be careful. Can we just... not tell Dad yet?"

Her grin widened—feeling a strengthened bond between us always put her at ease. "Sure, Sady baby."

With that, I climbed onto my bike and rode off, the cool breeze brushing against my face. For about ten minutes, I convinced myself I was just out for fresh air. But who was I kidding? I was going to see Greyson. And if Mom knew *the crush* was my teacher—a grown man—her supportive attitude would have gone up in flames, along with him, knowing her.

I took the same route as before, pretending I wasn't in a rush while speeding through the trails faster than any human could. When I arrived, he was sitting on his front steps, his bike leaning casually against a tree. He knew I would come.

As I hopped off my bike, he looked up with an expression that I hoped—no, *prayed*—was excitement. He took a few quick strides, closing the distance between us. My heart stuttered, my breath hitching in my throat.

"May I say how pleased I am that you chose to accept my invitation?" His voice was warm and smooth, carrying the kind of old-world charm that felt almost out of place in the modern world.

With practiced grace, he took my hand and brought it to his lips, pressing a light, courteous kiss to the back of it. The gesture was nothing more than polite—a gentleman's greeting—but there was something undeniably intentional about it. A quiet elegance, a sense of formality that made it clear he understood the significance of this meeting.

Still, the warmth of his touch lingered longer than expected, like the ghost of a forgotten tradition. The kiss he placed on the back of my hand sent a ripple of heat up my arm left my skin tingling.

"Why did you ask me to come?" The words spilled out fast, my brain struggling to keep up.

Greyson smiled, his blue eyes glinting with something I couldn't place. Mischief? Amusement? "Tell me, Miss Sady—why do you think I asked?"

His tone left no room for answers. Flustered and more than a little brave—or reckless—I decided to push back. My life had been throwing curveballs faster than I could catch them, and I was quickly running out of patience for mysteries.

"Last time I checked, I was your student, and you were my teacher." I folded my arms, channeling every ounce of defiance I could muster. "So tell me, am I just reading into whatever this is—"

"Despite my being your teacher, I am not that much older than you... sort of." His chuckle was soft, teasing. "And as long as I am your teacher, I promise nothing inappropriate will happen. What I'd like—if you'll allow it—is to get to know you better. To offer you something I think you're missing."

"And what is that, exactly?" I snapped, his cryptic answers were starting to grate on me. After the past few days, I was done with *cryptic*. "What do you think I don't have?"

"Why, Sady, isn't it obvious?" He grinned, the teasing note in his voice softening. "A friend. So please, if you please—call me Greyson."

I blinked, caught off guard. He was right, and yet it irritated me that he could see through me so easily. "I already have a friend," I said, my voice defensive. "Her name is Kelsey."

"Very well. Perhaps one friend is enough." His head tilted, his eyes watching me with a mix of amusement and something warmer.

It was impossible to stay mad at him. That smile—infuriating and charming in equal measure—dismantled my irritation bit by bit. Still, his words left me unsettled. Could I risk letting him in? Breaking every rule my parents had ever set? Especially when my feelings for him felt far from platonic?

Greyson climbed onto his bike, snapping his helmet into place with practiced ease. Flashing one of his signature winks, he whispered, "I dare you."

For a moment, I stood frozen, my brain short-circuiting. But then the thrill of the challenge sparked to life, and I gave him a subtle nod, hoping my hair hid the deepening shade of scarlet creeping up my neck.

"Good," he called over his shoulder as he took off. "Let's see if you can keep up!"

I stood there for only a few seconds, almost dumbfounded. If he thought he could win this one, he had a rude awakening. I just had to be careful to stay at a normal speed—the human one, that is.

He led us off the main trail and into rougher terrain. The ground was uneven, covered in roots and rocks that jutted out like nature's obstacles. It felt exhilarating. Whenever we reached a smooth patch, we rode side by side in comfortable silence. Keeping my focus on maintaining an average speed, letting him take the lead became easier and easier. My face was starting to hurt from smiling so much.

When he slowed down, a flicker of unease settled in my chest, a brief moment of uncertainty making me think our time had come to an end.

"Miss Sady." Peering over his shoulder, the exhilaration on his face was almost enough to stop my heart. "If you will join me—quietly, if you please."

He had already laid his bike on the ground, his hand reaching toward me in invitation. Puzzled, I followed suit, doing my best to move as silently as possible. When I allowed my fingers to touch his, a small electric shock ran through me, and I hoped he felt it too. Wait, no—I took that back. *Stop it, Sady.*

Moments later, we emerged into a clearing—a small, hidden glen bathed in dappled sunlight. My breath caught as I spotted the vixen. She was curled up near the base of an old oak tree, her litter of cubs tumbling and playing in the grass around her.

Greyson crouched low, his movements deliberate and calm. I mirrored him, feeling the gravity of the moment. Watching the fox family interact was like watching a living, breathing piece of art. The cubs yipped and nipped at one another, their playful energy filling the air with a sense of innocent joy.

"Beautiful, aren't they?" Greyson murmured, his voice so soft it barely reached me.

"Yeah," I whispered back. "It's... peaceful."

He nodded, his gaze fixed on the vixen as she nudged one of her cubs into the grass. For a moment, I forgot about all the chaos in my life—the prophecy, the changes, even my growing feelings for Greyson. Here, surrounded by nature and life, everything else seemed to fade away.

When the cubs began to tire and settle down, Greyson was a strange combination of proud papa and giddy little kid. He motioned for me to follow him back to our bikes. The ride back was quieter, the adrenaline of the trail replaced with a calm that mirrored the serenity of the glen.

As we approached his house, the sun was beginning to dip low in the sky. He dismounted, using the bottom of his shirt to wipe the sweat from his brow, giving me a fleeting glimpse of his deliciously sculpted abs—instantly sending my mind spiraling into very X-rated thoughts. *Damn it.* Sady, get a grip.

Those thoughts were swiftly replaced by panic.

I hadn't broken a sweat.

Damn it. He's definitely going to notice that.

While he was still blinded by his shirt, I tugged on my own and quickly poured some water from my bottle onto it. When he finally pulled his shirt down, I looked just as sweaty. And since I was still thinking about his bare skin, my face was flushed, too. *Problem solved—I hoped.*

"Why, Miss Sady, don't you look a mess."

He leaned in without warning and kissed me—along the top of my forehead.

"Uhm, thanks, Mr.—I mean, Greyson."

I turned slightly away, heat rising to my forehead. His kiss felt like sunlight breaking through the clouds.

"Miss Sady, out of curiosity..." He leaned against the column on his front porch. "Do you have a curfew?"

"Why? You asking for a sleepover?" The words slipped out, bypassing any filter. *Damn my smart-ass mouth.*

"Haha, that would be a solid no, and Miss Sady, I am disappointed in the inappropriate suggestion." His turn to blush—a beautiful shade of red. So, he wasn't completely immune. "I was wondering if I could interest you in a snack?"

And my mind immediately twisted his words into something entirely X-rated. Again.

I swallowed hard, my voice catching in my throat. "I already had dinner, and I, uhm... I should head home."

"Very well." He straightened, his grin softening into something warmer. "Be safe, and I'll see you in class tomorrow."

He stepped toward me, his arms wrapping around me in a brief but firm hug. The warmth of his body seeped into mine, and for a moment, I allowed myself to lean into it. But as my ear rested against his chest, I noticed something strange.

His heartbeat was slow. *Too* slow. And irregular, like a broken clock struggling to keep time. After that bike ride, it should have been pounding strong and steady.

I hugged him tighter, focusing on the sound. There, deep within his chest, I felt something else—a small part of his heart was completely gray, almost black, with no blood pumping to or from it. A part of his heart wasn't beating. It wasn't *alive.*

I barely had time to process it when Greyson gently pulled back, placing his hands on my shoulders. "Now, Miss Sady," he said with a chuckle, though his tone was firm. "That bordered on the inappropriate."

"Sorry," I stammered, taking a step back. "I didn't mean—"

Turning toward the front door, he didn't even say goodbye.

I floundered back onto my bike, so stunned by what I'd felt that I barely registered the abrupt dismissal. To be fair, this wasn't the first time I had sensed something in another person's body. Last year, one of my classmates showed up several days in a row looking like she was one stomach flip away from disaster. On the third day, she accidentally bumped into me coming out of a bathroom stall, and in that moment of near full-body contact, my senses flared.

Inside her body, there was something growing. She was pregnant.

Unfortunately, I had the bright idea of opening my mouth and asking about it. That went *well*. She was shocked—then furious. Shouting at me that I was accusing her of being a slut, she stomped off, leaving me standing there still a bit stunned by what I had sensed, seen, or felt. It was about three months later when the entire school knew, because she had started to show.

When I told Mom and Dad about it later that day, we spent time pondering what this ability meant. Mom wanted me to explore it—by hugging more people. Dad, the more pragmatic one, suggested I *not* go around hugging strangers. So, given my already minimal interaction with other people, I so rarely had a chance to test this delightful, confusing, and uncontrollable talent of mine.

By the time I pulled my bike into the shed, exhaustion dragged at every muscle. For once, I was relieved that neither Mom nor Dad was hovering or pressing me with questions. True to her word, Mom was trusting my judgment—trusting that if anything important happened, I'd share it.

But standing there in the quiet of the shed, the events of the day spinning in my mind, it occurred to me—I wouldn't even know where to start.

Chapter 26

The weekend passed in a strange haze of normalcy—or at least as normal as life got in our household. Dad disappeared into his workshop for hours on end, emerging only for meals or to check on me with one of his gentle, knowing smiles. Mom, on the other hand, spent the better part of Saturday glued to her computer, immersed in some kind of research she refused to share. Whenever I tried to ask, she'd just wave me off with a distracted, "Soon, Sady baby."

I tried to focus on schoolwork but couldn't stop replaying Friday night in my head—Greyson's cryptic words, the kiss on my forehead, the warmth I'd felt through his hug. Every time I thought about it, my heart fluttered like I was riding a roller coaster. And speaking of hearts, I was still puzzled and confused by what I had felt when we hugged.

Kelsey texted a couple of times to check in, mostly with funny memes and her growing obsession with Paul Wesley from *The Vampire Diaries*. It was still odd that she hadn't mentioned the incident from the cafeteria, which was fine by me. Her look of fear was not something I wanted to ever see again. For now, I sent back the minimum required responses, feeling like my head was too full to carry a proper conversation.

By Sunday afternoon, the house had settled into a quiet rhythm. Dad's music from the workshop hummed faintly in the background, and Mom was once again in front of the computer. I curled up in the living room by the warmth of the fireplace with a book I wasn't really reading, glancing at the clock and counting down the hours until Monday.

Eventually, the weight of my eyelids became too much to fight. With a sigh, I abandoned the book and shuffled to my bedroom, the soft creak of the floorboards accompanying me. I collapsed onto the bed without bothering to turn down the covers, exhaustion pulling me under.

And then it was here. Monday morning arrived too soon, sunlight spilling through my window as if mocking the heavy weight I'd carried through the weekend. My stomach growled loudly, yanking me from sleep like a rude alarm clock.

Starving. Again.

But this wasn't normal hunger. It clawed at me, deeper and more insistent, stirring cravings I refused to acknowledge. I'd been vigilant all weekend, sticking to normal food even as this strange ache whispered for something else. I wouldn't give in now.

"Not today, *Satan*," I muttered, chuckling at my choice of words as I forced myself out of bed and into the bathroom. Grabbing a hair tie from my nightstand, I pulled my unruly waves into a messy bun and headed to the kitchen. Mom had already left for work, leaving the house quieter than usual. A part of me was glad—her absence meant I didn't have to field questions about my pale complexion or the shadows under my eyes. They hadn't really improved, despite a healthy sleep routine.

I rummaged through the pantry, pulling out a box of muesli and mixing it with coconut milk. A scoop of protein powder, along with some pumpkin seeds, went in for added calories and nutrients. Stirring mechanically, I perched on the edge of a stool and forced myself to eat. Each bite was tasteless, a chore.

The soft creak of the workshop door in the backyard pulled my awareness away from my churning thoughts—and toward a much bigger distraction.

Dad stood in the doorway, looking bleary-eyed and rumpled. His current uniform consisted of sweatpants and a hoodie—the same one he'd probably been wearing since yesterday and the day before. He looked like he'd been glued to his monitors all night, taking me in with a weary once-over as he leaned against the doorframe.

"Morning, kiddo," he said, his voice a little hoarse. He rubbed at the back of his neck, a telltale sign that he'd been staring at screens too long. "That doesn't look like enough."

"I'm fine, Dad," I said quickly, stirring my muesli in an effort to look busy. "It's packed with protein."

He didn't respond immediately, his gaze narrowing slightly as if searching for cracks in my reply. "You sure you're feeling alright?"

"Look who's talking," I shot back, raising an eyebrow as I took in his rumpled hoodie, dark circles under his eyes, and general air of exhaustion. "You look like you're about to declare war on the coffee pot."

He let out a soft chuckle, his tired eyes crinkling at the edges. "Fair enough," he admitted, his voice tinged with weariness. "I didn't sleep much. Another job came in."

"And?" I prompted, tilting my head as he poured himself a cup of coffee, his movements slow and deliberate.

"And although it looks pretty benign, I can't help but feel there might be a connection with Cassiel and that subway tunnel," he said, his words trailing off as if he wasn't entirely sure he should be sharing this with me.

"Oh?" I leaned forward, curiosity piqued despite the gnawing ache in my stomach.

"It's just a hunch," he said, rubbing the back of his neck. "But this one feels… off. Like there's more to it than what's on the surface. I've been reviewing the footage and data all night."

"Dad, you need to get some rest," I said firmly, standing and walking over to give him a quick hug. "You always do better after you sleep. Seriously, go crash for a bit."

"Are you still keeping my dagger close?" His expression turned serious, and the silence between us seemed to demand an answer.

And there goes normal out the window again.

"Oh, Dad, I haven't worn that in months," I replied, trying to keep my tone casual, though his sudden shift in concern had my nerves buzzing.

His brow furrowed deeply, the flicker of worry in his eyes unmistakable. "Sady doll, please wear it. There's been too much going on these last few weeks."

"Fine," I relented, though his tone left little room for argument.

He seemed to hesitate, his fingers drumming lightly on the counter before he spoke again. "What about your mother's necklace?"

I froze for half a second, reluctant to volunteer anything. The medallion wasn't exactly the kind of accessory I was eager to add to my outfit. "Do I have to?"

"Yes, you do." The look on Dad's face told me this wasn't a battle I'd win. "Humor me."

"Give me a minute!" I called over my shoulder, dragging my feet as I headed upstairs to comply with his parental request.

In my room, I reached for the dagger, its worn leather sheath a comforting weight in my hands. With practiced ease, I strapped it securely against my calf, the cool metal of the handle pressing against my skin.

I was surprised by how quickly it warmed, almost as if it were coming alive, syncing with me. Within seconds, its presence faded into the background—no longer a foreign object but an extension of myself. As though it had always belonged there, waiting.

The medallion was another story entirely.

It wasn't exactly the sort of thing a teenager would choose to accessorize with. Made from an obsidian-like metal, black with garnet swirls that seemed to shift subtly in the light, it was encased in beautifully interlaced knotwork. In the center was an embossed heart flanked by two raised wings, their details so intricate they appeared to flutter if you looked too closely.

As I held it in my hand, a faint warmth seeped into my palm—not the comforting kind, but a subtle reminder of the power it contained. This wasn't just jewelry. It was a weapon.

Sliding my thumbnail beneath the point of the heart, I triggered the hidden mechanism. The blade slid free, its edges jagged and barbed in a way that screamed intention. Ruthless. Efficient. Lethal.

This was Mom's handiwork. She'd crafted it while pregnant with me—one of her many talents in working with metals. It was exquisite, deceptively delicate in appearance yet impossibly strong. Like Mom herself. She'd known, even before I was born, that her child might need every edge available for survival.

And like the dagger, this too was made from the celestial metal which they came to earth with.

Fastening the medallion around my neck, I felt its weight settle against my skin, heavier than I remembered. Where the dagger seemed to meld with my body, the medallion felt foreign—an ever-present reminder of what it was, and what I might become.

"Sady doll, everything alright?" Dad's voice carried up the stairs, lighter now, but his concern still lingered at the edges.

"Fine," I replied, tugging my scarf off the back of my chair as I headed out the door. Wrapping it around my neck, I made sure it covered the medallion. The last thing I needed was to draw any extra attention

Dad emerged at the bottom of the stairs, arms crossed but stance softening. "Good. Just... be careful, alright?"

"I always am," I said with a half-smile, descending the steps. His brow arched skeptically, and I rolled my eyes. "Okay, mostly."

"Mostly isn't as reassuring as you think it is," he muttered, stepping aside as I passed. "Not these days."

The cool morning air greeted me like a slap as I stepped outside. Adjusting the scarf for warmth—and for secrecy—I tightened my bag over my shoulder and took a deep breath. Time to face the day.

Once I arrived at school, I kept my scarf wrapped snugly around my neck, despite the heat from the vents. The crowded hallways buzzed with chatter, but my mind felt miles away. *Get with it, Sady,* I told myself.

When I entered the classroom, Mr. Black was perched on the windowsill, arms crossed, watching as the class settled in. His observant blue eyes swept the room, a flicker of mischief in them as he began to speak.

"Students, our class has been chosen to present *A New History of Halloween* at a very special event this year." His gaze lingered on the groans and murmurs rippling through the room. "The bad news? We only have two weeks."

A voice piped up from the front row. "But Mr. Black, what about our essay next week? And the test?" Taylor, the most organized person in class, sounded downright horrified.

"Well," he replied with a smirk, "both are cancelled. The next two weeks will be dedicated to this project, which will count for fifteen percent of your final mark."

The class collectively exhaled in relief before he continued, outlining the expectations for our group work. He divided us into groups of five, listing names with precision, and I ended up with Michaela, Jamie, Kelsey, and Linda. It was a relief—I'd spoken to all of them before, and there was none of the awkwardness that usually happened when I got stuck with strangers. Linda, in particular, was the calming presence, her quiet humor and unshakable composure grounding the group even when the class chat exploded over a forgotten assignment. She'd joined us a few times during lunch in the cafeteria, fitting seamlessly with Michaela's loud antics, Kelsey's boundless enthusiasm, and Jamie's thoughtful observations—the only guy in our group and an aspiring writer who always seemed to be soaking in the chaos for future inspiration.

Mr. Black caught my eye briefly. A slight nod confirmed my suspicion—he'd paired us deliberately. I bit back a smile, appreciative despite myself.

Once everyone had moved into their groups, the first task was to elect a team leader. The leader would then draw the group's topic from a hat—a randomized twist to keep things interesting.

"Sady, you've got the highest test scores," Kelsey said, nudging me lightly. "You should be team lead."

I opened my mouth to respond, but the thought of stepping into the spotlight made my skin prickle. "Actually," I said quickly, "isn't it

Michaela's birthday? I think it should be her."

Jamie's face lit up, and he nodded enthusiastically. "Absolutely! I mean, no one's more into Halloween than Michaela. She's perfect."

Michaela's eyes widened, her cheeks turning pink. "Oh, you guys, really?"

"Totally," I added, grateful to shift the attention away from myself. "Besides, birthday-girl should get the honor."

Michaela stood, performing an exaggerated curtsy that drew a round of chuckles from the table. "Well, since my royal subjects insist..."

She marched to the front of the class, radiating confidence, and plunged her hand dramatically into the hat to select our fate.

The entire class watched—some eager, others apprehensive—as she unfolded the slip of paper.

The moment her eyes landed on the words, her enthusiasm was palpable. She bounced back toward our table, practically skipping. The energy thrummed all the way to the back of the room like an electric current.

Meanwhile, a strange tingling crawled up the nape of my neck. It was faint but persistent—like an itch just out of reach. For a brief second, my overactive imagination took over. *Maybe this is it.* Maybe one of the "paths" Ramira mentioned would lead me to become *Spider-Girl.* The thought of swinging between skyscrapers in New York City, webs flying, was so absurd I snorted out loud.

Kelsey caught that and gave me an equally absurd look, clearly asking what she'd missed.

Michaela's arrival back at our table drowned out my embarrassing moment, saving me from having to explain my internal Marvel crossover. She slapped the piece of paper down in front of us with a triumphant grin.

"Guys, seriously. Best topic ever!" she exclaimed, loud enough to turn heads. "Halloween and the ancient origins of Vampires!"

My stomach flipped—and not in a good way. *Of course* we'd get this topic. Because if there was anything I knew far too much about—more than anyone in this room—it was vampires. *Real* ones that is. The tingling at my neck deepened, as if mocking me.

"Hey, Mr. Black," I asked, not bothering to mask my skepticism. "Who exactly is this special presentation for?"

"Well, Miss Sady, I'm glad you asked," he said, meeting my gaze evenly. "The Royal Ontario Museum is hosting a special event at Casa Loma this Halloween, showcasing new perspectives. Your generation has access to global knowledge—what better way to reimagine the past?"

Global knowledge? Sure. My family's history and firsthand experience were not exactly *group project*-friendly, so I nodded mutely.

"Okay, let's get started," Kelsey said, trying to refocus us.

"Michaela, what's the plan?" Linda asked gently, her calm demeanor steadying the group as Michaela, still giddy, explained her vision.

"Kelsey, you're good at organizing, right?" Michaela said, delegating without hesitation. "Linda, you're amazing with visuals—can you brainstorm ideas for the display? Jamie, I want you on narrative. It needs your humor to keep it from being dry or corny. Sady..." She turned to me, her voice softening. "Could you dive into the history itself? You're so good with research."

I swallowed, nodding despite the unease bubbling in my chest. "Sure. Sounds good."

As the class wrapped up, a quiet feeling of something not quite right lingered. But then, sitting next to Linda at lunch, jotting down ideas, I realized something—I was with a team that felt safe, comfortable even. Maybe I could get through this after all.

My role in the project was to gather as much information as possible from different cultures with vampire myths. The thing was, I already knew most of it. And what I didn't know, I could cheat by asking Mom. Or Dad. But the truth didn't live in history books. Not the full truth. And not the right dates, most of the time. *Can I lie and just fake it?*

For the rest of the lunch period, I smiled and nodded through group discussions, doing my best to stay under the radar. Michaela's excitement over the topic was contagious, her energy filling every lull in conversation with suggestions and wild ideas. Linda's quiet but impressive visual ideas helped keep us on track, balancing out Michaela's more... unconventional thoughts.

"Okay, so for our presentation on historical vampires, I was thinking we could focus on Vlad the Impaler, Elizabeth Bathory, and maybe even the myths surrounding the Plogojowitz case," Linda suggested, sketching rough ideas in her notebook.

"There was also Sarah Stout, and Duchess of Bedford?" I offered, preferring to keep my input to a minimum but giving us some more obscure figures that my family had researched years ago. My parents had sought out any legends, any folktales and rumours of the centuries of Vampires before I was born. Moonlighting as Vampire Hunters, I suppose.

"Oh, and what about including Arminius Vambéry? I think he was Stoker's inspiration for Van Helsing?"

Jamie perked up, this was his genre loving all things heroes and villains. "Sady, that is a wicked idea."

Michaela's hand shot up as if we were still in kindergarten. "Ooh! What about Damon Salvatore?"

Jamie snorted, barely containing his laughter. "Michaela, you know The Vampire Diaries isn't exactly... historical."

She shot him a look, feigning outrage. "Excuse me, but have you seen Damon Salvatore? He's timeless. Honestly, he belongs in the history books."

I couldn't help but beam as Linda sighed dramatically. "As much as I love Ian Somerhalder's cheekbones, I don't think our teacher will go for that."

"But imagine it," Michaela insisted, waving her hands as if painting the scene in the air. "A slide dedicated to Damon: 'The Influence of Smoldering Eyes on Vampire Lore.'"

The whole group burst into laughter, and even I felt the strain slip a little.

"Fine, fine," Michaela relented, a playful pout on her lips. "We'll stick to real historical vampires. But if there's a costume component, I'm showing up in black leather and giving my best brooding stare."

"Noted," Jamie said, scribbling into his notebook. "Adding 'emotional support vampire' to our list of assets."

And just like that, for a moment, everything felt normal.

But beneath the laughter, every word about vampires scraped against raw nerves, each mention of blood and lore stirring memories I'd buried deep. While they joked about fictional monsters, I couldn't shake the knowledge that the real ones were all too close.

By the time the final bell rang, I was no closer to wrapping my head around the day's events than I had been that morning. *Vampires* as our Halloween project. Of course. Because if there was one topic I could speak on with firsthand experience, it was this.

As the school day ended, spilling students into the crisp autumn air, I lingered near the bike racks. Most of my classmates scattered quickly, eager to leave, but I couldn't seem to move. A restless energy churned inside me, gnawing at my insides with increasing intensity. The medallion around my neck felt heavier than it had that morning, its presence a constant reminder of all the things I wasn't saying aloud.

And then there was the hunger—coiling, growing deeper. Not for food. For something else. Something I was fighting every second.

Even knowing that Dad was likely still passed out from catching up on sleep, the thought of going straight home filled me with dread. I needed answers—answers I wasn't going to get from Dad's cautious reassurances or Mom's relentless research.

I needed to talk to Mr. Black. *Greyson*.

Pushing aside any doubts, I swung my leg over my bike and headed toward the trail leading to his house. The cool air brushed against my skin as I rode, keeping my pace deliberately measured. If anyone were watching, it would look normal—casual. But my thoughts raced far ahead of me, buzzing with questions I didn't even know how to ask.

When his house came into view, a sense of foreboding washed over me. There were no lights on inside except for the motion-sensitive ones outside, flicking on at my arrival. The windows were dark, the air heavy with an unnatural stillness. My heart sank. *Maybe he isn't home.*

I turned to leave, ready to scold myself for coming unannounced, when something sharp and overwhelming hit me—a scent curling into my senses like a vice.

Blood.

And based on the sheer strength of it, there had to be a lot.

Something was wrong. *Very* wrong.

My thoughts leapt immediately to Greyson. *Is he hurt? Injured?*

Worse?

Kicking my bike to the ground, I sprinted toward the house. My head buzzed with the rush of adrenaline as I bounded up the steps two at a time. The front door was locked, but the smell pouring from inside set off every alarm in my body. I didn't think—I acted.

With one solid push, the door splintered off its hinges, crashing inward.

The acrid stench of blood thickened the air, coating my throat, but I pushed the discomfort away. Scanning the dark entryway, I strained to hear anything—any sound, any sign of life.

"Greyson!" My voice trembled as I called out, echoing against the empty walls.

No answer. Just the faint creak of the house settling. A cold breeze brushed past me, and I realized the blood wasn't just a *smell*—it was a presence, almost tangible in its weight.

The staircase loomed ahead, and I instinctively glanced upward. That's when I heard it—soft, uneven breaths from the second floor. Relief surged through me, but it was fleeting.

Something wasn't right.

I launched up the stairs, landing less delicately—and more loudly—than I would have liked.

"Greyson, where are you?" My voice broke, desperate now. I followed the sound of his labored breathing to the bedroom at the end of the hall.

The door was ajar, dim light from the hallway spilling inside. Pushing it open anxiously, I stepped in—and stopped short.

Chapter 27

Greyson lay sprawled on a king-size bed with an elegant silver-velvet headboard, the black sheets beneath him rumpled, damp with sweat. But it was his pallor that gripped me—his skin, usually a warm sun-kissed hue, had turned ashen, stretched tight over sharp cheekbones. His chest rose and fell in shallow, uneven breaths, his half-lidded eyes unfocused and fever-glazed.

A thin tube trailed from his left arm, connected to a hanging IV bag. No—not just any bag. *Blood.*

Beside the bed, a wide tub of half-melted ice water sat atop a low table. Towels draped over its edges, some already damp and discarded in a heap on the floor. A fresh cloth lay folded next to the tub—evidence of an attempt to bring down his fever. But it was clear that effort had fallen short.

I hesitated in the doorway, confusion settling over me like a thick fog.

The damp towels, the incomplete attempt to cool him down—it all felt too... improvised. Like someone had started caring for him and then vanished, leaving him to manage on his own.

But why?

And if he'd been alone this whole time, how had he managed even this much? The thought sent a ripple of concern through me. Greyson was usually a whirlwind of energy—erratic, eccentric, always on the move. This was fragile. This was helpless. Alone.

"Who in the hell—" His voice was hoarse, barely above a whisper. "What—? Is that... Miss Sady?"

His chest rose and fell with each strained breath, and under the dim light, his skin looked not just pale, but ashen—like the color had been drained from it. It was the same sickly gray as his joggers. A blood transfusion, here, in his bedroom. Why wasn't he in a hospital?

Greyson let out a weak groan, the towel slipping slightly from his torso. I grabbed the fresh cloth, dipped it into the icy water, and pressed it to his burning skin. The cloth warmed almost instantly against his unnatural heat, so I folded ice into the fabric before replacing it, hoping to offer even a moment of relief.

He lifted a trembling hand as though to push me away, but it fell limply onto the bed. "Miss Sady..." he murmured, his voice barely a whisper. "You shouldn't... be here."

A feeble protest, nothing like his usual, unpredictable energy. His pallor, the rumpled sheets, the blood bag hanging beside him—it all felt wrong.

"Well, you shouldn't be doing... whatever this is," I shot back, harsher than intended. I gestured toward the IV stand, my frustration barely veiled behind the rising tide of worry. "You're hooked up to a transfusion in your bedroom, Greyson."

I hesitated, the words catching in my throat before I forced them out.

"This isn't normal."

His lips twitched as if to laugh, but no sound came out. His eyelids fluttered closed, his face contorted briefly in pain. "Normal... is relative, Miss Sady."

I stiffened, the icy towel still in my hand, his choice of words settling over me like a lead shroud. My chest tightened, but I pushed past the implications—this wasn't the time to dwell on cryptic remarks. He needed help.

"Miss Sady, please, do sit down." He managed a weak smile. "You look like you might faint."

That did it. My head jerked up, and before I could rein it in, the retort shot out. "Oh, you're concerned for my safety? That's rich, coming from the guy who looks like he's auditioning for a zombie movie."

The faintest trace of a smile flickered across his lips but vanished almost instantly, replaced by another wince of pain. I bit my lip, regretting the edge in my voice. This wasn't the time to snipe at him, no matter how frustrating his lack of answers was.

Greyson shifted slightly, grimacing as he adjusted himself on the bed. "By the way," he rasped, "was it really necessary to knock my front door off its hinges?"

I froze, caught red-handed—or perhaps door-handed. My cheeks burned. "I thought you were in trouble," I muttered, avoiding his gaze. "What was I supposed to do? Ring the doorbell?"

He let out another wheezy chuckle. "Miss Sady, I appreciate your enthusiasm for heroics." His smile faded. "But truly, you shouldn't have come."

Ignoring his weak protest, I reached out—not physically, but with the heightened awareness I had spent years honing. Tuning out the distant hum of the refrigerator downstairs, the faint rustle of trees outside, and even my own quickened heartbeat, I focused entirely on Greyson.

There it was. His heartbeat. Or what passed for one. It was faint and staggered, uneven in a way that sent a chill creeping through me. A slow, halting rhythm that didn't belong to someone human—or at least, not someone alive for much longer.

His eyes fluttered open again, catching me mid-focus. "What are you doing?" His voice was barely audible, but there was an edge to it—curiosity, or maybe suspicion.

"Checking your pulse," I replied briskly, straightening as if I hadn't just been caught using a not-so-human ability. "Which, by the way, is a disaster. You need—" I stopped short, realizing I had no idea what he needed. A hospital? More blood? A miracle?

Greyson let out another wheezy chuckle. "Miss Sady, I assure you—this is... routine."

"Routine?" I gestured wildly to the IV bag and his corpse-like complexion. "This is routine? You look like a vampire after a week-long juice cleanse, Greyson!"

His first name slipped out before I could stop it, and it hung in the air between us. His brows lifted faintly, the ghost of a smirk tugging at the corners of his mouth despite the exhaustion carved into his features.

"And yet," he countered, "you're the one who looks ready to pass out."

"Oh, don't worry about me," I shot back, grabbing another damp towel and dunking it in the ice water. "Focus on staying alive, or whatever it is you are supposed to be doing, and I'll focus on... not fainting."

His weak laugh followed me as I slipped into the bathroom, closing the door behind me with a quiet click. Out of his sight, I exhaled a shaky breath, gripping the cool porcelain sink.

I didn't need a new towel. Not really. The ice water tub was right there, but I needed the moment—just a sliver of space where his fever-bright eyes couldn't see through the fear I was barely holding back.

My hands trembled as I let the faucet run over the towel anyway, the water a distraction. Something deeper was happening here, and a quiet, gnawing part of me wasn't sure I wanted to know what.

When I returned to his bedside, the cloth dripping faintly as I pressed it gently to his forehead, he shivered under the touch. His lips parted as if to speak, but I wasn't about to let him waste his energy.

As soon as he opened his mouth, I plonked the cold towel right over his face, muffling whatever words he was trying to get out. The faint protest beneath the cloth made me smile briefly. At least he still had enough fight left in him to grumble.

"Greyson, I need to know what's going on." I pulled the towel away slowly, avoiding his eyes as I replaced it with a fresh, ice-cold one. "What is wrong? What else can I do to help?"

He took a shallow breath, his voice barely above a whisper. "Miss Sady, I was born with a very rare genetic heart condition. Since I was a child, I've endured regular blood infusions. The short version of a long story is that my blood platelets are in a constant state of decay and require frequent replacements."

I stilled, the gravity of his words sinking in. My heart clenched at the thought of him lying here like this regularly—alone.

"I've studied enough anatomy to know transfusions shouldn't be painful for the patient," I said softly, not adding that I'd probably read more medical textbooks than most pre-med students. Mom hadn't pushed me into it out of academic curiosity—it was part of my tactical training.

Know weaknesses, she'd called it. But somewhere along the way,

I'd learned more about healing than hurting. Maybe that wasn't her intention, but it became mine.

Greyson managed a weak nod. "That's true," he murmured, shifting slightly as if trying to sit up.

I placed a firm hand on his shoulder, gently pressing him back down. "Not so fast," I chided.

He sighed, conceding. "Most people feel nothing during this procedure, but thanks to my rare blood type, my body tries to reject the transfusion every time. So, every so often—months if I'm lucky—I end up like this." He gestured weakly to himself, his voice tinged with a resignation that made me more aware of the silence between us.

I said nothing, focusing instead on wiping the sweat from his arms, shoulders, and—against my better judgment—his perfectly defined abs. For once, I didn't blush. I was too focused on offering whatever relief I could.

"How much longer?" I asked, breaking the silence.

"Hmm? Oh, another hour or so. I think." His voice was fading again, but he kept his eyes on me, barely holding on.

"Okay," I said firmly. "I'm not going anywhere. I'll stay with you until it's finished."

"Miss Sady..." His voice was soft, insistent. "You don't have to stay."

I arched an eyebrow, meeting his gaze head-on. "Greyson, didn't you offer friendship?"

His lips parted slightly, as if unsure where I was going with this.

"Well, I believe this is what friends do."

Another ripple of pain tore through him, and this time, he couldn't suppress the cry that escaped his lips. His hands balled into fists, clutching at the blanket beside him. Instinctively, I reached out, brushing a cool cloth across his brow in a soothing motion.

"Sady," he rasped, his voice hoarse and strained, "you are... a beautiful soul. Thank you."

"Oh, shut up and just rest, okay?" I muttered, not meeting his eyes. Compliments had never been my forte, and something about the way he said it made me squirm in a way I had no interest in unpacking.

For now, I focused on the simple task of keeping him comfortable. I couldn't fix this—not the way I wanted to—but at least I could do this much.

His skin was getting hotter by the minute. His breathing grew uneven, punctuated by a wheezing rasp that sent a tight knot of worry through me. I forced myself to ignore the cloying scent of blood hanging in the air like an unwelcome guest, clinging to focus. Nearly thirty minutes crawled by, and just as I dared to hope the worst was over, Greyson's body convulsed. His limbs shook, and a fit of harsh, wracking coughs ripped through him, leaving him hunched forward, gasping for air.

I reached for the tub of ice water, but it had all but melted—the remaining water tepid and useless. The damp towels were warm to the touch, offering no relief.

Panic flared. I bolted to the kitchen, yanking open the freezer. The last tray of ice cubes and a few frozen bags of peas and corn became my makeshift cooling supplies. I sprinted back upstairs, knowing I'd only been gone a few seconds, but my heart still hammered with dread at what I might find.

It was worse than I feared.

Greyson was half-collapsed on the edge of the bed, dangerously close to toppling over completely. Dropping the ice and frozen veggies onto the nearest dresser, I rushed to his side, steadying him with only a fraction of my strength before easing him back onto the pillows. His weight was solid, heavier than I expected, and in the process, our faces ended up inches apart.

"Miss Sady, when did you get here?" he muttered, his voice hoarse and slurred. His fevered gaze flickered over my face, unfocused, searching. A pause. Then, barely above a whisper—"Wait, is it really you?"

He's delirious. Well isn't that just *great*.

"Greyson, you're burning up," I said softly, trying to keep my voice calm despite the alarm bells ringing in my head. As I maneuvered him back onto the bed, his right hand lifted, brushing against my cheek. A familiar tingling sensation rippled through me. Not now, *damn it*.

"I'm afraid I may be hallucinating," he mumbled, his flushed cheeks and sweat-dampened brow made his fever painfully obvious. I grabbed the towel, now cool again, and gently wiped away the beads of sweat clinging to his skin. His focus latched onto me, unfocused yet oddly intense, as if he were trying to anchor himself in reality.

"You move really fast," he murmured, his voice slipping into a slur. "And if you broke my door, that means you're really, really strong."

A shiver ran through me, not from fear but from the unsettling mix of clarity and confusion in his words. His expression wavered between awe and disbelief, as if he wasn't entirely sure I was real.

"Greyson, you've got a fever and are talking more nonsense than usual," I said, keeping my tone light even as a twinge of guilt wormed its way through me.

His lips curled into a weak, lopsided smile. "You look real. You feel real." His eyelids drooped, and his voice dropped to a whisper. "But what if you're not?"

Fixing that door was going to be an absolute priority before he regained full awareness. Years of moving—and the inevitable home repairs that came with it—had made me more than capable of remedying the situation. Hopefully.

"I may go to hell for this," Greyson interrupted my mental to-do list, his fevered words snapping me back to the present.

His voice was thin, threaded with a mix of exhaustion and something dangerously close to wonder. His glassy eyes drifted over my face, as if he were trying to decide whether I was real or just another trick of his fevered mind.

Before I could react, he tugged me closer.

The world tilted as his lips brushed against mine—soft, burning, achingly warm. The kiss deepened, his arms pulling me tighter, and for a moment, the feverish heat between us eclipsed everything else. It was as if he was drawing the air from my lungs, leaving me breathless and tingling from head to toe. Just as I thought I might combust—whether from lack of oxygen or the fire coursing through me—he released me and sank back against the pillows.

His skin was noticeably cooler.

I stumbled backward, gripping the towel with trembling hands. My lips still tingled, and my mind whirled. Was it my imagination, or had his fever actually broken?

Ugh. Now who's delusional?

"I must say," he murmured, his voice softer now, the edges of his words blurring with exhaustion, "this hallucination is the loveliest I've ever had."

His lips curled into a faint, dreamy smile, and his glassy eyes wandered as if he were seeing something just beyond the edge of reality. It was both unsettling and strangely endearing—the way he seemed to drift between worlds, not entirely certain which one I belonged to.

He closed his eyes, his breathing finally steadying as exhaustion pulled him under. Mechanically, I continued wiping his arms and chest, trying to ground myself as the reality of what just happened washed over me.

That wasn't just any kiss.

That was my first kiss—.

And to him, it was just part of a hallucination?

"Tiny Sady..." he whispered, his words barely audible as he drifted toward unconsciousness. "I wonder what other gifts you inherited..."

My hands froze mid-motion. My breath caught in my throat. *Did he just—?*

The word *tiny* flickered through my mind, stirring an uncomfortable memory. A faint ripple of recognition ran through me, but I shoved it aside. Greyson needed my help, and I had a broken door to deal with before anything else.

Looking closely at his face, I noticed his breathing had steadied, and he seemed to be deeply asleep. *Good.* Time for me to clean up. Moving swiftly, I erased any evidence of my uninvited visit. Towels were rinsed, ice bags returned to the freezer, and the remaining frozen peas tucked away. By the time I was done, it looked as though no one had been here at all.

Except for one glaring problem. The door. The stupid front door.

I sighed, running a hand through my hair as I surveyed the damage. At first, I'd assumed it was just a normal door—something I could fix in a few minutes. But now, standing in front of the mess I'd made, I realized the truth. He wasn't kidding when he said I had to be strong.

Reinforced steel. Not wood.

What the hell? Who has a reinforced steel door on their house? I mean, other than my family.

I exhaled, rolling my shoulders. The door looked mostly

intact—except for the handle, the hinges, the lock—oh, and the entire right edge, where my forceful entrance had left a visible dent. *Okay. Not completely unfixable.* Taking a deep breath, I strengthened my shield and used all my power to bend the metal back into shape. My muscles strained with the effort, but after a few minutes, it looked... almost the same as before. *Almost.*

If you didn't look too closely, the metal seemed smooth enough. But beneath the fresh coat of normalcy, the edges weren't quite right—subtly warped, as if they had softened under extreme heat. A slight ripple in the surface hinted at something not entirely natural, a barely-there reminder of the force I'd used.

I bit my lip, hoping Greyson wouldn't notice. Or, at the very least, that he wouldn't look too closely.

Satisfied it would hold for now, I took the stairs two at a time for one last check on him. Still sleeping soundly, his face looked relaxed and peaceful in a way that made him almost unrecognizable. In class, with his quick wit and unpredictable energy, I'd guessed he was maybe thirty at most. But now, without the awareness in his features, without the usual smirk or challenge in his gaze, he looked younger. Almost boyish.

It was strange to reconcile this version of him with the whirlwind personality I'd come to know.

The bag of blood hanging beside him was empty now, and I hesitated before removing the IV drip from his arm. My fingers hovered over the tubing. I should do it. Leaving it in too long wasn't good, and I knew how.

For years, Mom had drilled me in emergency medical procedures—the kind you'd expect to learn in a combat medic's crash course rather than a suburban Red Cross class.

I knew how to set a broken bone, how to suture a wound, even how to handle a field transfusion. Weaving medical training into our lives as seamlessly as survival skills was Mom's speciality. She'd always said it was just in case, but as I stood over Greyson, those lessons felt less like preparation and more like prophecy.

With practiced precision, I pinched off the IV line, disinfected the site, and slid the needle out of his arm. I applied gentle pressure with a sterile pad, then wrapped his arm in a clean bandage. The motions were smooth, automatic, a small comfort in the midst of all the chaos.

And then it hit me.

A flicker of sapphire and brushed silver swept over me, a flash of color and sensation so brief it felt like the blink of a dream.

Ah, hell. Now?

The sensation left me frozen, my pulse pounding in my ears. It was faint, like a whisper on the edge of hearing, and I waited—half expecting something more. A word. A voice. A clue.

But there was nothing. Just silence.

A quick reach led me nowhere. Nothing to pin down, like it had been my imagination. Now who was the one hallucinating?

I needed to leave. Now. Making sure the door was secured behind me, I jogged over to my bike, still lying on the ground where I'd dropped it. As I pedaled toward home, my thoughts tangled into an impossible knot. *What the hell just happened?*

Between the blood transfusion, the strange Surge I felt, and—oh, right—the kiss, my head felt like it might implode.

I focused on the steady hum of my wheels against the pavement, letting the motion calm my nerves.

And then Mom's voice burst into my mind like a firecracker.

SADY BABY, WHERE ARE YOU?

The shock of her telepathic contact jolted me so hard I nearly veered into traffic. A car honked, blaring in my ears as I yanked the handlebars back under control.

ALMOST HOME, WAS WORKING ON SCHOOL STUFF.

I shot back quickly, forcing my heartbeat to slow. *Technically not a lie... I guess.*

OKAY, LOVE, SEE YOU SOON. I GOT TAKE-OUT. DAD IS STILL OUT LIKE A LIGHT.

Relief washed over me as her presence faded from my mind. *Good.* That gave me time to pull myself together.

I should tell them about the sapphire and brushed silver I sensed again. *That's important.* More important than... well, *other things.* Like my first kiss. With my teacher. Who had been delirious with a fever and probably wouldn't even remember it happened.

Right. I'd just tell them I sensed the colors while I was out on my bike. *Totally believable.* Besides, I did try to feel where it came from, and nothing. Like it never happened, but I had to trust myself on this one. It did.

Walking through the back door into the kitchen, I found Mom unpacking the food onto the counter. The sight of her immediately reassured me, though I barely had time to react before she scooped me into a hug, nearly knocking the wind out of me.

"Hey, Sady baby. Thanks for letting Dad sleep—I know he needed it." She pulled back, giving me a once-over before pressing a hand to my forehead, concern flickering in her eyes. "Whoa, you're burning up."

"Am I?" I forced a shrug. "Probably just from the bike ride. I took a detour to the quarry."

Her brow furrowed, but she nodded. "Oh, okay. Since when do you get that warm?"

Oh, brother. *Change the subject. Now.*

She beat me to it. "Never mind that for now. Ever since we saw that video of Cassiel you know your father has been shaken up, right?"

"Uhm, yeah?" Relief and unease tangled together. At least I didn't have to steer the conversation away, but her words stirred something tense inside me.

Then, without warning, she gripped my shoulders, her fingers tightening.

Her face was too close—close enough that I could see the raw urgency in her eyes.

"If they ever find us, and you have to make a choice—it has to be him. It must always be your father. Promise me."

"Whoa, Mom!" My voice wavered under the weight of her demand. She was shouting now, only in my mind, shaking me slightly, and the force of it was overwhelming. "No, I can't—"

COME HELL OR HIGH WATER, IF WE ARE UNDER ATTACK, YOU MUST CHOOSE SAM.

Her voice pushed into my mind, a desperate edge laced into every word. Tears streamed down her face, though she didn't sob. She wouldn't. Not in front of me.

IF SOMETHING HAPPENED TO HIM, I WOULD RAISE HELL ON EARTH. AGAIN. ONLY THIS TIME, THERE WOULD BE NO STOPPING ME. NOT EVEN FOR YOU.

Her words hit like a physical blow.

"Mom, stop it." I pleaded, desperate to understand, though part of me didn't want to.

She exhaled shakily, loosening her grip on my shoulders.

"Nothing is going to happen," I said, trying to believe my own words as I searched for something—anything—to defuse the tension. "Remember? Forever everlasting, right?"

Her expression softened slightly at the phrase, but her eyes remained troubled. For a fleeting moment, I thought about telling her everything—about Greyson, the sapphire and brushed silver, the kiss. But I couldn't. Not now.

Not when the weight of the unknown already threatened to crush us all.

"Mom, while I was out—" I shuffled my feet, doing my best to look casual and failing miserably. "I felt the sapphire and silver again. It was super subtle, just a flicker, and no words this time. Just the color, and it was so weak I couldn't get a pin on the direction."

"Really? Strange," she murmured, her hands settling firmly on my shoulders. Her gaze locked onto mine, her eyes searching. "But you said before you get absolutely no hostility from it, right?"

Her thumbs rubbed small, absent circles against my collarbones, a motion that might have seemed comforting if not for the way her fingers dug in just a little too hard. I knew that look—the one that meant her mind was racing, filing through every possibility, every threat.

"Yeah," I managed, forcing my voice to stay steady. "Nothing but warmth, and completely benign. It was... so brief, I kinda questioned if it was just my imagination."

Her brow furrowed, a tiny line creasing the space between her eyes. "Brief and benign, huh?" she echoed, as if testing the word on her tongue. "You're sure?"

I swallowed, her scrutiny pressing down on me. "Positive."

"And you made sure Ramira saw this too, when you connected with her?"

"Yes, Mom, I did."

For a heartbeat, neither of us moved. She didn't blink, didn't breathe, just held me there under the razor's edge of her focus. I felt like a specimen under glass, every instinct in me fighting the urge to squirm away.

Her lips parted, a question forming—but then—

"Whoa, ladies of my love!"

Dad's voice cut through the tension, warm and entirely oblivious, a splash of normalcy that shattered whatever unspoken interrogation was about to unfold.

"How long have I been asleep?"

"Sam, my love, it's nearly eight o'clock." Mom glided toward him, rising onto her toes to press a kiss to his lips. "I brought takeout."

"Oh good, I'm starving." His arms wrapped around her waist, pulling her closer. The unmistakable energy between them was like a flashing neon sign. Even a blind man could see where this was headed.

Oh, brother. Time to make myself scarce.

"Uhm, I'll just eat in my room, okay?" Grabbing the takeout box labeled with my name, along with some utensils, I didn't wait for a response. They were too wrapped up in their little moment to notice my exaggerated eye roll anyway.

Once in my room, I sat on the windowsill, the box of food beside me. I thought I was starving, but now I was just picking at it, my appetite lost somewhere in the chaos of my thoughts. The north-facing window had become my go-to spot for stargazing, a way to clear my head and find calm. But here in the city, the stars were drowned out by light pollution, leaving me staring at a dull, empty sky.

Fitting, really.

My brain whirled, a cacophony of problems all vying for attention.

School, my parents, Greyson, this inexplicable connection—how was I supposed to deal with all of it? Normally, I loved solving puzzles, but this one felt like a ten-thousand-piece nightmare with no corner pieces. So, where do I start?

Googling Greyson's heart condition.

The next hour of research yielded nothing useful. Every article, forum, and obscure journal only deepened the enigma that was Greyson—and the unsettling truth of what my heightened senses revealed. A faint warmth prickled under my skin, and I wondered if I had been staring at my screen too long.

Exhaustion draped over me like a heavy blanket, and I didn't even bother taking my barely-eaten takeout container back to the kitchen. My limbs felt leaden as I collapsed onto my bed, the cool sheets barely registering against my overheated skin. Sleep claimed me, swallowing my frustration—and the nagging thought that something wasn't quite right with me either.

This time, my dream carried me to the peak of a mountain, where I stood alone, surrounded by an endless expanse of rolling hills. They rose and fell like waves frozen in time, stretching toward the horizon.

Far below, a ravine cut through the land, swallowed in shadow. But the darkness wasn't still—it shifted and churned as an eerie mist began to roll in.

Obsidian streaked with oxblood red crept across the landscape like an oil spill, thick and relentless, swallowing everything in its path.

Panic gnawed at the edges of my ribs as I realized it wasn't just covering the ground—it was consuming it.

I turned, searching for an escape, but the entire mountain was surrounded. The dark swirls climbed steadily, snaking toward me with slow, unshaken certainty.

There's a connection, isn't there?

Mom's colors had changed—no more black. The void-like obsidian had faded, replaced by something earthier, steadier—a muted brown, rich but subdued. The oxblood red that once pulsed with raw intensity had softened, streaked with threads of Dad's gold, weaving through it like light breaking through old cracks.

And yet, even now, the sight of the colours she used to be, what she used to be, sent chills down my spine.

The mist thickened, rising higher. I could feel it in my lungs, heavy, clinging, seeping into the cracks of my skin.

Lightning split the sky, striking dangerously close. My breath caught as static prickled over my arms, the scent of rain tinged the air.

From the point of impact, three distinct swirls of color emerged.

First, sapphire slid south, steady and deliberate, cutting through the mist like a river carving its path through stone.

Then, muted mauve drifted north, clumsy yet elusive, slipping through the storm without resistance, never lingering long enough to be caught.

Finally, rich moss-green wrapped around me first, warm and grounding, wrapping through my limbs like a presence that had always been there. Like it had always been a part of me. It was comforting—but only for a moment.

The mist kept rising.

And then, I woke up.

CHAPTER 28

Waking up before the dream ended, drenched in a cold sweat, the heat from last night had already faded. A strange heaviness lingered in my limbs, like the echo of something that was never supposed to be there. Sheets tangled around me, damp as if caught in a current while I slept. My skin prickled—not quite cold, not quite warm. Just... *off*.

Pushing the thought away, I rubbed my eyes. The dream slipped from my mind, its remnants clinging to my mind like dew on spiderwebs caught in the morning sun.

Greyson. Would he be at school today?

Dragging myself out of bed, I stepped into the shower, letting the hot water wash away the tension clinging to me. The warmth should have been soothing, but it only reminded me of the strange heat still lingering under my skin.

When I finally made it downstairs, my hair was still damp, and the realization of how late I was hit me hard. Mom had already gone—I could tell because Dad was in the kitchen, gripping his coffee like it was the only thing keeping him upright.

If she were still home, he'd be moving around—circling her in that weird mating ritual way they always seemed to do. But now? He looked drained. Not a sloucher by nature, here he was, leaning against the counter slouched low enough that I wasn't staring at his sternum—but further up, to his collarbones.

"Morning, Dad," I said carefully, trying not to startle him.

"Ah, crap!" He jerked, hot coffee sloshing over his hand and forearm.

I was already moving, grabbing a towel and turning on the faucet. "I'm sorry!"

But he just shook his hand off, sending droplets flying, then stepped past me to run it under the water. He barely even looked at it.

"It's fine," he said, drying his arm on a dish towel. "Guess I need to be more awake before handling hot beverages."

There wasn't a single mark on his skin, of course. Not even a hint of irritation.

I sighed, tossing the towel onto the counter. "You could at least pretend it hurt," I mumbled, half amused, half exasperated.

His mouth twitched like he was about to argue, but instead, he just took a slow sip of coffee—carefully this time.

Just as he was about to say more, a buzz came from his back pocket—his phone. A job. I recognized the subtle shift in his expression, the way his brow furrowed ever so slightly as he checked the screen. He leaned down to give me a quick hug, his phone still in hand.

"Do you need anything from the store?" he asked, his voice distracted. "I'm heading out at lunch."

I hesitated for half a second. "Actually... yeah. Can you grab me some of that 100% organic dark chocolate from Healthy Planet? Oh, and more of that matcha tea with moringa."

That got his attention. He blinked at me, phone forgotten for the moment, and gave me a long, scrutinizing look.

"Let me get this straight," he said, crossing his arms. "You're eighteen. You have unlimited access to request literally anything from the store. And what do you ask for? Health food?"

"What can I say?" I shrugged. "Antioxidants are important."

He exhaled, shaking his head in mock disappointment. "Most teenagers would be begging for chips, soda, candy—"

"Most teenagers aren't me," I cut in, smirking.

"Clearly." He pocketed his phone, sighing like this was truly a burden. "Fine. But I'm gonna have to smuggle this nonsense past the other dads in the snack aisle. If anyone asks, I'm buying beer and beef jerky."

I laughed. "Noted."

For a second, I considered skipping school and asking if we could have a daddy-daughter day—like we used to. Impromptu road trips for "important errands" that somehow always ended with overpriced smoothies and deep conversations.

I remembered Paris, the last time we'd managed it. We'd spent the afternoon wandering through tiny bookstores and sampling too-sweet macarons from a bustling street vendor. He'd pulled me onto a carousel, insisting that age was just a number and that even immortals needed a break sometimes.

But even as the thought crossed my mind, I knew today wasn't one of those days. Reality pressed in too hard, smothering the spark of spontaneity before it had a chance to catch fire.

The moment passed, replaced by another.

I wanted to see Greyson. *Go figure.*

My backpack was ready, the dagger felt snug against my calf, whereas Mom's medallion felt like it was trying to drag me underwater. I hesitated, tempted to leave it behind, but something kept me from taking it off. Resigned, I grabbed an apple from the counter and headed out the door.

The bus ride seemed to stretch on forever, every stop lingering too long, every turn slower than it should have been. The city outside the window blurred past in streaks of gray and washed out color, like a painting left out in the rain. Even the hum of the engine felt distant, muffled. When we pulled up to the school, I blended in with the twenty or so other teenagers trudging up the grass hill to the front steps. The brown brick building loomed ahead, unimpressive as always.

Inside, the familiar hum of chatter and lockers slamming filled the air. I took a deep breath, but my nerves were on edge, buzzing beneath my skin for reasons I couldn't quite pin down.

Am I sweating?

Maybe it was just nerves. But why? There was no reason for my hands to feel clammy, for warmth to cling to me like I'd been running when I hadn't. I swallowed hard, pushing the thought away.

Reaching the door to our classroom, I let out a huge sigh of relief—so forceful I half-expected it to knock something over. Or someone.

But I barely registered the thought before I saw him.

Greyson's chair was occupied, the man himself looking up from a stack of papers. His sleeves were casually rolled up to his elbows, exposing forearms that looked entirely too at ease in this chaos. Rose-tinted glasses perched on his nose, giving him a deceptively relaxed appearance—like some bohemian professor with all the time in the world.

But beneath the soft hue of the lenses, I could see the dark circles shadowing his eyes, the kind that spoke of a sleepless night and too many secrets. To anyone who didn't know him, he'd look perfectly fine. But I caught the subtle bruise on the inside of his right elbow—a fading reminder of yesterday's blood transfusion—and the slight tightness at the edges of his smile.

He looked effortless, easy. But I knew better.

The room was still empty, the usual morning chaos yet to spill in through the door.

As I stepped inside, I tried to keep my nerves in check. *Tried* being the key word—because the second Greyson looked up at me, it was game over.

"Morning, Mr. Black!" I said, aiming for casual. "How are you?"

"Well, Miss Sady," he drawled, effortlessly cool, leaning back in his chair like he had all the time in the world. "I did have a rough night, but the dreams were pleasant. And you?"

Please don't blush. *Please don't blush.*

"Uhm, I'm fine. Thanks." The words tumbled out faster than I had intended, while darting toward my desk, eager to escape the pull of his gaze.

"Been out for any bike rides lately?"

Damn it all to hell. What do I even say to that? My mind raced, searching for an answer that doesn't scream *I spent the evening patching up your steel-reinforced front door after breaking in.* But I can't bring myself to turn around because I knew my face would betray me. The flush rising up the back of my neck was a precursor which warned me of the inevitable.

"Hey, Converse-Girl, glad you're here early. Can I ask you about the sources for our research project?"

Jamie's voice cuts through the tension like a life preserver. If I wasn't so flustered, I might've hugged him for the save.

"Hey, dude, sure," I said, turning toward him and deliberately not looking at Greyson. "What's up?"

"So, Michaela and I were going through the specifics of our assignment and noticed that we're supposed to research—or at least discuss—any biblical references related to our topic. Have you come across anything like this from the sources you've been researching?"

I blinked. "Crap, where was that in the assignment?"

Jamie laughed. "Exactly my reaction when Michaela brought it up. But it's there."

"You've got to be kidding me."

I didn't have to feign surprise. The thought of this new criteria for our project struck a little too close to home for comfort. Isn't this supposed to be a history class? When did we cross over into theology and philosophy?

"Yeah, and Michaela remembered you saying something about your parents—or maybe just your dad—being, like, religious history nerds or something?"

Right. I forgot I'd said that. "Ah, yeah, I guess you could say my dad used to be in the priesthood before he met my mom."

It's close enough to the truth to explain his encyclopedic knowledge. And mine, by proxy.

Jamie nodded, then gestured vaguely like he was trying to piece together a thought. "So… any chance you could handle that part? None of us have a clue where to start, and honestly, it might help us get an edge."

"Sure," I said, pulling out my books. "Pops will love to give me the inside scoop. It will be getting him to shut up that will be the prob—" Then a thought struck me, and I paused. "Wait—what edge? Why do we need one?"

"Did you even read the assignment?" Michaela's voice chimed in from behind me, her tone half-teasing, half-exasperated.

I turned and found her standing just behind my shoulder, her raised brow making it clear she overheard everything. "Ah, sorry. I've been kind of distracted."

"Everything okay?" Kelsey asked, placing a hand on my shoulder. She must've been eavesdropping too because her sudden closeness caught me completely off guard.

How did I not hear them coming? With everything that's been happening to me—the heightened senses, the superhuman abilities—how did they bust through my personal space bubble? Their proximity sends a pang of irritation through me, but I quickly shoved it aside.

"Yeah, I'm fine," I said, forcing a smile.

"You know you can talk to us, right?" Kelsey's voice was soft, but the squeeze of her hand on my shoulder spoke volumes. Her touch carried a quiet sincerity, a kind of care that caught me off guard. For a moment, I was torn between brushing it off and saying something real. The decision was taken from me as the bell rings, cutting through the moment and offering an easy escape.

As we shuffled to our seats, Kelsey leaned over, her eyes catching on something. "Whoa, Sady—I've never seen that necklace before. It's really cool."

Frowning, I glanced down—and sure enough, the medallion had somehow slipped free from beneath my sweater, resting against my chest as if it wanted to be noticed.

"Oh, uhm, thanks," I muttered, quickly tucking it back under the fabric. "It's kind of a family heirloom. From my mom's side."

Kelsey's grin was as wide as ever. "It's beautiful. Like, old but in a really elegant way, you know?" Her voice was genuine, not even a hint of jealousy or sarcasm—just pure admiration.

I managed a small smile, the medallion's weight suddenly more present against my skin. "Yeah, it's been in the family for aeons."

Kelsey's expression softened, her fingers absentmindedly brushing the chain of her own simple necklace. "I wish I had something like that from my mom."

Her words hung in the air, a gentle reminder of the gaps in both our lives—different losses, different stories, but somehow still woven from the same threads.

As the lesson started, I cleared my throat just loud enough for her to hear and nudged her arm lightly. "Hey, Kelsey?"

"Yeah?"

I hesitated for half a second, then pushed forward. "I was thinking... if you want, maybe come to my place after school to go over notes for the project."

Her eyes widened, and for a moment, she just stared at me, like she was waiting for the punchline. When it didn't come, she blinked. "You're sure?"

"Yeah, of course." I offered a small, tentative smile. "I'm pretty sure my house is quieter than yours sounds."

Kelsey's face shifted from disbelief to something softer—relief, maybe? Then, just like that, her face lit up with a brilliance that was almost blinding.

"That sounds great. Yes, please, Sady."

"No problem." My heart was pounding like I just agreed to do something life-changing, but I managed to hold the smile. "Let me just check with my parents first."

Kelsey nodded, her excitement evident, but she didn't push further.

The moment was quickly swept away as Mr. Black started the lesson, his voice pulling our attention to the front of the room.

For the rest of the class, I tried to focus, but my thoughts kept drifting. Every so often, I caught Kelsey's gaze flicking my way, her soft smile reassuring me that I made the right decision. Still, my stomach fluttered with a strange mix of anticipation and anxiety.

When the bell finally rang, I took my time packing up my things. Kelsey lingered by my desk, waiting for me. "So, let me know what your parents say, okay?"

"Of course," I replied, trying to sound casual. "I'm sure it will be fine."

We walked together into the hallway, dodging the usual chaos of students rushing to their next class. The din of lockers slamming and overlapping conversations filled the air. Kelsey touched my arm briefly before turning toward the science wing. "See you in third period?"

"Yeah, see you then."

I watched her go, her auburn bob swaying with each step, catching the light in warm, coppery flashes.

As soon as she was out of sight, I ducked into the nearest bathroom. It was quieter here, the muffled hum of the hallway offering a brief reprieve. Locking myself in a stall, I pressed my back against the door and exhaled slowly. *Time to contact the parental units.*

Leaning my head back against the cool metal of the stall, I took a deep breath and let my mind reach outward. The mental pathways I had been honing for years felt like second nature now, but there was always a faint flicker of exertion when I connected with more than one person. I was the only one in the family who could do it—Mom and Dad could reach out to me, and to each other, but bridging all our minds together? That was my specialty.

And it wasn't just limited to my parents. With a bit more focus, I could loop Ramira into the connection as well. Her mental presence was always a bit different—sharper, more disciplined—but when I managed to link all four of us, the sensation was nothing short of incredible. Like weaving individual threads into an unbreakable strand.

But right now, I needed just Mom and Dad. One crisis at a time.

MOM? DAD?

SADY BABY. I'M AT WORK, SO LET'S MAKE THIS QUICK, OKAY?

Mom's voice was brisk but not impatient, and I could practically feel the rustle of papers in the background.

SADY DOLL, WHAT'S UP?

Dad's tone was its usual calm, like he'd been waiting for me to reach out.

I shifted my weight nervously, though neither of them could see me.

SO, I WAS THINKING...

SPIT IT OUT, LOVE.

Mom's curiosity was tinged with amusement, but there was also a faint edge of impatience.

I INVITED KELSEY OVER TO WORK ON OUR SCHOOL PROJECT AFTER CLASS. JUST HER. AT THE HOUSE. IS THAT... OKAY?

There was a pause, and I braced myself. Mom's shields flickered with an emotion—concern, maybe? Meanwhile, Dad's end of the line hummed with his steady, grounding presence.

WELL, IT'S A HUMAN, RIGHT? HARDLY ANYTHING TO BE CONCERNED ABOUT.

Leave it to Mom turning this into...well, this.

MOM! SHE IS NOT AN IT!

I groaned internally, but there was no mistaking the fond

exasperation in my tone.

Sady doll, we've been monitoring everything closely. All quiet on the front. You've never invited anyone over before, I think it's a good step.

Dad promised, his warmth radiated through our link.

Mom sighed, her thoughts softening.

Okay, sweetheart. Just make sure you stay alert, alright? If anything feels off—

I'll let you know immediately.

I finished for her, feeling a bit like a kid promising to look both ways before crossing the street.

Sady baby, I will likely be late anyways. Sam, do please make sure you are wearing a baggy sloppy shirt so the poor girl doesn't faint. Oh, and try to slouch or hunch or something. And remember to blink.

Mom faded with a girlish giggle.

Yes, Dad. Please try to look normal?

I have no idea what you two are talking about but I will dutifully follow instructions.

Ok, we'll come on the bus. See ya.

Their chuckles trailed off as I severed the link. For a moment, the silence felt unbalanced, like the bathroom walls were going to tip over. *Or me.* Remembering Kelsey's hopeful smile, I pushed off the door, determined to get through the rest of the day.

Math class had always been painfully dull for me. Numbers just made sense—effortless, logical, like pieces of a puzzle clicking into place. No ambiguity, no guesswork, just patterns waiting to be recognized.

My past math classes had been far more advanced. Rigid, yes, but at least they had been challenging. Here, the curriculum felt sluggish, like we were moving in slow motion through concepts I mastered years ago. It was not my teacher's fault—technically, I should be taking college-level courses by now—but my transfer records were a nightmare, and the school stuck me in this class "until we can reassess."

So naturally, my mind started to wander. Feeling restless, or reckless, depending on your perspective, I decided to practice my reach.

Pulling energy from deep within, I constructed my shield carefully, layering it like a protective cocoon before trying something new. Instead of the usual grid-by-grid technique Mom insisted on, I let my senses flow outward in soft, concentric circles—reminiscent of the swirls from my dreams.

Within seconds, I found Mom and Dad. *Easy*. But then, the faint flicker of sapphire and brushed silver caught my attention again. It was so elusive I couldn't pin it down. Was he shielding himself? How curious. It was definitely male, though. Of that, I was certain.

Damn. The swirling technique felt almost effortless. There was no familiar tug warning me to conserve my energy. This didn't feel nearly as draining, and it's even easier to navigate than the latest feather-touch technique.

Bloody hell, the moss-green aura was closer—Louisiana by the range. She felt stronger, more vibrant than before, pulsing with warmth that felt familiar. *Better back off before I get noticed.*

Shifting focus, I scanned New York City for the bloodsuckers. Sure enough, there they were, huddled together. Wait—there was someone new. Those odd muted mauve vibes threading through the stone-gray veins of marble. Could it be New Orleans boy? That had to be him.

Moving further south, I stretched towards the Amazon rainforest, hoping to find Remiel again. Sliding more rapidly now, I found my reach in that same part of the jungle where I previously located the group of moss-greens. But there was nothing. *What the hell?*

Or was there? Slowing down enough to hover, to pause. Wow. A massive shield acting like a two-way mirror masked the area, cloaking whatever—or whoever—was beneath it. Intrigued, I probed cautiously.

Gotcha.

There, at the center. His aura was breathtaking—bronze-gold woven with velvety browns, shifting in deliberate, unshaken currents of energy. *Wow, was this how Dad used to be? Before...Mom.*

I didn't dare linger. The shield stirred at the edges, like someone shifting their angle in my direction. *Time to pull back—now.*

"Miss Smith, care to join your classmates?"

Mr. Allen's voice snapped me back to reality.

Crap. I yanked my senses back too quickly, and the backlash hit me like a freight train. The headache was immediate and brutal, making my knees wobble. Blinking against the sudden dizziness, I looked around and realized the classroom was empty. The bell must have rung while I was distracted.

Stumbling to my feet, I slung my bag over my shoulder and headed out. My steps were shaky, my temples throbbing, but I knew Kelsey was probably waiting for me outside. Just one foot in front of the other.

Then two things happened at once.

CHAPTER 29

First, the headache had amplified quickly, the pounding and blinding making me stumble. Second, I turned the corner and crashed into something—or rather, someone. The familiar scent hit me before I even opened my eyes.

"Miss Sady!" Greyson's hands were warm as they steadied me, one on each shoulder. "What on earth have you been doing?"

"Math equations!" I blurted out, sounding unconvincing and far too rushed, while wondering if I might vomit on that lovely shirt he was wearing.

"Math equations?" He raised a skeptical eyebrow, his smirk tinged with concern. "Well, Miss Sady, those must have been some particularly vexing equations."

"Why?" My voice was wary now, my nerves unraveling.

"Uhm, have you looked in a mirror?" His tone was light, but the genuine worry etched into his expression made me pause.

"Why?" The word slipped out again, and I cringed internally. I sounded like a toddler trapped in the endless *but why* phase, but the pounding in my skull made it hard to think straight, let alone form coherent sentences.

"Because your face is the most fascinating shade of grey—like old parchment left too long in the damp, I can't be sure." His brow furrowed. "And your eyes—oh, what in my father's name have you been doing? Your eyes—!"

Damn it. I blinked rapidly, trying to clear my blurry vision. "Oh, I, uhm... I have a migraine. This sometimes happens. It's fine."

His worry deepened, but I was already backing away, desperate to escape. "I have to go," I stammered. "I'm meeting Kelsey."

Before he could say anything else, I pivoted and walked quickly down the hall, willing myself not to look back. The last thing I needed right now was more questions.

I ducked into the nearest bathroom, pushing open the door with more force than necessary. The fluorescent lights hummed overhead as I stepped up to the mirror, bracing my hands against the sink. My reflection stared back at me, pale but flushed at the same time—like my body couldn't decide whether I was overheating or freezing. It was no leap of the imagination to assume the flush had been brought on by the close proximity of Greyson, and the touch of his hands on my shoulders. The pale? That was another matter.

My eyes were indeed bloodshot, the whites threaded with angry red lines. But as I blinked, I could almost see it—the faintest retreat of crimson, like ink swirling in water, slowly clearing. Not perfect, but better.

Great. *Just great.*

I swiped a hand under my eyes, smoothing away any lingering exhaustion, then twisted on the faucet and splashed cold water on my face. The shock of the cold water jolted me back to the present, snapping my focus into place. I inhaled deeply, gripping the edges of the sink. *Get it together, Sady.*

When I opened my eyes again, the redness had eased a little more. Small progress, but I'd take it.

After a final once-over—good enough—I dried my hands and pushed back out into the hall, making my way toward the exit.

In true Kelsey fashion, I found her outside, perched on the grass, wriggling her bare toes into the autumn-kissed grass despite the autumn chill in the air. She looked perfectly content, her head tilted back toward the weak sunlight. Of course, I managed to stumble toward her in a very un-Sady-like manner, half-crumpling onto the grass beside her.

"Sady, are you okay?" Kelsey's warm voice was laced with concern as she leaned over, wrapping an arm around my shoulder to steady me.

"Just dealing with the tail end of a headache," I admitted, my words sluggish. "Came out of nowhere. But I'm okay."

Her brow knitted, worry etching lines into her usually bright expression. "Are you sure? We don't have to do the project today if you're not feeling up to it."

"No, I want to," I insisted, managing a weak smile. "Honestly, I'll be fine. I just need a minute."

"The bus will be here soon." Her big brown eyes widened slightly, catching the light in a way I hadn't noticed before. "We could reschedule?"

I shook my head, the movement making my vision swim for a second. "No, let's do this. I'm fine, I promise. It'll be good to focus on something normal."

She hesitated, her arm still loosely around me, but then she nodded. "Okay. But if you need to bail, just say the word."

"Deal."

I nodded gently, but my wobbliness must have been obvious. Without hesitation, Kelsey grabbed my backpack and helped guide my unsteady steps toward the bus stop. Her easy strength and quiet support felt comforting, and I found myself leaning into her kindness more than I'd like to admit.

Settling into the bus, guzzling my water bottle had already eased the sting of the headache. When we reached my house, it had faded to a dull throb. This new technique—whatever it was—seemed to have a faster recovery period than I was used to, though it was clearly not without its challenges. As for the bloodshot eyes which were already easing? Well, that could be blamed on lack of sleep.

We stepped off the bus, and a sudden thought struck me. I had forgotten to warn her about Dad.

"Uhm, Kelsey?" My voice faltered slightly as we approached the front steps. "Before we go in, there's something I should probably tell you about my dad. He's, uhm—"

"What about your Dad?" Kelsey cut in, her voice light, but there was a flicker of tension beneath it.

I paused, thrown off by the interruption. "Huh?"

She shifted slightly, adjusting the strap of her backpack like it was suddenly too tight. "You sounded... I don't know. Serious." She exhaled a small laugh, but it didn't quite reach her eyes. "Is there, like... something I should be worried about?"

Her reaction caught me off guard. What exactly was she expecting?

I hesitated for a second, then offered a reassuring squeeze of her hand. "Nah, nothing like that," I said lightly. "He's just... different. You'll see."

As we approached the front door, I felt the need to double-check with the old man himself directly.

DAD, WE'RE ABOUT TO WALK THROUGH THE FRONT DOOR.

PLEASE TELL ME YOU'RE DRESSED.

AH, SADY DOLL, I TOTALLY FORGOT. I'LL HAVE A SHIRT ON

BEFORE YOU GET INSIDE.

Rolling my eyes, I pushed open the door. "Kelsey, seriously, there's nothing wrong with him. It's just—" I paused mid-sentence, glancing at her. She looked... scared? Her hand gripped her bag tightly, and her usual bright demeanor had dimmed. Reaching out, I squeezed her hand, trying to reassure her. What could she possibly be so nervous about?

We stepped inside, taking off our shoes and dropping our bags near the door. I guided her toward the kitchen, but something nagged at me.

DAD, SOMETHING'S WRONG. KELSEY SEEMS ON THE VERGE OF PANIC. I DON'T KNOW WHY.

DON'T WORRY, SADY DOLL, I KNOW WHAT TO DO.

Turning the corner, I braced myself, unsure what 'knowing what to do' actually meant.

We found him sitting at the kitchen counter with a plate of my favorite cookies—flourless chocolate cashew. As promised, he was in baggy joggers and a loose sweater, though the sweater in question had a very suspicious butter stain dribbled down the front, like he had lost a fight with a baking sheet.

His sleeves were shoved up to his elbows, revealing a dusting of flour on his forearms, and somehow—there was even a streak of it in his hair, as if he had absentmindedly run a hand through it mid-baking disaster.

He was slouched forward in his chair, mid-chew, and looked utterly ridiculous. A melted chunk of chocolate clung to the corner of his mouth, and when he grinned, it was with a full display of chocolate-streaked teeth—like a toddler who had just raided a dessert tray and absolutely didn't regret it.

"Hi, girls!" He slid the plate across the counter. "I was trying to wait for you, but the smell was driving me crazy!"

I glanced at Kelsey out of the corner of my eye, just in time to see her smile break through her initial unease. Then she blushed.

Oh. *Oh.*

I knew that look. She was crushing on my dad.

Well... at least she wasn't scared anymore.

"Uhm, Kelsey? Meet Sam." I grabbed the plate of cookies, biting back a smirk. "Also known as Dad and the world's messiest baker. Thanks for these, Pops! We're gonna head to my room."

"Why do you insist on calling me that? It sounds like a popsicle?" His accompanying eye roll made him look even more sheepish, and just endeared him to Kelsey further.

"Because it bugs you, that's why." I retorted right back.

"Teeangers these days, am I right Kelsey?"

"Uhm, sure Mr Sam, I mean Tree, oh—" Rescuing her before she said anything else, I had to suppress a laugh, while balancing the plate of cookies in my other hand. We nearly tripped up the stairs in the process.

Dad waved us off with a cheerful grin, still chewing—still looking like a walking baking disaster.

We hadn't even made it to the first landing, when Kelsey squeaked, her cheeks now a vivid pink: "There is nothing wrong with your dad! Why would you try to scare me like that?"

I was about to respond, but she glanced back one last time. Unfortunately, Dad chose that exact moment to stretch by the fridge. His sweater lifted slightly, revealing his annoyingly perfect eight-pack abs. Yes, eight-pack. Not six.

Kelsey's squeak turned into something closer to a strangled gasp, and I groaned. "Oh, brother," I muttered under my breath, pulling her the rest of the way up the stairs.

Once we were behind the safety of my bedroom doors, and cookies safely deposited onto my desk, we pulled out our books and notepads to get started.

"Sady! Seriously, what kind of tree is your dad, huh?" Kelsey rolled her eyes, and before long, we were doubled over in giggles as we stumbled into my bedroom.

The laughter felt good—unexpected but good. For the next few hours, we managed to stay focused on our project, alternating between furious note-taking and exchanging messages with Michaela about our progress. Every now and then, Kelsey made a goofy face or cracked a joke, and I found myself laughing more than I had in ages.

At some point, my stomach let out an unmistakable growl, loud enough to make Kelsey snort-laugh. I pressed a hand to my belly. The hunger hit hard, a sudden drop in energy that had my head spinning

We needed fuel.

UHM, DAD, WE'RE COMING DOWN FOR SNACKS. ANY CHANCE YOU'RE STILL WEARING A SHIRT?

OF COURSE I AM, BUT I'VE MISPLACED MY PANTS!

DAD!!! CAN YOU NOT TRY TO TRAUMATIZE ME? UGH, THIS IS NO TIME FOR JOKES!

My mental shout was laced with exasperation.

I knew he was kidding, but still—.

BESIDES, SADY DOLL, YOU HAVE BIGGER THINGS TO WORRY ABOUT THAN ME.

And that was when I heard Mom's SUV pull into the driveway. *Oh, great*. I had been hoping to introduce just one parent today, but now I had to figure out how to explain my supermodel-of-a-mother to Kelsey.

The front door opened just as we reached the bottom of the stairs. Mom stepped inside, carrying a bag of groceries, her graceful movements momentarily faltering as her gaze landed on the only human in the room. Meanwhile, Kelsey's jaw dropped, and she froze mid-step. For a long moment, they both stared at each other in mutual surprise, and Dad and I stood back, trying not to laugh.

"Mom, this is my friend Kelsey from school I told you about earlier." I glanced at Kelsey, who still seemed awestruck. "Kelsey, this is my mom, Sera."

To all our surprise, Kelsey squared her shoulders, stepped forward, and boldly extended her hand. "Hi! Nice to meet you. Thank you for letting us work on our vampire project here. My house is full of dumb and loud boys, and we'd never have gotten anything done."

VAMPIRE PROJECT? YOU'LL HAVE TO FILL US IN LATER, SADY BABY.

Mom blinked, taken aback for only a moment, before taking the offered hand in her own and offering a small smile in return. "Oh, sure. You're always welcome here, Kelsey."

"Hi honey, glad you're home. I was wondering what two teenage girls might want for dinner, maybe we can all decide together?"

With still hunched shoulders, Dad walked over to Mom and gave her the most G-rated hug I had ever witnessed. Normally, they were all intense eye contact and lingering touches—the kind of couple that made people uncomfortable just by existing in the same room. But today? It was like they had been given strict instructions to act like co-workers who barely knew each other. Mom, as if overcorrecting, tried to hunch too, and somehow, they both ended up looking like two people failing miserably at appearing casual.

And then came the spectacular-but-epic-fail kiss attempt.

Dad, for reasons beyond my comprehension, leaned in to give her a completely innocent, harmless peck on the cheek—something I genuinely didn't think I had ever seen him do before. But Mom, because she apparently had the reaction time of someone dodging a launched projectile, turned her head too fast at the exact wrong moment and—

Smack.

They knocked foreheads. *Loudly.*

I sighed, turning to Kelsey with a straight face. "In case you were wondering, my parents have never mastered the art of subtlety."

Kelsey glanced at me, then back at my parents, and within seconds, we were both giggling uncontrollably. The sound was contagious, and my parents joined in, their laughter blending with ours in a way that made the moment feel bizarrely normal.

"Mr. and Mrs. Smith," Kelsey managed between giggles, "that was by far the funniest, cutest, and dorkiest thing I think I've ever seen!"

For a brief moment, I wondered if this had been their plan all along—to help her feel more at ease and to make themselves appear... well, a little more human. As I caught my breath, Mom's voice slipped into my mind, her tone dry but amused.

NOPE, DARLING OFFSPRING, THIS WAS NO PLAN. I DON'T KNOW WHAT IN THE TARTARUS THAT WAS.

"Well, Sady's new friend," Mom said, rolling her eyes at Dad with a mischievous glint, "I'd love to tell you we planned it that way, but sometimes the best moments happen when you least expect them."

Uh-oh. That was Dad's cue, and he didn't miss a beat. Taking Mom's free hand, he spun her around with a grand flourish, pulling her in close before dramatically dipping her backward. For a moment, it looked like he was about to kiss her romantically—which he did all the freaking time—but instead, he licked her face. Yes, *licked*. From her jaw all the way up past her eyebrow.

Mom's squeal of outrage was ear-piercing. I braced myself for flying kitchen furniture or utensils—because, historically speaking, this was usually when things started levitating. My eyes did a quick scan for the nearest knife block, and I mentally calculated how long it would take to dive behind the kitchen island, and drag my new friend to safety without injuring her in the process.

But instead of launching a spatula across the room or setting something on fire (not unheard of, by the way), she smacked his shoulder and swatted at him, her indignation tempered by a laugh she couldn't quite hold back.

Seriously, did they catch some rare supernatural flu? Because I had never seen them act like this.

Beside me, Kelsey let out a choked laugh, clutching her sides, but when she turned to me, her expression was something different. Something *softer*.

"Sady..." Her voice was lighter than before, but there was something else there—something wistful, like she wasn't just seeing my parents being ridiculous but seeing something she didn't quite know how to put into words. "Your parents really love each other."

I blinked, momentarily caught off guard.

"Uhm, yeah?" I replied, caught somewhere between mortification and disbelief. "Though I don't think that's the word Mom would use right now."

Kelsey just smiled, her eyes lingering on them a moment longer, like she was memorizing the way they fit together.

And that was when it hit me. She wasn't just laughing at how ridiculous they were—she was taking it in, like someone glimpsing a life they had never had.

I swallowed past a sudden tightness in my throat, desperate to shake off the fragile ache of the moment.

"So," Dad said, slipping his feet into his boots and snatching Mom's keys off the counter, "how about some good old-fashioned fast food tonight before we take Kelsey home? I'll drive!"

"Really?" Kelsey asked, already swinging her backpack over her shoulder. "That sounds amazing."

Mom grabbed her jacket from the back of a chair, slipping it on as she joined us. "I could go for a milkshake," she said, her tone lighter than I'd heard all week.

"Family outing, then!" Dad declared, twirling Mom's keys around his finger. "Everyone, into the car."

We piled into the SUV, Kelsey's backpack wedged between us in the back seat. Mom took the passenger side, already queuing up one of her eclectic playlists, the kind that bounced between classic rock and ancient choral music without warning.

As we pulled out of the driveway, the air inside the car buzzed with an unexpected, but much-needed, sense of normalcy. Kelsey leaned over, whispering, "I didn't think I'd be getting the full family experience tonight."

I grinned. "You've seen nothing yet. Just wait until Mom starts singing along."

Sure enough, as soon as we hit the first stoplight, Mom was belting out an off-key rendition of *Bohemian Rhapsody,* and Dad joined in with dramatic hand gestures. Kelsey's giggles filled the back seat, and for a little while, the world outside the car faded away.

Before I knew it, we were pulling into the parking lot of a Burger King near the highway. The glow of neon lights spilled through the windows, and the promise of fast food warmth chased away the last threads of tension.

After seeing the huge crowd of what clearly were two football teams inside the dining area, we made the unanimous decision to eat in the car. It didn't take long for the aroma of burgers and fries filled the car, blending with the slightly less enticing scent of my plant-based option. Dad and I had gone meatless, as usual, but no one commented on it. For the first time in what felt like forever, everything seemed... normal.

Sitting in the parking lot with greasy wrappers, ketchup packets, and the stray bits of lettuce from my Impossible Whopper scattered across laps and the console, I realized this might actually be the most ordinary moment I had ever had in my entire life.

Dad broke the quiet munching with his calm but slightly gruff voice. "Kelsey, I hope you don't mind me prying," he began, twisting in his seat to glance back at her. "Sady mentioned that you live with your father and four brothers?"

There was a gentleness in his tone, the kind he usually reserved for sensitive topics. It wasn't just curiosity—it was the way he always tried to understand the people around him, to make them feel seen.

"Oh, what about your mom?" Mom chimed in casually, her tone light.

Kelsey froze mid-bite, her wide eyes darting briefly to Mom before settling on Dad.

"Oh, uhm, Mr.—"

"You can call me Sam if you like," Dad said gently, cutting off her hesitation.

Kelsey swallowed, her voice dropping to barely a whisper. "Oh, uhm, well... my mom died when I was just in first grade."

Dad's demeanor shifted, warmth replacing the concern in his eyes.

"I'm so sorry to hear that, Kelsey," he said, his voice quiet and genuine. He reached out, resting a gentle hand on her knee—a small, comforting gesture.

The reaction was immediate. Kelsey jerked back with a shriek, her whole body recoiling as if he'd burned her. The suddenness of it sent a jolt through all of us, and even the crinkle of fast-food wrappers fell silent.

"Whoa, it's okay!" Dad withdrew his hand instantly, his own surprise evident. His eyes darted to Mom, then to me, searching for an anchor in the sudden storm. "No harm intended," he added softly, his voice as steady as he could manage. "You're safe here, Kelsey. Always."

Mom shifted in her seat, turning slightly to offer Kelsey a reassuring smile. I reached out too, brushing my fingers against her arm. "You're good, Kelsey," I murmured. "We've got you."

Kelsey's breathing slowed, the initial shock melting into a shaky nod. "I—I'm sorry," she stammered, her cheeks flushing. "I didn't mean to— It just caught me off guard."

"No need to apologize," Dad said, his tone warm and unruffled. "We all have our moments. You're safe with us, I promise."

I didn't even think. Instinct took over, and I scooted closer to her, wrapping an arm around her shoulders in a small hug. She relaxed almost immediately, her shoulders sagging as she let out a shaky breath.

The atmosphere gradually eased back into something lighter. We finished our food while Mom launched into one of her many stories from our time living on the Faroe Islands. Her storytelling was direct and to the point, as always, but full of dramatic hand gestures and poignant pauses for effect.

"...so, you see, Kelsey, when Sady realized she had two choices: stay stuck in the mud pit possibly forever, or let the mud keep her boots and possibly her—"

"Mom!" I interjected, mortified. "Kelsey does not need to know that her friend walked two miles in the warm summer rain wearing only her underpants and a sweater because a mud pit sucked her boots and—I'll remind you—it was overalls into oblivion!"

"Oh yes, she does!" Kelsey burst out, her laughter bubbling up so quickly it turned into hiccups. "That's priceless!"

The sound of her laughter filled the car, and I joined in, despite my embarrassment. It felt good to hear her laugh so freely, but the moment was cut short when her cell phone rang. The lighthearted energy instantly drained from her face.

"Oh shoot," she muttered, fumbling for the phone. "What time is it?"

Dad, who always seemed to know the time without looking at a watch, answered calmly. "Just after 8 o'clock."

"Uhm, Mr. Smith, could I please ask you to drive me home right now?" Her voice was suddenly timid, her eyes darting between the phone and the window.

Dad glanced at her in the rearview mirror, his easygoing expression shifting to something more attentive. "Of course, Kelsey. We had already planned to head that way anyway—no problem at all."

The drive back to her townhouse complex was only ten minutes, but each passing second seemed to weigh heavier on Kelsey. Her hands tightened around the straps of her backpack, knuckles turning white as we pulled into the driveway.

As soon as we stopped, the front door swung open, and a broad-shouldered figure filled the doorway, backlit by the sickly yellow glow of the hallway lights. His silhouette was overwhelming, his frame thick and heavy in a way that spoke less of strength and more of unchecked mass. There was something about the way he stood—rigid, unmoving—that made the air feel colder, like the house itself was holding its breath.

"Kelsey! Get in the house!" he barked before she even had a chance to open the car door. His voice was rough, leaving no room for argument.

"Coming, Dad!" she called back, plastering on a tight smile as she grabbed her bag and climbed out. She paused just long enough to glance over her shoulder, offering me one last smile before disappearing inside.

"What a lovely girl she is," Mom said softly, watching the now-closed door. "But I wonder why she got so nervous about the time. Surely at almost eighteen years old, she doesn't have an 8 o'clock curfew?"

"No idea, Mom," I replied, turning to look out the back window. Through the first-floor window, I spotted Kelsey waving down at me. Her smile looked genuine, but the way she quickly ducked out of sight left me with a nagging sense of worry.

Chapter 30

The next morning, I woke up feeling different. Kelsey had transitioned from schoolmate to—friend. One who giggle-snorted like me. *A friend*. Bounding down the stairs, feeling positively giddy, I noticed Mom's car was already gone and Dad's shadow was already disappearing into the workshop.

Strange. Normally, one of them would see me off to school. And Mom had started to become really inconsistent with our morning training routine. But no matter. Nothing was going to mess with my zen today.

The halls of school buzzed with the usual teenage chaos. Conversations about Halloween swarmed around me, tethering me back to reality and thoughts of the project.

And *vampires*.

"Hey, Converse-Girl." Michaela's voice rang out behind me, unapologetically loud. "Did you finish the research with Kelsey yesterday?"

"Yeah." I turned, noticing her newly dyed, luminous plum-purple hair. "Woah, nice choice!"

"I'm channeling my inner Morticia." She beamed.

"Hey, babe." Jamie swooped from behind her. "My dad's lending me old-school shoes and a tie. Total Gomez vibe!"

Michaela's face lit up, her plum-purple hair bouncing as she threw her arms around him. "You're the best! Now all I need are the perfect Morticia shoes."

I smiled faintly, but my attention kept drifting to Kelsey's empty desk. She hadn't texted me. A nagging sense of worry crept in.

"Hey, Earth-to-Sady!" Michaela turned her focus on me, grinning like she had just thought of the best idea in the world. "You're invited to my Halloween party, ya know."

"Uhm, thanks," I mumbled, already feeling awkward under her enthusiastic gaze. "I'll think about it."

The bell rang—literally saving me. Michaela pouted as Greyson strode in, his usual smirk in place.

"All right, everyone, settle down!" His voice commanded the room as he perched on the edge of his desk, effortlessly exuding authority. "I've got an exciting announcement this morning."

The classroom erupted into groans and nervous chuckles, but Greyson pressed on with an exaggerated grin. "You're all going to love this. The history department has been invited to co-host an exclusive presentation at Casa Loma's annual Halloween masquerade ball."

A ripple of murmurs spread through the class, and Michaela practically jumped out of her seat, but Greyson held up a hand. "Yes, Miss Michaela, the Casa Loma. This year's event is a collaboration between the Royal Ontario Museum and the United Nations as part of an international cultural exchange initiative. Our display will be one of the evening's highlights, showcasing global legends and folklore alongside exhibits from around the world."

A buzz of excitement filled the room. Even the half-asleep kids' curiosity was piqued. Even I couldn't help raising an eyebrow at that. The UN? What were we getting ourselves into?

"This is an opportunity to present real history," Greyson continued, his tone shifting to something more serious. "To engage with international scholars, and to bring a bit of our own perspective to a global stage. And yes, there will be costumes—but think historical accuracy, not Spirit Halloween."

Michaela's hand shot up. "Does this mean we get to wear period clothing?"

Greyson's grin widened. "Absolutely. And if you play your cards right, you might even get a sneak peek at the exhibits from other countries before the public does."

Something about this innocuous announcement felt ominous. *Stupid spidey-sense tingling again.*

"You'll be presenting interpretations of Halloween traditions, both historical and modern. That means everything from ghost stories to vampires to ancient rituals." Turning back to his notes on the front board, he pointed at the clusters of names. "You'll work in your assigned groups, but the final presentation will require everyone's input."

The class buzzed again, like a swarm of bees disturbed. Some students leaned in, whispers curling like smoke between them. Greyson raised a hand. "One more thing. The event's coordinator, Sera Smith—any relation to you, Miss Sady?"

I could feel every pair of eyes turn toward me, the room suddenly heavier with curiosity. A cough caught in my throat, my face flushing hot under the weight of their stares. I shrank deeper into my seat, trying to melt into the chair. The silence felt like it stretched forever, like I was the only one in the room. "Uhm... yeah," I muttered, my voice barely above a whisper. "That's my mom."

The room seemed to hold its breath, and then, as quickly as it had come, the tension broke. Greyson continued with the project details, but the words barely registered. My mind was still tangled in the awkwardness, my gaze flicking to Kelsey's empty desk. The silence had left something behind—a gnawing unease creeping in.

I sifted through the past weeks—every absence had come with an explanation. And always, a reassuring text. But today? Nothing.

What if something was wrong? The memory of her nervousness last night in the car replayed in my mind.

"...and that's all for today," Greyson's voice pulled me back to the present. "Remember, your research outlines are due Friday. Dismissed."

The scrape of chairs and the hum of voices filled the classroom as my classmates began gathering their things. Slinging my bag over one shoulder, I couldn't help but glance again at Kelsey's empty desk.

"Everything okay?" Greyson's voice was lower now, directed only at me. *How did he know what I was thinking*?

He held himself still, but the way his lips pressed together hinted at an underlying strain, like he was already bracing for whatever I might say.

"It's nothing," I said finally, trying to sound breezy. "I just... noticed Kelsey wasn't here."

Greyson's head tipped forward ever so slightly, his jaw tightening as if he were piecing something together. "Her father called in this morning," he said carefully, his tone as measured as ever. "Said she was feeling sick and wouldn't be in."

There was nothing overtly suspicious in his words, but the way his lips pressed into a thin line afterward sent a shiver of doubt through me.

"Oh." My response was flat, my mind racing. That explained her absence, but something still felt off.

"She came over to study and work on our project yesterday," I muttered, almost to myself, as Greyson moved toward his desk. "She was fine. We dropped her off at home just after eight o'clock last night."

Eager to escape, I hurried to the door. But as I reached the threshold, I caught Michaela and Jamie exchanging a quick, loaded glance.

"...her curfew is 8 o'clock!"

"You don't think her dad would..."

"Miss Michaela, would you care to share what you're whispering about?" Greyson's blunt tone cut through the murmurs of the retreating students, and both of them straightened guiltily.

"Uh, only that Jamie and I need to rethink our costumes," Michaela said, her smile a bit too wide. "We were thinking Cleopatra and Marc Antony?"

Her words tumbled out in a rush, the kind of hasty cover-up that only made Greyson's eyebrow arch higher. Jamie gave a half-hearted nod, his expression somewhere between agreement and silent pleading for the conversation to end.

Greyson's eyebrow arched. "Bold choice. I expect a historically accurate interpretation, of course."

Michaela's smile faltered for a split second before she nodded enthusiastically. "Absolutely! I mean, I've always wanted to rock a snake crown."

Jamie shot her a sideways look, and I bit back a laugh. Leave it to Michaela to spin a potential scolding into a costume pitch. A question formed on my lips, but the students surged out in a wave of backpacks and chatter.

Through the crowd, my focus stayed locked on Michaela and Jamie as they slipped into the hallway. Reaching them, I grabbed their sleeves—definitely not as gently as I could have.

"Hey!" Michaela yelped, yanking her arm free. "What's your deal?"

"What's going on with Kelsey, her dad, and this curfew?" I demanded, keeping my voice low. They exchanged another one of those loaded glances, and the unease that had been simmering all morning surged.

"Sady," Michaela began hesitantly. "It's not really our place to talk about."

"Make it your place," I snapped. "She's my friend. If something's wrong, I need to know."

Jamie sighed, rubbing the back of his neck. "It's not like that, okay? Her dad's just... strict."

"Strict how?" I folded my arms, refusing to let them dodge the question.

The pieces started to fit—the way Kelsey had checked the time last night, her apprehension when asking Dad to drive her, the way she bolted from the car. My stomach twisted.

"He has rules," Michaela said carefully. "Curfew at eight. No exceptions. And she's got four older brothers who... well, let's just say they don't help."

Jamie nodded. "Two of them have been in juvie. The other two probably should've been. Her dad's 'tight ship' is more like a prison."

"Guys, it's one thing to have a hard-ass parent, but why do I get the feeling there's a bigger problem?"

Silence. Furtive glances and shuffling of feet. I had no time for this.

"Guys?" I softened my tone, dropping the edge from my posture. Mom was a pro at this, and I'd learned from the best. "She was at my place last night. I need to know if I did something wrong—or if I can help."

Jamie ran a hand through his hair, his frustration evident. "Look, I know you're new here and don't have many friends," he said, his words harsher than he probably intended. "But haven't you noticed Kelsey misses school a lot? Or how she's always in long sleeves and turtlenecks—even when it's boiling outside?"

Memories snapped together—Kelsey in oversized sweaters during heatwaves, tugging her sleeves down when people got close. Details I'd noticed but hadn't thought about. Now they hit me hard.

I opened my mouth, unsure of what to say, when chaos erupted. The rugby team thundered through the hallway, teachers appeared, and we were herded to our next classes.

Separated by the bell.

Sitting in math class, I stared blankly at the equations scrawled across the board. Numbers usually grounded me, giving me something solid to focus on when my brain felt like it was spinning out of control. But today, even math couldn't hold my attention. It wasn't long before an idea took shape in the back of my mind.

After school, I would go to Kelsey's house. I could always say I was dropping off homework. I needed to see her, to make sure she was okay.

By lunchtime, I'd isolated myself, sitting alone in the cafeteria. My thoughts churned with frustration, guilt, and worry. Too much was happening at once—Kelsey's mystery, my stupid hunger, and then there was Greyson.

What did he remember about the kiss? My cheeks burned just thinking about it, both thrilling and mortifying.

Why hadn't Kelsey texted me back yet, if she was just sick?

I stabbed my fork into my salad, replaying everything since my first day at this school. For once, Greyson didn't dominate my thoughts, Kelsey was nudging him into second place.

Damn it, why was being a teenager so confusing? I groaned internally.

"S A D Y !"

I dropped my fork with a clatter as Michaela barreled toward me, Jamie trailing behind, and as I stood slowly, my senses flared alive and setting my teeth on edge.

"Shh... Michaela," Jamie hissed, ever the voice of reason. It wasn't working.

"No, damn it!" she snapped, clearly out of breath. "It's all over school—have you heard?"

"Uhm, obviously not?" I shot back, irritation creeping into my words.

"Two police cruisers and an ambulance were at Kelsey's house around 3 a.m.!" she blurted, nearly shouting. Subtlety was not her forte.

"What?!" My jaw clenched so tightly I thought I might chip a tooth, my hands already curling into fists.

"Yeah, the ambulance took someone to William Osler Hospital," she continued, her voice quieter now.

Someone.

"Was it Kelsey?" I asked, my voice slow and deliberate, each word fighting the tightness in my chest. I forced myself to breathe, though my body screamed to act.

"We don't know," Michaela admitted, her eyes darting to Jamie as if for backup.

Someone.

I didn't wait for more details. Snatching up my backpack, I left the rest of my lunch untouched and spun on my heel, heading for the exit. The bus was due in less than five minutes, and I could be at the hospital in thirty. If I had my bike, I could have—

"Sady, wait!" Michaela's footsteps chased me down. "We're coming with you."

"Fine," I muttered through gritted teeth, not stopping. "But don't slow me down."

Jamie and Michaela exchanged a glance, as though surprised by the intensity of my reaction. *They don't know.* She was, is, my first friend.

We hurried to the bus stop, our pace conspicuous. Anyone with half a brain would know we were skipping class.

"And where are you all headed on such a lovely day?"

Of course, it had to be that voice. Michaela and Jamie froze mid-step. I didn't.

"Mr. Black," Jamie started nervously, "we were just heading to the hospital to visit a friend..."

"This friend wouldn't happen to be Miss Kelsey, would it?" Greyson's tone was no longer teasing, but cautious, probing.

The bus was approaching. I didn't have time for this.

"We don't know! And that's the problem!" I spun around, my frustration boiling over as I growled through clenched teeth. "Two police cruisers and an ambulance were at her house."

Greyson's jaw dropped, his body stiffening as the easygoing teacher vanished. "The bus takes thirty minutes," he said, voice tight, pulling out his car keys. "I can get us there in half the time."

His graphite Smart car was as unassuming as a teacher's vehicle could get. Michaela and Jamie crammed into the tiny backseat, looking hilariously squished, while I sat in front. For once, I wasn't distracted by Greyson's scent. My mind was too tangled in the puzzle pieces.

I hadn't reached out to Mom or Dad yet, and I wasn't even sure how my shield was holding up. I felt like I was leaking energy. Not good.

Greyson pulled out of the parking lot with urgency. His calm, teasing demeanor was replaced with seriousness. Silence filled the car, broken only by the engine's hum and Michaela's restless fidgeting.

"What do you know about Kelsey's dad?" I asked, breaking the silence.

Greyson's jaw tightened, his eyes flicking to me briefly before returning to the road. "Her father's a police officer," he said, his tone clipped. "Strict."

Jamie, leaning forward from the backseat, added, "Her dad's not just strict—he's a hard-ass. And her brothers? Total nightmares."

Michaela's wide eyes shifted to me, something unreadable flickering across her face. "Kelsey's family isn't exactly... easy. She never talks about them, but when she does, it's like she's walking on glass."

Her words hung between us, fragile and unsettling. I nodded stiffly, the feeling lodged deep, unmoving. Kelsey was my friend—my first real friend—and that was all I cared about.

Silence settled over the car, even breathing felt too loud. I stared out the window, my mind racing through a thousand possibilities, none of them good.

The hospital loomed into view, its glass façade reflecting the fading sunlight. Greyson pulled into a parking spot with practiced precision, killing the engine as the pressure in the car seemed to thicken.

"Let's stick together," he said, his voice low but firm. "We don't know what we're walking into."

He had made it in under fifteen minutes. I didn't wait for him to finish parking. Throwing the door open, I bolted toward the entrance, leaving the others behind.

"Sady!" Michaela's shout was distant, her voice laced with worry. They were lagging, and I could hear Greyson's measured steps not far behind, but I was moving too fast. *Damn it.*

The automatic doors slid open, and I nearly collided with a receptionist sitting behind a sleek desk.

"May I help you, young lady?" she asked, her tone friendly but her countenance shifting to concern as she took in my disheveled state.

"Kelsey Hamilton's room, please," I managed, trying to keep my voice steady.

She typed quickly and gave me the room number.

Someone was here. My friend.

Her room was on the fifth floor. How the hell were all six elevators occupied? *Seriously*?

Without a second thought, I turned towards the sign indicating the stairs. Not even bothering to see how far Greyson, Jamie, and Michaela were behind, I slammed the metal door shut behind me.

The cool air in the stairwell whipped past me. My shoes barely touched the concrete, my momentum a blur. Logic nagged at the back of my mind—warnings about security cameras, nurses, the chaos I might cause—but instinct took over. *And instinct didn't care.*

Fifteen seconds later, I was in the fifth floor hallway which was eerily quiet. The muted sounds of the hospital—beeping monitors, distant voices—felt surreal against the stillness. Room numbers guided me down the corridor, each step quicker than the last.

I didn't bother to knock. My ears tuned in, searching for any sign of life. Only one heartbeat. One set of breaths—shallow and synchronized, too perfect to be natural. *Mechanical.*

Pushing the door open, I froze. I was completely unprepared for what I saw.

There she was. My friend.

Lying in a flimsy, washed-out gown, Kelsey's small body was dwarfed by the stark white bed. Her face was swollen, unrecognizable, her once-bright eyes hidden beneath egg-sized bruises. The puffiness made her almost unrecognizable, the raw tenderness showing just how fresh the damage was. A plastic tube taped to her nose seemed minor next to the larger one helping her breathe.

Her lips were split in at least three places, thin scabs of dried blood marking the trauma. My gaze drifted to the cast on her arm, and her leg, the way her fragile form lay too still, too delicate. The machine beside her beeped steadily, white, blue and amber lights blinking in sync. A ventilator.

My heart clenched, twisting in a way I didn't know was possible. *My friend.*

I took a shaky step closer, my hands trembling, nothing could have braced me for this. My legs felt like lead, and I slumped into the visitor's chair, not trusting them to hold me. Tears streamed silently down my face, hot and relentless.

The sound of the door opening startled me, and I turned to see a nurse, her face lined with worry, stepping into the room.

"Young lady, what are you doing in here?" She stood in the doorway, arms crossed, and I vaguely realized I hadn't signed in at the nurse's station.

"I'm her friend," I managed, my voice cracking. "Please, can you tell me what happened?"

The nurse hesitated, her hands practiced but tense as she checked the machines. Her expression softened as she took in my tear-streaked face.

"We are keeping her sedated, in a coma," she said quietly. "To protect her brain from the injuries." She gestured to the tubes and wires. "Her body needs rest to heal."

"What are the injuries?" I whispered, leaning forward, my breath hitching.

"That's all I can share unless you're family," the nurse said, her tone taking on a professional edge. "It's a police matter. I think it's best you let her rest now. Let me escort you out."

"No," I said, shaking my head, my voice barely audible. "No, she's my friend. Please, can't you—"

"It's a police matter," she repeated more firmly. Her stance softened just slightly when she saw the desperation in my face.

I wasn't leaving. I steeled myself, pulling the same body-language trick I had seen Mom do a thousand times—softening my posture, relaxing my shoulders, and giving off the illusion of being helpless and vulnerable. It always seemed to attract sympathy.

"May I please stay a while?" My voice cracked, just enough to sound fragile. Inside, I burned with determination. I had my own ways of finding answers. No way was I waiting for a police investigation. "I promise not to disturb her. I just want her to know she's not alone. That she's... loved."

The nurse hesitated, her gaze shifting from Kelsey's pale, unmoving form to my tear-streaked face. Her sternness wavered, the professional mask slipping just enough to reveal a flicker of empathy.

"Well, technically, only immediate family is allowed," she began, her tone firm but not unkind. Her fingers tightened around the clipboard, knuckles pale. "But it is still visiting hours for another two hours. I'll pretend I didn't see you, but keep it quiet, alright?"

A rush of gratitude washed over me. "Thank you. I promise."

The nurse gave a small, reluctant nod before stepping back, allowing me to stay by Keley's side.I nodded, a lump forming in my throat, as she turned and closed the door behind her. The moment I heard the latch click, I got up and locked it. *No interruptions.* This was going to require focus.

Pulling the chair closer to the bed, I sat on Kelsey's left side and took her cold, fragile hand. Her pulse was faint beneath her skin, but I focused on the steady rhythm of her heartbeat. *Could I even do this?* It had barely worked on Dad the one time Mom knocked him unconscious. *Don't ask.*

Taking a deep breath, I slowed my own heartbeat to match hers. *If you're listening, please let this work.* My silent prayer sent in a rare moment of desperation was the last thought towards anything other than Kelsey. *My friend.*

The steady rhythm of the ventilator and the hum of the machines around us faded into the background as I let my shield expand, creating a soft bubble around the two of us.

Threading my thoughts through the unseen network between us, I sent soft pulses like roots tasting the soil. Each vibration was a whisper, dissolving into the air, careful not to disturb. Her subconscious resisted at first—an erratic tangle of confusion and discomfort. I could feel it, like a network flooded with distress signals, tendrils of fear curling outward, searching for understanding.

KELSEY. IT'S SADY. I'M HERE.

I whispered the words into the space between us, but my thoughts extended further, threading gently through the vast, unseen web of her mind.

Another gentle pulse, this one carrying a rhythmic cadence meant to soothe and sync with her subconscious. Slowly, so slowly, I felt her mind begin to adjust. The resistance eased, and I began pulling faint tendrils of words and images from the chaotic vortex of her thoughts.

KELSEY? CAN YOU HEAR ME?

I sent the thought as gently as I could.

...SADY?

Her voice in my mind was faint, fragile, like a thread threatening to snap. But it was something. Relief washed over me.

YUP, IT'S ME.

Thank the stars this worked.

I'M HERE.

HOW...?

Her confusion tangled with fear, a cold knot tightening in the connection.

HOW ARE WE—?

Letting the full impact of our friendship weave across the connection, to show her, it was safe. That I was safe.

I'M NOT SURE HOW MUCH TIME I HAVE. DO YOU TRUST ME?

YES, OF COURSE. YOU'RE MY FRIEND. I DON'T UNDERSTAND—?

I interrupted softly, keeping the rhythm steady.

KELSEY... CAN YOU TELL ME WHAT HAPPENED?

Even in her thoughts, I felt the icy blade of fear slicing through her, sharp and unforgiving. It locked her in place, instinctively pulling her away from me. Gently, I sent another wave, soothing vibrations rippling from my subconscious to hers, easing the strain thread by thread. Bit by bit, the fear loosened, melting into something hesitant but real—a faint glow of trust.

And then she let go.

She hadn't meant to. She didn't know how to stop it.

The memories tore free, rushing through the fragile connection like a dam breaking. Each one slammed into me like a tsunami—raw, jagged, overwhelming. I couldn't catch my breath.

KELSEY, SLOW DOWN!

I tried to steady the connection, but her subconscious had taken over, dragging me back to the beginning.

The first memory she showed me wasn't a nightmare—not at first. She was so little—barely more than a toddler, maybe two years old. The world around her seemed impossibly big, shadows stretching long and cold. She clutched a pink stuffed bunny to her chest, its ears perky and its belly plump.

The room was dim, the kind of half-light that belonged to early morning or the edge of dusk. Her mother's voice drifted through the air, soft and soothing, singing a lullaby as she folded laundry. Kelsey's tiny fingers reached out, brushing the fabric of her mother's skirt, and for a moment, everything was warm. Safe.

Then, the memory shifted—sudden and jarring.

Her mother lay crumpled on the kitchen floor, blood pooling around her like ink spreading through water. Kelsey stood frozen, the stuffed, and now slightly worn bunny slipping from her grasp. Her father loomed above the body, his silhouette blocking out the light. An axe hung loosely in his hand, red splattered across the metal and his knuckles.

The look on his face—pleasure, satisfaction—was sickening.

I gagged, bile rising in my throat. The air in the memory felt thick, suffocating, and I struggled to breathe, to pull myself out of it. But Kelsey's tiny, terrified eyes held me there, refusing to let go.

Wave after wave of memories followed, each more horrifying than the last. Her father, instructing her brothers on how to treat women. How to treat *her*. And her brothers, taking those lessons to heart with twisted, malicious glee. And how he had protected them through his job. A police officer, sworn to protect the peace. What a joke. A sick joke.

The violence. The cruelty. It was endless.

By the time she showed me what happened last night, I was shaking with rage.

She had arrived home past her curfew by only minutes. That alone had been enough to set her father off, but then he had blamed me—and my dad—for what followed. He ranted about 'bad influences' and 'corrupting' her. The brothers had helped. The punishment had been swift and merciless.

Rage seared through me, my grip on her hand tightening as the scene played out in vivid, horrifying detail.

And then it all went black.

The banging on the door jolted me out of the connection. For a moment, I wasn't sure if it was the real world or another fragment of her subconscious, but the relentless thud pulled me back into my body.

"Miss Sady!" Greyson's voice was urgent, muffled slightly through the thick hospital door. "Please open the door!"

My vision blurred as I stumbled toward the door, my body unsteady from the emotional toll of connecting with Kelsey's subconscious. Whatever headache this experiment might bring, I knew I had to move fast. Unlocking the door, I pushed past Greyson—ignoring the concern etched into his features—and headed straight for the stairs.

He hesitated, glancing between me and the room, likely thinking I was retreating to the waiting area. Without a word, he stepped into the room to see Kelsey for himself.

I barely reached the stairs when the ding of an elevator drew my attention. The sound reverberated through my heightened senses like a blaring alarm.

Inside were five heartbeats. And I recognized their scent. From her memories. *My friend.*

Pivoting abruptly, not even bothering to keep my shield up, I was at the elevator doors before they had fully opened. Later, I would wonder if I had ever moved that fast in my life.

Inside were five men.

The largest of them stood at the center, clutching a bundle of wilting flowers. His greasy hair clung to his sweaty, ruddy face, and a dirty denim jacket strained over his massive frame. His belly hung low, obscuring his belt. The other four, younger but no less menacing, reeked of cheap cologne, stale cigarettes, and bitter whiskey. I didn't need a second look to know who they were.

My gaze snagged on something tucked under the big guy's arm—a stuffed bunny. Its once-white fur had turned a grimy gray, and one of its floppy ears hung by a few loose threads. My breath caught in my throat. It was the same bunny from Kelsey's memory, the one she'd clutched in those few precious moments of safety before everything went dark.

The man's meaty fingers squeezed the bunny's neck, the flowers crumpled against its matted fur. His lips twisted into a mockery of a smile, and I felt the temperature in the room plummet.

"Come to see our little princess," he drawled, and waggled the bunny in the air. The motion of which sent a fresh wave of bile rising in my throat. "Brought her favorite toy and everything."

I clenched my fists, my nails digging into my palms. The urge to rip the bunny from his hands—to wipe that twisted look off his face—surged through me, hot and undeniable.

These were her nightmares in the flesh.

The largest of them sneered, his greasy lips curling back to reveal yellowed teeth. "Get out of the way, girl!"

His voice—grating, condescending—barely registered over the pounding in my ears. My heightened senses locked onto the scent of blood. Theirs.

Sneering right back, I stepped into the elevator, and slammed my hand against the button to close the door.

"Hey now, what do you think you're—"

Blondie didn't finish his sentence.

My fist made sure of it. The impact reverberated up my arm with a satisfying jolt. His head snapped back, and the elevator walls rang with the dull thud of bone against metal.

That was the last thing I remembered. At least until the door opened again, and Greyson stood on the other side, his expression frozen in shock.

SADY!

Dad's voice roared through the telepathic link like a thunderclap.

SADY!

Mom's mental cry doubling over Dad's voice in my mind, urgent and panicked.

The blinding migraine ripping through my skull, and the accompanying blackout lifted, were momentarily interrupted by the sheer force of both of my parents reaching out to me—just long enough for me to register that my knees were buckling.

Only, there was no space for me to land.

The floor was occupied by the bodies of five men sprawled across the floor of the elevator, beaten and bloody but still alive. *I hoped.*

Greyson caught me as I stumbled forward, unconsciousness pulling me under.

COMING SOON

I'm the Child of Prophecy.
Spoiler alert:
It's not going well.

EVERFALLEN

Book Two in the *Legacy of Blood and Hope* series

Arrives **September 20, 2025**

The Autumn Equinox—the last breath before the fall. And I'm the one holding it. *(What could possibly go wrong?)*

Acknowledgements

To the ones who've stuck with me through every plot twist—whether you first heard me rambling about this book in 2020, counted down to its original October 2021 release (*yeah... about that*), or simply nodded along as I swore, *this time for real*—thank you. Your patience, encouragement, and gentle (and not-so-gentle) nudges kept this story from collecting dust in the archives of my brain.

Speaking of plot twists—to my family, who have witnessed every unexpected turn in my life and loved me through them all. If I've ever pulled off anything remotely brave, creative, or outright ridiculous, it's because I had you as my foundation. *Thank you* doesn't even cover it.

To my own offspring, Nate—our journey has been anything but predictable, more of a *choose-your-own-adventure* with detours, questionable choices, and a suspicious lack of road signs. You are, and always will be, my greatest (+favouritest) plot twist.

To Jenn B., who, after I sent her the first 25K words of this book (which I thought was lost for 10 years), simply asked: "Where TF is the rest?" That question alone kicked my ass into gear—so here it is.

To my editors, 'Mama' Mic and 'Boss Belle' Cassandra—you two are the real MVPs. Somehow, you wrangled the chaos of my brain and made sense of it all. There are not enough words (or properly placed commas) to thank you for that.

To Georgie Barnes—book cover designer extraordinaire. You get stories in a way not everyone does, and somehow, you took the scattered fragments of this one and turned them into something stunning. You saw this book in ways I didn't even know I needed—and made it even better.

To my MoonSister and her Super-man, if you don't see where you've left your mark in these pages, holler at me.

To the readers of my first novel, *Lady of Fire*—I know, I know. You were expecting *Lady of Water* next. Don't worry, she's still living in my head rent-free. She'll get her turn. Eventually.

To the false starts, the near misses, and the long pauses—and to the ongoing struggle of writing a book while accepting that *self-published author* isn't exactly a get-rich-quick scheme. Turns out, nothing chokes the muse quite like stress and existential dread, but somehow, the story still clawed its way into existence.

And finally, to you—the reader.

Whether you picked up this book out of excitement, curiosity, or because the algorithm bullied you into it, I appreciate you. Being a writer often feels like screaming into the void, hoping someone on the other side is listening—and here you are. So whether you're here for the fated bonds, the dangerous secrets, or just to yell at my characters for their *very* questionable life choices—thank you.

Maybe you saw yourself in these pages. Maybe you recognized something familiar—a feeling, a struggle, a family dynamic you wish you had (*or wish you didn't*). Maybe you're still figuring things out, just like some of these characters are. If so, welcome to the club. The journey doesn't end here, and trust me—some discoveries take a little longer than others. But that's a story for another time.

I'm so damn glad you're here.

About the Author

Once upon a time, a girl fell in love with stories. Spoken, written, imagined—it never mattered. Stories were magic. And loving them? That wasn't enough. She had to create them. So she did—backyard adventures, high school plays, and, eventually, books. Turns out, some things don't change.

Melanie Frome has always been drawn to the myths hiding in history, the magic in the mundane, the stories most people walk right past without seeing. It took a while (and a few scenic detours combined with questionable decisions) to figure out she didn't need permission to be a writer—just stubbornness, curiosity, and a gut instinct that said, "This way."

Born in Scotland, raised everywhere else, she eventually found her way back—this time, on purpose. Edinburgh, with its ghosts, stories, and cobblestone whispers, feels like home.

She's lived enough lives to know this—losing yourself in the wrong things will break you. She's been there. That's why she chooses differently now. Work that fuels her. Movement, creativity, and making space for stories to thrive. It's not about balance. It's about alignment. And for her, that means doing what keeps the fire burning—without burning out.

Because keeping the fire lit is what makes the story worth telling.

Also by
Melanie Frome

Lady of Fire | Immortal Elements Book One

Printed in Great Britain
by Amazon

62498429R00262